Hegel's Career and Politics

Hegel's Career and Politics

The Making of the
Most Famous Philosopher in Germany,
1788-1831

Mehmet Tabak

Hegel's Career and Politics:
The Making of the Most Famous Philosopher in Germany, 1788-1831

© 2019 Mehmet Tabak

All rights reserved. No part of this publication may be reproduced, distributed, or transmitted in any form or by any means, including photocopying, recording, or other electronic or mechanical methods, without the prior written permission of the author, except in the case of brief quotations embodied in critical reviews and certain other noncommercial uses permitted by copyright law.

Published in New York City by the author.
Printed in the United States of America.

ISBN: 978-1-939873-04-0 (Paperback)
ISBN: 978-1-939873-05-7 (Hardback)
ISBN: 978-1-939873-06-4 (E-book)

Library of Congress Control Number: 2019932493

Tabak, Mehmet.
Hegel's Career and Politics: The Making of the Most Famous Professor in Germany, 1788-1831 / Mehmet Tabak

Includes bibliographical references and index.

1. Georg W. F. Hegel (1770-1831). 2. Career—Academics—Biography. 3. Politics—Germany—The Restoration. 3. Political Philosophy—Theory of the State—Ethical Life. I. Title.

First Edition, 2019.

This book is dedicated to my brothers, Erdem and Etem,
my sisters-in-law, Debbie and Dilek,
my nieces, Hannah and Gülten,
my nephew, Hüseyin,
and the loving memory of my brother, Cemal.

Contents

Acknowledgements ix
Preface xi
I. Twelve Aimless Years, 1788-1800..1
   1. Tübingen Years, 1788-1793...1
      1.1 Desultory Student..1
      1.2 The Myth of the Revolutionary Hegel 4
   2. Bern Years, 1793-1796 7
      2.1 Indecision, Depression, and Abortive Plans to Study Philosophy..........7
      2.2 Hegel's Politics in Bern—or the Lack Thereof..................................11
   3. Frankfurt Years, 1797-1800 13
II. Floundering *Privatdozent:* Jena Years, 1801-1806 18
   1. The Making of a *Privatdozent*..18
   2. Incoherent Lecturer 21
   3. Schelling's "Talented" Hitman 24
   4. In Search of a New Post and a Guardian...26
   5. Hegel's Final Battles in Jena..32
III. Political Writings, 1798-1807 36
   1. Cart's Confidential Letters 36
   2. On the Political Crisis of Württemberg...38
   3. The German Constitution 40
      3.1 Hegel's Main Concern 40
      3.2 Hegel's Nationalism..44
      3.3 Lessons to be Learned from Machiavelli and Richelieu 46
      3.4 "Representative" Government...49
      3.5 Subordinate Rights 51
   4. Ethics and Politics in the *Natural Law* Essay..53
      4.1 Critique of Hobbes and Fichte 53
      4.2 Ethical Life..56
   5. Jena Lectures on Ethical Life and the State, 1805-1806 60
      5.1 Public Authority, the Ruler, and the Tyrannical Lord.......................60
      5.2 War Against other States and Civil Society (Once Again) 63
   6. The *Phenomenology*: Ethicality and the Revolution 65
      6.1 Dumb Generality as Ethicality 65
      6.2 The French Revolution and the Reign of Terror 69
IV. Bonapartist Newspaperman and Rector, 1806-1815...................................76
   1. Love at First Sight...76
   2. Bonapartist "Newspaperman," 1807-1808..78
      2.1 Making Sense of Hegel's Bonapartism 78
      2.2 Servile Professor Wannabe 84
   3. Nuremberg Years, 1808-1816..87
      3.1 Unsatisfied Gymnasium Rector 87
      3.2 The "Liberators" and the "Rabble" 91
      3.3 Joining the "Liberators" 94
V. Receptions of the *Phenomenology* and the *Logic*, 1807-1815 99

1. Receptions of the *Phenomenology of Spirit* 99
2. Receptions of *The Science of Logic* 108
VI. Hegel's Restoration, 1815-1818 113
   1. Restoration Politics and Academics 113
   2. Berlin University is Hiring: Hegel or Fries? 115
   3. Hegel's Other Campaigns and Triumph 120
VII. Apologist-Careerist Professor of Heidelberg 129
   1. Restoration Politics and Academics in Baden 129
   2. Making New Friends and Enemies 132
   3. Political Works, 1817-1818 138
      3.1 On Württemberg's Constitutional Crisis 138
      3.2 Heidelberg Lectures on the State 147
VIII. The Initiation of a Prussian State Philosopher, 1818-1820 154
   1. Why Prussians Hired Hegel 154
   2. Why Hegel Went to Prussia 159
   3. Pledging Allegiance to the Prussian State 162
   4. Decrees, "Demagogues," and Non-Heroics 163
      4.1 The Karlsbad Decrees 163
      4.2 Decrees and "Demagogues" in Prussia 168
      4.3 Hegel's Non-Heroics 172
IX. The Philosophy of Right 179
   1. The Infamous Preface 179
      1.1 Exposing and Denouncing the "Demagogues" 179
      1.2 The Existing State (the Actual) is Rational 181
   2. Morality, Evil, and Revolutionary Disorder 183
   3. Ethical, Patriotic Individual 187
   4. The Rational State 189
      4.1 The State As "the March of God in the World" 189
      4.2 Organic Constitution of the Monarchical State 191
      4.3 External Sovereignty, War, and the Military Class 206
X. Making Friends and Enemies 210
   1. Receptions of the *Philosophy of Right* 210
   2. Requesting the Promised Rewards 215
   3. Overshadowing Schleiermacher (and Savigny) 217
   4. Victor Cousin: Hegel's "Demagogue" Friend 223
XI. Receptions of Hegel's Lectures 229
   1. Incoherent Genius and Mystic 229
   2. "Mystifying Charlatan" 234
   3. Obnoxious Philosopher 241
XII. The Most Powerful Philosopher and His Vanguard Party 246
   1. Hegel's Society 246
   2. More Tantrums before the Calm 252
   3. Long Live the King, the Prussian State, and Hegel! 258
XIII. The Philosophy of History 263
   1. Preliminaries 263
   2. The Cunning of Hegel 264

   3. Ranking Races and Nations 266
   4. The Emergence of the Divine, Rational State in Germany 271
XIV. Hegel's Final Struggles..278
   1. Hegel's Reaction to the July Revolution 278
   2. Hegel's Last Apologia: "The English Reform Bill"..................................282
   3. Hegel's Last Foe 287
   4. Two Deaths, One Funeral 291
      4.1 First Death..291
      4.2 Second Death 292
      4.3 Hegel's Funeral 294
Epilogue: "The Consensus View"..297
Bibliography 304
Index 323

ACKNOWLEDGEMENTS

Kashif Azam, Jaella Brockmann, John Feldmann, John Fousek, Benjamin Groc, Kirra Klein, Dena Motevalian, Shinasi Rama, and Nicolette Teta have given me very valuable feedback on the earlier drafts of this book. Jaella Brockmann and Ali Yalçın Göymen have patiently helped with the translations of various German texts. I sincerely thank them all. I am also grateful to the enduring love and support of my wife, Akiko Moriyama-Tabak.

PREFACE

As its title obviously suggests, this book focuses on Georg Wilhelm Friedrich Hegel's career and politics. The working assumption, which is to be illustrated throughout this study, is that his career and politics were intimately related, and that this relationship tells us something significant about how he became a famous philosopher. What may be less obvious is why a topic on which much has been written needs to be reexamined. To explain this bluntly, the image of Hegel, both in terms of his career and politics, has been significantly distorted in various ways, especially during the last eight or so decades. This book, then, presents a radically different image of Hegel's career and politics than what is available in much of the existing *contemporary* literature.

Hegel's late rise to academic prominence is often treated as a teleological outcome. According to this popular perspective, which is often adopted rather intuitively, everything Hegel had written during his "formative" years, however juvenile, incomplete, and even incoherent, portended the "great" philosophical "system" he would construct in his mature years. Thus, everything he had written along the way is seen as a step in the "development" of his philosophy. Likewise, his prolonged failure to gain academic success and recognition is commonly explained as the "late blooming" of a genius. In short, it is readily assumed that he was destined to become the most famous and powerful philosopher in Germany from the outset. Consequently, how he had managed to accomplish this feat is seldom questioned, and so is little understood. Against this common, teleological narrative, this study illustrates that Hegel's rise to prominence was very unlikely until it happened, and how and why this happened had little to do with his intellectual merits.

Briefly and schematically put, Hegel was at best an unimpressive college student at Tübingen. After his graduation, he had worked as a live-in private tutor for seven years in Bern and Frankfurt (1788-1800). At the age of thirty, the famous philosopher of the future had nothing but rather incoherent, fragmented thoughts and writings in his possession. As he himself well-understood, he had failed to make something of himself and thought it was about time to seek help (Chapter 1).

In 1801, Friedrich Schelling, his much more accomplished friend from Tübingen, helped Hegel become a *privatdozent* (an unsalaried, non-titular professor) at Jena University, even though he was utterly unprepared and unqualified. Consequently, and unsurprisingly, Hegel's career at Jena (1801-1806) may be safely summed up in three words: a dismal failure. During this period, he came to be known mainly as an incoherent lecturer and writer, as well as Schelling's slanderous sidekick. At the end of 1806, Hegel was basically penniless and without any real prospects to become a salaried professor at a university, even though he desperately wanted to become one. His other friend, Immanuel Niethammer, came to his rescue (Chapter 2).

With Niethammer's help, Hegel had worked as the editor of a provincial newspaper in Bamberg (1807-1808), and then as a gymnasium rector and teacher in Nuremberg (1808-1816). Despite his tireless lobbying efforts, he was still unable to become a salaried professor; this prospect seemed very unlikely until 1815 (Chapter 4). Relatedly, the publication of two of his major works, the *Phenomenology of Spirit* and *The Science of Logic*, during this period only helped reinforce the negative perception of his intellectual and academic merits, contributing to the ongoing disinterest in hiring him (Chapter 5).

Hegel's misfortune was reversed rather rapidly in 1816. This study illustrates how this reversal had much to do with the emergence of the Restoration in Germany and with Hegel's support of the same. However, an adequate understanding of the link between his politics and career prospects requires tracing the various shifts in his political sympathies. A secondary, but important nevertheless, goal of this tracing is to debunk the popular claim that Hegel's political views were inspired by the ideals of the French Revolution, and so were rather liberal and progressive.

To begin with, the popular legend that Hegel was an ardent supporter of the principles of the French Revolution in his youth cannot be documented (Chapter 1). What is demonstrably false is the related claim that he had supported these principles throughout his life. This book amply illustrates that he had in fact *opposed* the Revolution and its principles until the end of his life, the very few, spurious, anecdotal exceptions notwithstanding. Otherwise put, at least after 1798 (he did not have any discernable political views before that), Hegel had always espoused illiberal and authoritarian politics. This claim will be justified through an analysis of Hegel's eleven political, or politically relevant, works. The analysis of his works, including his lectures, will also reveal that he was not much of a philosopher.

Hegel's politics can be tellingly divided into three periods, and thus into three distinct, *illiberal* political sympathies. During the first period (1798-1806), and from a visibly nationalistic perspective, he had lamented the disunity of the Germans, the absence of a centralized, strong state in Germany, and its invasion by foreigners. Relatedly, he had yearned for a strongman, even a "tyrant," to unite the Germans in the Empire under a centralized state. Philosophically speaking, he had consistently defined "freedom" as uncritical, blind obedience to the state (Chapter 3).

After the invasion of much of Germany by Napoleon, and the related dissolution of the German Empire, Hegel became a Bonapartist in 1806.

Preface

This is the second period. However, his support for Napoleon should not be exaggerated. In other words, despite the rich academic chatter about his "infatuation" with the emperor, Hegel's Bonapartism is *mostly* contained in a handful of private letters. Moreover, his support for the Napoleonic institutions during this period is often *erroneously* interpreted as his support for the ideals of the French Revolution. As this study illustrates, what essentially differentiates this second period from the first is Hegel's support for the invasion of Germany, that is, its domination by a foreign despot (Chapter 4). Apart from this, we cannot say much about the details of Hegel's Bonapartism since he did not write any political texts during this Bonapartist period.

That Hegel's support for Napoleon was tied to his career ambitions is seldom, if at all, acknowledged in the existing literature. This fact will be demonstrated in Chapter 4, along with the fact that his Bonapartism had lasted until Napoleon's (first) demise in 1814. Hegel had already, and opportunistically, switched sides by the time the institutions of the Restoration were firmly forged into existence in 1815. Thereafter, until his death in 1831—hence the third period, Hegel was an enthusiastic apologist for the reactionary Restoration regimes, both in his written works and other activities, such as his lectures, relationships to the authorities, and hostile acts he had repeatedly and publicly directed against the opponents of such regimes. (Note: Hegel's "politics" also refers to his personal politics)

This is not a mere coincidence: Hegel's fortunes had suddenly improved during the first year of the Restoration when the authorities were becoming increasingly concerned about the "demagogic" university professors and students. This broader political context had created the conditions in which the likes of Hegel appealed to the authorities. Thus, in 1816, Hegel came close to receiving an offer from Berlin University and received two offers, one from Erlangen and the other from Heidelberg. He chose Heidelberg (Chapter 6). In the existing literature, the intimate relationship between the said context and Hegel's sudden appeal is either flatly rejected or completely ignored, even though the available evidence conclusively shows that Hegel himself was fully aware of this relationship and was prepared to use it to his personal advantage.

During his brief career at Heidelberg (1816-1818), Hegel had used his professorial pulpit, pen, and personal connections to further advance his career and augment his income. This entailed publicly defending the Restoration regimes, attacking their liberal-republican opponents ("demagogues"), and negotiating with various authorities for a higher office than what he now, as a salaried professor for the first time in his life, took to be "the precarious function of teaching philosophy at a university" (Chapter 7). Hegel's heightened ambition was helped significantly by the

Preface

intensification of both "demagogic" activity and its repression in 1817, as he was now widely known as an apologist for the authorities.

The following claims, which most Hegel scholars today deny, are amply documented in Chapter 8. The Prussian authorities decided to recruit Hegel at a time when they were beginning to crack down on the "demagogues," promising him a very good salary and "higher offices," both of which Hegel himself had actively sought. Hegel was officially hired in 1818 and went to Berlin as a philosopher of the Prussian state, with the aim of advancing his renown and career by functioning as the servant of this state. To his credit, he was quite forthcoming about his servility.

The repression of "demagogic" activity had reached its peak after the implementation of the Karlsbad Decrees in September 1819. Hegel published his *Philosophy of Right* in 1820. In it, he not only glorified the repressive Restoration states in Germany, especially the Prussian one, but also egged the authorities on to punish the "demagogic" professors. Otherwise put, it is simply wrong to read this philosophically impoverished text as either a defense of political liberalism or a critique of the Prussian state (Chapter 9).

If it was not already, it now became clear to both Hegel's opponents and masters that he was an apologist for the Prussian state. Indeed, this was also Hegel's self-image (Chapter 10). His lectures on world history also glorified, even deified, the Germanic states of the Restoration period, especially the Prussian one, from a nationalistic and racist perspective (Chapter 13). When the July Revolution of 1830 alarmed the authorities and Hegel himself, he published an essay, "The English Reform Bill," to once again glorify the Prussian state, criticize the English one, and to warn everyone against the liberal revolutionaries (Chapter 14, section 2). This was his last apologia for the Prussian regime. He died the same year and was ceremoniously buried as the most prominent philosopher of the Prussian state, at least according to his acolytes.

From the outset, Hegel's main aim in Berlin was to gain more power and influence; increasing his income was also important to him. In a rather mysterious manner, he had managed to become a very popular lecturer, even though just about everyone thought he was incorrigibly incoherent. Some of his epigones even imagined that he was able to induce their spiritual transfiguration. It was also believed that he was a "demagogue proselytizer." However, many remained unimpressed. Some took him to be a "mystifying charlatan." Others thought he was an obnoxious slanderer. Yet, despite the persistence of formidable opposition to both his disagreeable personality and so-called philosophy, his influence in the academic universe grew steadily, largely due to the support he had received from the Prussian minister of culture and education. For instance, he was given almost absolute authority in the determination of academic appointments, which he had used very effectively to build a cultish Hegelian "party." With the support of the said ministry, his party also published its own journal, the main task of which was to defend Hegel and attack his opponents. By 1831, he came to be known to many as the most powerful academic in Prussia, if not entire Germany (Chapters 10 to 14).

Based on the preponderance of the evidence it supplies, this study concludes that Hegel was a barely coherent charlatan, a slanderer, and a very ambitious sycophant. He had undoubtedly managed to become very famous and powerful within his sphere of activity, but not the "great" thinker he was then, and still is, said to be by his admirers. This latter fact, I believe, makes his rise to academic prominence a fascinating story, which is essentially the story of how an untalented sycophant benefitted from the repressive political context in which he had pursed his insatiable ambitions. It is equally fascinating that he has been depicted as both a great thinker and a liberal critic of the Prussian regime by many Hegel scholars during the last eight or so decades, to the extent that this distortion is nowadays called a "consensus among knowledgeable scholars" (Epilogue).

The present study is a product of extensive and rigorous research, which corrects many distortions found in similar studies. For this reason, it should be of interest to anyone interested in Hegel's life, career, and politics. It should also be of much interest to those interested in the period and the political geography covered herein, namely, the Napoleonic and post-Napoleonic (the Restoration) Germany. In this regard, this study devotes much attention to the politics of this period and, especially, how they had significantly shaped the academic world in Germany. Differently put, I examine the making of Hegel's career and politics within its broader historical and political context. I do this, I believe, more comprehensively and accurately than any other existing book on Hegel, convinced that one cannot make adequate and accurate sense of his career and politics by ignoring, or else giving short shrift to, this historical and political context.

The analysis of Hegel's political works offered in this book is not meant to be a comprehensive study of his so-called "political philosophy." I mostly focus on his key political ideas, especially his conception of the state and its relationship to individuals. In so doing, I deliberately ignore some of the philosophical themes covered in his works that many Hegel specialists find interesting. However, the narrower focus I adopt is advantageous in the sense that it allows us to understand his politics more effectively than would otherwise be the case in a more comprehensive account. Relatedly, as everyone agrees, Hegel was a notoriously unclear writer. I have endeavored to render his works accessible to a non-specialist audience, and so have sought to avoid overwhelming the reader with Hegelian jargon.

Chapter One

I. TWELVE AIMLESS YEARS, 1788-1800

1. Tübingen Years, 1788-1793

1.1 Desultory Student

Hegel was born on August 27, 1770, in Stuttgart, a city in the duchy of Württemberg. According to his sister, Christiane, he was sent to the German School, then to the Latin School, and finally to the Stuttgart Gymnasium, and that he had performed remarkably well at all three levels of his early education.[1] In September 1788, he graduated from the Gymnasium and was picked, along with four other students, to give a graduation speech on September 25. The topic of his speech was the "corrupted" state of education in the "backward" Turkey (the Ottoman Empire). His speech was primarily an homage to Duke Karl Eugen for offering his subjects a much superior system of education than what was then available in Turkey.[2]

On October 27, 1788, a month after his graduation, Hegel entered Tübingen University. To be more precise, he enrolled in the Protestant Seminary—the *Stift*. The *Stift*, which had about three hundred students, was hardly an exemplary learning center. Most students were expected to serve as preachers or school teachers upon graduation. According to his own autobiographical sketch, Hegel had studied "philology under the supervision of [Christian F.] Schnurrer and philosophy and mathematics under [Johann F.] Flatt and [August F.] Beckh" during his first two, and theology "under the supervision of [Johann F.] LeBret, [Johann L.] Uhland, [Gottlob C.] Storr and Flatt" during his remaining three years at Tübingen. In accordance with the wishes of his parents (some say contrary to his own wishes), Hegel's aim was to become a preacher.[3] In other words, and in today's terminology, his major in college was theology, not philosophy. For

---

[1] Günther Nicolin (ed.), *Hegel in Berichten seiner Zeitgenossen* (Hamburg: Felix Meiner, 1970), #1. Henceforth cited as *Berichten*.
[2] Johannes Hoffmeister (ed.), *Dokumente zu Hegels Entwicklung* (Stuttgart: Friedrich Frommanns Verlag, 1936), 52. Henceforth cited as *Dokumente*.
[3] Reprinted in Herman Nohl (ed.), *Hegels theologische Jugendschriften* (Tübingen: J. C. B. Mohr, 1907), viii-ix.

I. Twelve Aimless Years, 1788-1800

reasons that remain unclear, the successful student from Stuttgart would soon falter at Tübingen, graduating from it neither as a preacher nor as a competent philosopher.

Friedrich Hölderlin entered the same university at the same time as Hegel. Friedrich Schelling arrived there two years later. He was fifteen at the time, and so was five years younger than both Hegel and Hölderlin. It is said that the three were distant relatives.[4] They certainly knew each other. However, the popular portrayals of them as very close friends cannot be documented. The available evidence, which is relatively scarce, suggests that Hölderlin and (especially) Schelling did not belong to Hegel's immediate social circle. Indeed, according to Karl Schelling's biography of his father, Schelling and Hegel did not socialize much, though they shared similar intellectual interests and likely conversed about them to some extent.[5] It seems that Hegel had socialized a lot with his other friends, playing cards and consuming much wine.[6] He would retain these two hobbies until the end of his life.

Hegel's academic performance started to deteriorate during his initial years at Tübingen. As one recent biographer puts it, "the official documents up till 1791 remark upon a certain deterioration in his conduct ... His frequent absence from lectures is also duly noted."[7] It is very likely that he had continued to behave similarly during his remaining two years there. For instance, in September 1793, Schnurrer, who was at the time the ephor of the *Stift*, informed one of his friends that Hegel was absent from the university for "almost all of this summer." He regarded this as proof of Hegel's lack of discipline.[8]

According to Karl Rosenkranz, Hegel, Hölderlin and some other students (perhaps before Schelling's arrival) had studied Plato, Kant, Jacobi, and Hippel together.[9] Very likely, this was an ordinary study group, consisting of students enrolled in "Flatt's course on 'Metaphysics and Natural Theology' in the summer term of 1790."[10] Based on his "intimate" friendship and familiarity with Hegel, Phillip F. Leutwein recalled many

---

[4] John E. Toews, *Hegelianism: The Path Toward Dialectical Humanism, 1805-1841* (Cambridge: Cambridge University Press, 1980), 20.
[5] Karl. F. Schelling, "Schelling's Leben," in *Aus Schelling's Leben: In Briefen, 1775-1803*, ed. G. L. Plitt, 1-179 (Leipzig: S. Hirzel, 1869), 69-70. Also see Walter Jaeschke, *Hegel-Handbuch: Leben, Werk, Schule* (Stuttgart: J. B. Metzler, 2010), 5-7.
[6] Jaeschke, *Hegel-Handbuch*, 6.
[7] Horst Althaus, *Hegel: An Intellectual Biography*, trans. Michael Tarsh (Cambridge, UK: Polity Press, 2000), 8.
[8] *Berichten*, #25.
[9] Karl Rosenkranz, *Georg Wilhelm Friedrich Hegel's Leben* (Berlin: Duncker und Humblot, 1844), 40.
[10] H. S. Harris, *Hegel's Development: Towards the Sunlight, 1770-1801* (Oxford: Clarendon Press, 1972), 98.

I. Twelve Aimless Years, 1788-1800

years later that Rousseau was Hegel's philosophical "hero." "Metaphysics" was not of much interest to him. Moreover, Hegel was only dimly acquainted with the philosophy of "father Kant"; he had shown no interest in Leutwein's conversations with Schelling and others on the philosophies of "Kant, Reinhold, and Fichte." (As we will see shortly, Hegel himself would later confirm his lack of knowledge of these philosophers.) Overall, Hegel had often engaged in "eccentric" behavior, which displeased the *Stift* officials, and exhibited "desultoriness" with respect to his academic productivity, reading habits (described as "eclectic"), and intellectual interests.[11] Otherwise put, his interest and competence in philosophy were much more limited than what some of his biographers would have us believe.[12]

As a theology student, Hegel was required to deliver sermons at the communal student dinners.[13] His sermons were deemed barely coherent, and his style of delivery awkward at best.[14] The official report on Hegel's matriculation exam also described him as a poor orator. Moreover, his examiners deemed his knowledge of philology "*non ignarus*," and his interest in philosophy "*nullam operam impendit.*"[15] Another official report, dated September 20, 1793, also underscored Hegel's failure to impress his examiners during his consistorial exam. His explanation and delivery of 1 *Corinthians* 11:14 were deemed unsatisfactory, though the report also noted the "modest progress" he had made in theology. It also stated that Hegel was now permitted to work as a private tutor (*informator domesticus*) in Switzerland.[16]

Hegel needed this official permission from the university, and from the local government by extension, to work as a private tutor. This is to say, he had already arranged to work as a private tutor before his graduation from the university, likely knowing all along that he was not about to become a preacher. A few months before he was officially matriculated, a Bern

---

[11] *Berichten*, #8.
[12] *Pace*, among others, Georg Lukàcs, *The Young Hegel: Studies in the Relations Between Dialectics and Economics*, trans. Rodney Livingstone (Cambridge, MA: The MIT Press, 1975), 4. Oddly, Lukàcs claims two pages later that "in Tübingen and Berne Hegel did not concern himself with philosophical problems in any intensive manner."
[13] The written versions of some of these sermons are reprinted in *Dokumente*, 175-92.
[14] See Rosenkranz, *Georg Wilhelm Friedrich Hegel's Leben*, 26; Althaus, *Hegel: An Intellectual Biography*, 11; Terry Pinkard, *Hegel: A Biography* (Cambridge: Cambridge University Press, 2000), 282.
[15] Reprinted in Eduard Zeller, *Theologische Jahrbücher in Verbindung mit Mehreren Gelehrten*, vol. 4 (Tübingen: Ludwig Friedrich Fues, 1845), 205. Zeller claims to have seen the official report, and so rejects the claim that *multam*, rather than *nullam*, was inscribed in the original document. Regardless, we will see shortly that, by Hegel's own admission, *nullam* is more apt.
[16] Ibid., 206.

I. Twelve Aimless Years, 1788-1800

patrician, a certain Captain Carl Friedrich von Steiger, was seeking a private tutor for his two children. To make the long story short, while checking the references of another prospect, one David von Rütte, Steiger's contact in Tübingen, came across Hegel's name. After exchanging a few letters on the conditions of his employment, Hegel agreed to tutor the children of the Steiger family.[17] Luckily for Hegel, Rütte did not consult Schnurrer, who, upon learning Hegel's plans to become a tutor, predicted to one of his own friends that the undisciplined Hegel would make a poor tutor.[18] At any rate, Hegel left for Bern in late 1793.

1.2 The Myth of the Revolutionary Hegel

If one were to simply examine the available documents, without consulting the secondary literature, one would not ordinarily include a section on Hegel's politics, not to mention revolutionary activities, in a chapter that deals with his *Stift* years. Perhaps one would simply note that these years overlapped with the French Revolution of 1789 and the beginning of the Reign of Terror (1793) and that what Hegel thought about these events is not known. In other words, this section is necessitated by the widespread legend that Hegel was an ardent supporter of the revolution. It debunks this legend.

We know enough to conclude that, much like the youth in other German universities, some Tübingen students had celebrated the arrival of the new "age of freedom" with the French Revolution. However, there is no credible evidence to endorse the legend that Hegel himself was a sympathizer.[19] In fact, "there is not a single contemporary statement," either by Hegel or anyone who knew him, "on his position on the Revolution."[20] Even much less credible is the claim that he was the ringleader of a revolutionary student "club," the existence of which itself is in much doubt. Alas, lack of evidence has not deterred many scholars from assuring their readers that Hegel was a revolutionary activist.[21]

---

[17] Johannes Hoffmeister (ed.), *Briefe von und an Hegel*, 4 volumes (Hamburg: Felix Meiner, 1952-1960), #2 and #3. Henceforth cited as *Briefe*, followed by the Latin numerical to indicate the volume number, in this case, *I*.
[18] *Berichten*, #25.
[19] In 1826, while drinking with some "young people" in Berlin, Hegel apparently boasted about his enthusiasm for the French Revolution. *Berichten*, #457. I do not count this boasting, made thirty-three years after he left Tübingen, as a reliable piece of evidence. There is a similar story about him doing the same thing in 1820, in Dresden. I will prove conclusively in Chapter 8 that this story is false.
[20] Jaeschke, *Hegel-Handbuch*, 7-8.
[21] *Pace* Wilhelm Dilthey, *Die Jugendgeschichte Hegels und andere Abhandlungen zur Geschichte des Deutschen Idealismus* (Leipzig: B. G. Teubner, 1921), 13-14; Lukàcs, *The Young Hegel*, 10; Xavier Léon, *Fichte et son temps*, vol. 1 (Paris: Armand Colin, 1922), 173; Jacques D'Hondt, *Hegel In His Time*, trans. John Burbidge (Peterborough, Ontario:

I. Twelve Aimless Years, 1788-1800

This legend entered the existing literature, I believe for the first time, in Albert Schwegler's 1839 publication, in which he claims to have heard the story about Hegel's activism from Leutwein, the "old man." After asking him about Hegel's response to the political events of the period, writes Schwegler, Leutwein

> told me that Hegel had been the most enthusiastic orator for freedom and equality, and that he ... had raved all young minds for the ideas of the Revolution. One Sunday [spring] morning, the old man went on to say ..., Hegel and Schelling, with a few other friends, went to a meadow not far from Tübingen, and had erected a freedom tree.[22]

Schwegler's account has been justly deemed incredible by other scholars before. As we have seen earlier, Leutwein's own account mentions Hegel's lack of interest in the "Kantian *enragè*," which is usually linked to the Jacobin sympathies, due to Karl Diez's influence, at the *Stift*.[23] It does not say anything about either Hegel's alleged revolutionary activities or involvement in the planting of a "freedom tree." Regardless, the original source of this popular "tree" story is neither Leutwein nor Schwegler.

The "freedom tree" story has become one of the most well-known Hegel legends, in which Hölderlin has also been subsequently included. A popular and more embellished version of it has it that Hegel, Hölderlin, and Schelling erected a "freedom tree" on July 14, 1793, and circled around it, dancing and singing *La Marseillaise* to celebrate the Bastille Day. This date, which associates the alleged incident with a relevant reason for a celebration of the alleged kind, contrasts with the account Schwegler attributed to Leutwein, which has it that the incident occurred during a fine Sunday morning in spring.

This brings us to the original source of the story: Schnurrer's report to the Duke of Württemberg. The report was meant to debunk the allegations sent to him "from Ulm": "it was generally said and believed in those parts that the students [no names are mentioned] in the *Stift* had set up a Freedom Tree right before my very eyes."[24] It is highly likely that Schnurrer had investigated the rumors before denying their factuality to his own superiors, and so had unintentionally helped spread the rumors among the denizens of Tübingen. In short, the legend, which was debunked by Schnurrer himself, originated in Ulm, forty-four miles away from Tübingen.

Broadview Press, 1988), 171; Althaus, *Hegel: An Intellectual Biography*, 10; Pinkard, *Hegel: A Biography*, 24.
[22] *Berichten*, #9.
[23] Ibid., #8.
[24] Quoted in Harris, *Hegel's Development: Towards the Sunlight*, 115, n. 2.

I. Twelve Aimless Years, 1788-1800

Even if we assume that an incident of the alleged kind took place, Hegel was certainly not involved in it. As (in an unrelated context) Schnurrer informed one of his friends on September 10, 1793, Hegel had been "absent" from the university for "almost all of this summer," that is, the summer during which the alleged incident supposedly occurred. In other words, he was in Stuttgart at the time "under the pretext" of seeking a "cure" for his illness.[25] For this and other reasons, H. S. Harris has convincingly rebuked the factuality of this very popular, cute story about the "freedom tree."[26] Long before Harris, Schelling's son also noted that, after consulting some "informed contemporaries," he could not confirm it.[27]

I suspect that Schelling, and Hegel by extension, was implicated in the fictitious incident later because of his involvement in another incident. It is reported, on the strength of persuasive evidence, that Schelling had gotten himself into not-so-serious trouble with the Duke of Württemberg for allegedly translating *La Marseillaise*.[28] No such charges were ever leveled against Hegel, and there is no evidentiary reason to believe that he was even a suspect. Yet, an author volunteers the verdict that, due to their support for the French Revolution, "Duke Karl Eugen ... placed Hegel and his friends under secret police surveillance."[29] In fact, there is no reason to believe that even Schelling himself was put under such surveillance.

The upshot is that Hegel's alleged revolutionary sympathies during his Tübingen years cannot be confirmed, and some of the allegations in this regard may be safely discarded as fabrications. Some of Hegel's friends and acquaintances were certainly sympathetic to the Revolution. As for Hegel himself, the most plausible verdict is that he did not share their enthusiasm. As we know from his juvenile writings from this period, his strongest sympathies were with Christ and what he took to be the true religion. In his "The Tübingen Essay," written in 1793, we find precisely this Hegel, who also happens to be a critic of the "men of Enlightenment."[30] There is not even a hint of a revolutionary in this essay or in any of his other surviving juvenile essays and personal notes.

But some of Hegel's revolutionizers[31] remind us that Jean Jerome Kolb, a French student at Tübingen, wrote the following in Hegel's album: "*Vive*

---

[25] *Berichten*, #25,
[26] Harris, *Hegel's Development: Towards the Sunlight*, 115 n. 2, 116 n. 4.
[27] Schelling, "Schelling's Leben," 31.
[28] Ibid., 31 ff.
[29] David MacGregor, *Hegel and Marx: After the Fall of Communism* (Cardiff: University of Wales Press, 2014), 52.
[30] G. W. F. Hegel, "The Tübingen Essay," in *Miscellaneous Writings of Hegel*, ed. Jon Stewart 44-71 (Evanston, IL: Northwestern University Press, 2002).
[31] See, for example, Pinkard, *Hegel: A Biography*, 24.

I. Twelve Aimless Years, 1788-1800

la liberté! Vive Jean Jacques [*Rousseau*]!"[32] This appears to be the most formidable evidence to support the legend that Hegel was an "enthusiastic orator" for the ideals of the Revolution, though it obviously does not amount to much. Besides, this revolutionary image of Hegel, whose nickname was the "old man," strikes me as an oxymoron.[33] So, let me conclude by conceding that Hegel likely had some conversations about "*la liberté*" with his friends, and might have even approved their enthusiasm. But he himself was not enthusiastic enough to leave any written, or otherwise, evidence for us to declare him a sympathizer, not to mention a firebrand.

2. Bern Years, 1793-1796

2.1 Indecision, Depression, and Abortive Plans to Study Philosophy

There is not much to report on Hegel's life in Bern, Switzerland. As noted earlier, at the end of 1793, he moved to Bern to work for the Steigers. The available records indicate that his life in Bern was filled with unimpressive events and chores.[34] Initially, he had isolated himself from his Tübingen friends. It took him more than a year to send his first letter to Schelling, which confirms that their relationship was not as intimate as many today assume.

Hegel wrote his first letter to Schelling on the Christmas Eve of 1794. The latter's recent academic achievements and recognition, which he learned from a journal, sparked Hegel's desire to renew his "amiable" relationship with the successful Schelling. Differently put, Schelling's success reminded Hegel of his own failure. "I am not [intellectually speaking] completely idle but my occupation, heterogeneous and often interrupted as it is, does not allow me to achieve anything proper," he informed Schelling. Hegel even admitted to having failed to accomplish anything noteworthy at Tübingen, where he had "let" the opportunity to do so "slip by." Now, Hegel told Schelling, "I am" looking "for a situation—not in Tübingen—where I could bring to fruition" my academic

---

[32] For this and other similar entries, see Rosenkranz, *Georg Wilhelm Friedrich Hegel's Leben*, 34 ff.
[33] A sketch of Hegel by another student, found in Hegel's *Stammbuch*, represents him as a curled-up old man, supporting himself with two canes (one in each hand), with the caption, "May God help the old man!" Source: http://idb.ub.uni-tuebingen.de/diglit/Mh858. (Last access: January 14, 2019).
[34] See Hegel's letter to Steiger. *Briefe I*, #12.

I. Twelve Aimless Years, 1788-1800

endeavors.[35] The significance of his exclusion of Tübingen will be explained shortly. What should be underscored here are two things: he was already planning to leave Bern and he had not made any notable progress in his studies. Also, and this will become more evident shortly, Hegel was hoping that Schelling would help him get out of his present situation.

In January 1795, Hegel once again complained to Schelling about his own lackluster academic progress: "My remoteness from various and sundry books and the limitation of my time do not allow me to work out many of the ideas which I carry around with me." He also mentioned his renewed interest in improving his own knowledge of Kant's philosophy and admitted to being unfamiliar with the recent discussions on Kant's philosophy, including "the efforts of Reinhold." After a few vague comments on Fichte's philosophy, he lamented, "if I should come to the point of developing my opinion more extensively, I will subject it to your criticism but shall ask in advance your indulgence."[36]

Hegel repeated the same themes in his third letter to Schelling, written on April 19, 1795. He blamed his tardiness in replying to Schelling, "in part," on the "diverse occupations" imposed on him by his employer. "Yet what prevented me even more from replying sooner," he explained, "was the wish to send you a thorough critique of the writing you sent me ..., to show you at least that I have fully grasped your ideas. Yet I lacked time for a thorough study of these ideas." In other words, Hegel was unable to study even an essay, not to mention lengthy philosophical debates. Thus, we also read the following in his letter: "I shall undertake the study of Fichte's science of knowledge during the summer, when I generally will have more leisure to develop some ideas that I have long carried around with me; in connection with them, however, I lack the use of a library, which I would really need." In addition to Hegel's repeated confessions to the effect that he had not yet developed his own ideas, what needs to be noted here is his repeated desire to be "reunited" with Schelling.[37] Indeed, it is fair to say that procuring Schelling's help in this regard was one of the main motivations behind Hegel's correspondence with him.

On August 30, Hegel once more exalted his friend's philosophical virtues, thanking Schelling for giving him much-needed philosophical guidance and enlightenment: "What previously floated before my mind darkly and in undeveloped form has been illuminated by your writing in a most splendid and satisfactory manner," he said. Yet, and oddly, he also confessed to not being able to fully grasp Schelling's instructions: "You

---

[35] Clark Butler and Christiane Seiler (trans.), *Hegel: The Letters* (Bloomington: Indiana University Press, 1984), 28-29 (*Briefe I*, #6). Henceforth cited as *Letters*.
[36] *Letters*, 30-31 (*Briefe I*, #8).
[37] Ibid., 35-36 (#11).

I. Twelve Aimless Years, 1788-1800

cannot expect [competent] observations from me on your writing. In this matter I am but an apprentice" (of Schelling, to be sure). Moreover, his own "works are not worth speaking of," and so cannot at this time be submitted to Schelling's superior judgement. Hegel then repeated his ongoing desire to be reunited with Schelling and Hölderlin. He was recently informed by Hölderlin that the latter "has been in Tübingen." "How I would have wished to have been the third man there," daydreamed Hegel, adding that, in his "solitude," hearing something from his friends improved his spirits immensely.[38] Hegel had clearly felt isolated and lonely in Bern, and needed the help of his friends to join them, or else to simply get out of Bern.

Hegel's fifth and last letter from Bern to Schelling is lost. However, we can be quite certain that it repeated the main themes of the previous four letters. This verdict is confirmed by Schelling's June 20, 1796, reply to Hegel's lost letter. We also learn from his reply that Hegel was now in a state of depression. In response to Hegel's confession in this regard, the pompous Schelling advised him to "snap" himself "out of it as soon as possible." Hegel's lost letter also informed Schelling of his present plans to leave (with Hölderlin's encouragement) Bern for either Frankfurt or Weimar, and likely expressed his wish to be reunited with Schelling. In this regard, Schelling's reply was unpromising, as he merely expressed his willingness to help Hegel "plan" his future, should his present Frankfurt and Weimar plans falter.[39] In other words, Schelling had nothing concrete to offer Hegel with respect to his current predicaments and plans. Tellingly, Hegel did not reply.

Hegel's next letter to Schelling is dated November 2, 1800, which means that he would not correspond with him for more than four years. This is the letter in which he enjoined Schelling to help him move to Jena. I will discuss this letter later. What needs to be pointed out here is that Hegel's previous letters to Schelling were insincere. The upshot is that Hegel saw no reason to communicate with his "dear friend" after the latter had proven to be less-than-enthusiastic about assisting him with his current pleas for help.

Besides, Hegel was already soliciting similar help from Hölderlin, and would soon receive a positive reply from him, as we will see shortly. However, before we move on, it is worth mentioning another fact that highlights Hegel's insincerity in relation to Schelling. In his letters to him, Hegel had consistently agreed with Schelling's negative attitude toward the Tübingen establishment, disparaging the despotism and idiocy of the faculty and officials there. Indeed, as we have seen, Hegel also mentioned his strong

---

[38] Ibid., 41-43 (#14).
[39] *Briefe I*, #17.

I. Twelve Aimless Years, 1788-1800

desire "for a situation" in which he "could bring to fruition" his nonexistent philosophy, noting specifically that he had no desire to do this "in Tübingen."[40] Yet, it turns out, he had been simultaneously expressing his desire to work there as a "teaching assistant" in his letters to Hölderlin.

Hegel's hypocrisy did not escape Hölderlin's attention. In his November 25, 1795, reply to Hegel's lost letter, Hölderlin politely disparaged him for this reason, telling him that an assistantship at Tübingen would amount to a "betrayal committed against" Hegel himself, for he would associate with the "paltry [*armseligen*] people" of that institution.[41] During this time, Hölderlin himself was seeking employment as a private tutor in Frankfurt, and thought a similar post in the same city would suit Hegel better. After securing such a post for himself, he had arranged one for Hegel as well. He conveyed the latter news to Hegel on October 24, 1796. After describing the perks that would come with Hegel's employment by Johann Noë Gogel, a wealthy wine merchant, Hölderlin revisited the issue of Hegel's desire to work at Tübingen. "To me," he wrote, the kind of "stipend" Hegel expected to receive for his assistantship at Tübingen "stinks allover Württemberg ... like a stretcher in which all sorts of warms are stirring." "Seriously, dear," added the poet, "you cannot willfully put your mind [*Geist*] to such an insufferable test."[42]

Hegel replied positively in November, indicating that the prospects of reuniting with his "dearest" friend allowed him to unhesitatingly accept the offer and "renounce the other prospects that have presented themselves" to him. We do not know anything about "the other prospects" that had "presented themselves" to Hegel. Perhaps the statement was merely a reference to his earlier wish to work at Tübingen, though it also suggests that he might have had been communicating with some people there about this prospect. At any rate, Hegel announced, very joyously, that he would be in Frankfurt sometime in January 1797.[43]

However, despite his jovial and optimistic letter to Hölderlin, Hegel was still unable to "snap" out of his depression. This was not lost upon his sister, Christiane. On his way to Frankfurt, Hegel had stayed with his family for about two months in Stuttgart. Christiane observed in her diary that, after "three years in Switzerland," her brother came home in a very "introverted" state and seemed "jolly" only in a "cozy circle."[44] Many years later, in 1810, Hegel himself would confirm that he was indeed depressed "to the point of exhaustion ... for a few years," linking his depression to

---

[40] *Letters*, 29 (*Briefe I*, #7).
[41] *Briefe I*, #15,
[42] Ibid., #19.
[43] *Briefe I*, #20.
[44] *Berichten*, #30.

I. Twelve Aimless Years, 1788-1800

his inability to philosophically organize, and make sense of, what appeared to him at the time as chaotic phenomena.[45]

Since Hegel would fall into similar states of mind in Frankfurt and Jena, scholars have been disputing which "few years" he had in mind in this letter. Be that as it may, Hegel left Bern deeply unhappy. Surely, his isolation and lack of achievement must have contributed to his gloomy mood. However, there is no evidence-based reason to think that he left because he was disturbed by the Steiger family's oligarchical influence in Bern.[46] Bluntly put, Hegel did not leave Bern for political reasons, though we have enough evidence to think that he did not exactly approve of the way the nepotistic Bernese oligarchy conducted its political business (see Chapter 3).

2.2 Hegel's Politics in Bern—or the Lack Thereof

As Horst Althaus rightly reports, with one exception, "nowhere in the surviving letters from the Bern period does Hegel explicitly refer either to the revolutionary events unfolding in France or to the effects of the same in Berne, even though the Revolution was taking a drastic turn at this time."[47] Indeed, this is also true of his writings from this period. The exception is found in the letter Hegel wrote to Schelling on the Christmas Eve of 1794. In it, Hegel mentioned, rather casually, that the Jacobin Jean-Baptiste Carrier was recently "guillotined" (on December 16) and that his trial "has revealed the complete ignominy of Robespierre's party."[48] This rare comment on it proves Hegel's ongoing disinterest in the Revolution and suggests that, to the extent that he was interested in the revolutionary events, he disapproved of the Jacobins.

Another piece of information we have about Hegel's political sympathies from his Bern years is contained in his April 16, 1795, letter to Schelling. Referring to Schelling's recent writings, he wrote: "insofar as I have grasped them, I see in them a completion of science which will give us the most fruitful results. I see in them the work of a mind of whose friendship I can be proud and who will make a great contribution to the most important revolution in the system of ideas in all Germany." Then, he offered the following prediction: "From the Kantian system and its highest completion [by Schelling], I expect a revolution in Germany ... The aura of prestige surrounding the heads of the oppressors and gods of this earth is disappearing," as the "philosophers are [belatedly] proving the

---

[45] *Briefe I*, #158.
[46] According to the imaginative Pinkard, Hegel was dismayed by his employer's opposition to "the French Revolution" and advocacy for "an alliance with the Prussians and Austrians" against the French. Pinkard, *Hegel: A Biography*, 51.
[47] Althaus, *Hegel: An Intellectual Biography*, 21.
[48] *Letters*, 29 (*Briefe I*, #7).

I. Twelve Aimless Years, 1788-1800

dignity of man. The people will learn to feel it" eventually and will consequently "demand ... their rights." Moreover, "this enlivening power of [philosophical] ideas, even when they are in themselves still limited—such as the idea of the fatherland, of its constitution, and so forth—will lift hearts, which will learn to sacrifice for such ideas."[49]

It is difficult to miss Hegel's attempt to curry favor with Schelling, with whom, as the same letter noted, he was hoping to be reunited. Even if we assume that he had sincere hopes for a "revolution" in Germany, it is not clear what he wanted it to achieve. What kind of an "idea of the fatherland" and of "constitution" did he have in mind? What "rights" were people expected to "demand"? The most plausible answer to these questions is that Hegel himself was unclear about these issues in 1795. Thus, in the same letter, he gave a vague answer to our questions: "the spirit of constitutions has presently made a pact with self-interest and has founded its realm upon it."[50] This comment suggests that Hegel was displeased with *all* contemporary constitutions. It also hints at his opposition to particularism, with which both liberal and feudal constitutions would be critically identified by Hegel a few years later.

In fact, Hegel's "theological" writings from this period[51] may be read as various attempts to disparage self-interest *tout court*. However, there is not even a hint of a call for a revolutionary change in them, meaning that Hegel's anticipation of a "revolution" in his letter to Schelling was an isolated and vague outburst. Relatedly, his "theological" works offer only a few tangible political solutions, some of which appear to be self-contradictory. For instance, in one passage, he maintains that religion must now be treated solely as a private matter, and that the state should neither have its own religion nor regulate it.[52] In another, he even suggests that the state has a duty to protect the "right" of its citizens to choose and exercise their own religion.[53] Yet, he also argues that the separation of religion and the state is a recipe for disaster, and so praises what he believes to be the ancient-Greek way of integrating religion and the state into a single totality. This view is clearly defended in a "Frankfurt fragment:" "if the principle of the state is a complete whole, then church and the state cannot possibly be separate ... The whole of the church is a mere fragment only when man in his wholeness is shattered into a political man and a church man."[54] In his "Positivity of Cristian Religion" (Frankfurt), he claims, rather approvingly,

---

[49] Ibid., 35-6 (#11).
[50] Ibid.
[51] See G. W. F. Hegel, *Early Theological Writings*, trans. T. M. Knox (Philadelphia: University of Pennsylvania Press, 1971).
[52] Ibid., 112.
[53] Ibid., 123-24.
[54] *Dokumente*, 281-82.

I. Twelve Aimless Years, 1788-1800

that "religion is the best means" the state could use to legitimize itself in the eyes of its citizens.[55]

In short, Hegel left Bern for Frankfurt in January 1797 with a pile of rather incoherent manuscripts in his suitcase. Although some of his future admirers would find philosophical jewels in them,[56] Hegel himself thought otherwise. As he had told Schelling on numerous occasions, he was not able to develop his own views in Bern. Surely this self-assessment is even more applicable to his political views. If so, the claim that Hegel's self-assessment was simply due to lack of self-confidence is untenable. Even more untenable is the claim that he did not publish any of his Bern-Frankfurt writings because of "fear of censorship, of the courts, of hostile public opinion," and "not because he judged them inadequate."[57]

3. Frankfurt Years, 1797-1800

There is not much to report on Hegel's personal life in Frankfurt. It seems that he did not communicate with many people during this period, and that very few people cared to know what he was up to in this lively city. Of the six (!) surviving letters he had written during this approximately four-year period, one, written in late 1800, was sent to Schelling. It contained Hegel's big decision to move to Jena. It should not be concluded from this later decision that he was determined to pursue an academic career at a university from the moment he set foot in Frankfurt. That decision would be made, rather unexpectedly, after four more years of isolation and self-disappointment.

The other five letters were sent to Nanette Endel. Hegel met Nanette when he visited his family in Stuttgart before coming to Frankfurt. She was living with, and working for, the Hegels at the time. It is likely that Hegel's sister included Nanette in the "cozy circle" in which she thought her depressed brother had felt more comfortable and gregarious during his stay in Stuttgart. Hegel's relationship to Nanette had romantic implications, though it is difficult to ascertain the extent of their commitment to each other.

---

[55] *Hegel, Early Theological Writings*, 98.
[56] For an exceptionally readable discussion of Hegel's early theological writings, see Thomas A. Lewis, *Religion, Modernity, and Politics in Hegel* (Oxford: Oxford University Press, 2011), 16-134. Although Lewis' discussion of the confused Hegel is suspiciously too clear, I still could not get what Hegel's early theological writings teach. As Lewis himself charitably puts it, "Taken together, the developments [which developments?] of this decade constitute a fruitful succession of failures" (ibid., 17). A "fruitful succession of failures" is an interesting, perhaps a dialectical, way to put it—I guess.
[57] *Pace* D'Hondt, *Hegel In His Times*, 171.

I. Twelve Aimless Years, 1788-1800

Hegel's letters to Nanette give us a glimpse of his social life in Frankfurt. Apparently, he had initially enjoyed the cultural benefits of the vibrant, commercial city. For instance, he mentioned going to the theatre and participating in dancing events. "Here in Frankfurt I feel I am becoming more harmonious with the world," he wrote. However, and as if to be dialectical, his letters also exhibit a distaste for the Frankfurt socialites, claiming that it is "impossible to ... improve such people." He specifically complained about the consumerism of the Frankfurt socialites, and even expressed his desire to isolate himself from all human beings. It seems that he had at some point started to seek refuge in nature to "protect" himself "from the hazards of associating too intimately with them."[58] Hegel's last letter to Nanette was written on May 25, 1798.

Of his social life during the remaining two years in Frankfurt, we know even less. For instance, Hegel's relationship with Hölderlin in Frankfurt is somewhat of a mystery. In other words, there is no evidence to support the claim that they had "engaged in a constant, intense discussion of politics, poetry, and philosophy, and camaraderie."[59] It is not even clear whether, for instance, he had read Hölderlin's *Hyperion* (1797), though he did own a copy. Also, all the efforts by Hegel's revolutionizers to make him an active member of the so-called "Bund der Geister," which included Hölderlin, Isaak von Sinclair, and Jakob Zwilling, are unsubstantiated exaggerations.[60] What we can say for certain is that Hegel and Hölderlin had at least some interaction before September 1798, the month in which Hölderlin left Frankfurt under duress, likely much less interaction shortly thereafter, and none after the early months of 1799. Thus, regardless of the nature, extent, and intensity of their friendship in Frankfurt, it terminated after two years.

Hölderlin was involved in a love affair with Susette Gontard, his employer's wife, and was banished from the Gontard household when Susette's husband became aware of their affair. Consequently, Hölderlin moved to Homburg in late 1798, and had only intermittently visited Frankfurt to meet with Susette secretly. In one of her letters, she informed Hölderlin that he could learn from Hegel when she was alone.[61] Her letter to Hölderlin was written at the beginning of 1799. We do not know whether Hegel had in fact facilitated their secret rendezvous. What we know is that he and Hölderlin ceased to communicate with each other

---

[58] *Briefe I*, ## 22-25, 27.
[59] *Pace* Pinkard, *Hegel: A Biography*, 76.
[60] Jaeschke, *Hegel-Handbuch*, 16-17. However, Jaeschke thinks that, "despite the lack of direct evidence, Frankfurt-Homburg circle of friends had great importance for the development of Hegel's philosophy—especially for his mainly religious-philosophical manuscripts on the spirit of Christianity ..." and, more vaguely, for Hegel's political writings from this period (ibid.).
[61] *Berichten*, #38.

I. Twelve Aimless Years, 1788-1800

during this period; they would never see or even directly corresponded with each other ever again. The reasons for their separation are not clear to me. It is possible that they found little interest in each other, personally or otherwise. It is also speculated that Hölderlin's mental illness and obsession with Susette had contributed to their alienation from one another.

On January 15, 1799, around the same time Susette sent her letter to Hölderlin, Hegel himself received an important letter from his sister, informing him of the death of their father.[62] The impact of this news on Hegel is not known since he had very rarely spoken or written about his father. In March, seven weeks after receiving his sister's letter, and thus notably after his father's funeral, Hegel went to Stuttgart to collect his share of the inheritance, which amounted to "3154 gulden" and some change.[63] The inheritance was split between Hegel, his sister, and younger brother, Georg Ludwig, who died in 1812.[64] (Hegel never mentions his brother to anyone in any of his surviving letters.) Hegel's inheritance was large enough to change the course of his life.

By 1799, Hegel had once again become "unhappy" with his situation,[65] though his letters to Nanette suggest that he had been unhappy and isolated for a while. The extent of his unhappiness during this period is difficult to gauge. However, he clearly wanted to get out of his present situation, which he must have regarded as a dismal failure. He was in the habit of comparing his achievements with those of others. By this time, Schelling was already a celebrated philosopher and a professor at Jena, and Hölderlin was a renowned author and poet. Although it took Hegel another seventeen months to reach this decision after receiving it, his inheritance gave him the necessary financial encouragement and independence to move on. In late 1800, he decided to seek Schelling's help in this regard.

That Hegel had not communicated with Schelling since 1796 is itself a very revealing fact. His November 2, 1800, letter resembled all his previous letters to his successful "friend." First, Hegel noted his desire to move to Bamberg, where he might, he reasoned, settle and independently devote himself "to works and studies already begun." This was the same story he had been telling Schelling since 1794 about his "works." Then, he exalted Schelling's accomplishments and predictably went on to express his desire to join him in Jena. Oddly, or perhaps expectedly, Hegel described his request as an "unselfish endeavor."[66] Schelling's reply to Hegel is not

---

[62] *Briefe I*, #28.
[63] Althaus, *Hegel: An Intellectual Biography*, 35.
[64] Georg Ludwig Hegel was a military officer in the Württemberg royal force and died during Napoleon's Russia campaign in 1812.
[65] This is how he would remember his Frankfurt life in 1810. *Briefe I*, #167.
[66] Ibid., #29.

I. Twelve Aimless Years, 1788-1800

available, though he evidently understood his intended message and subsequently invited him to Jena. Hegel joined him in January 1801.

Schelling's own journey to Jena was the opposite of Hegel's. He earned his master's degree in 1792 by defending *his own* thesis, something expected of the successful students, not the likes of Hegel. His dissertation was deemed worthy of publication. Indeed, given its "impressive quality," it "occasioned reviews questioning whether it was actually authored by a seventeen-year-old student and not an established biblical scholar." He had published several more well-received essays during the next three years. In 1795, he defended his doctoral thesis, giving him the necessary formal qualification to teach at a university. In the ensuing two years, Schelling had worked as a private tutor for an aristocratic family, which gave him the opportunity to independently pursue studies in mathematics, physics, chemistry, and medicine at Leipzig University. By the end of 1797, he was already a celebrated philosopher. He was invited to Jena by Schiller and Fichte to attend an event during the same year, with the intention of introducing him to Goethe, who was at the time in charge of Jena University. "Schelling charmed Goethe and they spent the next few days engaged in experiments in optics. In June [1798], on Goethe's insistence, Schelling received the formal invitation to become a professor in Jena." In October, he began teaching there. He was twenty-three.[67]

What were Hegel's accomplishments and qualifications? Basically, he had written a bunch of fragmented "works," "carried around" with him equally fragmented thoughts,[68] and possessed an official report that rated him, at best, a mediocre college graduate (in today's terms), who had much difficulty with expressing himself. Yet, he would soon move to Jena to

---

[67] Bruce Matthews, "Schelling: A Brief Biographical Sketch of the Odysseus of German Idealism," in *The Palgrave Handbook of German Idealism*, ed. Matthew C. Altman, 435-56 (New York: Palgrave, 2014), 437-43. A discussion of Schelling's philosophy, which changed in important ways throughout his life, falls outside the scope of this study. For competent and accessible accounts, see Werner Marx, *The Philosophy of F. W.J. Schelling: History, System, Freedom* (Bloomington: Indiana University Press, 1984); Andrew Bowie, *Schelling and Modern European Philosophy: An Introduction*, London: Routledge, 1993); Dale E. Snow, *Schelling and the End of Idealism* (Albany: SUNY Press, 1996).

[68] According to Rosenkranz, Hegel had studied a German translation of James Steuart's *Principles of Political Economy* and Kant's *Metaphysics of Morals* and penned down impressive commentaries on them. These commentaries have been lost. Rosenkranz, *Georg Wilhelm Friedrich Hegel's Leben*, 86 ff. Alas, the truth is that Hegel's knowledge of political economy remained substandard and obscure throughout his life (is there any *evidence* to the contrary?), and that he consistently misunderstood, or else misrepresented, Kant's philosophy.

I. Twelve Aimless Years, 1788-1800

teach at a university. We will follow Hegel's career at Jena University in the next chapter.

Hegel's interest in politics had increased while he was in Frankfurt (circa 1798), as evinced by the several political tracts he had worked on during this period. I will discuss them in Chapter 3.

Chapter Two

II. FLOUNDERING *PRIVATDOZENT*: JENA YEARS, 1801-1806

1. The Making of a *Privatdozent*

Hegel arrived in Jena on January 21, 1801. Strangely enough, Schelling was prepared to help him become a *privatdozent* (an unsalaried lecturer), even though he was utterly unqualified and unprepared to teach philosophy at a university. Indeed, he did not even have the necessary formal qualifications to teach. Thus, the arrangement at hand was a recipe for an impending disaster. Hegel himself would prove this with his dismal performance at Jena University during the ensuing six years.

To begin with, Hegel had to fulfill the formal requirements for his *habilitation*, which would license him to teach. Given that the existing requirements at Jena were somewhat uncertain, he tried to get away with doing as little as possible in this regard. On August 8, he requested that the faculty in charge of the process recognize his Tübingen *Magister's* (master's) degree (1790) as equivalent to the doctor's degree in Weimar.[1] Hegel procured his degree after two years of college education by defending someone else's work, which was allowed under Tübingen's regulations. In the moment of a hurried confusion, caused by Hegel's intense campaign to start lecturing as soon as possible, the issue of his degree fell through the cracks. Suddenly, Hegel was referring to himself as "Doctor of Philosophy" in his correspondence and getting some of his counterparts to do the same. Thus, his doctoral degree was basically invented by Hegel himself.

However, Hegel was still required to defend an original dissertation before a committee of academic peers. Since he basically had nothing to defend, he first tried to obtain approval to teach before his defense.[2] As a compromise of sorts, the authorities at the university leniently allowed him to defend some theses of his own choosing, with the expectation that he

---

[1] Clark Butler and Christiane Seiler (trans.), *Hegel: The Letters* (Bloomington: Indiana University Press, 1984), 87. Henceforth cited simply as *Letters*. Also, Johannes Hoffmeister (ed.), *Briefe von und an Hegel*, 4 volumes (Hamburg: Felix Meiner, 1952-1960), #30a. Henceforth cited simply as *Briefe*, followed by the Latin numerical to indicate the volume number, in this case, *IV*.
[2] *Letters*, 87 (*Briefe IV*, #30c).

II. Floundering Privatdozent: Jena Years, 1801-1806

would complete and submit his dissertation shortly thereafter. On August 27, 1801, his thirty-first birthday, Hegel "defended" his twelve theses. I find most of them quite absurd and even comical, but will merely quote them here for the readers' purview, without further commentary:

I. Contradiction is the rule of the true, non-contradiction is the rule of the false.
II. The syllogism is the principle of Idealism.
III. The square is the law of nature; the triangle is the law of mind (*mens*).
IV. In true Arithmetic there is no room for addition other than unity's being added to the dyad, and no room for subtraction other than the dyad's being removed from the triad, and no room for the triad that is a sum, nor for the unity that is difference.
V. Just as the magnet is the natural lever, so too the gravitation of the planets toward the sun is the pendulum of nature.
VI. The idea is synthesis of the infinite and the finite, and the whole of philosophy consists in ideas (*est in ideis*).
VII. Critical philosophy lacks Ideas; it is an imperfect form of Skepticism.
VIII. The matter of the postulate of reason, which critical philosophy exhibits, destroys this very philosophy, and is the principle of Spinozism.
IX. The state of nature is not unjust; on that ground one must leave it.
X. The principle of moral science resides in our having to revere fate (*reverentia fato*).
XI. Virtue excludes innocence of action (*agendi*) and of passion (*patiendi*).
XII. Absolute morality is in every respect incompatible with virtue.[3]

We do not know how Hegel defended these theses, or even whether he defended them at all. In fact, his defense (disputation) was merely a formal gathering, the outcome of which was predetermined. In other words, his committee consisted of his friends. His defender was Karl Schelling, the philosopher's younger brother, who was a student at Jena at the time. His so-called "opponents" were Thomas Schwarzott, a student from Bamberg, Friedrich Immanuel Niethammer, Hegel's and Schelling's friend from

---

[3] Hegel, "Philosophical Dissertation on the Orbits of the Planets (1801), Preceded by the 12 Theses Defended on August 27, 1801," trans. Pierre Adler, *Graduate Faculty Philosophy Journal* 12, nos. 1–2 (1987): 269–309, 276-7.

II. Floundering Privatdozent: Jena Years, 1801-1806

Tübingen, and Schelling himself. Hegel expectedly passed the sham defense without any trouble.[4]

However, he still had to complete and submit his dissertation. The theme of his dissertation, titled *Dissertatio philosophica de Orbitis Planetarum* (*Philosophical Dissertation on the Orbits of the Planets*), was even stranger than the idea that he could teach philosophy at a university, for Hegel knew very little about this subject and what he knew was seriously flawed. In the first part of his brief and badly-written dissertation, he criticized Newton's science, which he would continue to castigate until the end of his life without understanding it (see Chapter 11). In the second part, he offered a "philosophical construction" of the *concept* of the solar system, with some support from Kepler's science and, above all, the Schellingian "true" philosophy. The very brief third part of his dissertation argued against the recent predictions (based on the Titus-Bode series), maintaining that there could not be a celestial body between Mars and Jupiter. He deduced his "proof" for this claim from a revised version of the number-series Plato gives in the *Timaeus* (written c. 360 BC!) As it is well known, his modification of Plato's series involved some basic math mistakes.[5]

Sadly, Hegel was not even aware of the fact that a dwarf "planet" had already been discovered by Giuseppe Piazzi on January 1, eight months prior to his defense. Unsurprisingly, then, his dissertation is still treated by his critics as proof of his ignorance and charlatanism, though some Hegelians have tried to salvage it, along with the reputation of its author. What is worse, the delusional Hegel thought it was a great achievement, and so proudly sent a printed copy of it to Ernst II, the duke of Saxe-Gotha-Altenburg. The duke was well-versed in astronomy and physics—hence the reason why Hegel sent him his dissertation. Indeed, the duke had established the famed Observatory of Gotha and employed the services of Baron Franz Xaver von Zach, one of the most important astronomers of the period. Upon reading Hegel's dissertation, the duke appropriately wrote "*Monumentum insaniae seculi decimi noni*" ("the monument of insanity of the nineteenth century") on it, and then forwarded it to Zach. Zach, in turn, called Hegel's enterprise "literary vandalism," adding that the likes of Hegel should "learn before they can teach."[6]

---

[4] Johannes Hoffmeister (ed.), *Dokumente zu Hegels Entwicklung* (Stuttgart: Frommanns Verlag, 1936) 312-14. Henceforth cited as *Dokumente*.
[5] Hegel, "Philosophical Dissertation on the Orbits of the Planets (1801)," 269–309. For a very informative (charitably critical) account of Hegel's dissertation, see Olivier Depré, "The Ontological Foundations of Hegel's Dissertation of 1801," in *Hegel and the Philosophy of Nature*, ed. Stephen Houlgate, 257-81 (Albany: SUNY Press, 1998.)
[6] Quoted in Clifford J. Cunningham, *Bode's Law and the Discovery of Juno: Historical Studies in Asteroid* (Cham, Switzerland: Springer, 2017), 23.

II. Floundering Privatdozent: Jena Years, 1801-1806

At any rate, Hegel handed his quickly-written dissertation to the university authorities on October 18, 1801. We do not know if any of them had even read it. What we know is that it was basically smuggled in to satisfy the official requirements for his *hablitiation*. However, the same day, and on procedural grounds, another member of the Jena faculty, the "logician and metaphysician Henning, claimed to have uncovered serious irregularities and expressly demanded the immediate withdrawal of Hegel's teaching license 'because there has been deception [favoritism] involved.'"[7] Thus, Hegel's relationship with some members of the Jena faculty was off to a rough start as it was rightly suspected that favoritism was involved in his *habilitation*.

Hegel intuitively knew how to get around this problem. With Schelling's help, he arranged to meet the person ultimately in charge of what went on at the university. Hegel and Goethe met at 11 pm on October 21.[8] Although what transpired between them during that meeting is not known, Hegel clearly wanted to ingratiate himself to his big boss. From that moment onward, he and Goethe would remain on friendly terms, which suggests that his first meeting with Goethe went well. Likely, Hegel pleased the anti-Newton Goethe with his own criticism of Newton.

2. Incoherent Lecturer

During the winter semester of 1801-1802, that is, soon after he submitted his dissertation, Hegel started offering "Logic and Metaphysics" by himself and two other courses with Schelling, namely, "Introduction to the Idea and Limits of True Philosophy" and "*Disputatorium*," in which students were required to defend and critique different theses every week. According to one Bernhard Rudolf Abeken, who took these courses, Hegel began his own lectures by quoting the inscription on Dante's gates of hell: "Abandon all hope, ye who enter here." Upon hearing this, Abeken "cried the bitterest tears," thinking that his previously held convictions on "God, faith, salvation, and immortality" were incompatible with "the new doctrine," preached by Schelling and Hegel. The *Disputatorium*, again according to Abeken's later recollection, involved the refutation of such theses as: "'In art, history ideally repeats itself; the task of an art history would then be to show how unity in art corresponds to diversity in history,'" and "'epic and tragedy relate to each other as identity and totality; lyrical poetry stands in the middle [as the middle term] and exhibits duplicity." Apparently,

---

[7] Horst Althaus, *Hegel: An Intellectual Biography*, trans. Michael Tarsh (Cambridge, UK: Polity Press, 2000), 61-62.
[8] Günther Nicolin (ed.), *Hegel in Berichten seiner Zeitgenossen* (Hamburg: Felix Meiner, 1970), #43, #44. Henceforth cited simply as *Berichten*.

II. Floundering Privatdozent: Jena Years, 1801-1806

Abeken's friend dropped the class after failing to dispute such propositions, wisely concluding that it would be best to stay away from this academic field.[9] Another student, Ignaz Paul Vital Troxler, the future discoverer of the phenomenon known as "Troxler's fading," noted some five decades after taking Hegel's courses that his "Logic and Metaphysics" soon fell apart, and so was terminated.[10] However, it seems that he himself had enjoyed the discussions carried out in the *"Conversatorium* under Hegel's direction."[11]

We do not have many details about the ultimate demise of Hegel's own course, though it is reasonable to assume that it had much to do with his incoherence. As Hegel himself would admit many years later to a friend, he had not yet achieved "clarity" in presentation, and so was "bound in the oral presentation to the letter of ... [his] notebook,"[12] meaning that his lectures were based on reading out loud, and dictating, his "philosophical" writings to his unfortunate students.

This confession helps us establish one of the main reasons behind Hegel's bad reputation: the various notebooks he had used for teaching purposes were themselves incoherent. (He refused to use the published works of others, believing that only his own thoughts were worth teaching.) Thus, Hegel's reputation as an incoherent lecturer at Jena had much to do with his impoverished philosophical writings, which cannot be described as anything other than mostly gibberish.[13] Have you read them?

Hegel's incoherence had also to do with him being an ungifted orator, which was duly inscribed on his matriculation certificate from Tübingen. This problem did not escape Goethe's attention. On November 27, 1803, he informed Friedrich Schiller that he had spent a few "pleasant" hours with some of the Jena faculty, including Hegel. Hegel "is a very good man," noted Goethe, but is significantly handicapped and disadvantaged because of his poor skills of "expression."[14]

Schiller responded to Goethe's concern three day later. Without knowing Hegel personally, he ventured to guess that it would be difficult to teach Hegel "what he lacks" in this respect. Still, he prescribed forging a relationship between Hegel and Karl Ludwig Fernow, a newly-hired

---

[9] *Berichten,* #48.
[10] Ibid., #50.
[11] Ibid., #49.
[12] *Briefe II,* #262.
[13] Translations of four such notebooks can be found in the following three volumes: G. W. F. Hegel, *System of Ethical Life and First Philosophy of Spirit,* trans. H. S. Harris and T. M. Knox, 97-177 (Albany, NY: SUNY Press, 1977); G. W. F. Hegel, *The Jena System, 1804- 5: Logic and Metaphysics,* trans. John W. Burbidge and George di Giovanni (Kingston and Montreal: McGill-Queen's University Press, 1986); G. W. F. Hegel, *Hegel and the Human Spirit: A Translation of the Jena Lecture on the Philosophy of Spirit of 1805-6,* trans. Leo Rauch (Detroit: Wayne State University Press, 1983).
[14] *Berichten,* #78.

II. Floundering Privatdozent: Jena Years, 1801-1806

aesthetics professor at Jena. The latter had already proven to be a popular and lucid professor during his first semester. However, he was rumored to be a superficial thinker. Thus, speculated Schiller, if brought together, the German Hegel would be forced to learn from the "French" Fernow "a teaching method, while Fernow would be forced out of his "superficiality."[15] Some of Goethe's letters and diary entries from this period suggest that he took Schiller's suggestion seriously, as he had brought Hegel and Fernow together on multiple social occasions.

However, Schiller's (silly) plan was doomed to fail from the start since Hegel was not enamored with Fernow's charm and popularity. On November 16, 1803, that is, two weeks prior to Schiller's letter to Goethe, Hegel sent a letter to the newly-married Schelling, who was in Stuttgart at the time. With a dose of envy, he informed Schelling that "Fernow could not find a large enough auditorium for the students registering [for his class]." However, it was rumored, and Hegel was eager to report it, that Fernow's lectures simply consisted of reading "Kantian definitions" to his students.[16]

A rather strange phenomenon was also at work, especially during the last two years of Hegel's career at Jena. According to Georg Andreas Gabler, a student who became a Hegel admirer during this period, Hegel was deemed incoherent by most students. He kept speaking about "the Absolute" of "the new philosophy." As Gabler recalled, his teaching was mostly "garbled chaos," which was expressed in a "strange and unfamiliar ... language and terminology," leading many students to declare the whole thing "'nonsense.'" Despite this, or perhaps because of it, a few students thought he was some sort of a mystical genius.

> These true disciples ... had the greatest esteem for the Master. They exhibited an almost idolatrous worship for everything that emanated from him. He was to them a higher being ... This worship extended to everything, even the least of what one could learn from the man's life and deeds, every move, every manner of conduct and behavior, every utterance. Behind every word that one could catch [from his mouth] was [assumed to have] a deep meaning, implying a profound truth.

For instance, after Hegel referred to Schelling as his "friend" on one occasion, these disciples started to wonder whether "friend" meant something "completely different from its common meaning."[17] This strange phenomenon of worshipping the incoherent philosopher would reach its apex during his career at Berlin University (1818-1831).

---

[15] Ibid., #79.
[16] *Briefe I*, #42.
[17] *Berichten*, #92.

3. Schelling's "Talented" Hitman

As noted earlier, Hegel arrived in Jena on January 21, 1801. The available evidence suggests that he had stayed at Schelling's residence at least until the end of 1801.[18] This arrangement likely played an instrumental role in their initial collaboration, which basically involved promoting Schelling's philosophy and attacking everyone else's, clearly under Schelling's direction. In effect, Hegel was the younger Schelling's subordinate.

The first attack was staged primarily against Fichte in *The Difference between Fichte's and Schelling's Philosophy* (1801).[19] Anticipating Fichte's reaction to all this, Schelling informed him on October 30, 1801, that, "just today, a book by a very talented person was published which bears the title: *The Difference between Fichte's and Schelling's System of Philosophy*; I had no part in it, but also could in no way whatsoever prevent it."[20] At best, this was a dishonest claim, for Schelling had "unquestionably" played an important role not only in urging its publication but also helping Hegel, his roommate at the time, with its composition.[21]

It seems that Fichte had never read the "talented" Hegel's essay. However, his correspondence with Schelling during this period, which mostly involved discussions on how each misunderstood the other, clearly indicates that he had sensed Schelling's intention to disparage his philosophy with Hegel's assistance. It also seems to be the case that Fichte did not want to stage a battle on this front. Thus, he offered a truce on January 15, 1802:

> I would obviously desire that both you and Hegel do not raise anything further against this point of dispute …, at least until my new presentation has appeared, which will be published at Easter. I … want to make … solely Spinoza into my opponent. This is not to spare you—I am not so petty to think that you require this—but simply to avoid causing further offense."[22]

In his subsequent replies, Schelling accepted Fichte's call for a truce, though the rupture between them had already been cast in stone.

---

[18] *Letters*, 89 (*Briefe I*, #32).
[19] G. W. F. Hegel, *The Difference Between Fichte's and Schelling's Philosophy*, trans. H. S. Harris and Walter Cerf (Albany, NY: SUNY Press, 1977). There are good reasons to believe that Hegel tried to use the *Difference* essay in lieu of a dissertation, though this effort did not pan out as he had hoped.
[20] J. G. Fichte and F. W. J. Schelling, *The Philosophical Rupture between Fichte and Schelling: Selected Texts and Correspondence (1800–1802)*, eds. Michael G. Vater and David W. Wood (Albany, NY: SUNY Press, 2012), 65.
[21] Walter Jaeschke, *Hegel-Handbuch: Leben, Werk, Schule* (Stuttgart: J. B. Metzler, 2010), 20.
[22] *The Philosophical Rupture between Fichte and Schelling*, 73.

II. Floundering Privatdozent: Jena Years, 1801-1806

Hegel's *Difference* essay quickly earned him the reputation of being Schelling's sidekick and hitman. For instance, Karl Böttiger read it as essentially Schelling's work, adding that "Schelling has now fetched a stout warrior to Jena through whom he gives notice to the astonished public that even Fichte stands far below his own viewpoint."[23]

Hegel and Schelling also founded the *Critical Journal of Philosophy*. They were its sole editors and contributors. The main aim of the *Journal*, as its first issue declared, was to stage polemical attacks against other philosophers. In his December 30, 1801, letter to Caroline and Wilhelm Friedrich Hufnagel, Hegel revealed this aim in the following, colorful words: "Its tendency in part will be to ... put an end and limit to unphilosophical rubbish. The weapons the *Journal* will use are very diverse. One may call them cudgels, whips, and bats. It is all for the good cause and glory of God."[24] The "unphilosophical" tribe included basically all contemporary philosophers except, of course, Schelling and Hegel. However, the "talented" Hegel's bizarre mission to whip the "unphilosophical" tribe into submission, and all this for the "glory of God," would soon go awry, as he would wind up whipping himself.

The academic community at large quickly understood the intended aim of the *Journal*. For instance, on March 22, 1802, Friedrich Jacobi informed Friedrich Bouterwek of "the appearance of the first issue of a new critical journal, edited by Schelling and a certain Herr Hegel, who is quite unknown to me, in which most violent anger prevails, so it seems."[25] Friedrich Köppen was Jacobi's source for this troubling information regarding the slanderous journal of angry Schelling and a certain Herr Hegel.

The more he had published, the more Hegel came to be known as Schelling's mouthpiece. This opinion was further publicized by Köppen in his review of Schelling's philosophy. The author of *Faith and Knowledge*,[26] he wrote, "whether he be Herr Hegel or some other individual, had to write as he did, according to the principles of Schelling's system." Therefore, reasoned Köppen with some sarcasm, the "name Hegel" should be used "to refer simply to an individuality belonging to the system of Schelling."[27] Thus, in accordance with Schelling's identity-philosophy, Hegel had no independent individuality of his own. Köppen himself was very familiar

---

[23] Quoted in H. S. Harris, "Introduction," in G. W. F. Hegel, *The Difference Between Fichte's and Schelling's Philosophy*, trans. H. S. Harris and Walter Cerf, 1-75 (Albany, NY: SUNY Press, 1977), 67 n. 10.
[24] *Letters*, 89 (*Briefe I*, #32).
[25] *Berichten*, #58
[26] G. W. F. Hegel, *Faith and Knowledge*, trans. H. S. Harris and Walter Cerf (Albany, NY: SUNY Press, 1977).
[27] Quoted in H. S. Harris, *Hegel's Development: Toward the Sunlight* (Oxford: Oxford University Press, 1972), xlviii.

II. Floundering Privatdozent: Jena Years, 1801-1806

with such relationships of subordination. In his November 26, 1803, letter to Karl Gustav von Brinkmann, Friedrich Schleiermacher, the famed theologian and philosopher, compared Hegel's subordinate relationship to Schelling to that of Köppen's similar relationship to Jacobi.[28]

Köppen's ambivalence on the author of the essay had a legitimate basis, as the name of the author of each article was concealed. Thus, the readers had to guess the author of each essay. Indeed, simply based on its "bad style," Jacobi concluded in a letter to Reinhold that *Faith and Knowledge*, in which Hegel targeted Jacobi himself, must be Hegel's work. In the same letter, Jacobi complained about having much "trouble in comprehending" the writing of the "wretched Hegel."[29]

Friedrich Schlegel was even less forgiving of Hegel's incoherence than Jacobi. In March 1804 (perhaps after trying to read Hegel's *On the Scientific Ways of Treating Natural Law*—published in two installments in 1802 and 1803[30]), he complained bitterly about the "disgusting Hegelisms [*Hegeleien*]." "I will not read anything written by this man again," wrote Schlegel in protest to his brother, August.[31]

Sometime in 1803, if not before, Schelling himself came to resent his collaboration with Hegel. For instance, he agreed *almost* entirely with August Wilhelm Schlegel's castigation of Hegel's *Faith and Knowledge*.[32] Schelling also complained about Hegel's editorial skills, holding him responsible for the blemishes in one of his own published essays, which he asked Hegel to "polish" before printing it while he was away.[33] It is also reasonable to conclude from the general context that Schelling had begun to resent his collaboration with the slanderous Hegel, perhaps because he thought it was becoming an impediment to his own career prospects. He was, after all, in search of a better post for himself elsewhere since Jena was now becoming an increasingly unattractive institution.

4. In Search of a New Post and a Guardian

Schelling, Niethammer and Heinrich Paulus—another friend from Tübingen, left Jena for the University of Würzburg sometime in 1803, leaving Hegel behind. Also, the *Critical Journal* was discontinued after

---

[28] *Berichten*, #77.
[29] Ibid., #65.
[30] G. W. F. Hegel, *On the Scientific Ways of Treating Natural Law, on its Place in Practical Philosophy, and its Relation to the Positive Science of Right*, in *Hegel: Political Writings*, eds. Laurence Dickey and H. B. Nisbet, 102-85 (Cambridge: Cambridge University Press, 1999).
[31] *Berichten.*, #83a.
[32] Ibid., #66.
[33] Ibid., #68.

II. Floundering Privatdozent: Jena Years, 1801-1806

Schelling's departure. Evidently, the publisher was unwilling to let Hegel run it by himself for the obvious reasons. With Schelling's departure and the discontinuation of the *Journal*, Hegel's brief appearance under the academic limelight abruptly ended, though his image as Schelling's incoherent sidekick and hitman would remain in effect for many years to come, despite his concerted efforts to undo it.

The "exodus" of the faculty from Jena during this period was a more general phenomenon, as many other professors had also left. Despite it, neither the remaining faculty at Jena nor Goethe was inclined to promote Hegel to one of the salaried positions vacated by the departure of these professors. Hegel lingered on in obscurity during the ensuing year. Without any signs of promotion from the Jena authorities, he started to take the matters into his own hands more rigorously than ever before. In other words, the "exodus" seems to have served as a wakeup-call to Hegel as he now realized that his career prospects stood on very shaky grounds at Jena.

On September 7, 1804, Hegel sent a letter to Johann Gries, an independent literary figure, poet, translator, and a socialite, asking him to lobby on his behalf for the "chair" of philosophy now available at Heidelberg University. Hegel met Gries when the latter had stayed in Jena for a while, and assumed, mistakenly it turned out, that his gregarious "friend" had already established himself in Heidelberg, and so could effectively speak in his favor.[34] This was just the beginning of Hegel's ceaseless, but unsuccessful, lobbying efforts to become a salaried and tenured professor.

Shortly after sending his letter to Gries, Hegel learned that "a few" of his colleagues were about to be "appointed to professorships in philosophy" at Jena. On September 29, he politely, but not without a dose of indignation, informed Goethe that he also deserved to be appointed, since he was "the oldest [or the most senior (*älteste*)] *Privatdozent* in philosophy locally [i.e., at Jena]." This was certainly not a legitimate academic reason for an appointment of the requested kind. Hegel needed to improve his lecturing skills and add an original book to his lackluster résumé. Of the former requirement, he informed Goethe that he had been doing better lately and that he expected to attract more students in the upcoming semester. Of the latter requirement, he acknowledged that his "literary works" were currently "too insignificant for [him] to dare present them to" anyone, though he expects to "complete ... a purely scientific elaboration of philosophy" very soon.[35] In short, as was the case with his *habilitation*, Hegel once again requested an academic promotion without satisfying the normal expectations for it.

---

[34] *Briefe I*, #48.
[35] *Letters*, 685 (*Briefe I*, #49).

II. Floundering Privatdozent: Jena Years, 1801-1806

Among others, Jakob Fries was one of the *privatdozents* the faculty decided to promote, bypassing the utterly unaccomplished Hegel. In other words, Fries' promotion had much to do with his academic accomplishments.[36] For instance, he was already the author of an influential book in which he took the post-Kantian idealists to task and even bothered to mention Hegel's name in it.[37] Generally speaking, Fries would go on to become a well-known and respected philosopher, only to be overshadowed by Hegel after 1818, and this for largely political reasons,.[38]

As Hegel came to realize that his prospects at Jena were unpromising, he simultaneously turned towards Niethammer for help and started to distance himself from Schelling. For instance, he did not reply to Schelling's July 1804 letter, which, quite inexplicably, invited him to contribute to a projected journal, the *Yearbooks of Scientific Medicine*.[39] (Hegel's next letter to Schelling is dated January 3, 1807.)

"I do not know if my compliments to the Schelling family can be given to you since I do not know if they will be delivered," wrote Hegel to Niethammer on December 10, 1804. This gossipy comment implied that the Niethammers and the Schellings were not on very friendly terms. Likely, Hegel had in mind either a certain unhappy affair Schelling had caused at Würzburg, which put him at odds with Niethammer, or the speculated fact that the Niethammers did not approve of Schelling's marriage. (In fact, Hegel himself never approved of Caroline Schelling, who divorced August W. Schlegel to marry the younger Schelling.) Hegel then wondered whether Niethammer knew anything about a possible professorial position at Erlangen and elsewhere, adding that, "since it is so very tentative, I will say nothing further, knowing that with you it is in good hands."[40]

On March 4, 1805, Hegel informed Niethammer that he was unable to pay back, in full, the sixty Thalers he borrowed from him recently. He also noted that his earlier appeal to Goethe finally bore fruit; he was recently promoted to a vaguely-defined professorship (*außerordentliche Professor*), clearly at Goethe's charitable insistence. Understandably, Hegel's report did

---

[36] When I refer to other persons' "accomplishments," I have in mind primarily the perspectives of their contemporaries. I do not claim anywhere in this book that Fires, Schelling, or anyone else was or was not a great philosopher.

[37] If I am not mistaken, Fries mentions, in passim, Hegel twice in the entire book, and depicts him as a proponent of Schelling's identity-philosophy. In one mention, he criticizes Hegel for leaving unanswered the question of how he transitions "from the standpoint of the absolute to the finite and [shows] the necessity of the finite." Jakob Fries, *Reinhold, Fichte und Schelling* (Leipzig: A. L. Reinicke, 1803), 183.

[38] For a very useful, accessible, biographically-informed article on Fries' philosophy, see David E. Leary, "The Psychology of Jakob Friedrich Fries (1773-1843): Its Context, Nature, and Historical Significance," *Storia E Critica Della Psicologia* 3, no. 2 (1982): 217-48.

[39] *Briefe I*, #47.

[40] *Letters*, 102-03 (*Briefe I*, # 52).

II. Floundering Privatdozent: Jena Years, 1801–1806

not contain even an ounce of enthusiasm on his part, since his promotion did not come with a salary.[41] It was merely a formal embellishment of the unimpressive title of *privatdozent*. Consequently, and now under increasing financial duress, Hegel directed his lobbying efforts to other universities, such as Heidelberg, with more urgency than ever before.

Sometime before August 1805, Hegel contacted Johann Heinrich Voss, who was famous for translating Homer. "Since a new hope is arising for science in Heidelberg, and since you certainly have as much interest in science as you yourself devote to it," wrote Hegel, "I dare place in your hands my wish to take an active part in it and ask you to espouse my cause." Tellingly, without mentioning his name, Hegel also castigated Schelling in the same letter, claiming that the latter professed "ignorance" and a form of horrid "formalism." Clearly, he opined that the perception of him as Schelling's disciple was undermining his career prospects. As was the case in his appeal to Goethe, Hegel also confessed that he had nothing to show as proof of his qualifications: "As far as my intentions in philosophy are concerned, I of course necessarily wish that the only thing capable of providing a basis for judgment—my works up to now—were [already] laid down as a foundation. For I myself recognize them as [only] slightly finished." Without any tangible evidence to promote his cause, Hegel could only offer flattery and a pretentious promissory note. He wanted, he said, to make philosophy "speak German," just as Luther made the Bible and Voss made Homer speak German.[42] On August 24, Voss politely declined to help.[43]

Hegel had also contacted two of his former students for the same post. One of them was Karl Kastner, who was now a chemistry professor at Heidelberg. On November 15, Kastner informed Hegel that his own effort on Hegel's behalf was unsuccessful also. Still, he urged Hegel to send a copy of his work-in-progress to the university administrators, and to include a letter to explain how his philosophy "unequivocally defends *religion*." As crucially, Kastner informed him of a criticism brewing in the background at Heidelberg, which he himself shared: "Schelling's *Philosophy of Nature* pleased me immensely. However—keep this between us—it appears to me that it contains a certain weakness, as he constantly withdraws behind the Absolute."[44] This piece of information further reinforced Hegel's conviction that, if he was to receive an offer from Heidelberg, he had to distance himself from Schelling.

The second former student Hegel contacted was Christian Lange, who

---

[41] Ibid., 104 (#54).
[42] Ibid., 106-08 (#55).
[43] *Briefe I*, #56.
[44] Ibid., #57.

II. Floundering Privatdozent: Jena Years, 1801-1806

also reported back, on December 4, his failure to secure Hegel a position at Heidelberg. However, his letter informed Hegel of the theologian Karl Daub's interest in him, noting that the latter likes his writings. Lange also encouraged Hegel to hurry up and publish a book, which would certainly "not fail to have a great effect" on his prospects at Heidelberg.[45] A publishable book Hegel did not have. Instead of him, and with Voss' endorsement, the university hired none other than Fries, who had by now published multiple, well-received books. Fries was now, if not previously, one of Hegel's chief enemies.

After defeating them at Ulm and Austerlitz in late 1805, the French forced the Austrians to make territorial and other concessions, which were formalized with the Treaty of Pressburg, signed on December 26. With this new arrangement, Ferdinand III, an Austrian prince, became the duke of Würzburg. Consequently, for personal, political, and religious reasons, Niethammer, Schelling, and Paulus left Würzburg in 1806. Hegel, on the other hand, saw a multifaceted opportunity in their departure. In his January 14, 1806, letter to Niethammer, he wondered whether new prospects for him might now emerge at Würzburg. Another political development was also of interest to Hegel. On the same day, the duke of Württemberg, Friedrich II, was recognized as King Friedrich I with Napoleon's help. As Hegel noted, Friedrich at once (on January 1) abolished "the Provincial Diets." Given this new scenario, Hegel informed Niethammer, "I have thought about writing to [Württemberg Privy Councilor] Baron [Ludwig Timotheus] von Spittler, but really do not know if he is still active in university matters." Finally, he expressed his wish to have "a garrison of [Prussian] officers" in Jena, who would be "obliged to occupy themselves with the sciences," and so would help "increase the number of students" at Jena. If implemented, he believed, this scenario would improve his own career prospects there.[46]

Remarkably, Hegel showed no interest in the political implications of these developments. Every event, however large or small, real or imagined, presented itself to him as a career opportunity, or the lack thereof.

On October 13, 1806, Napoleon invaded Jena. (I will discuss Hegel's very favorable impression of Napoleon in Chapter 4.) Expectedly, Hegel's very-pressing personal issues forced him to relegate the invasion of Jena to a secondary status. Thus, in his letter to Niethammer, mailed the same day,

---

[45] *Letters*, 100 (*Briefe I*, #58). During this period, Daub was under Schelling's spell. Before that, he was a Kantian. It is said that Daub regarded "the most absurd assertions as philosophically justified." Otto Pfleiderer, *The Development of Theology in Germany Since Kant, and Its Progress in Great Britain since 1825*, trans. J. Frederick Smith (London: Swan Sonnenschein, 1890), 132.

[46] *Letters*, 108-09 (*Briefe I*, #59).

II. Floundering Privatdozent: Jena Years, 1801-1806

Hegel surmised that his manuscript (the *Phenomenology of Spirit*) might not be delivered before the deadline (October 18) set by his publisher. This meant that he was not going to receive the much-needed payment for his book, which was certainly written in a hurry to both boost his academic credentials and improve his dire financial situation. Relatedly, Hegel viewed himself as the foremost victim of the French invasion:

> If I get through today alright, I shall perhaps still have suffered as much or more than others. From the general outer appearance [of things], I must doubt whether my manuscript, which went off on Wednesday and Friday, has arrived. My loss would indeed be all too great. My other acquaintances here have not suffered anything. Am I to be the only one?[47]

It is difficult to appreciate Hegel's assessment of himself as the most-suffering individual among his acquaintances during Napoleon's Jena campaign. On October 13 and 14, when the more decisive twin-battles of Jena and Auerstedt took place, many homes in the region were either looted or set on fire and many people had lost their lives,[48] as Hegel himself would soon report to Niethammer in another letter.

With this letter, written on October 18, Hegel included the last installment of his manuscript except its Preface, which would be written in early 1807. After providing a brief update on who did and did not suffer at the hands of the French troops in Jena (apparently, his own residence was plundered by the French soldiers), he informed Niethammer that, according to his counsel, Ludwig Christoph Asverus, Göbhardt (Hegel's publisher) could not legally "raise objections in the case of a delay of these last *few* sheets [included in the letter and mailed on the deadline] caused by *intervening circumstances.*" Given that the war had freed him of his teaching obligations at Jena for the time being (the university was temporarily closed for the obvious reasons), Hegel also proposed to go to Bamberg, where both Niethammer[49] and the publisher resided at the time, so that he could personally oversee the editing process of his manuscript. And there was the most pressing issue: "I am compelled ... to ask you to send me money without fail. I need it most urgently," wrote Hegel.[50] A subsequent letter to Niethammer suggests that the expected money was sent

---

[47] Ibid., 114-15 (#74).
[48] F. N. Maude, *The Jena Campaign, 1806* (London: Swan Sonnenschein, 1909).
[49] During this period, Niethammer was working for the Bavarian government as an administrator of Protestant school and church affairs in Bamberg. He would acquire a more prominent governmental position in 1808.
[50] *Letters*, 116 (*Briefe I*, #76).

II. Floundering Privatdozent: Jena Years, 1801-1806

and received shortly thereafter, as was the last installment of the manuscript. Likely, the money Hegel received was already spent before its arrival.

5. Hegel's Final Battles in Jena

As we have seen, Hegel's efforts to procure a salaried teaching post were unsuccessful. In relation to his prospects at Jena, the reluctant Goethe was now his only hope. Clearly, the poet-minister was still concerned about Hegel's well-being. For instance, mostly out of pity for his destitute situation, he managed to procure a tiny stipend (100 Thalers) for him in July 1806.[51] However, he was unwilling to ignore his unsatisfactory academic performance and grant him a salaried post. Evidently, he still expected, and wished to see, "a careful presentation" of Hegel's "manner of thinking" in his forthcoming book.[52]

After staying with Niethammer in Bamberg to oversee the editing of the *Phenomenology*, Hegel returned to Jena in December 1806. Upon returning to Jena, and in a state of despair, he found a recent publication, which was sent to him by its author from Munich, Bavaria. The author was Schelling, and the publication a harsh critique of Fichte's recent works. Hegel quickly remembered how much he admired and missed Schelling. At least this is what his January 3, 1807, letter conveyed to the latter. He apologized for not corresponding with his friend for such a long time. Unsurprisingly, he went on to utter the real purpose of his letter: "I would hope to hear what is new in the works" in Bavaria, adding that, "since you are close to the source, perhaps you will learn more definitely what intentions are entertained there and at the same time can judge whether prospects may open up there for me. In such a case I may call upon your friendship, news, advice, even help."[53] It is as if Hegel copied the contents of the letter from his Bern letters to Schelling.

Schelling's lengthy reply of January 11 was not very encouraging: "When I heard from Niethammer that you were in Bamberg, I hoped you would stay there, and was very surprised to receive a letter from you in Jena." Moreover, having received the news about its impending publication from Hegel, and unaware of the fact that it insulted him, Schelling advised Hegel to send the *Phenomenology* to various authorities in Bavaria and to inform them of his motivation to work at the new (expected to open soon) Bavarian university.[54]

---

[51] *Briefe I*, #64. The amount of 100 Thalers is indicated in Hegel's August 6, 1806, letter to Niethammer (ibid., #67).
[52] Quoted in Althaus, *Hegel: An Intellectual Biography*, 87.
[53] *Letters*, 73-74 (*Briefe I*, #82).
[54] *Briefe I*, #83.

II. Floundering Privatdozent: Jena Years, 1801-1806

We will follow this renewed correspondence between Hegel and Schelling shortly.

During the same month, the desperate Hegel received the news of a vacancy created by the departure of "Professor [Franz] Schelver" from Jena to Heidelberg. At the end of the same month, he sent a letter to Goethe, asking him to allocate Schelver's salary to him. In exchange, he would fulfill Schelver's duties. However, there was a minor problem with Hegel's proposal: Schelver was a *botanist*. In his letter, Hegel assured Goethe, a reputable botanist himself, that he had some previous experience in the field of botany, as he had pursued botanical studies previously and even possessed "herbarium in Switzerland." If given the opportunity, he would like to "move into the currently unoccupied apartment of the Ducal Botanical Garden" and temporarily inspect and help maintain the garden. In so doing, he would learn even more about botany and "could soon deliver botanical lectures as well as ones on philosophy."[55] Naturally, Hegel's farfetched proposal, clearly concocted out of desperation, was ignored; the vacant position was filled with a qualified botanist, Siegmund Friedrich Voigt.

There was an additional reason for Hegel's desire to move into the apartment of the Ducal Botanical Garden: he wanted to get away from Christiana Burkhardt, his housekeeper and landlady. On February 5, she gave birth to their son, Ludwig Fischer. This situation likely gave Hegel an additional reason to discount his prospects at Jena since he wanted to avoid marrying Christiana and take care of his own son.[56] Consequently, the philosopher of "ethics," defined as selflessness, fled the scene.

At any rate, Hegel was now in an abject condition, for which, it is fair to say, he himself was solely responsible. Niethammer, who had by now become Hegel's new guardian, came to the rescue. As his February 20 letter to Niethammer indicates, Hegel accepted the offer, procured for him by the former in short order, to become the editor of a provisional newspaper, the *Bamberger Zeitung*.[57] However, Hegel was not enthusiastic about this prospect at all.[58] Even though it offered him a much-needed relief from his abject financial situation, it was not the kind of a job he had been hoping to obtain during the last six or seven years. Indeed, it appeared to confirm his failure to become a "respectable" professor, to which he clearly felt entitled.

At about the same time, and in response to his own inquiries, Hegel

---

[55] *Letters*, 686-87 (*Briefe I*, #87).
[56] Allegedly, Hegel had promised to marry Christiana. However, "once he had left Jena, he didn't give much further thought to the whole matter." Althaus, *Hegel: An Intellectual Biography*, 86.
[57] *Letters*, 126 (*Briefe I*, #89).
[58] *Briefe I*, #90. This letter will be quoted shortly.

II. Floundering Privatdozent: Jena Years, 1801-1806

received some news from Kastner to the effect that a literary journal might be founded in Heidelberg. His friend Schelver, the botanist, also wrote back to him, expressing his personal hope that Hegel would procure a salaried teaching post at Heidelberg, in addition to editing the planned journal. However, the news that Hegel was an incoherent lecturer had also reached the academic circles in Heidelberg. Schelver assured him that he would do all he could to reverse Hegel's unfortunate reputation and that he himself should also refute it. Regarding the founding of the literary journal, Schelver requested from Hegel a report on the kind of journal he would like to put together, should he be appointed its editor, and comment on the current philosophers, including Schelling. There was an additional element in this request. "I fear," he wrote, that Georg Friedrich Creuzer and Karl Daub might invite Shelling, rather than Hegel, to fill the vacant post.[59]

Hegel quickly put together an elaborate plan, called "Maxims for the Journal of German Literature." One gets the sense from reading it that he wanted his counterparts at Heidelberg to believe that, unlike what he had done with the *Critical Journal*, he would not use the new journal as a tool of slander. Still, he could not resist slandering several philosophers, including Schelling. The latter has been encouraging a form of arrogant and confused "formalism," which he, Schelling, himself is only now "beginning to solemnly renounce," Hegel wrote in his plan.[60]

That Hegel was acting as an opportunistic calculator is brought to sharper relief in his correspondence with Schelling. On February 23, he informed the latter about his new prospect in Bamberg: "I have been offered a deal that pays more than staying here [in Jena]." "For me," he added, "this is, for the time being, the prime consideration. Even if the business itself does not seem completely suitable [for a philosopher such as Hegel], nor even completely respectable in the eyes of the world, at least it is not dishonest." The double-dealing Hegel then urged Schelling to publish a prestigious "scientific journal" in Munich under the auspices of the Bavarian Academy of Sciences. Of course, Hegel would be the editor of the journal.[61] In his reply, Schelling once again advised Hegel to first establish himself through his own efforts in Bavaria before pursuing such grand projects. Besides, if pursued, Jacobi and his posse would likely control the journal, and would certainly not allow Hegel to run it, said Schelling.[62]

Hegel's attempt to juggle both Schelling and the faculty at Heidelberg

---

[59] Ibid., #86.
[60] G. W. F. Hegel, "Maximen des Journals der deutschen Literatur," in G. W. F. Hegel, *Gesammelte Werke: Jenaer kritische Schriften*, eds. Hartmut Buchner and Otto Pöggeler, 509-14 (Hamburg: Felix Meiner, 1968).
[61] *Letters*, 75-77 (*Briefe I*, #90).
[62] *Briefe I*, #93.

II. Floundering Privatdozent: Jena Years, 1801-1806

at the same time bore no fruit. Subsequently, in March, he requested a leave of absence from the administrators at Jena and moved to Bamberg, clearly begrudgingly, to work as the editor of the *Bamberger Zeitung*. We will follow his post-Jena story in Chapter 4.

Chapter 3 examines Hegel's political works, written during the period extending from 1798 to early 1807.

Chapter Three

III. POLITICAL WRITINGS, 1798-1807

1. Cart's Confidential Letters

Depending on what one counts as his own, this chapter examines five or six of Hegel's political works, or the relevant parts of such works, all written during the period extending from 1798 to early 1807. Briefly stated, one purpose of this chapter is to show, as clearly as possible, how Hegel espoused decisively illiberal political views during this period. Its second main aim is to illustrate the sense in which these views belong to the first phase of his political sympathies. Its third aim is to help the reader appreciate why his own contemporaries (and the present author) thought he was not much of a philosopher.

It is evident that Hegel had become more interested in politics in 1798 than he had ever been previously. However, Hegel's authorship of some of the works attributed to him is doubtful. One such work is the so-called "The Earliest [or Oldest] System-Program of German Idealism,"[1] assumed to be written in 1796 or 1797. Most scholars accept that, although written in his handwriting, Hegel was not its real author. In my view, which is hardly original, the document expresses Hölderlin's thoughts, and that Hegel had copied the text in Frankfurt.[2]

Another work is also attributed to Hegel on what I believe to be rather dubious grounds. Hegel, it is widely believed nowadays, had translated from French into German, appended a preface and running commentary to, and anonymously published Jean-Jacques Cart's book (*Confidential Letters*) on the oppression of the people of the Vaud by the Bernese aristocracy. The German translation of Cart's book[3] was attributed to Hegel, for the first

---

[1] (Attributed to) G. W. F. Hegel, "The Earliest System-Program of German Idealism," trans. H. S. Harris, in *Miscellaneous Writings of Hegel*, ed. Jon Stewart, 110-12 (Evanston, IL: Northwestern University Press, 2002).
[2] For a very informative discussion of the history and debates on the authorship of this document, as well as a very compelling defense of Hölderlin's authorship of it, see Eckart Förster, "'To Lend Wings to Physics Once Again': Hölderlin and the 'Oldest System-Programme of German Idealism," in *European Journal of Philosophy* 3, no. 2 (1995): 174-98.
[3] The title of the original was *Lettres de Jean-Jacques Cart à Bernard Dumuralt, Trésorier du Pays de Vaud, sur le droit public de ce Pays, et sur les événements actuels* (Paris:

III. Political Writings, 1798-1807

time, in the Meusel's *Das Gelehrte Teutschland* (1805). What we find in this lexicon of German literature is a brief biographical entry, which merely notes that Hegel had previously lived in Bern and Frankfurt and was now a *privatdozent* at Jena. It lists the translation of Cart's book as Hegel's only publication, without mentioning any of the essays he had published from 1801 to 1803.[4] This, then, is not a very reliable piece of evidence.

The entry was copied by the editors of future such lexicons, though it had remained entirely unknown to Hegel scholars until Hugo Falkenheim noticed it in 1909. Subsequently, he popularized the view that Hegel was the anonymous translator.[5] Another piece of information has been used to add credence to Falkenheim's claim: Hegel's April 16, 1795, letter to Schelling contains a paragraph, the contents of which resemble a comment made by the anonymous translator.[6] In these comments, the translator, like Hegel in his letter, disapproved of the political intrigues of the Bernese oligarchy in similar terms.

There are also many reasons to dispute the claim that Hegel was the anonymous translator. I will not bore the reader with all such reasons. Suffice it to mention several significant ones. A copy of the translation of Cart's book (not the original in French!) was found in his house after his death. It was subsequently auctioned off by his family and disciples without anyone suspecting that he had translated it. Although he was in the habit of keeping all his notes, no notes on Cart's book were ever found among his belongings. In fact, he had never mentioned either Cart's name or the case of the Vaud in any of his works and personal correspondence. This also means that he never identified himself as the translator. There is also no compelling reason to explain why he would be interested in translating it. Finally, both Cart and the anonymous translator defend certain views and institutions, such as the "old rights," which cannot be attributed to Hegel.

But let us now suppose that Hegel was the anonymous translator. Falkenheim used the translator's comments to illustrate why Hegel did not espouse any revolutionary, radical ideas during his Frankfurt period.[7] There is thus much truth in Falkenheim's verdict since one cannot infer from the translator's comments that he was "committed" to a "radically democratic"

Imprimerie du Cercle Social, 1793). The German translation is titled *Vertrauliche Briefe tiber das vormalige staatsrechtliche Verhaltnis des Waadtlandes zur Stadt Bern: Aus dem Franzdsischen eines verstorbenen Schweizers* (Frankfurt: Jägersche Buchhandlung, 1798).
[4] Günther Nicolin (ed.), *Hegel in Berichten seiner Zeitgenossen* (Hamburg: Felix Meiner, 1970), #86. Henceforth cited as *Berichten*.
[5] Hugo Falkenheim, "*Eine unbekannte politische Druckschrift Hegels,*" in *Preussische Jahrbucher* 138 (1909): 193-210.
[6] Clark Butler and Christiane Seiler (trans.), *Hegel: The Letters* (Bloomington: Indiana University Press, 1984), 35 (*Briefe I*, #11). Henceforth cited as *Letters*.
[7] *Pace* Raymond Plant, *Hegel* (New York: Routledge, 1973), 52-53.

III. Political Writings, 1798-1807

society and politics. Instead, both Cart and the translator favor the restoration of "the old rights" of the people of the Vaud, as well as a more just administration of criminal law, complaining specifically about the fact that "criminal justice is entirely in the hands of the government."[8] (Hegel, we should note, never defended the separation of the judiciary power from the executive power.) In the final analysis, regardless of whether he was the anonymous translator or not, we know for certain that Hegel was not committed to a "radically democratic" or "liberal" society in 1798. This claim will be sufficiently illustrated in the ensuing section.

2. On the Political Crisis of Württemberg

Since 1797, Württemberg had been governed by Duke Friedrich II, whose power was limited by the oligarchic Permanent Committee of the Provincial Diet. In 1798, Friedrich's decision to join the war against France faced fierce opposition from the standing committee of eight members of the diet (the *Ausschuß*), who refused to finance his war efforts. To overcome this opposition, the duke decided to summon the diet itself, which had not met for several decades. He dissolved the diet when it also refused to endorse his war efforts. In short, what we might call a "constitutional crisis" set in. (As noted earlier, after joining Napoleon's side, Friedrich would abolish the existing constitution in 1806.)

In response to this crisis, Hegel decided to publish an essay in 1798, the same year in which the translation of Cart's book was published in Frankfurt. He initially and misleadingly titled it *The Magistrates should be Elected by the People* (or *Citizens*). For reasons that are not entirely clear, the publisher(s) declined to print Hegel's essay.[9] What matters for our purposes more than such reasons is what the surviving fragments of the now-lost manuscript reveal about Hegel's political views.

In the surviving fragments, Hegel mostly criticizes "everyone" for seeking "only his limited advantage or the advantage of his class [or estate]." He exhibits a strong distaste toward the consultants (the lawyers), who are regarded as the primary culprits in nourishing selfish behavior in Württemberg. The "men of nobler aspirations and purer zeal," who are not identified, are called upon to work for the common good, and to remove the "unjust" parts of the existing constitution, which happens to be "still robust." Accordingly, Hegel merely recommends the "peaceful" removal of simply those "unjust" factors of the existing constitution that make

---

[8] *Vertrauliche Briefe*, 116-17.
[9] For various speculations on this issue, see Rosenkranz, *Georg Wilhelm Friedrich Hegels Leben*, 91; Harris, *Hegel's Development: Toward the Sunlight*, 427, 433; Pinkard, *Hegel: A Biography*, 75.

III. Political Writings, 1798-1807

Württemberg unstable.[10] These factors are not spelled out, which adds credence to Rudolf Haym's verdict that Hegel's essay was too vague with "its results," and so was not worth publishing anyway.[11]

The ensuing paragraphs of Hegel's essay, or of what has survived of it, basically amount to more moral preaching. He repeatedly disparages all parties involved in the political turmoil for their particularism and selfish behavior. He then associates the mentality and behavior of the people, "the common herd," with ignorance and the absence of "collective spirit." For this reason, *fears* Hegel, "popular elections would serve only to bring about the complete overthrow of the [existing] constitution." (He certainly had the lamentable French Revolution in mind.) Fearing this potential outcome, he proposes, as "the chief priority," that "the right of election" be placed "in the hands of a body of enlightened and upright men," not the common people, "the herd." In the last sentence of the surviving text, he goes even further by suggesting that no "kind of an election might give us any expectation of an assembly of this kind, however carefully one defined active and passive [kinds of] eligibility."[12]

This last verdict is Hegel's answer to a question he himself poses, which is noted by Haym: whether "it would be advisable to allow an unenlightened, habitually obedient mob," which is "dependent on the impression of the moment, to elect its representatives in a country that had a hereditary monarchy for centuries."[13] As we have seen, Hegel's answer is negative, and this helps us understand why his publisher "friend,"[14] who was clearly in favor of a representative body with meaningful legislative power, thought publishing Hegel's essay would do more evil to the progressive cause than good.[15]

Thus, the surviving fragments of Hegel's pamphlet do not endorse its reading as a liberal, republican, progressive, democratic, or revolutionary text.[16] Rather, and to repeat, they amount to little more than moral

---

[10] G. W. F. Hegel, *The Magistrates should be Elected by the People*, in *Political Writings*, eds. Laurence Dickey and H. B. Nisbet, 1-5 (Cambridge, UK: Cambridge University Press, 1999), 1-2.
[11] Rudolf Haym, *Hegel und seine Zeit. Vorlesungen über Entstehung und Entwicklung, Wesen und Wert der Hegelschen Philosophie* (Berlin: R. Gaertner, 1857), 67.
[12] Hegel, *The Magistrates should be Elected by the People*, 3-5.
[13] Haym, *Hegel und seine Zeit*, 66.
[14] A portion of the publisher's letter to Hegel is copied in Rosenkranz, *Georg Wilhelm Friedrich Hegels Leben*, 91.
[15] These conclusions force us to regard the second title found on Hegel's manuscript, namely, *On the Recent Domestic Affairs of Württemberg, Especially on the Inadequacy of the Municipal Constitution*, more appropriate. There is a scholarly dispute on who wrote this second title and on why it was written.
[16] According to Harris, "it is virtually certain ... that [Hegel] shared the hope [with his radical friends in Stuttgart] ... that a renewal of the war [with France] would lead to a

III. Political Writings, 1798-1807

preaching and a call for vaguely-described peaceful "change," which should not include popular (or even any) elections. By the same token, Hegel evidently opposes, even fears, a popular revolution in this essay. Unless the still "robust constitution" is "peacefully" changed in some way, warns Hegel, a "terrible outburst" of "vengeance" will be inflicted by the "ever-deceived, ever-oppressed mass."[17] This claim somewhat tenuously links Hegel to the anonymous translator of Cart's book, who also warns of a similar revolutionary outcome in his Preface.

The conclusion we must now draw is that, during his Frankfurt period, Hegel was not the supporter of the ideals of the French Revolution of 1789 he is nowadays imagined to be. For the most part, he did not have strong political views, though it is evident that he had become increasingly more interested in politics by 1798. However, he was not able to go beyond rather conservative, timid, and vague suggestions for political change. Soon after his failed attempt to publish his essay on the constitutional problems of Württemberg, Hegel became more visibly illiberal and undemocratic, as we are about to see.

3. The German Constitution

3.1 Hegel's Main Concern

It is widely accepted nowadays that *The German Constitution* was written over a period of several years, extending from late 1798 (or early 1799) to 1802.[18] This means that a portion of it was written-revised while Hegel was

---

revolution in Southern Germany, and he was ready and eager to support a minority government of patriots in a Republic of Württemberg established by French arms." Harris, *Hegel's Development: Toward the Sunlight*, 433. Similarly, Pinkard claims that one of his publisher "friends" informed Hegel that "the actions of the French in Württemberg had discredited all apologies for, and the defenses of, the Revolution in Württemberg, and that Hegel's manuscript [allegedly a revolutionary text] would therefore serve only to set back the cause of [radical] reform rather than to help it." Pinkard, *Hegel: A Biography*, 75.

[17] Hegel, *The Magistrates should be Elected by the People*, 2.

[18] *The German Constitution* was edited and published for the first time in 1893 by Mollat. G. W. F. Hegel, *Kritik der verfassung Deutschlands*, ed. Georg Mollat (Munich: Kassel, 1893). In 1913, Georg Lasson published a different (rearranged) version of the fragmented manuscript. G. W. F. Hegel, *Die Verfassung Deutschlands*, in *Hegels Schriften zur Politik und Rechtsphilosophie*, ed. Georg Lasson, 3-136 (Leipzig: Felix Meiner, 1913). For two translations, see G. W. F. Hegel, *The German Constitution*, in *Political Writings*, trans. T. M. Knox, 143-242 (Oxford: Oxford University Press, 1964); G. W. F. Hegel, *The German Constitution*, in *Political Writings*, eds. Laurence Dickey and H. B. Nisbet, 6-101 (Cambridge: Cambridge University Press, 1999). In this chapter, I will cite the latter translation, and will occasionally revise it without further notice.

III. Political Writings, 1798-1807

in Jena.[19] For the reasons I will provide shortly, this unpublished manuscript cannot be objectively read as a liberal, progressive, or anti-nationalistic text.[20] Overall, *The German Constitution* belongs to what I call the "critical phase" of Hegel's political sympathies, which is characterized by his disillusionment with the Germans and the German Empire's constitution-state, and by his desire to unite the Germans under a centralized state—by all means necessary, capable of defending itself.

The central theme of *The German Constitution* was suggested to Hegel by the Second Congress of Rastatt (November 1797-March 1799). We know this because the earliest known fragment of this manuscript begins with a reference to it. More specifically, Hegel begins the fragment by lamenting the concessions the German Empire[21] was forced to make at the Congress after suffering a humiliating defeat at the hands of the French forces. The concessions included ceding the control of some of the "most beautiful lands" of Germany and "millions of its children" to the French Republic, as well as the "burden of heavy debt," resulting from the war reparations the French demanded to end the hostilities. Hegel regards this settlement as an epic humiliation of the German nation, and critically links its current woes to the Empire's weak constitution and the selfish behavior of the Germans.[22] These themes are repeated in his other fragments, written later. In fact, it is safe to assume that his later interest in this topic, and hence his revision of the manuscript, was further rekindled by similar German failures, which resulted in the equally humiliating Treaty of Lunéville (1801).[23]

---

[19] See H. S. Harris, *Hegel's Development: Toward the Sunlight* (Oxford: Oxford University Press, 1972), 436, n. 1.; H. S. Harris, "Introduction to the *Difference* Essay," in G. W. F. Hegel, *The Difference Between Fichte's and Schelling's Philosophy*, trans. H. S. Harris and Walter Cerf, 1-75 (Albany, NY: SUNY Press, 1977), 67, n. 6.

[20] Pace Z. A. Pelczynski, "An Introductory Essay," in *Hegel's Political Writings*, trans. T. M. Knox, 3-137 (Oxford: Oxford University Press, 1964), 56 ff; Shlomo Avineri, *Hegel' Theory of the Modern State* (Cambridge: Cambridge University Press, 1972), 34-61. Unlike Avineri, Pelczynski does not defend the legend that Hegel opposes nationalism in *The German Constitution*.

[21] Following Hegel, I will refer to the "Holy Roman Empire of the German Nation" simply as the German Empire or Germany. "Holy Roman Empire of the German Nation" was formally adopted in 1512, likely due to both the growing dominance of the German states in the Holy Roman Empire and the Empire's loss of certain non-German territories, such as Italy and Burgundy. See Joachim Whaley, *Germany and the Holy Roman Empire: Volume I: Maximilian I to the Peace of Westphalia, 1493–1648* (Oxford: Oxford University Press, 2012), 17.

[22] Johannes Hoffmeister (ed.), *Dokumente zu Hegels Entwicklung* (Stuttgart: Friedrich Frommanns Verlag, 1936), 282.

[23] For a translation of this treaty, see Frank Maloy Anderson, *The Constitutions and Other Select Documents Illustrative of the History of France, 1789-1901* (Minneapolis: The H. W. Wilson Company, 1904), 290-94.

III. Political Writings, 1798-1807

Consistently with the spirit of the first fragment, the first sentence we encounter in the Lasson edition reads: "Germany is no longer a state."[24] In the Mollat edition, it reads: "The form of German constitutional law is deeply rooted in what has made the Germans most celebrated, namely, their drive for freedom." These two sentences are closely related: according to Hegel, the German drive for freedom largely explains why Germany is not a state, though its archaic and anarchical constitution is also to be blamed for this predicament.

Hegel assesses the "health" of a state primarily within the context of the anarchical system of states. This is to say, the power of the state "generally reveals itself ... in the turmoil of war," which is unavoidable. In his view, an entity is not really a state unless it is powerful enough to defend and govern itself. Its power determines its right both domestically and internationally. Thus, "in the war [and in the subsequent peace treaty] with the French Republic, Germany has found by its own experience that it is no longer a state," and is thus without right, for it has been defeated, occupied, and humiliated by this and other "foreign ... conquerors."[25]

Once more, Germany's predicament is causally linked to "the obduracy of the German character," which prevents the Germans from sacrificing "their particular characteristics to society," from uniting under a common political authority ("the universal"), and so from discovering "freedom in common." We already observe an illiberal tone in Hegel's voice, which becomes more obvious when he defines this "freedom in common" as "free subjection to a supreme political authority."[26] In this manner, Hegel's desire to have a proper state in Germany is associated with "free subjection" to the authority of the state, which is seen as a precondition for "freedom in common" from the yoke of foreign powers.

According to Hegel, "no major war has been waged among the European powers in which German valor has not invariably won honor, if not laurels, and in which rivers of German blood have not been shed." Indeed, reports Hegel with a sense of Teutonic pride, "at every opportunity" the Germans prove "their courage and ... show themselves worthy of their ancestors and of the ancient military fame of the Germans." Yet, "no land is more unprotected, more incapable of self-defense" than the German Empire. In the final analysis, the so-called "Imperial Army" is "less useful in war than any army in the rest of Europe." The selfish particularism of the Germans and their unwillingness to subject themselves to a common authority are given as the causes of this lamentable dilemma.[27] The issue of

---

[24] Hegel, *The German Constitution*, 7.
[25] Ibid.
[26] Ibid., 10.
[27] Ibid., 26-30.

III. Political Writings, 1798-1807

the army receives one of the very few concrete proposals from the mostly lamenting Hegel. He wants "amalgamating the whole military strength of Germany into a single army." "The Emperor would, of course, have supreme command of this army." Also, "in this army, every major prince would be a general by birth, and each would be in charge of his own regiment and appoint its officers."[28] So, at least in this regard, Hegel wishes to keep the nobility and the emperor firmly in charge.

Alas, "the German political authority is in the same position *in financial matters* as it is in respect of military power." This is especially a major problem in post-feudal Europe, where "finance has become an essential part" of political and military power. This development requires the fiscal system to be "under the direct control of the supreme political authority." The Germans (individuals, estates, and states/statelets) resist such an authority. Consequently, an actual "financial power," which "is essential to a state in our times," is also missing in Germany. For these reasons, the Germans merely constitute not a state but an unorganized "mass," which "is unable to defend its independence against external enemies."[29]

Hegel also laments the presence of the same problem of German independence and particularism in the juridical system of the Empire. This system is not based on "universal laws in the strict sense; on the contrary, the relationship of each estate to the whole is a particular matter," he says. By "universal laws in the strict sense," Hegel means the laws that issue from the central authority. Thus, he reasons, the absence of such "universal" laws "has an essential effect on the nature of the [supreme] political authority," for it renders this authority "powerless." For all these reasons, and more, "Germany does not internally constitute a political authority," and so cannot be regarded "as a state." Instead, it must be conceived "as a mass of independent states [or estates]," in urgent need of being "completely under the control of a single government."[30]

The religious division also finds an undesirable expression in the Imperial constitution, argues Hegel. Before the rise of Protestantism in Germany, "the whole still retained certain a cohesion," which resulted from "an inner bond of disposition [*Gemüter*]" the local rulers had toward one another. The source of this cohesion was "religious unity." In the ensuing paragraphs, Hegel enumerates, in a rather jumpy manner, many factors he holds responsible for the loss of religious unity. Ultimately, though, he holds "the rise of Imperial cities" and the concomitant rise of "civic consciousness [*bürgerliche Sinn*], which cares only for individual interests," responsible for the lamentable disunity. According to Hegel, "the universal misery of

---

[28] Ibid., 98.
[29] Ibid., 30-35.
[30] Ibid., 40-42; 44-49.

III. Political Writings, 1798-1807

the wars of religion, especially the Thirty Years War [1618-1648]" was a result of this religious disunity.[31] As disagreeable as this division is to him, Hegel does not propose the abolition of different religious persuasions in *The German Constitution*. We will return to this issue shortly.

3.2 Hegel's Nationalism

The loss of "territories ... over the passage of several centuries," Hegel complains, "make up a long and melancholy list."[32] "Germany," he says in another context, "has been ...plundered, robbed, scorned, despised, and usually diminished [in territorial terms] in peace ... by foreign powers." Consequently, and for a long time now (since the Peace of Westphalia, 1648), it "has ceased to decide independently the course of its internal affairs; it has handed over its fate to others,"[33] especially, now, to the French Republic. It is worth repeating here that everything Hegel says in *The German Constitution* contradicts the claim that, circa 1798, he was in favor of a French invasion of Germany or Württemberg.[34]

As we read through the manuscript, it becomes more and more obvious that Hegel wants a centralized, essentially *German*, state. For instance, he criticizes "the constitutional lawyers" for defending "the Holy Roman-German Empire's claims to Hungary, Poland, Prussia, Naples, etc." According to Hegel, such claims or rights are "politically insignificant," since they "do not pertain to the German Empire as such." Although his reasoning is not as tight as one would like it to be, Hegel here differentiates the rightful claims of the *German* Empire from those of the (rather bogus) universalistic Holy Roman Empire (the other appellation of the German Empire). The upshot is that the *German* Empire

> could have neither the interest, nor the will, nor latterly the power to assert what might be considered appropriate to the Emperor's role as sovereign, and to uphold so unnatural [*unnatürliche*] a union of territories which are separated by their geographical position as well as by the individuality [i.e., the specific character] of their peoples.

A "natural" German state should consist only of "German" territories. "Hungary, Poland, Prussia, Naples, etc." cannot belong to it. [35] (Interestingly, the Hegel of this period regarded Prussia as a foreign state.)

---

[31] Ibid., 50-51
[32] Ibid., 35.
[33] Ibid., 83.
[34] *Pace* Harris, *Hegel's Development: Toward the Sunlight*, 433; Frederick Beiser, *Hegel* (New York: Routledge, 2005), 214-15.
[35] Hegel, *The German Constitution*, 35-36.

III. Political Writings, 1798-1807

Hegel proceeds to discuss various losses of German territory to foreign powers since the Peace of Westphalia (1648). Some of these losses were based on "chimerical claims and wholly unreal rights." Others entail "genuine loss to the Empire." These latter are the many territories Hegel regards as *German*. They were ceded, he repeats, to Sweden, Spain, Prussia, and France through various peace treaties. "Finally, the Peace of Lunéville [1801] has not only deprived Germany of numerous rights of sovereignty in Italy; it has also robbed it of the entire left bank of the Rhine." Hegel regards the latter a genuine loss.[36] This thought is expressed from a different angle once more: "It must be reckoned as even more of a loss that foreign princes have become the owners of German Imperial territories, and hence also members of the German Empire." This has been happening for a while, which has not only urged "the dissolution of the Empire into independent states," but "also granted foreign powers the right to interfere in the internal affairs [of Germany]."[37]

Interestingly, Hegel mainly blames the treasonous Germans for the predicament in which Germany has found itself. With the German allies of the French in mind, he says that it is an act of "extreme malevolence if one party in a state ... calls on a foreign power for help." Thus, regardless of the situation in which they find themselves, "the [natural] principle that ... [Germans] ought ... to form a single state [among themselves] still prevails," even if this "union is itself the product of tyranny." This is because such a national political union is "the most sacred of human aims."[38] As we will see shortly, Hegel indeed yearns for a tyrannical unification of Germany in *The German Constitution*.

While the relatively indeterminate nature of the manuscript leaves room for debate on the precise nature and intensity of his nationalism, the claim that its author was not a nationalist (or was an anti-nationalist) is clearly false.[39] On a further note, Napoleon, who had played a crucial role in forcing the emperor's (Francis II) hand to accept the Peace of Lunéville on February 9, 1801, is mentioned only once in *The German Constitution*, and this in passim.[40] This fact indicates that Hegel was not a Napoleon admirer during this period. This issue will become more relevant in the ensuing chapters.

Hegel's nationalism, as we have seen, is intimately related to the main task of his manuscript, in that he wants to unite the fragmented Germans under a centralized state. In this context, three additional questions arise:

---

[36] Ibid., 36-40.
[37] Ibid., 58.
[38] Ibid., 59.
[39] *Pace* Avineri, *Hegel's Theory of the Modern State*, 35 ff.
[40] Hegel, *The German Constitution*, 87.

III. Political Writings, 1798-1807

How, or by what means, is Germany to be united? What sort of a state is it to have, if it is to be able to defend itself? What kind of rights and freedom should Germans have?

3.3 Lessons to be Learned from Machiavelli and Richelieu

Once again, the most urgent problem Hegel wants to solve in *The German Constitution* is the statelessness of Germany, and this is where Machiavelli's ideas, as Hegel interprets them, come handy.[41] Much like Hegel, Machiavelli had witnessed the dissolution and humiliation of his country, Italy, and responded to this misfortune of his country by calling upon his prince to unify it by means of force, says Hegel. In his wording, "deeply conscious of this state of universal misery, hatred, upheaval, and blindness, an Italian statesman, with cool deliberation, grasped the necessary idea of saving Italy by uniting it into a single state." Accordingly, Machiavelli "appealed ... to his prince to assume the exalted role of savior of Italy and to earn the fame of bringing its misfortune to an end."[42] Clearly, Hegel has in mind the last chapter of *The Prince*.[43]

Following what he takes to be Machiavelli's teaching, Hegel argues that "a state should be formed by a nation," and that "freedom is possible only when a nation is united into a state by means of compulsory association." This is a rational lesson the Germans have failed to understand, despite all the suffering caused by "the Seven Years War ..., the recent war with France ..., and by the French [revolutionary] frenzy of freedom." Thus, Hegel wants a Machiavellian prince to eliminate all divisions in Germany and to crush the Revolution-inspired disobedience to the state. This, which was also Machiavelli's "noble purpose," should be achieved by any means necessary. Those who see in Machiavelli's "work nothing but a foundation for tyranny or a golden mirror for an ambitious oppressor," those who claim that his "means are repugnant" and "unholy," notes Hegel, miss the greater purpose. Given the horrid condition of Germany, "there can be no question of any choice of means; gangrenous limbs cannot be cured with lavender water ... A life which is about to decay can only be reorganized by most violent means [*gewaltsamste Verfahren*]."[44] What matters ultimately to Hegel is the right of the state to exist; any action to secure this end is justified; the end justifies the means. Indeed, "the state has no higher duty

---

[41] There is much truth in Cassirer's claim that Hegel "dreamed of being a second Machiavelli." Ernst Cassirer, *The Myth of the State* (New Haven: Yale University Press, 1946), 122.
[42] Hegel, *The German Constitution*, 79.
[43] Niccolò Machiavelli, *The Prince*, trans. James B. Atkinson (Indianapolis: Hackett, 2008), Ch. 26.
[44] Hegel, *The German Constitution*, 80.

III. Political Writings, 1798-1807

than to preserve itself and to destroy the power of such offenders [as those who oppose its authority] in the surest way it can."[45]

Germany needs a strongman to implement such drastic measures, since the Germans, for whom the idea of unification is "something utterly alien," are incapable of forming a state by themselves. In fact, claims Hegel falsely, this is a generally valid assumption for all peoples and all times, since the formation of a proper state "has never been the fruit of deliberation, but only of force." Thus, Hegel here opposes the (usually liberal) contractarian theories, which maintain that a legitimate state must be based on the voluntary agreement of its constituents. Accordingly, he adds that the Germans "would have to be brought together into a single mass by the power of a conqueror. They would have to be compelled to regard themselves as belonging to Germany." This (unidentified) conqueror, this *German* "Theseus," is also to act as the ruler, who has the capacity to hold "the direction of the state's power within his hands." A German Theseus of this kind would also "have to possess enough magnanimity to grant the people [or the nation] he had created ... a share in matters of common concern."[46]

As we will see in the next section, the "share in matters of common concern" Hegel has in mind here is an oligarchical system of representation, dominated by the nobility and the emperor, without popular elections, and so has little to do with "the French frenzy of freedom" he disparaged earlier. Also, the claim that Hegel had in mind Napoleon as the "conqueror" in this context cannot be taken seriously since much of *The German Constitution* is a nationalistic lamentation of the French invasion of various parts of Germany. In other words, the "conqueror" in question is urged to subdue *his own* nation; he is not a foreigner; he is a "patriot," who must compel his countrymen "to regard themselves as belonging to Germany."[47]

Hegel goes on to suggest that his patriotic conqueror must learn from Cardinal Richelieu, the chief minister of Louis XIII. He must thus be able to overcome the kind of "hatred ... Richelieu and other great men ... brought upon themselves" by destroying "the particular and distinctive characteristics of their fellows." Hegel, who is nowadays described as a "liberal," even thinks such characteristics are symptoms of "the profound perversion [*Verkehrtheit*]" of "the social nature [*Natur*] of man." Once his social nature is perverted, "he uses his powers" to cause more isolation (individualism, particularism) from the others, and even "asserts his separation to the degree of madness, for madness is nothing else but the complete separation of the individual from his own kind [*Geschlecht*],"

---

[45] Ibid., 81.
[46] Ibid., 100-01.
[47] Ibid., 101.

III. Political Writings, 1798-1807

namely, his nation. Luckily, "the German nation [*Nation*]" is not capable of the degree of madness one encounters "in the Jewish nation," and in those societies (Revolutionary France) in which extreme isolation has led to everyone murdering each other "until the state is shattered." Still, in Germany, too, "particularism—privilege and self-preference—is so intimately personal that the concept and insight into necessity [into what human nature necessitates] are much too weak to effect any action" in favor of national unity. Genuine "concept and insight," proposed by Richelieu, Machiavelli, and now Hegel, are so frowned upon by the particularistic Germans that they "must be justified [and imposed] by force; only then will they [the Germans] submit to them."[48] They must be taught a lesson.

What, then, were Richelieu's great accomplishments?

Hegel portrays Richelieu, whom Montesquieu justly called a "despot,"[49] as a great statesman. His ensuing apology for Richelieu dovetails his foregoing apology for Machiavelli. He had proven his greatness, claims Hegel, when he crushed "the great nobles and the Huguenots" in France, and "thereby raised [the French state] to be one of the most powerful states." In Germany, he gave the estates "free rein," and so abolished its "existence as a state." Thus, from a *realpolitik* standpoint, he wisely gave "the principle of monarchy" to France and "the principle of forming a mass of distinct states [and estates]" to Germany, and so deliberately enjoined its dissolution.[50]

Hegel's claims about Richelieu's actions and motives are not without merit. In a 1632 memorandum, Richelieu described the goal of the French intervention in the Holy Roman Empire (i.e., Germany) unambiguously: "to ruin the House of Austria [of the Habsburgs] completely, ... to profit from its dismemberment, and to make the [French] king the head of all the Catholic princes of Christendom and thus the most powerful in Europe."[51]

But, claims Hegel with exaggeration, the actions Richelieu had taken against the Huguenots should not "be regarded as suppression of freedom of conscience." While he "eradicated" both their "armed fanaticism" and claims to an independent "state, he left the Huguenots their freedom of conscience, their churches, worship, and civil and political rights, on an equal footing with the Catholics." In this manner, Richelieu discovered and exercised that form of "toleration which was implemented more than

---

[48] Ibid.
[49] "If this man's heart had not been bewitched with the love of despotic power, still ... arbitrary [and despotic] notions would have filled his head." Charles De Montesquieu, *The Spirit of Laws*, trans. Thomas Nugent (Kitchener, Ontario: Batoche Books, 2001—originally published in 1748 and translated in 1752), bk. 5, sec. 10.
[50] Hegel, *The German Constitution*, 75-76.
[51] Quoted in Andreas Osiander, "Sovereignty, International Relations, and the Westphalian Myth," *International Organization* 55, no. 2 (2001): 251-87, 260.

III. Political Writings, 1798-1807

a century later as the product of a more cultivated humanity and as the most splendid achievement of philosophy and more refined manners."[52] Differently put, Richelieu invented the very policy Frederick II (Frederick the Great) of Prussia and Joseph II of Austria would implement a century later.

Rather than *constitutional* rights, Frederick II offered "grace" to the Catholic minority in Prussia, and Joseph II did the same to the Protestants in the predominantly Catholic Austria. What they did was consistent with "the higher natural right of freedom of conscience and the non-dependence of civic rights on faith."[53] Thus, Hegel clearly endorses a non-constitutional policy of religious "tolerance," based on the monarch's "grace." The monarch's "grace," like God's, is not an obligation, *we* note, and so may be withdrawn, especially when things go awry.

Hegel, in short, is unwilling to grant constitutional guarantees (rights in this sense) to the estates and individuals, as we will further establish shortly. Beforehand, however, we need to investigate the kind of "share in matters of common concern" he thinks the magnanimous strongman should "grant the people" or nation he is urged to create by Hegel.

3.4 "Representative" Government

Hegel had always (at least after 1798) defended the existence of representative institutions. It should be further clarified that such institutions had existed in Germany, and elsewhere, long before the French Revolution, as Hegel himself notes on multiple occasions in *The German Constitution*. Thus, when Hegel mentions representative institutions approvingly in this manuscript, or elsewhere, one should not immediately jump to the conclusion, as many of his liberalizers tend to do, that he supports the kind of representative institutions the French had tried to implement during the Revolution.

According to Hegel, "German freedom used to mean simply the independence of the estates from the Emperor." This undesirable freedom amounted to "the abolition of the political association [*Staats verbandes*]." In the past, says he with much and typical exaggeration, the only known alternative to this disunity was "slavery and despotism." However, since the French Revolution, that is, "for the last ten years, the whole of Europe has fixed its attention on the terrifying [*fürchterlich*] struggle of a people for freedom," which has now become a Europe-wide movement.

---

[52] Hegel, *The German Constitution*, 76-77. Unlike what Hegel carelessly asserts here, Richelieu did not give equal rights to the Protestants and Catholics. For a very informative discussion, see R. J. Knecht, *Richelieu* (New York: Routledge, 2013), Ch. 5.
[53] Hegel, *The German Constitution*, 52-53.

III. Political Writings, 1798-1807

Consequently, political "concepts have inevitably undergone a change," and so lost "their former emptiness and indeterminacy."[54]

"It is evident," Hegel says, that the miserable effects of this "blind clamor for freedom," unleashed by the French Revolution, have "taught us enough" to resist such freedom. This is because this "bloody game" of freedom, which has caused many nations to "plunge into an abyss of misery," has produced "the realization that a firm government is necessary for freedom." However, despotism (i.e., the complete absence of representation) has also fallen out of favor. What has emerged is the realization that "the people must take part in the making of laws and in the most important affairs of the state." One striking aspect of Hegel's proposal in this regard is his tendency to reduce such "important affairs" to the "approval for a proportion of national taxation, especially for extraordinary taxes." Also, the people now expect "the government ... [to] act in accordance with the laws." In short, "without such a representative body, freedom is no longer conceivable."[55]

Hegel's liberalizers cannot quote the last sentence often enough; they assume that it vindicates Hegel's republican liberalism. What Hegel himself prescribes, however, is something else. Hereditary monarchy is one of "the necessary attributes of a state," he says, adding that the monarch "would have to" (or must) receive "the cooperation of the parts [i.e., estates]." Tellingly, he does not here, or elsewhere, say that the monarch must cooperate with the latter. Likewise, military expenses are to "be borne by the provinces," and should be "approved annually by the provincial assemblies, all of which would combine to perform this task."[56]

Such assemblies are to be populated by representatives "selected" from the districts of the provinces. These delegates should merge with the "Cities Bench of the Imperial Diet" to form a single body. The College of [Imperial] Electors and the College of Princes, the other two colleges of the Imperial Diet, are also to be retained in Hegel's scheme, which is clearly modeled after the existing Imperial system. As a matter of principle, Hegel believes that "if the representatives were drawn exclusively from princely houses and the noblest families, their talents and brilliance would give an exalted status and appearance to such a princely assembly." To be sure, "the Emperor," the noblest of all by birth, should "be placed at the head of the German Empire."[57] For his part, "the monarch looks after national affairs, especially in so far as they concern external relations with other states; he is

---

[54] Hegel, *The German Constitution*, 92.
[55] Ibid., 93-94.
[56] Ibid., 98-99.
[57] Ibid., 99-100.

III. Political Writings, 1798-1807

the center of political power, and everything which requires legal enforcement emanates from him."[58]

Basically, then, Hegel's "representative" system is a monarchical oligarchy in which the nobility, led by the emperor, controls both the army and the "representative" institutions. There is not even a single word on popular elections in Hegel's proposal. Also, it seems that the main, if not the only, task of the Hegelian representative institutions is to "approve" the taxes necessary to fund the military, and this annually. He does not in this (or in any other) context consider the issue of what should happen if the representative bodies refuse to approve the required funds for common defense, demanded by the monarch. He merely assumes that they would, or should, give their consent. After all, "free subjection" to the central authority, he told us earlier, is what "freedom in common" requires. Hegel would repeat this claim until the end of his life.

Overall, the system of representation Hegel proposes in *The German Constitution* is a sketchy outline, which raises more questions than it answers. However, it is clearly *not* modeled after the representative system implemented in France soon after the Revolution of 1789.

3.5 Subordinate Rights

On the issues of rights and laws, *The German Constitution* contains several paragraphs in which Hegel seems to argue that their specific form is irrelevant to the formation of a viable state. Such things may "be present in the most diverse ways," he says, insisting that "there may even be complete irregularity and disparity in such matters" within a single state (or empire). He then adumbrates a long list of institutions and practices that he regards as irrelevant to the formation of a "mass" into a state, which basically includes just about everything proper political theorists would regard as relevant.[59]

Before giving us the list, Hegel gives us the following, minimal, definition of the state: "A mass of people can call itself a state only if it is united for the common defense of the totality of its property." To clarify, he has in mind the defense of the *territory* of the whole nation, "the totality of its property," and not private property. This requires two things: "a common military force and a [centralized] state power." Accordingly, he now maintains, "if the universal political authority demands of the individual only what is necessary for itself ..., it may in other respects grant the citizens [*der Bürger*] their living freedom and individual [*eigenen*] will, and even leave considerable scope for the latter." Once again, "what is

---

[58] Ibid., 62-63.
[59] Ibid., 17-20.

necessary" or "indispensable to the whole" is common defense.[60] In fact, with the likes of Fichte in mind (likely written in Jena), he goes on to disparage "those political theories" that subordinate "everything" to "the immediate activity of the supreme political authority."[61] Such comments as the ones just quoted have misled some of Hegel's liberalizers to claim that he proposes a "minimal," liberal state in *The German Constitution*, as if not subordinating "everything" to its authority qualified it as a "minimal," liberal state.

A calmer, closer look at what Hegel just told us would reveal that he leaves the issue of what the state may demand of its citizens open-ended, and here, too, he remains committed to the lessons he draws from Richelieu. We already observe elements of this in what he just told us in the previous paragraph: the state is to "grant," as it sees fit, what might "even" turn out to be "considerable" scope for free activity. No liberal talks this way, and Hegel goes on to prove that he is no liberal. Thus, immediately after his objection to "those political theories," he asserts the following: "It is self-evident that the highest political authority must exercise ultimate control of the internal relations of a people and of their organization." This means, apparently in a "self-evident" manner, that "state power must be concentrated in one center," namely, the "government," which would undertake both the "decisions [legislation]" and their "execution."[62]

Hegel proceeds to grant conditional freedom to the people once more. *If* the people "respect" the government's authority, *if,* furthermore, this authority "is secure in itself and immutably sanctified in the person of a monarch chosen by birth and [or which is] in accordance with natural law, the political authority may freely allow [!] the subordinate systems and bodies [estates]... to a large share of the relationships which arise in society." Hegel's conditional defense of the people's or the estates' freedom becomes even more decisively illiberal in the following sentence: the state "must secure itself above all these [concerns for rights and freedoms], and to this end, it must not spare the subordinate systems of rights and privileges [of both the estates and citizens]."[63] In this sense, Hegel regards "a people as fortunate if the state allows [!] it considerable freedom in subordinate activities of a universal [or general] kind, and ... a political authority as infinitely strong if it can be supported by a greater spirit of freedom [i.e., duty to obey it], untainted by pedantry, among its people."[64]

---

[60] Ibid., 15-17.
[61] Ibid., 21.
[62] Ibid.
[63] Ibid.
[64] Ibid., 25.

III. Political Writings, 1798-1807

What ultimately matters to Hegel, who takes himself to be a student of Machiavelli and Richelieu, is the preservation of the state, in relation to which the rights and freedoms of its denizens are both subordinate and dispensable. This view is clearly expressed in another passage: "The services and duties of individuals" should be "determined by the needs of the whole," which is to be decided by "the state." When the state accepts the contrary scenario, it necessarily confirms that "it has been deprived of its power." Indeed, all private rights and possessions "rest on the power of the state." Consequently, "if the state loses all authority [or power]" over them, such rights and possessions become "very precarious."[65] Based on this poor reasoning, which implies that any limitation of the power of the state is tantamount to depriving it of all its power, Hegel asserts that the preservation of private rights necessitates their dispensability and subordination to the needs and authority of the state. The upshot is that Hegel thinks there are no such things as "inviolable ... private rights [*Privatrecht*]," since the "right of the state" is "superior" to such rights. In fact, he further reasons, "if the state is to exist, it cannot treat [private] rights" as inviolable.[66] These are decisively illiberal thoughts, it goes without saying.

4. Ethics and Politics in the *Natural Law* Essay

4.1 Critique of Hobbes and Fichte

On the Scientific Ways of Treating Natural Law was self-published, in two installments, in the *Critical Journal* in 1802 and 1803.[67] One of Hegel's main aims in the *Natural Law* essay is to critique two existing "sciences" of natural law or right *(Naturrecht)*, namely, empiricism (of Hobbes) and the idealism of Kant and Fichte. His second main aim is to construct his own, Schelling-inspired speculative "system" of natural law or political philosophy. This section mostly focuses on his second aim. In my attempt to make sense of it, I will inevitably make Hegel's essay appear much clearer than it really is. In other words, the whole thing is a philosophical and linguistic disaster.[68]

---

[65] Ibid., 11-12.
[66] Ibid., 67.
[67] G. W. F. Hegel, *On the Scientific Ways of Treating Natural Law, on its Place in Practical Philosophy, and its Relation to the Positive Science of Right*, in *Political Writings*, eds. Laurence Dickey and H. B. Nisbet, 102-85 (Cambridge: Cambridge University Press, 1999). Nisbet's translation will be occasionally altered without further notice.
[68] "The difficulties of the work in German are legendary." James Schmidt, "Recent Hegel Literature: The Jena Period and the Phenomenology of Spirit," *Telos* 48 (1981): 114-41, 116.

III. Political Writings, 1798-1807

According to Hegel, the "empirical science" of natural right (or law) ultimately winds up creating a system of determinations, based on the conversion of the *many* into *one*. But it is precisely this relation of "the one and the many which this empirical knowledge cannot overcome." Consequently, what emerges from the empiricists' inquiry is a "formal totality" in which the parts (many individuals) are not truly united. Differently and politically put, the anonymous empiricist takes the atomistic and antagonistic society of individuals living in the chaotic state of nature as an *a priori* principle. In this conception of "the state of nature," individuals are "thought of as embroiled in a war of mutual annihilation." It now becomes clear that Hegel's unnamed empiricist is Hobbes, whose theory of the state of nature as a state of total war justifies the absolute political state, the Leviathan. According to Hegel, this "absolute totality" is merely an "external" determination, which Hobbes allegedly superimposes onto the chaotic "multiplicity as a further and alien factor." Therefore, their "relationship ... can only be that between ruler and ruled," of total "domination and obedience."[69]

Hegel merely and unthinkingly *asserts* his own solution:

> The absolute Idea of ethical life ... contains both majesty [the political state] and the state of nature [many individuals] as altogether identical, for majesty itself is nothing other than absolute ethical nature [of the individuals]; and there can be no thought, in the real existence [*Reellsein*] of majesty, of any loss of absolute [ethical] freedom (which is what we should understand by 'natural freedom') or of any abandonment of ethical nature ... On the contrary ..., individuality as such is ... completely at one with absolute ethical majesty; and this genuine, living, non-subjugated oneness is the only genuine ethical life of the individual.[70]

Here, the ethical "substance" of all individuals is identified, all-too-readily, with the state, which is "the absolute substance." In this manner, he has allegedly shown the identity of human substance (or essence) with the state. Thus, by obeying the state, individuals obey themselves, and not an alien, external power, claims Hegel. Otherwise put, Hegel has no qualms with Hobbes' absolute state. Rather, his problem with the latter's theory is that it makes this authority "external" to the individual. Hegel allegedly solves this problem with a jargon-laden, tautological definition.

Two forms of consciousness in Fichte's philosophy, Hegel goes on to

---

[69] Hegel, *Natural Law*, 107-13. Cf. Thomas Hobbes, *The Leviathan*, ed. J. C. A. Gaskin (Oxford: Oxford University Press, 1998), Chaps. 13-17.
[70] Ibid., 113-14.

III. Political Writings, 1798-1807

argue, "remain totally opposed to one another." Here, he wants to explain how Fichte's system of right (law) creates a scenario in which the general will, the will of the government, restricts the activities of individuals.[71] Hegel calls this scheme of things "coercion."[72] Once again, the problem is "externality," and not coercion per se. Thus, his critique of Fichte is essentially the same as his critique of Hobbes, as Fichte, too, is disparaged for putting individuals under the authority of an alien will.[73]

Hegel now acknowledges that his opponent wants to ensure that the government does not become despotic. For this purpose, Fichte creates a system of reciprocal coercion: "the governed are coerced [restricted] by the government and the government by the governed." This is a reference to Fichte's defense of popular elections (representation) and the separation of the legislative and the executive powers. But this scenario might produce a perpetual struggle between two equal powers. Fichte's solution to this specific problem is the institution of the *ephorate*. Hegel cannot see how this institution would solve the problem it is supposed to solve, for the "ephors are likewise just as much private wills as the others."[74] It is as if Hegel himself could conceive of rulers who are not "private wills."

Moreover, as Fichte himself acknowledges, the government may not accept the supervision of the ephors. Should this happen, argues Fichte, the people (the highest authority in Fichte's theory) should rise against the

---

[71] "The principle of any judgment of right is that each is to limit his freedom, the sphere of his free actions, through the concept of the freedom of the other (so that the other, as free in general, can exist as well). The concept of freedom at issue here (which, as already stated above, has only formal meaning) yields the concept of original right, that is, of that right that should belong absolutely to every person as such." Johann G. Fichte, *Foundations of Natural Right*, ed. Frederick Neuhouser, trans. Michael Baur (Cambridge, UK: Cambridge University Press, 2000), 102 (§10). For an accessible and useful summary of Fichte's theory of government, see Allen W. Wood, "Fichte's Philosophy of Right and Ethics," in *The Cambridge Companion to Fichte*, eds. David James and Günter Zöller, 168-98 (Cambridge: Cambridge University Press, 2016), 176-78. For his early political thought, see Frederick C. Beiser, *Enlightenment, Revolution, and Romanticism: The Genesis of Modern German Political Thought, 1790—1800* (Cambridge: Harvard University Press, 1992), 57-83; Reidar Maliks, *Kant's Politics in Context* (Oxford: Oxford University Press, 2014), throughout.
[72] Hegel, *Natural Law*, 132-33. The problem Hegel tries to identify here pertains to the well-known (before and after Hegel noticed it) problem of transition from the self-positing individual (subjectivity), as the bearer of rights, to the social membership of the same. For a very interesting attempt to avoid this problem on Fichte's terms, see Nedim Nomer, "Fichte and the Relationship between Self-Positing and Rights," *Journal of the History of Philosophy* 48, no. 4, (2010): 469-490.
[73] Also see G. W. F. Hegel, *The Difference Between Fichte's and Schelling's Philosophy*, trans. H. S. Harris and Walter Cerf (Albany, NY: SUNY Press, 1977), 148-49; G. W. F. Hegel, *Faith and Knowledge*, trans. H. S. Harris and Walter Cerf (Albany, NY: SUNY Press, 1977), 183.
[74] Hegel, *Natural Law*, 134-35.

III. Political Writings, 1798-1807

government. Hegel would have nothing of this: "what could one do with such a mob, which also interferes in all private affairs, which is itself remote from public life, and whose education has not equipped it to be conscious of the collective will or to act in the spirit of the whole, but to do precisely the opposite?" Hegel's reference to the "recent" actions of a "government" in this context indicates that his opposition to Fichte's theory is inspired by his fear of, and opposition to, the French Revolution and its institutions.[75] In short, Hegel opposes a government based on both checks-and-balances and popular representation and shows much disdain for the rational capacities of "the people." As we will see in due course, the allegedly "progressive" Hegel had always detested "the people," also known to him as the "herd," "the mob," and "the rabble."

4.2 Ethical Life

4.2.1 War, Death, and Ethical Life

Hegel's own solution, once again, is "the absolute ethical totality." "We shall make the positive presupposition," he adds thoughtlessly, "that the absolute ethical totality is nothing other than a *people* [or a nation]." In this presupposed totality, "the individual proves his oneness with the people in a negative sense—and in an unambiguous manner—only by [incurring] the danger of death." To make this "negative" unity possible, Hegel first needs to create belligerent states and wars, so that individuals may practice Hegelian ethics and validate his speculative "science" in so doing. Here, Hegel allegedly proves that war is "absolutely necessary," since absolute ethical life cannot sustain itself without it. Reversely put, "war preserves the ethical health of peoples" by inducing

> their indifference to determinate things [such as property, rights, and so on]; it prevents ... the people from becoming habituated to them, just as the movement of the winds preserves the seas from that stagnation which a permanent calm would produce, and which a permanent (or indeed 'perpetual' peace [*a la* Kant] would produce among peoples.[76]

Hegel would repeat this perversity until the end of his life, as we will repeatedly observe in due course. Alas, this is not the most disturbing part of his war-ethics nexus; he recommends that the state should wage war against its own people periodically, in order to keep them ethical. Thus, he now turns his attention to the internal relations of a "people." He discusses

---
[75] Ibid., 135.
[76] Ibid., 139-41.

III. Political Writings, 1798-1807

such relations primarily in terms of "political economy."[77] There is nothing worthwhile here to consider, except his conclusion that civil society must be punished occasionally. "Since this system is [rooted] entirely in negativity and [indeterminate] infinity," he claims meaninglessly, "it follows that ... it must be treated wholly negatively by the ... [state], and [so] must remain subject to the dominance" of this ethical-political will. Translation: the state must "prevent" civil society from becoming "an independent power." This further means that the state must not treat the property rights of individuals as inviolable, for this "would indeed rule out a negative treatment of the system of possession and would give it complete latitude to become absolutely firmly established. Instead, the ethical whole [i.e., the state] must ensure that this system remains aware of its inner nullity."[78] Thus, the Hegelian ethical life is ultimately sustained by two kinds of war waged by the state: one against other states and one against its own people.

Hegel goes on to divide his society into three "classes [or estates—*Stände*]." Why three classes? They are, claims the incorrigibly "speculative" Hegel, "formed in accordance with the absolute necessity of the ethical." This "necessity" was earlier linked to the willingness to die for one's community in a war. The same link now supplies the rationale for Hegel's first and most essential (or ethical) class. This "is the class of the free, the [collective] individual of absolute ethical life." It is to be drawn from the ranks of the nobility. It is "free" in the sense that its members are completely, selflessly, and courageously devoted to the preservation of the whole. The practical side of their "freedom" is expressed through their "work, which is directed ... towards death, and whose product is again not something individual, but the being and preservation of the whole of the ethical organization." The second class consists of "those who are not free [or are unethical], and which has its being [*ist*] in the differentiation [*Differenz*] of need and work and in the right and justice of possession and property; its work deals with matters of detail and consequently does not entail the danger of death." The third class, the peasantry, "is solely concerned with the earth as an element; its work confronts it with the whole [sphere] of need as its direct object." In a nutshell, this unthinking generality, which lacks "differentiated understanding," reinforces "the first class with its numbers and elemental being" in wars in Hegel's system, and so also faces death rather crudely. The lower two classes are to also "relieve the first class" of its "need to earn its living."[79]

Hegel thinks the second class, which exists in the sphere of political economy and clings to its private rights, is the class that should be

---

[77] Hegel, *Natural Law*, 141.
[78] Ibid., 141-42.
[79] Ibid., 147-48.

III. Political Writings, 1798-1807

periodically reminded of "its inner nullity." By drawing some lessons from Edward Gibbon's account of the fall of the Roman Empire, he argues that the equality "between the [first and second] classes" led to "the demise of freedom" in the Roman Empire. Consequently, the ethical union "'insensibly sunk into the languid indifference of *private life*.'"[80] According to Hegel, this state of affairs "immediately introduces the formal legal relationship [*Rechtsverhältnis*], which fixes individual being and posits it absolutely" as a bearer of inviolable rights. This lamentable scenario constitutes the "corruption and universal debasement" of the community, based on the "system of property and right," to which "belong the inherently [in Hegel's eyes] subordinate and purely formal questions concerning the rightful basis of property, contract, etc., but also the whole endless expansion of legislation at large" to regulate conflicts arising from private rights and interests. Due to its intrinsic nature, this "system must simultaneously develop as a universal condition and must [consequently] destroy free ethical life."[81]

Hegel thinks the rise of the second class at the expense of the first, accompanied by the individualistic "system of property and right," is also responsible for the ongoing dissolution of Germany. Relatedly, he also disparages "the vacuity of the rights of man," proclaimed and implemented, I surmise without any doubt, during the French Revolution.[82] Such dangerous and unworthy things as these do not belong in Hegel's ethical life.

4.2.2 *Moralität* versus *Sittlichkeit*

The ensuing material is from the second installment (1803) of the *Natural Law* essay. The famous Hegelian distinction between "morality" (*Moralität*) and "ethical life" or "ethicality" (*Sittlichkeit*) is explicitly drawn here for the first time. Typically, Hegel begins his new endeavor with a jargon-laden definition of ethical life, with which we are already familiar:

> For since real absolute ethical life comprehends and unites within itself infinity (or the absolute concept) and pure individuality in general and in its highest abstraction, it is immediately the ethical life of the individual; and conversely, the essence of the ethical life of the individual is quite simply the real (and hence universal) absolute ethical life—the ethical life of the individual is one pulse-beat of the whole system, and is itself the whole system.[83]

---

[80] Ibid., 149. Edward Gibbon, *Decline and the Fall of the Roman Empire*, vol. 1, ed. J. B. Bury (London: Methuen, 1925), 56-57.
[81] Hegel, *Natural Law*, 149-50.
[82] Ibid., 178-79.
[83] Ibid., 159.

III. Political Writings, 1798-1807

All this pretentious jargon says is that the essence of the individual is identical with the ethical life of his or her people. This readily confirms to Hegel that the lived ethical life of the community is the external actuality of the ethical individual's inner essence. This circular explication allegedly vindicates "a linguistic indicator, namely that it is in the nature of absolute ethical life [*Sittlichkeit*] to be ... an *ethos* [*Sitten*]," since "both the Greek word [*ethos*] for ethical life and the German word [*Sitten*] express its nature admirably." This meaning of *Sittlichkeit*, Hegel further argues, is so incontrovertible that "the newer [individualistic] systems of ethics" were forced to adopt "the word 'morality' [*Moralität*] instead." Differently put, since the philosophers of morality "make a principle out of individuality," they could no longer use the term *Sittlichkeit*, for this term refers to the absolute, Hegelian ethical whole in which individuality vanishes.[84]

But Hegel goes further than this self-satisfying tautology and claims that morality, understood as the individualistic (subjective) outlook and life, debases ethical life—of the Hegelian kind. For this reason, it amounts to "natural wrong [*Naturunrecht*]" since it urges the "ethical nature" of the individual to plunge "into the utmost corruption and misfortune."[85] Also, and unsurprisingly, he associates morality with "the second class [*Stand*]." "Morality in the usual sense" is thus a "reflection" of "the *bourgeois* or private person."[86]

The "private person," endowed with rights, Hegel now argues, is a historical product. This, in turn, suggests to him that the malady at hand can be reversed. This requires Hegelian "*education* [*Erziehung*]," at least of children. The aim of this sort of education, as "the wisest men of antiquity" tell Hegel, consists in their habituation to live "in accordance with the customs [or ethics—*Sitten*] of one's country." He goes on to add that the "*system of legislation*" must express the existing, "living customs [*Sitten*] of the present ... perfectly." This will somehow clarify "what is right and what has actuality within a people by looking at its laws." These laws "must also ... be perfectly united with the form of particularity [i.e., with individuals' psyche]," so that they "may be perceived and worshiped as the god of the people; and this perception itself must, in turn, have its active expression [*Regsamkeit*] and joyful movement in a cult."[87]

After taking the contractarian theories of the state to task, which allegedly nullify "the absolute majesty of the ethical totality," the cultist Hegel once again attacks Fichte's "machine" state, claiming that the latter's "constitutional law ..., as a perfect police-force," could "permeate the

---

[84] Ibid.
[85] Ibid., 160.
[86] Ibid., 160-61.
[87] Ibid., 162-63.

III. Political Writings, 1798-1807

being of each individual completely, thereby destroying civic freedom—and this would be the harshest despotism." In other words, "Fichte wishes to see the entire activity and being of the individual as such supervised, known, and determined by the universal and the abstraction to which he stands opposed."[88] Presumably, Hegel has avoided Fichte's "despotism" by advising individuals to joyfully worship the laws derived directly from the customs of their nation. With the same move, he also takes himself to have successfully overcome the indeterminacy or emptiness involved in Kant's moral doctrine, which preaches obeying self-given universal laws (morality in this sense).

Hegel is not even aware that his accommodationist demand contradicts his other major demand, which calls for the repression of the particularistic, individualistic customs and laws of the modern (bourgeois) society. In other words, he both defends ethical relativism and opposes the historically relative customs and laws associated with bourgeois society.

These are the wicked and confused thoughts, as they appeared in 1803, of the very same man who has been repackaged and marketed in recent decades not only as a liberal thinker but also as a profound philosopher of "freedom."

5. Jena Lectures on Ethical Life and the State, 1805-1806

5.1 Public Authority, the Ruler, and the Tyrannical Lord

The manuscript, which contains Hegel's Jena Lectures (1805-1806),[89] makes the barely readable *Natural Law* essay look like a literary jewel. For this reason, very few people have read it, and even fewer have commented on it in an elaborate manner.[90] I will only consider its last part, which is

---

[88] Ibid., 170-71.
[89] G. W. F. Hegel, *Hegel and the Human Spirit: A Translation of the Jena Lectures on the Philosophy of Spirit of 1805-6*, trans. Leo Rauch (Detroit: Wayne State University Press, 1983). Henceforth cited as *Jena Lectures*.
[90] For general remarks, see H. S. Harris, *Hegel's Development: Night Thoughts: Jena, 1801-1806* (Oxford: Oxford University Press, 1983); Pini Ifergan, *Hegel's Discovery of the Philosophy of Spirit: Autonomy, Alienation, and the Ethical Life: The Jena Lectures 1802-1806*, trans. Nessa Olshansky-Ashtar (London: Palgrave, 2014); Paul Franco, *Hegel's Philosophy of Freedom* (New Haven: Yale University Press, 1999), 67-80. These lectures have attracted the interest of the scholars especially interested in Hegel's conception of recognition. See Axel Honneth, *The Struggle for Recognition: The Moral Grammar of Social Conflicts*, trans. Joel Anderson (Cambridge, UK: Polity Press, 1995); Ludwig Siep, "The Struggle for Recognition: Hegel's Dispute with Hobbes in the Jena Writings," in *Hegel's Dialectic of Desire and Recognition: Texts and Commentary*, ed. J. O'Neill, 273-88 (Albany, NY: SUNY Press, 1996); Robert R. Williams, *Hegel's Ethics of Recognition* (Berkeley: University of California Press, 1997), 93-108.

III. Political Writings, 1798-1807

more directly relevant to his so-called "political philosophy" than its other parts.

Let us begin with the following line: The government is "the power over life and death."[91] This means that it is the absolute power over the lives of individuals. Through this power, says Hegel, the government gains the "trust" of individuals and instils "fear" in them. Somehow, this combination of trust and fear brings about not only my "agreement" with the will of the government but also the confidence that "it is my real self"; I am confident that, through it, "it is I who rule," even though I am in reality ruled by the "lord, public force, and ruler," says the philosopher of silly contradictions and tricks.[92]

These three forms of authority are now to be justified by definitional fiat. "Public force" is the community's "insurmountable strength against the individual and is his necessity and the power oppressing him." This is a good thing since true ethical freedom is precisely the suppression of the individual's subjectivity. However, this ethical power is "effective only insofar as it is united into a unity, only as [universal-individual] will," namely, the will of the ruler—the monarch. Thus, adds the great dialectician, "individuals have to make themselves into the universal will through the negation of their own will." This is a "scientific" way of saying, individuals (the people) should not make the universal will; or, they should make it negatively by *not* making it.[93]

Thus far, we have covered Hegel's "scientific" exposition of the concepts of "public power" and "the ruler." The following pertains to "the lord," the founder of a nation-state.

Hegel now takes a swipe at Rousseau, who "imagines" that "the civil union" rests "on a primordial contract, to which each individual is presumed to have given his tacit agreement," as well as his agreement to obey "every subsequent action [law?] of the community." As if it were meant as a historical account, he finds Rousseau's theory of social contract historically inaccurate, adding that "all states were established through the noble force of great men."[94] Consequently, he proves his ability to both misunderstand the purpose of Rousseau's *prescriptive* theory of social contract and conjure up historical facts.[95] Be that as it may, what emerges

---

[91] Hegel, *Jena Lectures*, 145-46.
[92] Ibid., 151-53.
[93] Ibid., 153-54.
[94] Ibid., 154-55.
[95] Jean-Jacques Rousseau, The Social Contract *and Other Later Political Writings*, ed. and trans. Victor Gourevitch (Cambridge: Cambridge University Press, 1997). The fuller title of Rousseau's book is *On the Social Contract; or, Principles of Political Rights*. For a very useful, historically informed commentary, see David Lay Williams, *Rousseau's Social Contract: An Introduction* (Cambridge: Cambridge University Press, 2014).

III. Political Writings, 1798-1807

here is Hegel's life-long opposition to Rousseau's attempt to link the legitimacy of political power to the will, or the consent, of the citizens.

Hegel's "great man" claim is related to the rulership of the aforementioned "lord." In other words, all states were, and must be in the future, founded by a noble great man, who has something about him that compels the others to "call him their lord." They "must obey" him "even if they do not want to." Knowing and expressing the "absolute will" is what is "preeminent in the great man ..., so that all flock to his banner [and] he is their god." "Theseus," who "established the Athenian state," is once again given as an example of such a great man. However, without mentioning his name, Hegel also praises Napoleon (some scholars understandably think he has Robespierre in mind), who "sustained the state" through "a fearful force" during "the French Revolution." "This force," which is "tyranny," or "pure frightening domination," adds he, "is necessary and just, insofar as it constitutes and sustains the state."[96]

Drawing his inspiration from Machiavelli once again, from whom he also heard about Theseus, Hegel asserts that "no concepts of good and bad, shameful and vile, malicious cunning and deceit" can be properly applied to the actions of the state, which is "absolute spirit." As far as "the constituting of the state" is concerned, such acts as "assassination, fraud, cruelty, etc., carries no sense of evil," says Hegel, adding that it is in this "great sense that Machiavelli's *The Prince* is written." Moreover, Machiavelli's theory, like Hegel's, is driven by "deep feeling for the misery of his fatherland"; "patriotic inspiration underlies his cold and prudent teaching." How patriotic he must have been when he called for the "death" of the "leaders" of various principalities, and for "the fear of death for the rest." As it is the case in *The German Constitution*, here, too, Hegel's apology for Machiavelli is tied to his own "patriotic" desire to see the organization of Germany into a strong, centralized state through the efforts of a tyrannical "lord." But the stubborn Germans would refuse to accept the absolute will and "pure force" of a "lord" or a "tyrant." Thus, "the state," led by a great lord, "must have the courage ... to take completely tyrannous action" whenever and wherever it is necessary.[97] Obviously, Hegel still wanted to unify Germany circa 1806. Obviously, too, he was still yearning for a tyrant-lord he could worship. Indeed, he had a fetish of this kind throughout his life.

In the final analysis, in Hegel's conception of it, tyranny functions as the founding principle of his desired state. "Through tyranny, we have the ... education [of individuals] toward obedience," adds he. Once the people are properly "educated" to obey the state, tyranny becomes "superfluous,"

---

[96] Hegel, *Jena Lectures*, 155.
[97] Ibid., 155-56.

III. Political Writings, 1798-1807

and so is "replaced by the rule of law." To those who make obedience their second nature, "the law itself is no longer an alien force, but rather the known universal will." Thus, they are no longer oppressed, as they are in Fichte's republic, for they intuitively obey the laws given by the state and the lord. This "educated ... obedience" is the "underlying ... existent essence" of the law in the Hegelian ethical community. However, since the individual "may not conceive and understand how he is sustained in [the state]," the law still implies tyrannical force. "Thus, the universal [the will of the state] has a negative and a positive significance simultaneously" in this sense.[98]

5.2 War Against other States and Civil Society (Once Again)

In the ensuing few paragraphs, Hegel compares the ethical life of an imagined ancient Greek polis with the freedom of modern individuals. First, he claims that the ancient Greek polis expressed "the beautiful [and] happy freedom of the Greeks, which is and has been so envied." Then, he asserts that "a higher level of abstraction" or "distinction" than the one found in the Greek polis exists in modern states. After some confused thoughts about the system of "hereditary monarchy" and the representation of the people in modern times, he adds abruptly that "it is bad for a people when it is the government, as bad as it is irrational."[99]

Next, Hegel once again refers to a "higher principle of the modern era," allegedly "unknown to Plato and the ancients." He likely has in mind the "principle" of "hereditary monarchy." Then follows a description of the "ancient polis," which confuses the life of the guardians Plato imaginatively proposes in the *Republic* with the actual life of ancient Greeks. In this life, Hegel alleges, "the common morality" was the basis of the "immediate unity of the universal and the individual," which means that "no part separated itself from the whole."[100] Moreover, unlike the system proposed in "Plato's *Republic*" and what existed in "Sparta," modern individuals choose their own professions, based on their own "outlook."[101] This seems to be yet another modern "higher principle." How all this adds up, or what it is supposed to add up to, is difficult to divine.

We were just led to believe that the differentiation of modern individuals into different professions, and so their distribution into various classes or estates, stems from their own choice and outlook. However, Hegel now maintains pretentiously that this differentiation is the work of the spirit, as it seeks to know its "own existence and activity" in each

---

[98] Ibid., 156-57.
[99] Ibid., 157-60.
[100] Ibid., 160-61.
[101] Ibid., 161-62.

III. Political Writings, 1798-1807

distinct class.[102] I will not bore the reader with the details of Hegel's silly discussion of classes. Suffice it to say briefly that he presents five classes in this manuscript. Apart from adding the class of bureaucrats, what is different about his new scheme of classes is the way they are ordered, as he now wants to dialectically advance from the lower to the higher classes, whereas as the reverse was the case in his *Natural Law* essay.

First, and the lowest, is the mentally and labor-wise "crude" peasantry.[103] Then, Hegel brandishes "the *Bürger* class," by which he seems to mean the artisans and manufacturers. Its members are mainly concerned with their property rights, and so are individualistic.[104] The third is the "*mercantile class*," which mainly cares about "money."[105] These lowly classes fail to meet Hegel's ethical expectations. For the first time, Hegel here presents "the universal class" of civil servants, and places it above the other three classes just discussed. Since this "public class works for the state," it has "the absolute moral [ethical] outlook" both in his "knowing" and "activity." It turns out, this class also fails to count as "absolute actual self."[106]

The "military class" is the highest of all. Hegel now needs to justify the necessity of this class, and so abruptly, but unsurprisingly, turns his attention to the sphere of interstate relations. This sphere is the "real ... state of nature," since there is no power above the states in it. Hegel typically opposes Kant's notion of "permanent peace," and denounces emphatically the appeal to "morality" in regulating interstate relations. Since these relations exist in a state of war, the military class is necessary to defend each state. In war, says Hegel, this class exhibits its willingness to sacrifice itself, since it faces "the danger of death." In short, "the end" of the military class is "the maintenance of the totality [i.e., the state] against the enemy who is out to destroy it."[107]

For some speculative reason, the external war reminds Hegel of the "ethical" need to wage war against the classes themselves. "In war," says he, "the government ... shakes up the organization of its classes—as well as the all-embracing systems of right, of personal security and property." In other words, the external war reveals to Hegel's consciousness the necessity of absolute and tyrannical power of the state over classes and individuals, their rights, personal security, and property. "All this," says he, "vanishes in the power of the universal [i.e., the political state or government]."

---

[102] Ibid., 162-63.
[103] Ibid., 163-64.
[104] Ibid., 165-66.
[105] Ibid., 166.
[106] Ibid., 167-70.
[107] Ibid., 170-71.

III. Political Writings, 1798-1807

Consequently, "the individual's rootedness in his own [particularistic] existence, this sundering of the totality into atoms, here suppresses itself. The individual has his absolute freedom [in his submission to the will of the government], and this itself is the strength of the government." Thus, the "subjugation and coercion" of the entire community under "pure power" reemerges here as the fundamental constituting-principle of Hegel's ideal ethical and free life.[108]

The question is not whether Hegel was a progressive/revolutionary liberal or a conservative liberal (with a small "c," it is often said). Rather, it is whether he supported an authoritarian state, absolute tyranny, or a combination of both. That he was not much of a thinker goes without saying, so I believe. In fact, one would be apt to characterize his thoughts as largely absurd, rather than simply second-rate.

6. The *Phenomenology*: Ethicality and the Revolution

6.1 Dumb Generality as Ethicality

The *Phenomenology of Spirit* contains rather extensive discussions on morality, ethics, and politics.[109] This section focuses on a few of them, and so is not meant as a comprehensive study of Hegel's book, the overall aim and coherence of which is still a matter of scholarly dispute.[110] First, I deal

---

[108] Ibid., 171-72. For an interesting discussion of the founding act of ethical life in Hegel, see Ido Geiger, *The Founding Act of Modern Ethical Life: Hegel's Critique of Kant's Moral and Political Philosophy* (Stanford: Stanford University Press, 2007).
[109] G. W. F. Hegel, *Phenomenology of Spirit*, trans. A. V. Miller (Oxford: Oxford University Press, 1977).
[110] The following is a small portion of the works published on the *Phenomenology*: Alexandre Kojève, *Introduction to the Reading of Hegel: Lectures on the Phenomenology of Spirit*, trans. James H. Nichols, Jr. (Cornell: Cornell University Press, 1980); Jean Hyppolite, *Genesis and Structure of Hegel's Phenomenology of Spirit* (Evanston, IL: Northwestern University Press, 1974); Philip J. Kain, *Hegel and the Other: A Study of the Phenomenology of Spirit* (Albany, NY: SUNY Press, 2005); Ludwig Siep, *Hegel's Phenomenology of Spirit*, trans. Daniel Smyth (Cambridge: Cambridge University Press, 2014); Charles Taylor, *Hegel* (Cambridge, UK: Cambridge University Press, 1975), 125-221; Terry Pinkard, *Hegel's Phenomenology: The Sociality of Reason* (Cambridge, UK: Cambridge University Press, 1994); Michael N. Forster, *Hegel's Idea of a Phenomenology of Spirit* (Chicago, IL: Chicago University Press, 1998); Jon Stewart, *The Unity of Hegel's Phenomenology of Spirit: A Systematic Interpretation* (Evanston: Northwestern University Press, 2000); William F. Bristow, *Hegel and the Transformation of Philosophical Critique* (Oxford: Oxford University Press, 2007); Robert B. Pippin, *Hegel on Self-Consciousness: Desire and Death in the Phenomenology of Spirit* (Princeton: Princeton University Press, 2011). For a collection of essays on various aspects of the *Phenomenology*, see Kenneth R. Westphal (ed.), *The Blackwell Guide to Hegel's* Phenomenology of Spirit (Oxford: Wiley-Blackwell, 2009). For a review of the academic altercations on the question of the

III. Political Writings, 1798-1807

with is his conceptions of ethical life and ethical consciousness, which basically repeats the same ideas we have encountered in his previous works. Second, I discuss his treatment of the Revolution, which he treats as the complete "historical" alienation and destruction of the ethical spirit.

As it is the case in his other writings, the *Phenomenology* also imagines the ethical in contrast to, or as a critique of, morality, especially its Kantian manifestation.[111] An infamous example of such a critique is the following:

> Suppose something has been entrusted to me; it is the property of someone else and I acknowledge this because it is so, and I keep myself unfalteringly in this relationship. If I should keep for myself what is entrusted to me, then according to the principle I follow in testing laws, which is a tautology, I am not in the least guilty of contradiction; for then I no longer look upon it as the property of someone else: to hold on to something which I do not regard as belonging to someone else is perfectly consistent. Alteration of the *point of view* is not contradiction ...[112]

Clearly, this pedestrian argument is meant as a response to Kant's "deposits" argument. Alas, his understanding of Kant's argument is deeply flawed. Kant's argument is roughly and briefly the following. If the unauthorized appropriation of someone else's deposit ("property") were accepted as a universal principle, then no rational person would entrust

---

Phenomenology's overall coherence, see Schmidt, "Recent Hegel Literature: The Jena Period and the *Phenomenology of Spirit*," 135-40; and Gary Dorrien, *Kantian Reason and Hegelian Spirit: The Idealistic Logic of Modern Theology* (Chichester, UK: Wiley-Blackwell, 2012), 186 ff. These works constitute a small portion of the existing literature on the *Phenomenology*.

[111] For a variety of views on Hegel's relationship to Kant, see Paul Guyer, "Thought and Being: Hegel's Critique of Kant," in *The Cambridge Companion to Hegel*, ed. Frederick C. Beiser, 171-210 (Cambridge, UK: Cambridge University Press, 1993); Robert B. Pippin, *Hegel's Idealism: The Satisfactions of Self-Consciousness* (Cambridge: Cambridge University Press, 1989); Allen W. Wood, *Hegel's Ethical Thought* (Cambridge: Cambridge University Press, 1990); Karl Ameriks, *Kant and the Fate of Autonomy: Problems in the Appropriation of Critical Philosophy* (Cambridge, UK: Cambridge University Press, 2000); Dieter Henrich, *Between Kant and Hegel: Lectures on German Idealism* (Cambridge, MA: Harvard University Press, 2003), 299-331; Robert M. Wallace, *Hegel's Philosophy of Reality, Freedom, and God* (New York: Cambridge University Press, 2005); Stephen Houlgate, *The Opening of Hegel's Logic: From Being to Infinity* (Lafayette, IN: Purdue University Press, 2006); Beatrice Longuenesse, *Hegel's Critique of Metaphysics* (Cambridge, UK: Cambridge University Press, 2007); William F. Bristow, *Hegel and the Transformation of Philosophical Critique* (Oxford University Press, 2007); Sally Sedgwick, *Hegel's Critique of Kant: From Dichotomy to Identity* (Oxford: Oxford University Press, 2012); John McCumber, *Hegel's Mature Critique of Kant* (Stanford, CA: Stanford University Press, 2014).

[112] Hegel, *Phenomenology*, §437.

III. Political Writings, 1798-1807

others with their property. Consequently, there would be no deposits to appropriate. It is also important to note Kant's following clarification: "I cannot adduce my inclination (e.g., in the present case my avarice) as a principle of determination fitted to be a universal practical law; for this is so far from being fitted for a universal legislation that, if put in the form of a universal law, it would destroy itself." Hegel, however, treats the whole matter as if it depended on the "avarice" of the deposit-keeper in his/her isolation. Interestingly, Kant opined that "the commonest understanding can distinguish without instruction what form of maxim is adapted for universal legislation, and what is not."[113] Apparently, Hegel did not possess such an understanding.

If read independently (not as a critique of Kant), Hegel's argument basically asserts that individuals are incapable of absolutely determining what is right or wrong, just or unjust, and so on. However, he does not treat the issue at hand as unresolvable. His own solution typically takes little thought: A given content "is right because it is what is right."

> That something is the property of another, this is fundamental; I have not to argue about it, or hunt around for or entertain thoughts, connections, aspects, of various kinds; I have to think neither of making laws nor of testing them. All such thinking on my part would upset that relation, since, if I liked, I could in fact just as well make the opposite conform to my indeterminate tautological knowledge and make that the law.[114]

With the help of this and other similar moves, Hegel believes to have shown that his critique has dialectically brought about, or necessitated, the "superseding" of both "*willing* and *knowing* by this particular [reflecting, moral] individual." In this way, he declares triumphantly, consciousness "has put its merely individual aspect behind it." [115] Accordingly, consciousness acquires its most certain reality in "the *realm of ethical life* ... of a people or nation," wherein "the laws [and customs] proclaim what each individual is and does." In other words, such a nation abides by the following ancient wisdom: "The wisest men of antiquity have ... declared that wisdom and virtue consist in living in accordance with the customs of one's nation." He, and only the dialectical Hegel can do this, refers to this totality as "a free nation."[116]

---

[113] Immanuel Kant, *Critique of Practical Reason and Other Works*, trans. Thomas Kingsmill Abbott (London: Longmans, Green & Co., 1879), 160.
[114] Hegel, *Phenomenology*, §437.
[115] Ibid., §§435-36.
[116] Ibid., §§347-52.

III. Political Writings, 1798-1807

It becomes rather clear at this point, and in what follows, that Hegel does not simply *describe* how the ethical concepts and behavior of individuals are given by their own culture, as some scholars would have us believe. For one thing, he frequently takes a critical attitude toward modern individualism and its philosophers. This criticism, as we have seen earlier, and will encounter again shortly, often reaches its highest pitch when he calls upon the state to periodically wage war against civil society (*bürgerliche Gesellschaft*). Otherwise put, Hegel takes the declaration of the "wisest men of antiquity" as a prescription. In so doing, he contradicts the very "wisdom" he has learned from the ancients, for he calls upon the state to act against the existing, modern, individualistic-particularistic customs.

Another ancient piece of wisdom informs Hegel's "ethical" solution to the "antitheses" of moral reason: "Sophocles' *Antigone* acknowledges ... [the customs and laws] as the unwritten [eternal] and infallible law of the gods." Therefore, one should not try to "inquire after their origin," for this would violate their sacrosanct, absolute nature, argues Hegel. Otherwise, such an inquiry would render these absolute laws "conditioned and limited." Nor should the individual try to validate them, for such inquiry would question "their unshakeable, intrinsic being, and regard them as something which, for me, is perhaps true, but also is perhaps not true." The cultish Hegel thus prescribes unconditional obedience to the existing laws, calls this obedience "ethical disposition," and repeats that it "consists just in sticking steadfastly to what is [given as] right [or law], and abstaining from all attempts to move or shake it, or derive it." To ensure that we do not misunderstand him, he repeats that "as soon as I start to test them, I have already begun to tread an unethical path." This implies to Hegel that the individualistic-subjective (moral) reason destroys the ethical order. Only "by acknowledging the *absoluteness* of the [eternal ethical or customary] right [or law], I am within the ethical substance."[117]

After repeating similar thoughts in the ensuing few paragraphs, Hegel presents a scenario in which the government may allow the community to "organize itself into systems of personal independence and property, of laws relating to persons and things." That is, it may allow individuals, families, etc., to pursue their "particular ends," such as "those of gain and enjoyment." These particularistic interests may even "articulate" themselves "into their own special and independent associations" or corporations. It turns out, this liberalization of society is a dialectical ploy to justify the ethical necessity of the state. Thus, we suddenly encounter Hegel's old prescription of keeping civil society ethical: "in order not to let them become rooted and set in this isolation, thereby breaking up the *whole* and letting the [ethical] spirit evaporate, the government has from time to time to shake them to their

---

[117] Ibid., §437.

III. Political Writings, 1798-1807

core by war." By staging wars against its own people periodically, claims Hegel, the government would also prove "itself to be the real power of the community and the force of its self-preservation."[118]

6.2 The French Revolution and the Reign of Terror

"The *Phenomenology* is psychology thrown into confusion and disorder by history, and history brought to ruin by psychology."[119] Hegel's admirers love to hate this claim, which belongs to Haym. In my view, it is an apt characterization of Hegel's famous work. More narrowly stated, its second part ("history brought to ruin by [speculative] psychology") is an apt characterization of Hegel's discussion of the French Revolution. The problem at hand is only compounded by Hegel's life-long misunderstanding of Rousseau,[120] as well as his dual-attempt to equate Rousseau's theory with the institutions and practices of the Revolution and its culmination into the Terror.[121] While it is true that the revolutionaries often appealed to the authority of Rousseau, one cannot assume that they, as it were, used the *Social Contract* as a blueprint for constructing new political institutions.[122] Given Hegel's propensity to pretend otherwise, one also wonders if he knew much about the Revolution itself. Thus, one often

---

[118] Ibid., §455.
[119] Rudolf Haym, *Hegel und seine Zeit: Vorlesungen über Entstehung und Entwicklung: Wesen und Wert der Hegelschen Philosophie* (Berlin: R. Gaertner, 1857), 243.
[120] Stern enumerates multiple ways in which Hegel's critique of Rousseau in the *Phenomenology* is unfair to the latter but settles on the supremely *academic* conclusion that "Rousseau is arguably less significant here than is traditionally supposed." As far as I can tell, he cannot quite explain if there is anything "significant here" at all. In the final analysis, it seems to me that Stern wants to conceal both Hegel's embarrassing misunderstanding of Rousseau and his imaginary explanation of the Revolution as an enactment of the latter's political philosophy. Robert Stern, *The Routledge Guidebook to Hegel's Phenomenology of Spirit* (London: Routledge, 2013), 179 ff. Wokler, on the other hand, correctly observes that Hegel both misunderstood Rousseau and incorrectly identified him as the ideological founding-father of the revolution. However, to my mind, Wokler is also guilty of too much academic balancing (a.k.a. "objectivity"), which urges him to portray Hegel's analysis of the Revolution as both a great philosophical analysis and fundamentally flawed. Robert Wokler, "Contextualizing Hegel's Phenomenology of the French Revolution and the Terror," *Political Theory* 26, no. 1 (1998): 33-55
[121] Hegel would repeat this barbarous thought in his *Philosophy of Right*: when Rousseau's (allegedly) individualistic principles were "invested with power" during the French Revolution, "they induced, for the first time in human history, the monstrous spectacle of the overthrow of the constitution of a great, actual state," which then produced "the most terrifying" terror. G. W. F. Hegel, *Grundlinien der Philosophie des Rechts oder Naturrecht und Staatswissenschaft im Grundrisse*, ed. Eduard Gans (Berlin: Duncker und Humblot, 1833), §258R; also see §29, R.
[122] For a very thoughtful analysis of the relationship between Rousseau and the Revolution, see Joan McDonald, *Rousseau and the French Revolution 1762-1791* (London: Bloomsbury, 2013).

III. Political Writings, 1798-1807

wonders whether he misinterprets Rousseau or the Revolution. One also encounters many silly "logical" (or psychological) explanations of events, expressed with barely coherent sentences, giving credence to Adorno's claim that "Hegel's texts are antitexts."[123] Equally problematic are the claims of various scholars that Hegel defends the ideals of the Revolution in the *Phenomenology* (or elsewhere).[124]

At some point in the *Phenomenology*, Hegel produces an "inner revolution" by submitting the utilitarian consciousness to dialectical torture. From this "inner revolution," he alleges effortlessly, "there emerges the actual revolution of the actual world." The "new shape of consciousness" that undertakes this revolution is called "*absolute [unrestricted] freedom.*"[125] After reading some gibberish, we realize that the "*absolute freedom*" he has in mind is based on what he takes to be Rousseau's conception of the general will, even though his name is not mentioned.

Hegel proceeds to depict the Revolution, which is also not explicitly identified as a historical event, in such a way that cannot be found in either Rousseau's theory or the facts of the Revolution:

> [The concept realizes itself in such a way] that each individual consciousness raises itself out of its allotted sphere, no longer finds its essence and its work in this particular mass, but grasps itself as the Notion [concept] of the will, grasps all masses as the essence of this will, and therefore can only realize itself in a work which is work through and through. In this absolute freedom, therefore, all social groups or classes, which are the spiritual beings into which the whole is articulated, are abolished.[126]

---

[123] Theodor W. Adorno, *Hegel: Three Studies*, trans. Shierry Weber Nicholsen (Cambridge: The MIT Press, 1993), 119.

[124] Habermas' chapter on Hegel's alleged elevation of "revolution to the primary principle of his philosophy" is a famous example of how the claim cannot be demonstrated because it is false. In Habermas' chapter, one finds many extravagant dialectical formulations, such as: "Hegel did not curse the French Revolution and its children into oblivion; he celebrated them into oblivion;" "Hegel celebrates the revolution because he fears it;" "Hegel's philosophy of revolution is his philosophy as the critique of revolution;" "He has to legitimize the revolutionizing of reality without legitimizing the revolutionaries themselves;" "Hegel was able to legitimize the revolutionary order and still at the same time to criticize revolutionary consciousness," etc. Jürgen Habermas, *Theory and Practice*, trans. John Viertel (Boston: Beacon Press, 1973), Ch. 3. The lack of direct evidence in Habermas' account is remarkable. For an attempt to resolve the "contradictions" posited by Habermas, see Karlheinz Nusser, "The French Revolution in Hegel's *Phenomenology of Spirit*," in *The Phenomenology of Spirit Reader: Critical and Interpretive Essays*, ed. Jon Stewart, 282-306 (Albany: SUNY Press, 1998).

[125] Hegel, *Phenomenology*, §582.

[126] Ibid., §585.

III. Political Writings, 1798-1807

What is one to make of this speculative monstrosity? Instead of declaring it a bundle of gibberish, one author charitably explains that Hegel here "abstracts from the actual events because strictly speaking these events fall outside the scope of the *Phenomenology*."[127] That Hegel abstracts from the actual events is evidently true since anyone who thinks and writes about events necessarily abstracts from them. What needs to be explained is whether the abstraction has any relevance to the event of which it is assumed to be an abstraction. Besides, as we are about to see, some of "these events" do fall into "the scope of the *Phenomenology*."

The individual bearer of this consciousness of "absolute freedom," Hegel also claims, believes that "the world is for it simply its own will, and this is [also] a general will." "And what is more, this will is not the empty thought of will which consists in silent assent, or assent by a representative, but a real general will, the [direct, actual] will of all *individuals* as such." Consequently, "each ... always does everything, and what appears as done by the whole is the direct and conscious deed of each."[128] This fictional "abstraction" is supposed to explain the sense in which "all social groups or classes ... are abolished." Now, it is true that Rousseau opposed representation, though this cannot be said of the revolutionary institutions at the national level. Apart from this conformity with Rousseau's opposition to representation in the *Social Contract*, the rest of Hegel's "abstraction" is a figment of his imagination. He seems to believe that "all social groups and classes" were really abolished during the Revolution. "The particular spheres of labor," he says, "which would be further distinguished as more specific 'estates' or classes," were opposed as a restriction on absolute freedom. It turns out, Hegel's everyone-doing-everything claim is also related to the institutions and activities of the revolutionary government. More specifically, he argues that the revolutionaries also opposed the division of powers "into legislative, judicial, and executive powers," adding once again that this consciousness does not "let itself be cheated out of reality, the reality of itself making the law and accomplishing, not a particular work, but the universal work [i.e., all work of the state] itself."[129]

From this fabrication of Rousseau's theory and/or historical events, Hegel effortlessly deduces the dictatorship of Robespierre, logically known as "a One." The upshot is that, when everyone (the many) attempts to do

---

[127] Karin De Boer, "Hegel's Non-Revolutionary Account of the French Revolution in the Phenomenology of Spirit," *Epoché: A Journal for the History of Philosophy* 22, no. 2, (2018): 453-66, 459.

[128] Hegel, *Phenomenology*, §584.

[129] Ibid., §588. There were, it is true, thousands of clubs and communes during the revolutionary years throughout France, the existence of which, of course, does little to justify Hegel's "abstraction." For an impressive account, see Michael L. Kennedy, *The Jacobin Clubs in the French Revolution, 1793-1795* (New York: Berghahn Books, 2000).

III. Political Writings, 1798-1807

everything, nothing is done. This scenario allegedly produces its anthesis, as its deed "must concentrate itself into the One of individuality and put at the head an individual self-consciousness; for the universal will is only an *actual* will in a self, which is a One." This scenario, or negation of the many, creates, as it must, its own negation, whereby the many are "excluded" from the will and deeds of "the One." But the supremely logical Hegel cannot decide how much exclusion is involved in this scenario: "But thereby all other individuals are excluded from *the entirety of this deed* and *have only a limited share in it* [emphasis added]."[130]

At this point, Hegel's chain of reasoning breaks down almost completely. However, the attentive reader should be able to discern another logically and factually false claim here, which is generously quoted by his admirers as a great insight: "Universal freedom, therefore, can produce neither a positive work nor a deed; there is left for it only *negative* action; it is merely *the fury* of destruction."[131] Everyone knows that there was much "*fury* of destruction" during the Terror. But the claims that there was only ("merely") destruction, and that this was a result of some logical necessity, are both absurd.[132] From this "abstraction," Hegel easily produces the equally exaggerated conclusion that the result was (he speaks in the present tense for "logical" reasons) the complete "destruction of the actual organization of the world." What is worse, "the sole work and deed of [such] universal freedom is ... *death*," indeed meaningless, aimless death. "It is thus the coldest and meanest of all deaths, with no more significance than cutting off a head of cabbage or swallowing a mouthful of water."[133]

Hegel goes on to repeat his argument for the rise of the Terror from a slightly different angle. "The government," which *pretends* to carry out "the universal will," is in fact "a specific will." For this reason, "it is absolutely impossible for it to exhibit itself as anything else but a *faction*." Consequently, the excluded people now interpret the will of the government as "a crime committed against it," and express their "intention" to "overthrow" it. For its part, the government cannot demonstrate the guilt of its opponents, for the government's accusation is leveled against "an

---

[130] Ibid., §589.
[131] Ibid.
[132] For a brief but effective account of the Jacobin accomplishments and destruction, see Eric Hobsbawm, *The Age of Revolution, 1789-1848* (London: Abacus, 1977), 89-94. For a reputable Marxist account of the Revolution, see Albert Soboul, *A Short History of the French Revolution, 1789-1799*, trans. Geoffrey Symcox (Berkeley: University of California Press, 1977). For a Tocquevillian account, see François Furet, *Revolutionary France, 1770-1880*, trans. Antonia Nevill (Oxford: Wiley-Blackwell, 1992). For a refreshing and provocative rejection of Hegel's "mere *fury* of destruction" claim, see Sophie Wahnich, *In Defence of the Terror: Liberty or Death in the French Revolution*, trans. David Fernbach (London: Verso, 2012).
[133] Hegel, *Phenomenology*, §590.

III. Political Writings, 1798-1807

unreal pure will," that is, the mere "*intention*" to overthrow it. As a result, the government declares that the opposition is "*suspected* ... of *being guilty.*" (Here, Hegel has in mind "the law of suspects," issued by The Committee of Public Safety in 1793.) Since the opponent is reduced to a mere "inwardness of [guilty] intention," reasons the unreasonable Hegel, the government's response to it necessarily "consists in the cold, matter-of-fact annihilation" of the opposition's "existent self." In other words, the government factually destroys the bodies of its opponents by killing them, since it cannot punish their non-factual, non-actual *intention*. "The *terror* of death" is the "negative nature" of (Robespierre's) government, meaning that it necessarily carries out its "*work*," or self-realization, through killing everyone opposed to it.[134]

Because of this utterly destructive experience, the "absolutely free self-consciousness" now finds its "reality quite different from what its own Notion [conception] of itself [initially] was." In other words, it first took itself as the expression of "the *positive* essence of personality," which was supposed to be "preserved" through "the universal will." Instead, through its own initiative, it found itself in a reality in which it is destroyed in cold blood by the abstract universal will, the will of the isolated government, which is its negativity. This reflects the foremost self-alienation of consciousness. Consequently, muses Hegel, consciousness becomes Kantian, as it "now knows itself" simply as "a pure knowing or pure will." With this, "there has arisen the new shape of Spirit, that of the *moral* Spirit."[135]

At this point in the *Phenomenology*, Hegel basically abandons the issues of politics and ethical life. However, there is no evidence to support the claim that he meant to abandon his earlier "state absolutism."[136] What we can say with certainty is that he thinks the spirit has migrated elsewhere after running its necessary, and necessarily disastrous, course in France; it has passed "over into another land of self-conscious Spirit where, in this unreal [or purely inner] world freedom has the value of truth."[137] This "another land" is Germany.

As for the principles of the Revolution, Hegel thinks, as we have seen, they are *necessarily* self-destructive. On the one hand, this means that its aims and institutions have historically been superseded by a "new shape of Spirit." On the other hand, and this by implication, it means that one ought not to bring back them back, for they would inevitably reproduce the same "*fury* of destruction." Nowhere in the *Phenomenology* does Hegel even

---

[134] Ibid., §§590-92.
[135] Ibid., §§592-93.
[136] *Pace* Franz Rosenzweig, *Hegel und der Staat*, vol. 2 (Munich: R. Oldenbourg, 1920), 19.
[137] Hegel, *Phenomenology*, §595.

III. Political Writings, 1798-1807

suggest that the liberal-republican principles of the Revolution should or would be realized in the future.

Relatedly, we should not forget that the author of the comments on "Absolute Freedom and Terror" is the same person who disparages individualism of all kinds throughout the *Phenomenology* and believes that the individuals living in an ethical community do not even question the given laws, never mind making them.[138] Overall, and this issue has not been sufficiently studied, Hegel belonged to the "conservative" philosophical trends in Germany, which had emerged as a critique of the Kantian "radicalism" in the immediate aftermath of the Revolution.[139]

To conclude this chapter, from 1798 to early 1806, Hegel had remained a poor thinker and writer. During this period, he had espoused decisively illiberal political views. Also, except in the *Phenomenology*, which is silent on this issue, Hegel had yearned for the unification of Germany and the organization of its parts under a centralized state. In 1806, the German Empire was dissolved. This fact might help explain why he did not bring

---

[138] As Shklar justly puts it, "Hegel's *Phenomenology* is a massive assault upon the 'subjectivity' of individualism, both epistemological and social." Judith N. Shklar, "Hegel's Phenomenology: An Elegy for Hellas," in *Hegel's Political Philosophy: Problems and Perspectives*, ed. Z. A. Pelczynski, 73-89 (Cambridge: Cambridge University Press, 1971), 74. Franco *academically* opposes this view: "Contrary" to Shklar's claim, "the Phenomenology cannot be seen *simply* as 'a massive assault upon the "subjectivity" of individualism' [emphasis added]." Paul Franco, *Hegel's Philosophy of Freedom* (New Haven: Yale University Press, 1999), 103, 113.

[139] For useful surveys of these trends, see Reinhold Aris, *History of Political Thought in Germany, 1789-1815* (London: George Allen & Unwin, 1936); George P. Gooch, *Germany and the French Revolution* (London: Longmans, Green, and Co., 1920); Klaus Epstein, *Genesis of German Conservatism* (Princeton: Princeton University Press, 1966); George Kelly, *Idealism, Politics, and History: Sources of Hegelian Thought* (Cambridge: Cambridge University Press, 1969); Frederick C. Beiser, *Enlightenment, Revolution, and Romanticism: The Genesis of Modern German Political Thought, 1790—1800* (Cambridge: Harvard University Press, 1992); Reidar Maliks, *Kant's Politics in Context* (Oxford: Oxford University Press, 2014). These debates were also informed by Edmund Burke's *Reflections on the Revolution in France and on the Proceedings in Certain Societies in London, Relative to that Event* (London: J. Dodsley, 1790).

That Hegel, like other German conservatives, also borrowed some of his key views on the Revolution from Burke is convincingly illustrated in J. F. Suter, "Burke, Hegel, and the French Revolution," in *Hegel's Political Philosophy: Problems and Perspectives*, edited by Z. A. Pelczynski, 52-72 (Cambridge: Cambridge University Press, 1971.) However, Despite the said obvious Burkean influences, there is no evidence to prove that Hegel had read Burke's *Reflections*. Likely, he had read either Gentz's heavily edited and supplemented translation of Burke's book, which he infused with "German" conservative, anti-revolutionary rationalism or the commentaries on this translation. See Friedrich Gentz, *Betrachtungen über die französische Revolution nach dem Englischen des Herrn Burke*, 2 vols. (Berlin: Friedrich Vieweg dem Aelteren, 1793). For a very informative account of Gentz's translation, see Jonathan Allen Green, "Friedrich Gentz's Translation of Burke's Reflections," *The Historical Journal* 57, no. 3 (2014): 639-59.

III. Political Writings, 1798-1807

up the double-issue of ethical life and the state in the post-Revolution Germany, though he did see Germany as the new home of the ethical spirit.

Chapter Four

IV. BONAPARTIST NEWSPAPERMAN AND RECTOR, 1806-1815

1. Love at First Sight

Contrary to what some notable Hegel scholars claim,[1] Hegel has nothing to say about Napoleon in the *Phenomenology*. However, as we have seen in the previous chapter, he (possibly) praised him, unnamed, in his 1805-1806 Jena lectures as a tyrant-savior of the French state. Overall, though, there is no evidence to prove that he had given any serious thought to Napoleon before 1806. This fact helps us limit the temporal scope of Hegel's Bonapartism.[2]

October 13, 1806, was the day Napoleon simultaneously conquered Hegel's city and heart. By then, the *Phenomenology* had been mostly written and sent to the publisher. This love-at-first-sight is documented in Hegel's letter to Niethammer, written the same day: "I saw the Emperor—this world-soul, riding out of the city on reconnaissance. It is indeed a wonderful sensation to see such an individual, who, concentrated here at a single point, astride a horse, reaches out over the world and masters it." Given that he had always admired "great" conquerors and tyrants, Hegel's sudden infatuation with Napoleon is not very surprising. Perhaps more surprising is the fact that this was also the first time he admired someone who invaded his own country. "Such advances as occurred from Thursday to Monday," he further reported, "are only possible for this extraordinary man, whom it is impossible not to admire."[3] This love affair, however, was one-sided, as the Emperor had never heard of Hegel throughout his life.

---

[1] Pace Jean Hyppolite, *Studies on Marx and Hegel*, trans. John O'Neill (New York: Basic Books, 1969), 58; Terry Pinkard, *Hegel's Phenomenology: The Sociality of Reason* (Cambridge: Cambridge University Press, 1994), 186.
[2] By "Bonapartism," I mean advocacy for a dictatorship or authoritarian centralized state, led by a strongman. In Hegel's case, the term also implies admiration for Napoleon as a "great man."
[3] Clark Butler and Christiane Seiler (trans.), *Hegel: The Letters* (Bloomington: Indiana University Press, 1984), 114-15. Also, Johannes Hoffmeister (ed.), *Briefe von und an Hegel*, 4 volumes (Hamburg: Felix Meiner, 1952-1960), *Briefe I*, #74. Henceforth cited as *Briefe*, followed by the Latin numerical to indicate the volume number, in this case, *I*.

IV. Bonapartist Newspaperman and Rector, 1806-1815

It is possible to read Hegel's endorsement of the French invasion as his preference for the more civilized foreign invaders over the less civilized Prussians, as his following comment implies:

> As I [myself] already did earlier [?], all now wish the French army luck; and, in view of the immense difference that separates not only its leaders but even the least of its soldiers from their enemies [i.e., Prussians], luck can hardly fail it. In this [manner], our region will thus soon be free of this [Prussian] deluge.[4]

However, it is not true that Hegel had been unhappy with the Prussian "deluge" before Napoleon's invasion of Jena. For instance, ten months earlier, on January 14, 1806, he wished to see more Prussian officers in Jena on purely personal, careerist grounds:

> The [Jena Faculty] Senate and the [Prussian] General do not seem to have hit upon the praiseworthy idea of transferring to us here a garrison of [Prussian] officers obliged to occupy themselves with the sciences until they espy an enemy, which anyhow will not happen so soon. I fear no way will remain to increase the number of students if such a remedy is not found.[5]

Sometime in April, Hegel even contacted Isaac von Sinclair, his acquaintance from Tübingen and Frankfurt, to see if there were any prospects for him at Berlin University, that is, in Prussia.[6] These pieces of evidence indicate that Hegel's personal interests were now beginning to shape his political wishes and allegiances. As we will see shortly, his support for Napoleon was also linked, but not reducible, to his personal interests.

Suffice it to conclude for now that Hegel's support for both Napoleon, the man, and the French invasion of Germany were only recently acquired. Otherwise put, the Battle of Jena marked the beginning of what I call the "second phase" (Bonapartism) of Hegel's political sympathies.[7] We will examine how his Bonapartism came into its own and subsequently disappeared in the ensuing sections of this chapter. It will be observed that it lasted until Napoleon himself was conquered, and so became useless to both himself and Hegel.

---

[4] *Letters*, 114-5 (*Briefe I*, #74).
[5] Ibid., 109 (#59).
[6] *Briefe I*, #60.
[7] The "first phase" refers to the period, and writings, discussed in Chapter 3. This is, broadly speaking, the "critical-nationalist" period, during which Hegel lamented both the fragmentation and weakness of the German Empire and its conquest by the foreigners, including the French.

IV. Bonapartist Newspaperman and Rector, 1806-1815

2. Bonapartist "Newspaperman," 1807-1808

2.1 Making Sense of Hegel's Bonapartism

As we have seen in Chapter 2, when Hegel reported his encounter with Napoleon to Niethammer, he was already in a destitute situation. Given the urgency of his situation, the latter had quickly arranged a job for him in Bamberg. As he described it to Schelling on March 13, 1807, bringing Hegel to Bamberg was nothing less than a drastic rescue operation: "I am glad that I have finally succeeded in rescuing him from the desolate Jena ... For the time being, he is at least saved [*gedeckt*] from hunger ...; in every respect it was good to pull him away from Jena."[8]

When Hegel was hired to manage it, the *Bamberger Zeitung* was an impoverished and faltering paper. As Niethammer informed him, the previous editor had managed the paper so "brilliantly that he had nearly lit its death-torch."[9] Moreover, the *Zeitung* was more of a provincial bulletin than a reputable newspaper. Moreover, it "was printed on absorbent paper in quarto format and consisted of simply two sheets," some portion of which was devoted to local news and some to advertisements. It even lacked an "official imprint to indicate the publisher's or the editor's name." Hegel's main task was basically limited to deciding the contents of the paper and ensuring that they complied with the Napoleonic censorship. (Bamberg, a town incorporated into the kingdom of Bavaria in 1803, was under Napoleon's sway at the time). Thus, Hegel was mainly tasked with ensuring that the reports in the beleaguered paper were pro-Napoleon and pro-Bavarian regime.[10] As we will see shortly, he had no qualms with supporting Napoleon. The same cannot be said about his attitude toward his new job; he would remain as determined as ever that becoming a salaried university professor was his "destiny.

The next piece of evidence (after his famous letter to Niethammer) we have of Hegel's Bonapartism comes from another letter, which was sent to one of his former students. It was written on January 23, 1807. In it, Hegel offered the following prediction, which may also be read as a predilection: "Thanks to the [blood?] bath of her Revolution, the French Nation has freed herself of many institutions which the human spirit had outgrown like the shoes of a child," and that, because of the Napoleonic invasion, these "other nations [he mentions the Germans in this context]" will be "forced

---

[8] Günther Nicolin (ed.), *Hegel in Berichten seiner Zeitgenossen* (Hamburg: Felix Meiner, 1970), #125. Henceforth cited as *Berichten*.
[9] *Briefe I*, #88.
[10] Horst Althaus, *Hegel: An Intellectual Biography*, trans. Michael Tarsh (Cambridge, UK: Polity Press, 2000), 106-07.

IV. Bonapartist Newspaperman and Rector, 1806-1815

to ... surpass their teachers [i.e., the French]."[11] Thus, in early 1807, Hegel expected the Germans to learn from, and surpass, the *Napoleonic* "institutions."

According to Shlomo Avineri, while in Bamberg, Hegel was pleased to see that "the principles annunciated by the French Revolution were being adopted in Germany." He derives this conclusion from Hegel's August 29, 1807, letter to Niethammer. In it, Hegel "calls Napoleon 'the great constitutional lawyer in Paris', who teaches the German princes the meaning 'of the concept of a free monarchy'."[12] In this letter, it is true, Hegel clearly endorsed "the concept of a free monarchy" *a la* Napoleon and identified "the great professor" in Paris as the only power capable of implementing it in Germany.[13] However, this fact highlights a problem in Avineri's claim, which is overlooked by many other Hegel scholars also. The problem is simple: Napoleon had already betrayed "the principles annunciated by the French Revolution" long before Hegel wrote this letter.

This is not the place to settle Napoleon's complicated relationship to the Revolution. However, a few comments on this issue are in order. From the outset, Napoleon was bent upon establishing a personal dictatorship, a task at which he was obviously successful, though he was assisted by his "collaborators"—some politicians and, especially, the military.[14] Surely, at least in France, he had reinforced the legal equality of persons and attracted much peasant support by maintaining the abolition of feudal property relations by the revolutionaries.[15] At the same time, however, with the stroke of a pen, he reinstated slavery in the colonies in 1802, reversing the measures taken by the Jacobins eight years earlier.[16] Before that, he had ruthlessly crushed all opposition, left and right, in France, though there is a debate on whether he had established a "police state" or a "security state."[17]

---

[11] *Letters*, 123 (*Briefe I*, #85).
[12] Shlomo Avineri, *Hegel's Theory of the Modern State* (Cambridge: Cambridge University Press, 1972), 66.
[13] *Letters*, 141 (*Briefe I*, #103).
[14] Isser Woloch, *Napoleon and His Collaborators: The Making of a Dictatorship* (New York: W. W. Norton & Company, 2001).
[15] For an excellent study of the abolition of feudalism during the Revolution, see John Markoff, *Abolition of Feudalism: Peasants, Lords, and Legislators in the French Revolution* (University Park: Pennsylvania State University Press, 1996).
[16] See Philippe R. Girard, *The Slaves Who Defeated Napoleon: Toussaint Louverture and the Haitian War of Independence, 1801-1804* (Tuscaloosa: The University of Alabama Press, 2001).
[17] See Howard G. Brown, *Ending the French Revolution: Violence, Justice, and Repression from the Terror to Napoleon* (Charlottesville: The University of Virginia Press, 2006); Peter Hicks, "The Napoleonic 'Police' or 'Security State' in Context," *Napoleonica: La Revue* 4, no. 1 (2009): 2-10.

IV. Bonapartist Newspaperman and Rector, 1806-1815

He got himself "elected" consul for life in 1802.[18] Then came the famous Code in 1803-1804. The Code was modern (which does not mean liberal) in many ways, but also "institutionalized the subservience of women in marriage and of workers in their places of employment."[19] "As early as February 1800, fifty newspapers were closed down, leaving only thirteen in circulation. By 1811, this number had been further reduced to four."[20] In accordance with the Code, all new books were subjected to censorship before their publication. Theatrical plays were also censored for their political and moral content.[21]

Aided by both his grip on power and military victories, Napoleon gave himself a higher title. The French Constitution of 1804 (of the Year XII) declared him the "Emperor of the French" (Title I) and made this title "hereditary in the direct natural and legitimate lineage of Napoleon Bonaparte, from male to male, by order of primogeniture, and to the perpetual exclusion of women and their descendants" (Title II). Napoleon's male family members were declared hereditary "princes" and, upon reaching the age of eighteen, granted the right to become members of the Senate (Title III). Along with the "princes," the powerful Senate was to consist of "titular grand dignitaries of the Empire" and other members, ultimately handpicked by the emperor himself (Title VIII). The "Tribunate" was rendered entirely powerless; it was also only indirectly representative. It could not make or even propose laws—it was merely a debating club (Title XI).[22] In short, for all intents and purposes, this constitution gave Napoleon, the Emperor, absolute power.

The foregoing information should allow us to better understand "the concept of a free monarchy" implemented by Napoleon, the "great professor of constitutional law ... in Paris," and now endorsed by Hegel, the not-so-great "newspaperman" in Bamberg.

In November 1807, Hegel revisited the issue of the "reorganization" of Bavaria in another letter to Niethammer. "So far," complained he, "we see the implementation of only one-half of the French imitations." This noblest half, which includes "the freedom of the people, participation in

---

[18] Philip G. Dwyer and Peter McPhee (eds.), *The French Revolution and Napoleon: A Sourcebook* (London: Routledge, 2002), 152.

[19] Ibid., 155.

[20] Ibid., 141. Also see Frank Maloy Anderson, *The Constitutions and Other Select Documents Illustrative of the History of France, 1789-1901* (Minneapolis: The H. W. Wilson Company, 1904), 282-83.

[21] For a classic survey, see Victor Coffin, "Censorship and Literature under Napoleon I," *The American Historical Review* 22, no. 2 (January 1917): 288-308. Also see J. Holland Rose, "The Censorship under Napoleon I," *Journal of Comparative Legislation and International Law, New Series* 18, no. 1 (1918): 58-65.

[22] Anderson, *The Constitutions and Other Select Documents Illustrative of the History of France, 1789-1901*, 343 ff.

IV. Bonapartist Newspaperman and Rector, 1806-1815

elections [and] ..., at least, a public exposition of all grounds of governmental decisions and measures for the insight of the people," is missing, lamented Hegel. Repeating his recently-acquired wisdom, he added somewhat optimistically that "Germany has already learned much from France" and the slow-learning "*allemands* will in time gain even more from [the French]." Which French? "The Emperor," whom Hegel once again expected to implement the "noblest" part of "the French imitations."[23]

In the meanwhile, Hegel had no intention of keeping his new job. In a letter to Karl Ludwig von Knebel, Goethe's friend and his acquaintance, he not only solicited local news from Weimer for his newspaper but also confessed that he would, "without hesitation," give up his editorship post "for the philosophy lecture hall, should an opportunity arise."[24] Hegel's letter to Knebel, written on August 30, 1807, was clearly meant as a reminder to the Weimar authorities that, if called to teach there with a salary, he would readily return to Jena University. Alas, Knebel only sent some local news.[25]

When his effort to receive a call from Jena bore no fruit, when, furthermore, nothing came of Niethammer's promise to find him an academic post, Hegel concocted a new plan to improve his status. This plan, which he sent to Niethammer on January 22, 1808, called for the publication of a political-literary paper, to be modeled after *Le Moniteur*, the official organ of the Napoleonic regime. His somewhat fragmented rationale for this scheme is given in the following portion of his letter.

> A critique in an ordinary literary review has a private character, which licenses the young men to reply ... in a quite boorish way. The real means to counter such wantonness is not available to you [i.e., Niethammer and the Bavarian government] because you have *no Moniteur*. The advantage of the *French Moniteur* is that it has the authority to put adolescent insolence in its place, to tame and shut up impudent mouths ... This aspect of such [censored] reviews, of course, may cause an outcry about repression of the freedom of thought and the press ... Yet ..., in all cases where such an outcry commands authority, it is not a question either of thinking or of the sciences. For thinking and science have nothing to do with the wanton immaturity which is alone impressed by such talk, and which can be held in check only by authority of some kind ... To put it pointedly, you have freedom of the pen and press—I almost said *Fress-Freiheit* instead of

---

[23] *Briefe I*, #108.
[24] Ibid., #104.
[25] Ibid., #109.

IV. Bonapartist Newspaperman and Rector, 1806-1815

Press-Freiheit—*but* you lack all *publicity* leading the government to lay before its people the condition in which the state finds itself.[26]

These sentences shed further light on Hegel's concept of "free monarchy" by means of "publicity." His desire to censor freedom of expression,[27] it goes without saying, coincided with Napoleon's dictatorial approach to freedom of the press, which also allowed the government to control the information about its activities. But we should not ignore the fact that the entire plan was designed to serve Hegel's personal interests: "So, set up a political-literary *Moniteur,*" he concluded, "and give me something to do with it."[28]

Hegel's outlandish proposal did not materialize. Instead, he received a letter from Niethammer, indicating that the Napoleonic Code might be adopted in the French-dominated parts of Germany. In his reply of February 11, Hegel welcomed the news. "But the Germans are still blind," and so "this will hardly happen voluntarily." "It is only from ... the will of the French Emperor," Hegel noted once again, "that matters can be set in motion." Relatedly, he wanted Napoleon to abolish "the characteristic *modes of centralization* and organization prevalent up to now [in Germany] ..., forms in which there is no justice, no guarantee, no popular participation, but only the arbitrariness and sophistry of a single individual [such as the king of Württemberg]." Hegel, we must also note, specifically mentioned the "importance" and the "hope" of introducing something like "the French or Westphalian constitution."[29]

We have already noted what the French-Napoleonic constitution entailed. The Westphalian constitution, which declared Napoleon's youngest brother, Jérôme I (born Girolamo Buonaparte), the first king of Westphalia, basically mimicked Napoleon's constitution.[30] In short, Hegel was as liberal and republican as the brothers Bonaparte. In fact, his ideas about the press and publicity were directly derived from Napoleon's policies in the German territories under his control. In the Rhineland territories, including Westphalia, Napoleon put "press censorship under the aegis of the Ministry of Police, creating a censorship department named, in somewhat Orwellian fashion, 'La Division de la Liberté de la Presse.'" Newspaper editors "were forced to take an oath of loyalty to the emperor.

---

[26] *Letters*, 155-57 (*Briefe I*, #112).
[27] Remarkably, Avineri reads Hegel's letter to Niethammer as a call for "tolerance of the freedom of the press," which issues from "the Napoleonic Code." Avineri, *Hegel's Theory of the Modern State*, 67.
[28] *Letters*, 157 (*Briefe I*, #112).
[29] Ibid., 159-60 (*Briefe I*, #117).
[30] *Constitution Des Königreichs Westfalen (15. 11. 1807).* http://www.dircost.unito.it/cs/pdf/18071115_germaniaRegnoVestfalia_ted.pdf.

IV. Bonapartist Newspaperman and Rector, 1806-1815

The most stifling of ... Paris's many regulations for the press was the requirement that all political news come directly from the official government organ, *Le Moniteur*."[31] In Bamberg, Hegel himself was implementing this sort of freedom of the press.

In contrast to Hegel, many liberal-republicans in Germany, who tended to be nationalists also, saw nothing but an egotistical, vicious dictator in Napoleon. If anything, they generally disliked him, including the ones in the Rhenish republic allied with him.

At a meeting of Cologne public leaders [in 1799], for instance, when the call went up, '*Vive la République, vive Bonaparte!*' the ardent Rhenish republican Michael Venedy shouted: 'What? You still believe in the [existence] of the Republic? With the [new] constitution, that went to the devil. Bonaparte is a dictator; out of a dictator will come a monarch, and out of the monarch a despot ... Franz Lassaulx was similarly pessimistic about the future under the new consulate [led by Bonaparte] ... 'Bonaparte is nothing but an ambitious soldier' [he said].[32]

Ernst Moritz Arndt, the historian, writer and poet, made a similar sentiment known in one of his books by addressing the following message to Napoleon: "You are a brave and fortunate adventurer, a craft schemer, and an eternal great abomination that terrifies the world ..., a conceited, faithless, greedy, and blood-thirsty tyrant who would dominate the world as you so easily dominate your French."[33] Arndt met Schleiermacher, his future brother-in-law, in 1809, after he fled from Rügen to Berlin to avoid persecution for his opposition to Napoleon and the French occupation.[34] For his part, the liberal Schleiermacher perceived the opposition to Napoleon as a defense of German freedom and character, as a battle for the very essence of "German ethical life."[35] "Upon learning that Napoleon had placed Halle in the Kingdom of Westphalia, ruled by Napoleon's brother Jerome, Schleiermacher wrote the following to a friend: 'I cannot accommodate myself to this government and must live under a German

---

[31] Walter M. Simon, *The Failure of the Prussian Reform Movement, 1807–1819* (Ithaca, NY: Cornell University Press, 1955), 155.
[32] Jon Vanden Heuvel, *A German Life in the Age of Revolution: Joseph Görres, 1776-1848* (Washington DC: The Catholic University of America Press, 2001), 85.
[33] Quoted in Alfred G. Pundt, *Arndt and the Nationalist Awakening in Germany* (New York: Columbia University, 1935), 75.
[34] Ibid., 71.
[35] Quoted in John E. Toews, *Hegelianism: The Path Toward Dialectical Humanism, 1805-1841* (Cambridge: Cambridge University Press, 1980), 57.

IV. Bonapartist Newspaperman and Rector, 1806-1815

prince, so long as there is one.'"[36] He then joined Heinrich Friedrich Karl von Stein, the liberal-reformer chancellor of Prussia, in a "conspiracy" to expel the French from Germany by means of a popular rebellion. When his police uncovered Stein's secret activities in August 1808, Napoleon ordered the confiscation of his estates in the new kingdom of Westphalia, and forced the Prussian king, Friedrich Wilhelm III, to sack him. He also declared Stein the enemy of France and its allies and ordered his arrest. Indeed, he went further and informed the Prussians that, if captured, Stein would be shot. Stein was informed of the despot's intentions, and so fled to Austria to save his life.[37] In short, Napoleon was despised by many prominent German liberal republicans, be it nationalists or not. Hegel, on the other hand, was an apologist for just about everything for which Napoleon stood, at least for now.

2.2 Servile Professor Wannabe

However, it would be a mistake to use several comments, found in several private letters to an official of Napoleonic order in Bavaria, Niethammer, as evidence of Hegel's intense interest in either reforming Germany or supporting Napoleon. Neither aim was his top priority; becoming a salaried professor at a university was. If anything, the publication of the *Phenomenology* (1807) had undermined his prospects in this regard, as it was generally received negatively (see Chapter 5). Thus, the increasingly agitated Hegel's "destiny" was now entirely in Niethammer's hands. This dependence forced him to adopt an increasingly servile attitude towards Niethammer. At the same time, he linked his "destiny" to Napoleon's success in Germany, not least because Niethammer's ability to "save" him, he thought, depended on the Emperor's own success. Thus, through the medium of Niethammer, Hegel had come to tie his own "destiny" to that of Napoleon.

This is revealed in Hegel's August 20, 1808, letter to Niethammer. He was now disgruntled by the fact that his name for a new academic post, "for sure, will not be on top" of the list of candidates. "However, as is only human," he reasoned, "I would consider ... [being on top of the list] one of the most important." He also complained that the ongoing "wretched war" was obstructing the development of "what is best—namely, the arts and sciences," especially since it was undermining additional "financial support" for the expansion of the system of education. "The prospects are

---

[36] Quoted in Theodore Vial, *Schleiermacher: A Guide for the Perplexed* (London: Bloomsbury, 2013), 18.
[37] Guy Stanton Ford, *Stein and the Era of Reform in Prussia, 1807-1815* (Princeton: Princeton University Press, 1822), 265 ff.

IV. Bonapartist Newspaperman and Rector, 1806-1815

getting dimmer" for both the expansion of the arts and sciences and, more importantly, Hegel's appointment to a university post.[38]

The "wretched war" refers to Napoleon's temporary defeat in Spain at the hands of the Austrians. The next prize for these belligerents was Munich. Hegel expressed confidence in Napoleon's ability to get there before the Austrians since "once Napoleon puts his troops on the march, he does not mean to have done so in vain." Hegel then wishfully linked his confidence in Napoleon's prospects against the Austrians to his own career prospects: "these prospects of war [expected to be successful] may perhaps become a motive for accelerating introduction of the new organization" of the system of education, which would then enable Niethammer to find him a professorial post at a university. "I am looking forward to my deliverance from the yoke of journalism," prayed Hegel in conclusion, "which has become even more oppressive for me through observing your own activity [or success as an education reformer] with a longing matched only by my confidence."[39]

In his September 15 letter to Niethammer, Hegel adopted the same servile, pathetic, manipulative tone he had recently adopted and utilized when in need: "We are here generally on the receiving end in relation to you, the Giver. Take my skipper into your favor, oh ye Stars, so that he may guide my little boat safely to port. Yet my own concern is really only a small boat in the wake of the flagship." (Who talks like this anyway?) Hegel's "small" concern was related to Niethammer's impeding "comprehensive plan" for educational reform, tied to Napoleon's success in the region. The plan included opening a "small university."[40]

Apparently, what made Hegel so "anxious to break away from ... [his] journalistic galley" was that "a short time ago ... [he] was subjected to another inquisition [!], which reminded ... [him] more precisely of ... [his] general situation." His job and salary were now in "jeopardy," he claimed with characteristic exaggeration. His precarious situation resulted from "a single article, which is found offensive" by the authorities because it reported the presence of "the three Bavarian camps" in the vicinity, related to Napoleon's campaign to repel the Austrian offensive mentioned earlier.[41] This was the same person who recently requested to become a Napoleonic censor in his own right.

At any rate, Hegel predictably linked the said "inquisition" to the main point of his letter, the usual demand for a university post: "So what is Julius [Niethammer's son] doing with himself? Are you going to send him to the

---

[38] *Letters*, 165-66 (*Briefe I*, #126).
[39] Ibid.
[40] Ibid., 167-69 (#127).
[41] Ibid.

IV. Bonapartist Newspaperman and Rector, 1806-1815

University with me? Who is the philology professor of whom you are thinking *in petto* as my colleague?"[42]

Hegel's already-thin patience was tested when, just two weeks after his previous letter, "still no word, not even a syllable" from Niethammer had arrived in response to his imagined university post, which would allow him to teach philosophy to Julius. "Tell me in but one line," he wrote with due urgency, "if there is still hope, or if I have to renounce such hope and, with it, Bavaria." However, given the perceived gravity of his situation, procuring a university post was no longer his only option; an appointment at "the gymnasiums or lyceums," previously suggested to him by Niethammer, would also do. Overall, Hegel had become immensely resentful when other academic appointments were being made while he remained a "newspaperman," and was now prepared to hold two supreme authorities responsible for his misfortune: "Every minute of my existence as a newspaperman is lost—wasted time for which God and you will have to render account and make compensation." Then followed another pathetic plea: "Be herewith implored to pour a drop of oil or water into this damnation, at least for the time being. Better still, pour rather the whole pot over my head as soon as possible."[43]

At the end of October 1808, the immensely-patient Niethammer responded to Hegel's pleas with a job offer: Professor of Preparatory Philosophical Sciences and Rector at the Nuremberg Classical Gymnasium. On October 28, Hegel replied with a much more cheerful letter than the ones he had sent recently. However, he was not entirely satisfied with the offer, and so accepted it conditionally. "In this connection," he thus reminded Niethammer, "you yourself noted repeatedly and explicitly that you are keeping the prospect [for a professorship] in Altorf open." He then urged Niethammer to upgrade and reorganize Altorf as a university for both Protestants and, above all, himself: "What a great future would be promised me if this plan were to materialize!" Hegel mailed the letter the next day, though not without adding another embarrassingly servile note to it: "You are my Creator, and I am your creature ... I bid you farewell out of both the friendship I owe you personally and the respect I owe you as my superior."[44] With this debt to his "Creator" in his pocket, which he also treated as a debt owed to himself, Hegel moved to Nuremberg in late 1808, carrying with him also his non-negotiable "destiny" to become a salaried philosophy professor at a university.

---

[42] Ibid.
[43] Ibid., 169 (#129).
[44] Ibid., 178-79 (#135).

IV. Bonapartist Newspaperman and Rector, 1806-1815

3. Nuremberg Years, 1808-1816

3.1 Unsatisfied Gymnasium Rector

Hegel moved to Nuremberg in December 1808. For a while, he had discharged his duties, both administrative and professorial, faithfully. However, as his early 1809 letters indicate, he was not fully satisfied with his salary and the amount of administrative work he had to perform to earn it. One gets the sense from these letters that he had held the ongoing war responsible for his personal and professional troubles.

Hegel continued to be his usual self throughout 1810, nagging about his situation and always wishing to obtain something better for himself, especially a salaried post at a university. On May 15, he called Niethammer's attention to the news that "a university at Regensburg as also of a comprehensive university in Munich" might be established. "If it is not too late, I want to ask if you can think of me," Hegel said. Otherwise, he should "at least be freed of the rectorship and merely retain the professorship so as to draw closer to ... [his] true vocation."[45]

By September, Niethammer's ongoing struggles in Munich with respect to educational reform had reached new heights. In this context, he demanded the resignation of Josef Wismayr, the High Councilor of school affairs; or else, he himself would resign. Hegel intuitively understood Niethammer's threat to resign as a threat to himself, for his own situation depended on Niethammer keeping his own post as the Central Commissioner of Education of Bavaria. On September 27, he expressed his grave concerns in this regard to Niethammer in no uncertain terms. "For years," he wrote, "we have awaited you as our savior, a savior who moreover has at least redeemed me from the mania and yearning for things and transformations to come," referring to his desire to become a university professor. However, Niethammer's recent "remarks" about his own "personal situation" drove Hegel back to his mania, and so "away ... from such freedom, from all expectation into quite the opposite state, indeed into fear." Hegel, in other words, "cannot persuade" himself "that this condition [i.e., Wismayr's resignation] will be met, that a minister can approve it."[46] In short, unless he backs off, Niethammer will go down, taking Hegel with him.

Although Niethammer eventually prevailed against Wismayr, the news of another threat to Hegel was now in circulation: his classical gymnasium was to be replaced with a "modern" one, with a more practical curriculum (of the kind Wismayr favored). Naturally, the news displeased Hegel. His

---

[45] Ibid., 211 (#161).
[46] Ibid., 223-43 (#165).

IV. Bonapartist Newspaperman and Rector, 1806-1815

October 27 letter to Niethammer approached the issue at hand with an entirely sarcastic and melancholic tone. After depicting his own anticipated situation in the direst possible terms, Hegel once again appealed to his savior's help: "I ask you in the name of all you have done for me thus far, in the name of all I have, of all the wounds endured and blood spilt [!], to bring me, your work, to completion ... So please, please—... Yours, Hegel."[47]

On November 3, Hegel was in a better mood, as his gymnasium was spared. "What a great sensation the allegedly forthcoming abolition of the local gymnasium has created here," he wrote to Niethammer, adding that "all social classes, ages, sexes, and persons both official and private share the same sensation of the harshness of this [proposed] measure against Nuremberg." He then imaginatively described the threat to shut down his gymnasium as an attack against all Protestants: "You yourself know better than anyone how highly the Protestants esteem their scholarly educational institutions, how these institutions are as dear to them as the churches ... One could not have attacked a Protestant population at a more sensitive spot than its schools." Then followed the usual pathetic plea: "In these windy November days I hope from you the breath of a living zephyr that you may soon blow my way,"[48] referring, of course, to an appointment at a university.

But nothing, so it seems, sufficed to satisfy Hegel. On December 22, he sardonically linked the "reprieve granted to ... [the] gymnasium" to the postponement of his own "destiny elsewhere," namely, at a university. In other words, the survival of the gymnasium "has come to number among the reasons for ... [his] own failure to advance," as there was now no compelling reason to transfer him elsewhere, preferably to a university. It did not help that Paulus was recently hired by Heidelberg University. The envious Hegel hastened to inform Niethammer that, as he "learned by accident," Paulus is "really Jewish." "In Germany, there must be many disguised Jews, just as in Portugal," he added. After the usual complaints to, and requests from, his "savior," Hegel—humorously, he believed—said: "to show that I am not of Jewish blood, I am sending you a few gingerbreads, and wish you happy holidays as well."[49] This anti-Semitic comment was meant more as an expression of jealousy, as an attempt to slander Paulus, than an attempt to alert Niethammer to the presence of the many "disguised" Jews in Germany.

Hegel waited until February 23, 1811, to once again badger Niethammer with another report on his prospects: "The authorities are

---

[47] Ibid., 224-26 (#168).
[48] Ibid., 226-28 (#169).
[49] Ibid., 229-31 (#173).

IV. Bonapartist Newspaperman and Rector, 1806-1815

thinking of seriously organizing Erlangen [University] by Easter ... There is talk in this connection of a philosopher being needed there; there is talk of me—but also of Schelling. May God and my destiny—and to me you are my destiny—touch rather the former!"[50] (As we will see in the next chapter, the relationship between Hegel and Schelling had completely deteriorated by this time.)

When nothing came of this request for a while, Hegel devised another plan to urge his "destiny" to "touch" him. On April 18, he informed Niethammer of his "bond with a good and very dear girl," namely, "Marie von Tucher." Marie belonged to an ancient patrician family in Nuremberg and was twenty-one years younger than Hegel, who was now almost forty-one. But there was a problem: "my happiness has in part been made contingent [by Marie's family] on my faculty appointment at Erlangen ... How nice it would be if we could be united in Erlangen."[51]

Understandably, Niethammer found Hegel's ploy both annoying and without substance. In his reply, he pointedly asked: "Do you as professor and rector of the Nuremberg gymnasium perhaps not consider yourself sufficiently respected and worthy to be publicly and solemnly received as a member of a family which, it is true, has assumed a very respected position in the former glory of the Imperial city of Nuremberg?" Moreover, and as if to expose his ploy, Niethammer revealed that he and his wife know Hegel's fiancée and her family well, and so are "absolutely" convinced that Marie's family would not give Hegel "reason for such concern." "So, do not allow such idle worries—not to speak of a certain vanity on your part, which so ill befits a philosopher—keep you from concluding your marriage as soon as possible," advised Niethammer.[52]

In July, Georg and Marie were planning their future together. However, Hegel could not conceive of a future in which he was not a salaried professor at a university. Thus, on July 13, he resolved at once to lobby his "Jewish" friend's wife, Caroline Paulus. He now complained that, despite raising his hopes in this regard, Niethammer had failed to procure a post for him at Erlangen. Somehow, this situation reminded Hegel that Caroline "and the lord and master [a reference to her husband's status in their family] are in Heidelberg and have thought ... [he] perhaps might be needed there." With this reference to her husband as the "master," Hegel thought he was teasing Caroline, who had feminist inclinations. "I may ask you to ask the master," he added annoyingly, "whether his friendship might accomplish something there, and whether he would view conditions there as favorable to me and to be preferred. How great would be my good fortune to find at

---

[50] Ibid., 232-33 (#176).
[51] Ibid., 239 (#181).
[52] Ibid., 239-40, (#183).

IV. Bonapartist Newspaperman and Rector, 1806-1815

last in Heidelberg my port of destination! You will not leave me without a reply, will you?"[53] A few days later, Caroline informed Hegel that the presence of Johann Jakob Wagner and Fries at Heidelberg rendered his prospects there unlikely.[54]

Not all of Hegel's complaints were exaggerated or invented, however. On August 16, he informed Niethammer that his salary was "now five months in arrears." This situation naturally induced Hegel to panic, for he had already made wedding arrangements. The gravity of the situation at hand forced him to make a sarcastic joke: "The beautiful gamecock has already been fattening for two weeks." If the wedding does not occur, "it will either suffocate in its fat or must be eaten in vain." Given the gravity of the situation, he minimized his requests from Niethammer in a passive-aggressive manner:

> So, this time I do not inquire even once about Erlangen, nor even about whether you are coming to the wedding, but only whether you can say anything definite about a decision on the gymnasium foundation forthcoming within three or four weeks, and thus whether I can count on something certain by then.[55]

Hegel's next letter to Niethammer indicates that the latter offered to loan him some money for his wedding expenses. However, Hegel already borrowed the needed money from another friend and, as he informed Niethammer, "the wedding is definitely set for the 16th of September." But Hegel was not about to forget the possible Erlangen appointment: "Is a decision on *Erlangen* possible or to be hoped for by ... [October]?" He also suspected that Niethammer's silence in this regard was a clear sign that the answer to this question must be negative.[56]

Among other places, Hegel also sought Niethammer's advice and assistance to obtain a professorship at Tübingen, for which position he had been lobbying for a while.[57] This request irked Niethammer, as it revealed to him Hegel's desire to teach at a reactionary university. "For me," he replied to Hegel on December 8, 1812, "a professorship in Tübingen would be intolerable, if only because of the ridiculous hood I would have to wear in public. I would in any case prefer to be a rector and professor with honor in Nuremberg [i.e., at the gymnasium] than a professor in Tübingen with such shame." However, the forgiving and patient Niethammer also had

---

[53] Ibid., 246-49 (#189).
[54] *Briefe I*, #191.
[55] *Letters*, 250 (*Briefe I*, #194).
[56] Ibid., 251 (#195).
[57] *Briefe I*, #197, #198.

IV. Bonapartist Newspaperman and Rector, 1806-1815

some good news for Hegel: "I have not failed here to tip the balance in my direction by succeeding in having you named to the [Municipal] School Councillorship attached to the Royal Commissioner's Office in Nuremberg with an official salary of 300 florins."[58] Hegel welcomed the news and retained this extra appointment and salary until 1816.

Before we move on, it is important to bear in mind how Hegel had desperately wanted to become a salaried university professor and that he was willing to go anywhere, including Tübingen. As he himself would note some years later, "the longer I stayed in Nuremberg, the more intense became my wish to have a university professorship again."[59] To put this in the vocabulary of detectives, this statement helps us understand the main "motive" behind many of Hegel's actions while he was in Nuremberg.

3.2 The "Liberators" and the "Rabble"

We can be quite certain that Hegel was still a Napoleon admirer when he moved to Nuremberg. As Gotthilf H. Schubert, Hegel's colleague at the gymnasium, reported many years later, Hegel "appeared" to everyone as "an unconditional admirer" of Napoleon, "the conqueror of nations." Schubert also speculated that Hegel had picked up this habit in Bamberg, where "all public papers praised Napoleon."[60]

On April 23, 1809, Napoleon defeated the Austrian forces at the Battle of Regensburg (a.k.a. the Battle of Ratisbon). Even though some supported Napoleon, many other Nuremberg residents did not. On May 7, Hegel "eagerly" congratulated Niethammer for his "deliverance from the enemy forces." In other words, Niethammer's, and Hegel's by extension, career would have been at stake had Napoleon failed against the Austrians. Before Napoleon's victory, the "enemy" had briefly occupied Nuremberg. Of this situation, Hegel reported that the

> jobless and homeless scoundrels ..., youths off the streets [that is, the rabble] ..., greeted the lance of the uhlans who entered Nuremberg with a [chant of] 'Long live our brothers!' The noise was enormous but rang hollow and immediately died away. The entire mob is surely now once and for all off our backs.[61]

However, Napoleon's campaign against the Austrians did not go as well as Hegel thought it did. Under the command of Archduke Charles, the Austrians had managed to defeat Napoleon's forces at the Battle of Aspern-

---

[58] *Letters*, 284 (*Briefe I*, #214).
[59] Ibid., 434 (*Briefe II*, #317).
[60] *Berichten*, 145.
[61] *Letters*, 196-98 (*Briefe I*, #147).

IV. Bonapartist Newspaperman and Rector, 1806-1815

Essling (May 21–22, 1809). Subsequently, on June 26, an Austrian patrol force briefly reentered Nuremberg, with the "rabble" cheering them on again. Three days later, the deeply-disturbed Hegel reported the "shameful events that have taken place" to Niethammer:

> On Monday an Austrian patrol force arrived here. The municipal militia made no move to maintain order; its commander has been shamelessly mistreated, beaten up, and disarmed by the rabble at the city's gate. This rabble opened the gates and with the most dreadful and vociferous cheers brought in the Austrians, stormed the police station, destroying windows, files—everything. The people tore down everywhere the Royal coat of arms ... In short, one cannot imagine a more abject civilian attitude and behavior.[62]

By early 1813, Napoleon's forces were already retreating toward the Rhine. A significant factor in this retreat was the major defeat of his Grande Armée at the hands of the Russians in late 1812. During this campaign, Napoleon had lost about 500,000 soldiers. Many were killed in the battle, many died for other reasons, such as cold weather, and many chose desertion. (Hegel's brother died during this campaign.) His forces had also killed almost as many people on the other side, not to mention the deaths of scores of civilian—due to war-related reasons.[63]

Consequently, and as thus emboldened, Prussia decided to join the advancing Russians in 1813, breaking the humiliating treaty it had signed with the French several months after the Battle of Jena in 1806.[64] This was a part of the broader initiative of what was dubbed "the Sixth Coalition." In February 1813, the Prussian king, who had now regained his bearings with Russian help, called upon his subjects to volunteer, or else be conscripted, to fight against the French.[65] In March, he released a public appeal to explain the importance of repelling the French yoke.[66] Many

---

[62] Ibid., 198-200 (#148).
[63] For a very informative account, see Philippe-Paul Comte de Ségur, *Defeat: Napoleon's Russian Campaign*, trans. J. David Townsend (New York: New York Review Books, 2008).
[64] For a historically interesting contemporary and official Prussian perspective, see *Napoleon's Conduct towards Prussia since the Peace of Tilsit: From the Original Documents Published Under the Authority of the Prussian Government* (London: Henry Colburn, 1814).
[65] For an excellent account, see Michael V. Leggiere, *Napoleon and the Struggle for Germany: The Franco-Prussian War of 1813*, vol. 1 (Cambridge: Cambridge University Press, 2015).
[66] For an English translation of the king's appeal to his people ("An Mein Volk"), see John Breuilly, *Austria, Prussia, and the Making of Germany, 1806-1871* (London: Routledge, 2011), 123-24.

IV. Bonapartist Newspaperman and Rector, 1806-1815

students and other folks from various parts of Germany joined what was then called a "patriotic war of liberation."[67]

On May 13, in a letter to Niethammer, Hegel sarcastically thanked the approaching "several hundred thousand Cossacks, Bactrians, Prussian patriots, and the like" for helping him and his colleagues receive their unpaid salaries, by which he implied that the Bavarian government was forced to satisfy its employees to prevent unrest. "What is best of all," he added, "is that we received this money without the Cossacks and Bactrians, or any of those other excellent liberators ... Thus, things go well for us only with the approach of the enemy."[68] In June, Hegel was still in denial about the prospects of "the enemy ... 'liberators,'" as the news of "21,000 men" encamped around Munich, ready to repel the "liberators" from Bavaria, gave him much hope.[69]

At the end of December 1813, and as Hegel's guest, Ludwig Döderlein, Niethammer's stepson, was in Nuremberg to observe the "liberators," who had recently freed the city from the French occupation. On December 23, Hegel conveyed his dismay with the "liberators" and the support they were receiving from the public to Niethammer, who was equally unhappy with this situation. "Ludwig ... was here, among other things, to see our liberators pass by," wrote Hegel sarcastically, adding that, "if *par hasard* there are any liberated individuals to be seen, I myself will stand up and watch!" He then described the "liberators," especially the Russians, as an uncivilized bunch, as thieves, who have "lice" and guzzle cheap "brandy." "Liberation," he went on to add, "should ... be liberation from the burdens of the previous system" in which there existed "several kings and princes," as well as a "special constitution" for each German principality. Hegel called this fragmented scenario "oppression," lamenting its return to the territories liberated from the French. Otherwise put, he wanted a common "*roi*" and a common constitution for all Germany. Whether this "*roi*" (king) should be Napoleon or someone else, he did not say. He concluded his letter on a rather pessimistic note, indicating a sense of frustrated resignation on his part: "I have decided to observe events for one more week and then let them take whatever course they will."[70]

However, despite these setbacks, Hegel continued to believe, wishfully as it turned out, that Napoleon was still invincible. On April 10, 1814, he reported the news of the "victory" against the French at the Battle of Fère-

---

[67] Evidently, many were inspired by nationalistic ideas. However, the extent and precise nature of German nationalism during the Napoleonic wars remain matters of scholarly controversy.
[68] *Letters*, 296 (*Briefe II*, #219).
[69] Ibid., 297 (#221).
[70] Ibid., 298-300 (#225).

IV. Bonapartist Newspaperman and Rector, 1806-1815

Champenoise (March 25) to Niethammer. After this decisive defeat, and unbeknown to Hegel, Napoleon's opponents forced him to abdicate unconditionally on April 6. Unaware of Napoleon's abdication, Hegel predicted that, "for all we know, this [March 25] victory only means that the Allies have escaped ruin" for the time being.[71]

A few days later, Hegel heard the news of Napoleon's abdication. In a letter to Paulus, written on April 18, he remarked—rather casually I would say—that he did not "want to ask" what Paulus had to say "of the great Napoleon. There would still be many things to be asked about this Liberation of ours which is said to have taken place."[72] Clearly, Hegel was not enthusiastic about this "Liberation" of theirs. However, unlike what many scholars claim, he was not devastated by the news of Napoleon's demise either. As we are about to see, Hegel would adjust to the new facts in short order and quite willingly. It was time to join the "liberators," the new victors.

3.3 Joining the "Liberators"

On April 29, 1814, Hegel informed Niethammer that the additional salary he was granted in December 1812 was in arrears. "The threatening danger" of losing this supplementary salary "struck" his wife "with actual horror" and allegedly induced her to have the following dream:

> She dreamt she found herself in a large encampment near Paris full of wild soldiers, Cossacks and Prussians, all mixed together. She was completely taken with fright. However, you [Niethammer] rode through the tumult and made way on all sides. My wife approached you on foot; and as she was about to be thronged, you kindly extended your hand down from your steed and gave a sign that she was under your protection. She thus escaped safe and sound, full of joyous gratitude. She then found herself with you in a temple where all was joy and contentment. I was not indifferent during this account to the fact that I did not enter the story even once. My wife wanted to excuse the fact by saying that I was enveloped in her. I am quite willing to be protected by you, through her, against Bashkirs and Tschuwaschens [the Chuvash people], and to be brought into the haven of peace.[73]

At the same time, having now lost all his moral bearings—to the point of creatively pimping his wife, Hegel also hinted at his intention to join the Prussians, if not the Bashkirs, etc., in the same letter. "It is a frightful

---

[71] Ibid., 303-05 (#229).
[72] Ibid., 305 (#230).
[73] Ibid., 306-07 (#233).

IV. Bonapartist Newspaperman and Rector, 1806-1815

spectacle to see a great genius [i.e., Napoleon] destroy himself. There is nothing more *tragic*," he first said. Then, he boasted about having predicted this outcome in the *Phenomenology*:

> I may pride myself ... on having predicted this entire upheaval. In my book, which I completed the night before the battle of Jena, I said on page 547: 'Absolute freedom—which I had previously described as the purely abstract formal freedom of the French Republic, originating, as I showed, in the Enlightenment—passes out of its own self-destructive actuality over into *another Land* ... of self-conscious spirit [i.e., Germany] ... The new form of *moral* spirit is at hand.[74]

Hegel, it is true, did predict the rise of "the new form of *moral* spirit" in Germany in the *Phenomenology*, but then went on to hold the view that "the great genius" was invincible until he was forced to abdicate in 1814. Be that as it may, the more relevant point is that he was now willing to link the "new form of ... spirit" with the post-Napoleonic order in Germany. More predictably, however, neither Napoleon's nor Germany's fate was Hegel's primary concern. What mattered the most to him was his unfulfilled dream of longstanding. Accordingly, he concluded his letter to Niethammer with his usual prayer, which now had a new political significance: "May the alleviation of my every headache over all current events big and small be attainable in connection with Erlangen,"[75] now under the jurisdiction of the Restoration authorities in Bavaria, most of whom were Napoleon's lackeys until recently.

On July 30, 1814, when nothing came of his anticipated Erlangen headache pill, Hegel wrote to Paulus for his "advice and, if possible, assistance" to obtain a professorship either at Heidelberg or Berlin, that is, in Prussia! Although the situation at the gymnasium "has improved" recently, "my wish to return to a university remains insurmountable," he wrote.[76] Hegel's wish was indeed "insurmountable." In his August 16 reply, Paulus expressed doubt about Hegel's prospects at Heidelberg, giving Hegel's mean-spirited disparagement of Fries in his *Science of Logic*—in that "infamous footnote" (see Chapter 5)—as an important reason why Fries would oppose his appointment. Regarding the vacancy at Berlin University, he legitimately claimed to be without any influence.[77]

In his reply to Paulus, written on October 9, Hegel went so far as to express some regret for the acerbic tone of the "footnote," which, though

---

[74] Ibid.
[75] Ibid.
[76] Ibid., 318-19 (#235).
[77] Ibid., 309-10 (#236).

IV. Bonapartist Newspaperman and Rector, 1806-1815

"merited" by its target, was nevertheless "disagreeable." Be that as it may, he reasoned, nothing, including Fries' opposition to his employment at Heidelberg, was "insurmountable," as the recent events (a reference to Napoleon's demise) have shown. Hegel was now willing to leave the "happy resolution" of his wishes to join Paulus at Heidelberg University partly "in the hands of friendship, but partly in the hands of the Great Congress as well!" Despite his ensuing critical comments on the ceremonial aspects of the Congress—all "the festivities and the twaddle," Hegel was serious about his fate being in "the hands of the Great Congress." More specifically, he was hoping that the Congress would declare the duchy of Baden, along with the Rhine Palatinate, a Bavarian territory, thinking that this would somehow improve his prospects at Heidelberg (situated in Baden).[78] Likely, he thought this arrangement would allow Niethammer to bypass Fries' objection to his appointment there. Hegel thus wanted the Congress to redraw the boundaries within the post-Napoleonic Germany to accommodate his career ambitions.

The "Great Congress" refers to the Congress of Vienna, which was already at works in late September, though it would formally begin in November 1814 and end in June 1815.[79] On October 26, Hegel complained about the lack of news from the "events" unfolding at the Congress to Niethammer. In an ambivalent manner, he then linked this slow progress to the indecision of the "gentlemen" (including Niethammer) in Munich, Bavaria, hoping that "they will know by the first of November" the fate of projected appointments to universities. Other places, he complained, seem more efficient, as several "philosophical professorships open at universities outside Bavaria" were likely to be filled soon. And, Hegel had "a few friends" intervening on his behalf. "May God help!" he prayed, and then suggested that he could not remain "indifferent" to these prospects elsewhere.[80] He was, in short, ready to abandon Niethammer.

On November 29, Niethammer explained to Hegel that, due to the growing opposition he was now facing in Munich from the forces of the Restoration, he was no longer able to help him.[81] This was a clear sign, if one was needed, for Hegel to establish more firm ties with such "few

---

[78] Ibid., 311-12 (#241).
[79] For excellent treatments, see Mark Jarrett, *The Congress of Vienna and its Legacy: War and Great Power Diplomacy After Napoleon* (London: I.B. Tauris, 2014); Brian E. Vick, *The Congress of Vienna: Power and Politics After Napoleon* (Cambridge, MA: Harvard University Press, 2014). For a more focused, politically oriented study, see Tim Chapman, *The Congress of Vienna 1814-1815: Origins, Processes, and Results* (London: Routledge, 1998). For a classic contemporary account, see M. de Pradt, *The Congress of Vienna* (London: M. Carey, 1816).
[80] *Letters*, 313 (*Briefe II*, #243).
[81] *Briefe II*, #244.

IV. Bonapartist Newspaperman and Rector, 1806-1815

friends." His "destiny" was now squarely in the hands of the Restoration authorities, and he understood this well.

Contrary to what some of his liberalizers would have us believe, by December 29, Hegel had become quite enthusiastic about the Congress, despite its "deficient" (slow) progress:

> It is a new, unforgettable experience for the peoples to see what their Princes are capable of when they convene to devote themselves in mind and heart to discussion of the welfare of both their own peoples and the world—all, to be sure, according to the most noble declared principle of universal justice and the welfare of all. For centuries we have only seen action taken by cabinets or individual men for themselves against others. The present phenomenon, however, is unique and calls for a brilliant result.[82]

On February 21, 1815, Hegel once more linked the progress at the Congress to his own prospects.[83] Five days later, Napoleon escaped from Elba and staged a comeback in March 1815. Initially, it seemed as if he was back with full force as Louis XVIII, installed to the French throne by the new victors, fled the scene on March 19. On April 23, Napoleon opportunistically issued a new, quite liberal, monarchical constitution, drafted largely by Benjamin Constant, to be submitted to a plebiscite. Elections to the new Chamber of Representatives would follow soon.[84] However, as he would be reminded in short order, Napoleon was outnumbered and outgunned. On June 18, he was defeated near Waterloo.[85] Seeing the writing on the wall, he abdicated for the second and last time.

On March 19, a day before Napoleon entered Paris, Hegel offered a pessimistic and somewhat cryptic assessment of Napoleon's return in a letter to Niethammer. Once more, what worried Hegel the most was the possibility that the new conflict would lead to the elimination of "all interest in sciences and scientific institutions," that is, his own prospects. He also regarded Napoleon's return as a non-serious event, "even if eagles are planted on the walls of Paris," a reference to Napoleon's earlier promise to his soldiers that, in victory, they would together plant the eagle, with the national colors and all, everywhere in France. Hegel concluded his letter on an ambivalent note about his own future. Given that these recent

---

[82] *Letters*, 313-14 (*Briefe II*, #245).
[83] Ibid., 314-15 (#246).
[84] Jarrett, *The Congress of Vienna and its Legacy*, 159, 161.
[85] For a very informative discussion, see Jeremy Black, *The Battle of Waterloo* (New York: Random House, 2010). Also see Edward Ryan, *Napoleon's Shield & Guardian: The Unconquerable General Daumesnil* (London: Greenhill Books, 2003), 285 ff.

IV. Bonapartist Newspaperman and Rector, 1806-1815

developments were "non-events and non-destinies," "nothing" further could be said about his own "hopes and wishes." However, "I also have reason to believe that no negative decision has been made either," he noted, referring, of course, to his own prospects in Bavaria.[86] As far as Hegel was concerned, all these momentous events acquired their significance in relation to his "insurmountable" desire to "return to a university."

As we will see in Chapter 6, Hegel would soon become an ardent supporter of the Restoration regimes in Germany, which came into being at the Vienna Congress under the auspices of the triple Holy Alliance (Russia, Austria, and Prussia), As he saw it, his "destiny" was now in their hands.

---

[86] *Letters*, 316 (*Briefe II*, #247).

Chapter Five

V. RECEPTIONS OF THE *PHENOMENOLOGY* AND THE *LOGIC*, 1807-1815

1. Receptions of the *Phenomenology of Spirit*

This chapter documents how the receptions of Hegel's two major publications by his contemporaries had been generally negative. This documentation will help us further understand why he was unable to become a tenured-salaried university professor during the period covered in the previous chapter. The question will then become: What happened after 1815? Why did his fortune suddenly change in 1816? This question will be answered more firmly in Chapter 6 than it was in Chapter 4.

In April 1807, a month after Hegel's arrival in Bamberg, the *Phenomenology* was finally released to the public. Hegel's book immediately received very high praise—from Hegel himself. In other words, "Hegel even went so far as to publish a 'notice' in ... [*Bamberger Zeitung*] about his new book that extolled its virtues." He then sent similar notices to various other journals.[1]

In one of them, printed on October 28, 1807, Hegel anonymously announced the publication of his book and mentioned several "good bookstores" where it could be purchased for "six florins." The *Phenomenology*, his advertisement added, "deals with the becoming of knowledge." He also called the readers' attention to "the Preface," in which "the author" disparages "the presumption and mischief of the philosophic formulas that are currently degrading philosophy." The advertisement also announced, prematurely, the impending publication of a "*second volume*," containing "the system of *logic* as speculative philosophy, and the other two parts of philosophy, the sciences of *nature* and *spirit*."[2] This indicates that, at the time, Hegel thought of the *Phenomenology* as the beginning of his would-be philosophical system. Indeed, the main part of the full title of the *Phenomenology* is *System der Wissenschaft*, and its cover indicates that

---

[1] Terry Pinkard, *Hegel: A Biography* (Cambridge: Cambridge University Press, 2000), 240.
[2] See G. W. F. Hegel, "Hegel's Advertisement for the Publication of *The Phenomenology of Spirit*," in *Miscellaneous Writings of G. W. F. Hegel*, ed. Jon Stewart, 281-2 (Evanston, IL: Northwestern University Press, 2002).

V. Receptions of the Phenomenology and the Logic, 1807-1815

Phänomenologie des Geistes is its "first part." He would change his mind in this regard several years later.[3]

Despite his pompous and belligerent public exaltation of the *Phenomenology*, Hegel privately showed some signs of dissatisfaction with it. He expressed this sentiment to Schelling on May 1, 1807:

> Working [my way] into the detail has, I feel, damaged the overview of the whole ... I need not mention—as you will find out for yourself all too easily—that even individual sections in many respects would still need further groundwork for them to be brought into subjugation *[unterkriegen]*. Make allowances for the greater want of form in the last sections by recalling that I actually completed the draft in its entirety in the middle of the night before the Battle of Jena.[4]

For the record, it is not true, nor could it have been, that Hegel "completed the draft in its entirety in the middle of the night before the Battle of Jena." Much of it, as we know, was written earlier and some of it after this battle. However, many parts of the *Phenomenology* do indeed exhibit visible signs of having been written in a great hurry, as if the author was trying to fill as many pages as possible within a short period of time. After all, the publisher promised "to pay him 18 florins a page," but was also pressuring Hegel to brandish the rest of the manuscript (about one-half of it) before he could pay him in full.[5]

At any rate, the main purpose of Hegel's letter was to ask Schelling to promote the *Phenomenology*: "I would not know anybody else by whom I would rather have this writing introduced to the public, and from whom

---

[3] In his 1812 "Preface" to his *Science of Logic*, Hegel still describes the *Phenomenology* as the first, perhaps a preparatory, part of his "system," rendering *Logic* its second part. G. W. F. Hegel, *Science of Logic*, trans. A. V. Miller (London: George Allen & Unwin, 1969), 29. However, in his *Encyclopedia of Philosophical Sciences*, published in 1817, Hegel outlines his "system" of philosophy in a way that significantly departs from the program he suggests here. For instance, he treats the science of logic as the first leg of his triadic "system" and subsumes phenomenology under the first section ("subjective spirit") of the third leg of his "system," namely, "the philosophy of spirit [or mind]." G. W. F. Hegel, *Philosophy of Mind: Part Three of the Encyclopaedia of Philosophical Sciences*, trans. William Wallace and A. V. Miller (Oxford: Oxford University Press, 1971). My view is that Hegel was never able to develop a coherent system.

[4] Clark Butler and Christiane Seiler (trans.), *Hegel: The Letters* (Bloomington: Indiana University Press, 1984), 79-80. Henceforth cited as *Letters*. Also, Johannes Hoffmeister (ed.), *Briefe von und an Hegel*, 4 volumes (Hamburg: Felix Meiner, 1952-1960), *Briefe I*, #95. Henceforth cited as *Briefe*, followed by the Latin numerical to indicate the volume number, in this case, *I*.

[5] See Butler's commentary, *Letters*, 109.

V. Receptions of the Phenomenology and the Logic, 1807-1815

I could prefer a judgment on it."[6] But securing Schelling's endorsement required an explanation: without mentioning his name, Hegel mocked Schelling's philosophy, with the usual "formalism" charge, in his Preface. Schelling's "absolute," he also famously quipped, is akin to "the darkness of night, in which all cows are black," implying that Schelling's philosophy collapses all differentiated knowledge into identity. Ironically, Hegel borrowed the (originally Yiddish) proverb from Schelling himself, who utilized it in 1802 to criticize the very conception of the absolute Hegel mockingly attributed to him. Schelling: "For most people see in the essence of the Absolute nothing but pure night and cannot recognize (*erkennen*) anything in it; it shrinks before them into a mere negation of difference (*Verschiedenheit*) ... I want to show ... how that night of the Absolute can be turned into day for knowledge."[7] Again ironically, Hegel himself has been famously criticized for similar reductionism.[8]

Hegel anticipated that his swipe at him would provoke Schelling's disapproval of his book. He thus told him that the Preface is not "too hard on the shallowness that makes so much mischief with your forms in particular and degrades your science into a bare formalism."[9] In other words, Hegel deceptively wanted Schelling to believe that his targets were those who misused Schelling's philosophy, and not Schelling himself. As we learned in Chapter 2, Hegel had recently, in early 1807, also asked Schelling to help him find a job in Munich while he was simultaneously disparaging his "formalism" to others privately.

Schelling was not in a hurry to reply to Hegel's dishonest letter of May 1, 1807. In his November 2 reply, he downplayed the significance of Hegel's criticism. "Given my own justly measured opinion of myself," wrote Schelling, "I would have to think too little of myself to apply this polemic to my own person. It must, therefore, as you have expressed in your letter, apply only to further bad use of my ideas and to those who parrot them without understanding, although in ... [the Preface] itself the distinction is not made." His letter also expressed dissatisfaction with Hegel's handling of certain concepts, such as "intuition," on which they

---

[6] *Letters*, 79-80 (*Briefe I*, #95).
[7] Quoted in Andrew Bowie, *Schelling and Modern European Philosophy: An Introduction* (London: Routledge, 1993), 55. Bowie provides a useful discussion of this issue in the subsequent pages. For a very interesting discussion of how the "night" analogy used by both Schelling and Hegel is linked to Novalis, see Li Sui Gwee, "Night in Novalis, Schelling, and Hegel," *Studies in Romanticism* 50, no. 1 (2011): 105-124. References to the "night" can also be found in Hegel's *Difference* essay.
[8] For a collective effort to defend Hegel against various versions of this charge, see Philip T. Grier (ed.), *Identity and Difference: Studies in Hegel's Logic, Philosophy of Spirit, and Politics* (Albany: SUNY Press, 2007).
[9] *Letters*, 79-80 (*Briefe I*, #95).

V. Receptions of the Phenomenology and the Logic, 1807-1815

were previously in agreement, so Schelling had mistakenly thought all along.[10] Although Schelling concluded his letter on a friendly note ("Write me again soon and retain your attachment for your true friend ..."), he was not at all convinced that Hegel did not target his philosophy in the Preface. One also gets the sense from his reply that, for the obvious reasons, he had no desire to promote Hegel's book. Hegel also sensed this, we must assume, and did not reply as a result. Once again, Schelling was of no use to him. This was their last correspondence, though they would, purely by coincidence, run into each other at a spa in Karlsbad in 1829.[11]

However, Schelling was not about to ignore the matter at hand completely. In his July 30, 1808, letter to Karl Windischmann, he referred to the *Phenomenology* as "tangled skein [*Weichselzopf*]," and recommended that the pious Windischmann, who was at the time writing a review of it, should not be too kind to Hegel's book.[12] His May 27, 1809, letter to Gotthilf H. Schubert was also very dismissive of the *Phenomenology*.[13]

On September 6, 1807, Jean Paul (Johann Paul Friedrich Richter), the author, informed Jacobi that "after his confused writing or thinking against" Jacobi in *Faith and Knowledge*, Hegel "surprised" him "very much by his clarity, style, freedom and vigor" in his "latest philosophical system." Moreover, he reported, Hegel "also broke away from the father-polyp Schelling, though these outgoing arm- and head-polyps can easily be put together in the father-polyp again."[14] What Jean Paul understood of the *Phenomenology*, or how much of it he had read, is not clear. My guess is that he had in his possession only the Preface, which Hegel had distributed for promotional purposes generously.[15] It seems that, merely on the strength of its polemical Preface, Hegel's work was bound to please those who opposed Schelling's philosophy or disliked him for other reasons.

Jacobi was not convinced by Jean Paul's off-the-cuff reference to Hegel's surprising clarity and rigor. On November 27, he complained to Fries about having difficulty with digesting Hegel's *Phenomenology*, hoping that Köppen, Jacobi's disciple, would soon review it for his benefit.

---

[10] Ibid., 80-81 (#107).
[11] Horst Althaus, *Hegel: An Intellectual Biography*, trans. Michael Tarsh (Cambridge, UK: Polity Press, 2000), 267.
[12] Friedrich Schelling, *Aus Schellings Leben in Briefen, 1803-1820*, ed. G. L. Plitt (Leipzig: S. Hirzel, 1870), 128.
[13] Günther Nicolin (ed.), *Hegel in Berichten seiner Zeitgenossen* (Hamburg: Felix Meiner, 1970), #143. Henceforth cited as *Berichten*.
[14] *Berichten*, #130.
[15] In July 1807, Jean Paul met Hegel in Bamberg, where he likely obtained a copy of Hegel's Preface. On March 3, 1821, he asked to borrow Hegel's *Phenomenology* from one of his friends, which suggests that he never had a copy of the whole book in his possession. *Berichten*, #340.

V. Receptions of the Phenomenology and the Logic, 1807-1815

Only then, reasoned Jacobi, might he be able to understand Hegel's cryptic book.[16] In short, one of the most prominent German philosophers of the period was unable to understand Hegel's *Phenomenology*.

On December 12, Fries replied to Jacobi with a brief private review. "Because of its language, Hegel's work is almost intolerable to me," said Fries. He then described the *Phenomenology* as "a general philosophical history of the human spirit or reason," which mimics "Schelling's natural philosophy" from the distinctive vantage point of the history of spirit. Fries went on to describe Hegel's mission in the *Phenomenology* as self-contradictory since he rendered all human knowledge both fluid and relative and claimed to possess "absolute knowledge." "If Köppen wants to get involved in the detail of this work with his review," he told Jacobi, "I wish him good luck!"[17]

Köppen, it turns out, took up the challenge. He had made a career for himself by attacking Schelling, and so was pleased to see Hegel, Schelling's former acolyte (as Köppen described him a few years ago), attack him. In the *Phenomenology*, he argued, Hegel exposed "the false formalism of the Schellingian *Naturphilosophie*," and so confronted his own philosophical past. However, he committed a major philosophical "'blunder'" by collapsing "'all speculative philosophy into [pure] logic'," even though Kant had shown that pure logic is empty.[18]

In a review published in the *Neue Leipziger Literaturzeitung*, an anonymous author also highlighted Hegel's failure to successfully critique Kant. Consequently, the reviewer opined, Hegel's attempt to convert the Schellingian speculative philosophy into pure logic not only prevented him from successfully distancing himself from Schelling but also urged him to adopt a false philosophical standpoint. The reviewer then linked this standpoint to the many "strange logical games" and unintelligible passages found in the *Phenomenology*.[19]

Although there was not much agreement on what it was about, or whether it targeted or mimicked Schelling's philosophy, the near consensus reached by the concerned academic community was that the *Phenomenology* was incoherent. "Even Hegel's friend, the botanist F. J. Schelver …, evidently stated publicly not only that he was unable to understand the *Phenomenology*, but also that it was 'devoid of scientific order.'"[20] Other negative reviews, some of which were published in

---

[16] Ibid., #131.
[17] Ibid., #132.
[18] Pinkard, *Hegel: A Biography*, 261-62.
[19] Ibid., 262.
[20] M. J. Petry, "Introduction," in G. W. F. Hegel, *The Berlin Phenomenology*, ed. and trans. M. J. Petry, xiii-xcvii (Dordrecht: D. Reidel, 1981), lxxxi.

V. Receptions of the Phenomenology and the Logic, 1807-1815

academic journals, also had helped further tarnish the reputation of the *Phenomenology* and its author.

However, there were also a few endorsements. One of them was Windischmann's review, which was published in *Jenaische Allgemeine Literaturzeitung* in early 1809. His "review is distinctly dull and pedestrian," and concludes "by admitting that he is not certain that he has understood what Hegel is driving at."[21] On April 27, 1810, Windischmann wrote a letter to Hegel to privately express his appreciation of the *Phenomenology*. "Your book," he told Hegel, will "be viewed as the elementary text of the emancipation of man, as the key to the new Gospel Lessing prophesized," adding that all this will be secured by the "magical power of the Impenetrable."[22] Hegel likely cringed when he read these lines since he previously (1807), and not entirely unjustly, criticized Windischmann for belonging to the "crude forest stream, which threatens to confound reason and science."[23] On May 27, he merely thanked Windischmann for his interest in the *Phenomenology*.[24]

Another positive review was written in 1810 by Karl F. Bachmann, Hegel's former student at Jena. He insisted that, rather than parroting it, Hegel's philosophy was the "opposite" of Schelling's, whom Bachmann admired also. Indeed, he noted in a juvenile manner, Schelling "might be regarded as the modern Plato" and Hegel "the modern Aristotle." By drawing upon his familiarity with Hegel's Jena lectures, Bachmann presented the *Phenomenology* "as a preparation for systematic philosophy and practical activity," to be put at the service of "the fatherland and the state." As taught by Hegel, and now praised by Bachmann, philosophy "must have a stimulating effect upon action, it must awaken nobility of sentiment, teach us to think effectively and act well; the system is a nourishment only to the manly and the valiant, the effeminate and the cheap-minded are destroyed by it."[25] In his more mature and wiser years, Bachmann would become one of Hegel's harshest critics.[26]

---

[21] Ibid., lxxvii. According to Pinkard, "Windischmann ... misunderstood just about everything about Hegel's book." Pinkard, *Hegel: A Biography*, 262.
[22] *Briefe I*, #155.
[23] G. W. F. Hegel, "Maximen des Journals der deutschen Literatur," in *Gesammelte Werke: Jenaer kritische Schriften*, eds. Hartmut Buchner und Otto Pöggeler 509-14 (Hamburg: Felix Meiner, 1968), 512.
[24] *Briefe I*, #158.
[25] Quoted and summarized in Petry, "Introduction," lxxxii.
[26] By 1816, Bachmann had already moved away from the teachings of both Schelling and Hegel. Five years later, he saw Hegel's logic as a lamentable threat to the Aristotelian logic, which (justified) claim he further defended in 1828. In 1833, he disparaged a key assumption of Hegel's system—the identity of thought and being, which Bachmann saw as hostile to empirical knowledge. By this time, he had become one of the chief targets of Hegel's acolytes, to whom he replied in his *Anti-Hegel*. Carl Friedrich Bachmann, *Über die Philosophie*

V. Receptions of the Phenomenology and the Logic, 1807–1815

Sometime in August 1810, Isaac von Sinclair urged Hegel's attention to his own forthcoming book. Since he was looking for allies to endorse it, he thought it wise to praise Hegel's *Phenomenology*, especially his disparagement of "the charlatanry of Schelling and his consorts," which is merely a "methodless" nonsense "hiding behind a silly enthusiasm" for philosophy. Oddly, or perhaps tellingly, Sinclair was able to issue this compliment to Hegel without reading his book. In other words, as he informed Hegel, he read about it in a review published in *Heidelberg Yearbooks*. Sinclair also expressed his hope to rekindle their "old friendship,"[27] dating back to their Tübingen years. Two months later, Hegel sent a copy of the *Phenomenology* to Sinclair and clarified in an enclosed letter that it is only the "beginning" of his system; the remainder of his "science" or philosophical system would be published later.[28] On April 16, 1811, Sinclair responded in kind by sending Hegel his newly-released *Truth and Certainty*,[29] asking him to help promote it.[30]

Sinclair's assessment of the *Phenomenology* was relayed to Hegel on February 5, 1812. It is ripe for judgment, he noted, despite Hegel's (copout) claim that it should not be judged yet since it is only "the beginning" of his "science." Expectedly, he found Hegel's "critical and polemical" Preface, that is, mostly his castigation of Schelling's philosophy, to be the most "excellent" part of his book. After comparing Hegel's method of exposition to his own, he concluded that they both share the same standpoint of Cartesian "doubt," which "could be developed from everything." More specifically, Hegel proceeds "from the uncertainty of things, of sensory perception, which in truth is doubt in the concrete, doubt as experienced." However, since Hegel has "not yet entered upon the path of construction," he is "unable to abandon the standpoint of experience," and so naturally remains within the realm of doubt or uncertainty. Even so, Sinclair found Hegel's "execution" astonishing, and so was enjoined to admire "the penetration of mind which has replaced the guiding thread of construction." Then, Sinclair admitted that he was able to follow, "with the greatest delight," only "through the first section," which means that he understood,

---

meiner Zeit, zur Vermittlung (Jena: Cröker, 1816); *Von der Verwandtschaft der Physik und der Psychologie: Eine Preisschrift* (Utrecht, Johannes Altheer, 1821); *System der Logik: Ein Handbuch zum Selbststudium* (Leipzig: F. A. Brockhaus, 1828); *Über Hegel's System und die Nothwendigkeit einer nochmaligen Umgestaltung der Philosophie* (Leipzig: Vogel, 1833); *Anti-Hegel* (Jena: Cröker, 1835). For an accessible and very useful discussion, see Frederick Gregory, *Scientific Materialism in Nineteenth Century Germany* (Dordrecht: D. Reidel, 1977), 17 ff.
[27] *Briefe I*, #162.
[28] *Briefe I*, #167.
[29] Isaac von Sinclair, *Wahrheit und Gewißheit* (Frankfurt: J. C. Hermann, 1811).
[30] *Briefe I*, #179.

V. Receptions of the Phenomenology and the Logic, 1807-1815

or thought he did, only one-fifth of Hegel's entire book. After this point, he found Hegel's attempt to "probe the depths of enigmas ... incomprehensible," adding that he "could only dimly understand ... what followed." After registering more complaints about Hegel's book, and with the anticipation of Hegel's forthcoming "science" in mind, Sinclair concluded his letter on a friendly and encouraging note: "I ... expect everything from your speculative philosophy."[31] He would be disappointed with Hegel's "science," as we will see in the next section.

As he wrote to Thomas Seebeck on November 28, 1812, Goethe was urged to read a portion of the following paragraph (not quoted in his letter) of the *Phenomenology* from Ignaz Paul Vital Troxler's comment on it:

> The bud disappears in the bursting-forth of the blossom, and one might say that the former is refuted by the latter; similarly, when the fruit appears, the blossom is shown up in its turn as a false manifestation of the plant, and the fruit now emerges as the truth of it instead. These forms are not just distinguished from one another, they also supplant one another as mutually incompatible. Yet at the same time their fluid nature makes them moments of an organic unity in which they not only do not conflict, but in which each is as necessary as the other; and this mutual necessity alone constitutes the life of the whole.[32]

This passage outraged Goethe: "It is probably not possible to say anything more monstrous. To want to annihilate the eternal reality of nature by a bad sophistical joke seems to me quite unworthy of a reasonable man." However, he hoped that the passage might have a different connotation in its broader "context," but could not "get hold of the book" to see it for himself.[33] Seebeck promised to investigate the matter at hand.[34] On December 13, he sent Goethe the entire paragraph.[35] Goethe, I suppose, now found out that the paragraph was meant as an analogy to illustrate how various philosophical systems relate to one another. In his reply to Seebeck, he still expressed dissatisfaction with Hegel's paragraph, but regarded the whole matter settled.[36]

For his part, as we have seen, Hegel confessed to Schelling soon after its publication that his book was unclear. However, when criticized by others for the same reason, he tried to explain away its obscure language as

---

[31] *Letters*, 289-90 (*Briefe I*, #199).
[32] G. W. F. Hegel, *Phenomenology of Spirit*, trans. A. V. Miller (Oxford: Oxford University Press, 1977), §2.
[33] *Berichten*, #159.
[34] Ibid., #160.
[35] Ibid., #161.
[36] Ibid., #163.

V. Receptions of the Phenomenology and the Logic, 1807-1815

the only proper language of true philosophy. This copout explanation is given in his November 21, 1807, letter to Knebel. In response to Knebel's friendly complaint about the relative absence of "intelligibility and clarity" in his book, Hegel claimed that a philosophical "subject matter does not permit ... clarity of exposition," and that he hoped his "obscure style" would help his readers achieve more profound philosophical comprehension.[37]

Henceforth, this explanation would become Hegel's readymade justification for his "obscure style," as can also be observed in his December 18, 1812, letter to Peter van Ghert, his former student at Jena, and a rare admirer at the time.

> I am sorry that there are complaints [in Holland] about the ponderousness of the presentation [in the *Phenomenology*]. It is, however, the nature of such abstract subjects that treatments of them cannot assume the ease of a common reader. Truly speculative philosophy cannot take on the garb and style of Locke or the usual French philosophy. To the uninitiated, speculative philosophy must in any case present itself as the upside-down world, contradicting all their accustomed concepts and whatever else appeared valid to them according to so-called sound common sense.[38]

Sound common sense and clarity were not the Hegelian sorts of virtues, as he here admits. Thus, he was regarded as the philosopher of unsound nonsense by many of his contemporaries. For this reason, or this being an important reason, Hegel's hope to obtain a salaried teaching post at a university was further undermined. This predicament was compounded by Hegel's uncontrollable urge to slander just about all philosophers, including the influential ones who might have had otherwise helped him procure a post.

For instance, as Hegel himself knew, many academic appointments in Bavaria were decided by Jacobi, who was helping his own acolytes with such appointments. As we have sufficiently established by now, he regarded Hegel as an incoherent slanderer; it did not help that Hegel had been attacking him since 1801. Hegel, of course, thought that such appointments were undeserved. Thus, when Köppen was appointed to Landshut University, Hegel thought the undeserving Köppen was unjustly hired with Jacobi's help. "Köppen's call to Landshut," he wrote to Niethammer in May 1807, "is, of course, quite characteristic; and what seems to me his

---

[37] *Letters,* 144-46 (*Briefe I,* #109).
[38] Ibid., 591 (#215).

V. Receptions of the Phenomenology and the Logic, 1807-1815

complete incapacity for any solid thought is all the more shocking because it shows how great is the power he [Jacobi] has courted."[39]

During this period, Hegel still thought, wrongly as it would turn out, that Niethammer could overcome the hurdles created by Jacobi and his allies. "I know I have your support, and know the worth of this support as well," he told Niethammer in the same letter.[40] However, both Niethammer and Hegel would soon realize that the latter's relationship with Jacobi needed to be improved. We will return to this issue in the next chapter.

For now, and to conclude this section, the claim that "Hegel's *Phenomenology* quickly established his reputation as Germany's leading philosopher" has no merit whatsoever.[41] In fact, a good number of the 750 copies of the first edition/printing of the *Phenomenology* remained unsold as late as 1829, even though its author was the most famous philosopher in Germany at the time.[42] If anything, the *Phenomenology* reinforced the existing image of Hegel as an incoherent and undeserving figure. His *Logic* would further galvanize this image of him.

2. Receptions of *The Science of Logic*

Fries published his *System of Logic* in 1811, which was generally well-received. Fries' success (recognition by others) annoyed the envious Hegel immensely, and he was not about to conceal this fact from Niethammer in his October 10, 1811, letter: "I feel sad that in the name of philosophy such a shallow man attains the honorable position he holds in the world, and that he even permits himself to inject such scribblings with an air of importance." This was the nicest thing the outraged Hegel was able to say about Fries and his book, which he proceeded to describe as "spiritless, completely shallow, threadbare, trivial, devoid of the least intimation of scientific coherence." Fries' "most-slovenly" logic, he added, amounts to little more than "lecture-hall twaddle, such as only a truly empty-headed individual in his hour of digestion could ever come up with."[43]

After adding more details to his private castigation of Fries' *Logic* and

---

[39] Ibid., 129 (#98).
[40] Ibid.
[41] *Pace* Kenneth R. Westphal, "Introduction," in *The Blackwell Guide to Hegel's* Phenomenology of Spirit, xvi-xxvii (Oxford: Wiley-Blackwell, 2009), xvi; Pinkard, *Hegel: A Biography*, 264. This misinformation might have been inspired by Gotthilf Heinrich Schubert's claim, written in 1855, that the *Phenomenology* was "one of the most admired literary achievements in the field of philosophy." *Berichten*, #145.
[42] See Hegel's letter to his brother-in-law, *Briefe IV*, #605a.
[43] *Letters*, 255-58 (*Briefe I*, #196).

V. Receptions of the Phenomenology and the Logic, 1807-1815

person, Hegel arrived at the more significant point of his letter to Niethammer:

> I hope to be able to bring out my work on logic by next Easter ... It might not be ill-advised for the authorities [such as Niethammer] to wait upon further treatments of logic before sanctioning and publicly introducing for instructional purposes the old logical shambles, which take their worst form in Fries' hands ... By fall my own labors for the lecture hall may likewise result in a more popular and easily accessible form, displaying more of the tone expected both of a general textbook and of gymnasium instruction.[44]

The promised "popular and accessible form," which Hegel hoped would be adopted as a textbook for schools by the Bavarian authorities, never arrived. In fact, it is fair to say, he was simply incapable of making his views, orally or in writing, popular and accessible. Instead, spurred by both his envy for Fries and the need to supplement his income and academic standing, he rushed to finish the first part of his *Science of Logic* (*The Doctrine of Being*). As he informed Niethammer on February 5, 1812,

> Nine sheets of my *Logic* have been printed. Before Easter, perhaps another twenty will be printed ... I am in it up to my ears. It is no mean feat in the first half year of one's marriage to write a thirty-sheet book of the most abstruse contents ... I would have needed another year to put it in proper form, but I need money to live."[45]

Hegel's *Logic*, so it seems, was largely ignored. It did, however, initially make the academic news for the following slanderous footnote it contains: The latest treatment of this science [i.e., logic] ... *by Fries* returns to the anthropological foundations. The idea or opinion on which it is based is so shallow ... that I am spared the trouble of making any notice of this insignificant publication."[46] This slander had no other explanation than Hegel's uncontrollable envy for Fries' success. It would provoke Fries to respond in kind in short order.

I believe to have sufficiently demonstrated elsewhere that Hegel's *Doctrine of Being* is a philosophical blunder.[47] However, as usual, what matters more for our present purposes is its reception by his contemporaries.

---

[44] Ibid.
[45] Ibid., 261 (#198).
[46] G. W. F. Hegel, *Science of Logic*, trans. A. V. Miller (London: George Allen & Unwin, 1969), 52, n 1.
[47] Mehmet Tabak, *The Doctrine of Being in Hegel's Science of Logic* (New York: Palgrave, 2017).

V. Receptions of the Phenomenology and the Logic, 1807-1815

The first negative review of *Logic*, or its first main part, had reached Hegel in the form of three letters from Johann Wilhelm Andreas Pfaff, Hegel's mathematician colleague at the gymnasium. In these letters, which I find very competent and thoughtful, Pfaff specifically took to task a central claim Hegel makes in *Logic*, that he proves his results immanently, without any presuppositions. This, Pfaff justly pointed out, Hegel failed to do.[48]

On October 12, 1812, Sinclair also sent his thoughts on *Logic* to Hegel. He apologized for his inability to give Hegel "a detailed verdict" on his "system" since he "cannot presently understand it." He then noted cautiously and politely that Hegel's presuppositionless method was unconvincing, and that, unlike his claim to the contrary, his system did not amount to a "self-identical whole."[49] Hegel responded to Sinclair's criticism in a now-lost letter, in which he likely defended his infamous claim that true philosophy cannot presuppose anything as its premise. In his reply, Sinclair adopted a franker tone than the one he expressed in his previous letter. "As you very justly remarked [in your letter]," he wrote to Hegel, your "beginning gives me much trouble." He found it especially problematic that Hegel pretended to begin "wholly out of the blue." Sinclair, on the other hand, defended the view that philosophy ought to at least presuppose itself, which presupposition he identified with "doubt."[50] Hegel replied sometime in January 1813 with a rebuttal of his own. He also noted that his "single and ultimate goal is to teach at a university," but his recently-raised hopes "for Erlangen" (by Niethammer) have been dashed.[51]

Several other surviving, private comments on Hegel's *Logic* are also negative. The following comment is found in August Twesten's June 6, 1815 letter to the famous theologian and philosopher Friedrich Schleiermacher: "One does not understand everything, and what one understands often comes across as little more than a sleight of hand, rather than a bold and truly profitable speculation." This comment followed a more positive one about Hegel's Introduction, which is admittedly somewhat clearer than the rest of his book.[52] Schleiermacher noted in his reply that the reviews he had seen gave him similar impressions of Hegel's *Logic* as the one Twesten reported, but he himself had not read it.[53]

Perhaps Schleiermacher had in mind Fries' scathing review of the first two books of Hegel's *Logic*. The review, published in the *Heidelberg Yearbooks*, basically accused Hegel of linguistic and philosophical

---

[48] *Briefe I*, #202, #204.
[49] Ibid., #210.
[50] Ibid., #211.
[51] Ibid., #218.
[52] *Berichten*, #168.
[53] Ibid., #169.

V. Receptions of the Phenomenology and the Logic, 1807-1815

vandalism. Fries also highlighted Hegel's inability to comprehend, much less competently critique, Kant's antinomies and Newton's science. It is "sad," he wrote, that "our author" bases his critique on a very "low level of scientific education [or understanding]" and on Goethe's "mistakes."[54] Upon reading his review, Jacobi congratulated Fries on his "excellent assessment" of Hegel's book, which he himself looked at "only once and put away forever" for the obvious reasons.[55]

"My poor innocent *Logic* and I are being ... pilloried in the *Heidelberg Yearbooks*," complained Hegel to Paulus on August 16, 1815, adding that this should not be seen as "just vengeance" for the slanderous footnote on Fries' *Logic* in his own *Science of Logic*. "I, as the aggrieved party ..., must find it trite and crude, all the more so inasmuch as the charge of ignorance made against me ought to be completely turned back against [Fries]."[56] Hegel's friction with Fries, although essentially apolitical at the time, would soon boost Hegel's career prospects in a very politicized context (see Chapter 6).

There was, however, also a strikingly positive assessment, privately sent to Hegel by one Nicolaus von Thaden, an obscure Danish civil servant, who was an avid consumer of Hegel news for reasons that remain a mystery. In his August 27, 1815, letter to Hegel, Thaden declared *Logic* "the book of books, a consummate masterpiece of the human spirit." He also lamented that Hegel's book was little known and, "at least publicly, not acknowledged by any writer for its true worth." In fact, the "three" reviews in circulation that he has seen are entirely negative. Thaden reasoned that Hegel's difficult writing style might have urged these, in Thaden's view, unfair reviews. He also assumed, quite correctly, that Hegel was bent upon increasing his renown, and so suggested that he should write on practical matters, especially on the state, to achieve his goal.[57]

The Final Act of the Vienna Congress was signed on June 9, 1815, nine days before Napoleon's defeat near Waterloo. Thus, the Restoration period was already in the works when Hegel received Thaden's letter and recommendation. It is unlikely that Thaden's suggestion had anything to do with this, but his claim that Hegel would acquire more fame by focusing "on practical matters, especially on the state," would prove prophetic in short order.[58] In other words, Hegel would soon publish a political pamphlet to defend the king of Württemberg, which would increase his

---

[54] Jakob Fries, "Wissenschaft der Logik von D. G. W. F. Hegel," *Heidelbergische Jahrbücher der Literatur*, no. 25 (1815): 385-93.
[55] *Berichten*, #170.
[56] *Letters*, 95 (*Briefe II*, 250).
[57] *Briefe II*, #251.
[58] Ironically, Hegel's *Philosophy of Right* would immensely disappoint Thaden in 1821 (see Chapter 10).

V. Receptions of the Phenomenology and the Logic, 1807–1815

fame, especially in the eyes of the authorities. This is to say, too, that Hegel's relatively unknown political pamphlet had played a much more significant role in helping advance his career than his two major books.

Chapter Six

VI. HEGEL'S RESTORATION, 1815-1818

1. Restoration Politics and Academics

As noted in Chapter 4, Napoleon's two abdications roughly overlapped with the Vienna Congress, which took place between November 1814 and June 1815. The German Confederation, erected from the ashes of the Holy Roman (or German) Empire, was one of the chief achievements of the Congress. It included thirty-nine German "states," which were dominated by Austria and Prussia, though the views and expectations of the Russian and English rulers were also taken into consideration, as were those of the lesser Germanic states and duchies. The Articles of the Confederation (1815) recognized each member as a "sovereign state," but also stipulated their commitment to unity and common defense. Perhaps unbeknown to anyone at the time, the common-defense clause would soon come to primarily mean coordinated activity against the liberal-minded domestic "enemies," active within the member states.

Famously, Article 13 stipulated that all member states "shall have an estate constitution (*landständische Verfassung*)." This article was included as a compromise of sorts to the denizens of the Confederation, who had been led to believe that their sacrifices during "the war of liberation" would be rewarded with political reform. Thus, all rulers agreed to implement Article 13, though only a few of them complied rather quickly in the ways they saw fit. On May 22, 1815, before the enactment of the Articles, Friedrich Wilhelm III issued an edict, promising to implement a constitution in Prussia, which would grant a national representative assembly.[1] However, a potent power would soon persuade the king to drag his feet, though it is not clear that he would have done otherwise without the influence of this power.

In other words, both the Confederation and its articles were overshadowed by the demands of a higher superstructure, known as the Holy Alliance. It was formed by Austria, Russia, and Prussia on September

---

[1] The edict is reprinted in Wilhelm Altmann (ed.), *Ausgewählte Urkunden zur Brandenburg-Preussischen Verfassungs und Verwaltungsgeschichte* (Berlin: R. Geartners, 1897), 87-88. Also see Walter M. Simon, *The Failure of the Prussian Reform Movement, 1807–1819* (Ithaca, NY: Cornell University Press, 1955), 109 ff.

VI. Hegel's Restoration, 1815-1818

26, 1815. They agreed to reintroduce Christian and monarchical principles of government throughout the post-Napoleonic Europe and, in connection with this, to "monitor and supervise political activity throughout Europe to guarantee conformity with those principles. The Restoration—the Metternich era—had begun."[2] The notorious Karlsbad Decrees, enacted in 1819, would be an extension of these principles.

Although these principles were not uniformly implemented everywhere, it is abundantly clear that the Austrian and Prussian rulers took the need to monitor political activity in Germany very seriously. Relatedly, the promised constitution now received a more cautious interpretation, especially from Metternich and his Prussian counterparts, who quickly envisioned it in a way that would severely limit popular participation in the affairs of the state.[3] In fact, they went further and opined that granting a constitution—any kind—would urge more radical demands for reform, ultimately threatening their own power, if not existence. Royal heads had been rolled not so long ago, so it was widely believed, after Louis XVI of France conceded to a constitution. Thus, the "Holy" rulers prioritized monitoring and supervising political activity, or else suppressing it, and in some cases (such as in Prussia) postponed the promulgation of a constitution indefinitely, while at the same time giving the impression that it was still their aim to do so.

They had legitimate, if exaggerated, reasons to believe that radical political activity was brewing in the background. For instance, with the blessing of the liberal Duke Karl August of Saxe-Weimar-Eisenach, the *Urburschenschaft*, a political student fraternity, was founded on June 12, 1815, by liberal-republican and nationalistic students at Jena University. Many of its members were veterans of "the war of liberation," who were

---

[2] Thomas P. Saine, "The World Goethe Lived In: Germany and Europe, 1750–1830," in *The Cambridge Companion to Goethe*, ed. Leslie Sharpe, 6-22 (Cambridge: Cambridge University Press, 2002), 21. Friedrich Gentz, the confidant, assistant, and adviser to Metternich, was the main official theoretician of the Holy Alliance. For a classical study on Gentz and his politics, see Paul Friedrich Reiff, *Friedrich Gentz, an Opponent of the French Revolution and Napoleon* (Urbana-Champaign: The University of Illinois Press, 1912). While the "Christian" principle was largely Tsar Alexander I's idea, the "monarchical" principle was added by Metternich. The impressionable king of Prussia went along. See Mark Jarrett, *The Congress of Vienna and its Legacy: War and Great Power Diplomacy after Napoleon* (London: I. B. Tauris, 2013), 173 ff. For a useful, succinct discussion of the Restoration period, see Mary Fulbrook, *Concise History of Germany* (Cambridge: Cambridge University Press, 2004), 104-15. For an informative biography of Metternich, see Alan Palmer, *Metternich: Councillor of Europe* (London: Faber & Faber, 2014). For his continental policing activities, see Donald Eugene Emerson, *Metternich and the Political Police: Security and Subversion in the Hapsburg Monarchy, 1815-1830* (The Hague: Martinus Nijhoff, 1968).

[3] See Simon, *The Failure of the Prussian Reform Movement, 1807–1819*, 212 ff.

VI. Hegel's Restoration, 1815-1818

now expecting the deliverance of the promised constitution. This organizational model was quickly adopted in other universities and grew into a Germany-wide movement known as the *Burschenschaften*.

Tellingly, in October 1815, a month after the formation of the Holy Alliance, the Prussian king conferred an honorary medal on an influential Berlin University professor, Theodor von Schmalz. Schmalz was rewarded for the several political pamphlets he had published several months earlier.[4] His aim in publishing them was to warn against the activities of "secret" nationalist-liberal "clubs," which allegedly preached French Jacobinism with German characteristics and sought constitutions with the sole aim of destroying the monarchical regimes. Even some very conservative, anti-revolutionary figures, such Barthold G. Niebuhr, found Schmalz's claims about the existence of such "secret" clubs incredible. However, especially given the presence of the "open" clubs, the Prussian king found them worthy of a stately medal, which bestowed upon the most-reactionary Schmalz the Order of the Red Eagle, Third Class.[5] Alexander I, the Russian tsar, congratulated the king for his action.[6]

In the words of a historian of this period, this was an "unmistakable sign that the winds of reaction were prevailing within the Berlin court."[7] Evidently, such winds were also blowing through the windows of the academic edifice. Although not reducible to it, Hegel's first Berlin campaign must be understood in this broader political context.

2. Berlin University is Hiring: Hegel or Fries?

Hegel's first Berlin campaign (1815-1816) coincides with the broader political context I just briefly described. As his July 30 letter to Paulus indicates, he was already interested in teaching at Berlin in 1814.[8] More

---

[4] Theodor Schmalz, *Berichtigung einer Stelle in der Bredow-Venturinischen Chronik für das Jahr 1808: Ueber politische Vereine, und ein Wort über Scharnhorsts und meine Verhältnisse zu ihnen* (Berlin: Maurerschen Buchhandlung, 1815); Theodor Schmalz, *Ueber des Herrn B. G. Niebuhrs Schrift wider die meinige, politische Vereine betreffend* (Berlin: Maurerschen Buchhandlung, 1815).
[5] Simon, *The Failure of the Prussian Reform Movement, 1807–1819*, 116-22.
[6] Alexander congratulated Wilhelm on the "success of the wise and vigorous measures" he had "taken to control the secret societies, whose excesses might have given" the king "good grounds for anxiety." Wilhelm downplayed the scope of the "anxiety," claiming that it was merely a "natural consequence of the disturbed state of political scene" in the aftermath of the war against Napoleon. Both the tsar and the king are quoted in Simon, *The Failure of the Prussian Reform Movement, 1807–1819*, 140, 141.
[7] Jon Vanden Heuvel, *A German Life in the Age of Revolution: Joseph Görres, 1776-1848* (Washington DC: The Catholic University of America Press, 2001), 213, n. 130.
[8] Clark Butler and Christiane Seiler (trans.), *Hegel: The Letters* (Bloomington IN: Indiana University Press, 1984), 308-12. Henceforth cited as *Letters*. Also see Johannes Hoffmeister

VI. Hegel's Restoration, 1815-1818

specifically, he wanted to fill the chair of philosophy Fichte had occupied until his death on January 27, 1814. It is likely that he had also contacted other people in Berlin during the same period. As he noted in his October 26 letter to Niethammer, there were several "philosophical professorships open at universities outside Bavaria," and that "it is to be thought that new appointments may be in the works. It seems that a few friends want to intervene on my behalf. May God help!"[9] By March 1815, the Berlin faculty and the relevant authorities were giving Hegel's candidacy serious consideration.

The number of "qualified" candidates for this post was quite small, as the declared intention was to find a speculative philosopher. To be more precise, two philosophy chairs were vacant, the second being that of practical philosophy, but the government decided to fill only the position for speculative philosophy. In addition to a few others, none other than Fries was also in the same loop, even though he was not a speculative philosopher. He was proposed by Wilhelm de Wette, his friend and disciple. De Wette, now a professor of theology, endorsed Fries' and opposed Hegel's candidacy with equal zeal.[10] However, as his March 4 letter to Fries indicates, some influential figures at the university, including Schmalz, strongly opposed Fries' candidacy and supported Hegel's. This support for Hegel's candidacy struck de Wette with horror, who not only favored Fries but also thought Hegel, with his "confused head," was unqualified and undeserving.[11]

Tellingly, Hegel's other supporters included Georg Nicolovius, a high-ranking official in the Prussian ministry of interior, who was at the time employed in the Department of Culture and Public Education, and Philip Konrad Marheineke, who would subsequently become Hegel's disciple and

---

(ed.), *Briefe von und an Hegel*, 4 volumes (Hamburg: Felix Meiner, 1952-1960), #235. Henceforth cited as *Briefe*, followed by the Latin numerical to indicate the volume number, in this case *II*.

[9] *Letters*, 313 (*Briefe II*, #243).

[10] De Wette was a theology student at Jena when both Hegel and Fries became *privatdozent* there in 1801. Although his main teacher was Paulus, he eventually gravitated towards Fries' philosophy. After 1806, he taught at Heidelberg as Paulus' and Fries' colleague. In 1810, de Wette became a theology professor at Berlin, when the university was still under the influence of the liberal philosopher-minister-reformer Wilhelm von Humboldt. For an excellent biography, see John W. Rogerson, *W. M. L. de Wette, Founder of Modern Biblical Criticism: An Intellectual Biography* (Sheffield, UK: Sheffield Academic Press, 1992).

[11] Günther Nicolin (ed.), *Hegel in Berichten seiner Zeitgenossen* (Hamburg: Felix Meiner, 1970), #167. Henceforth, cited as *Berichten*. The information I provide here about de Wette's letters to Fries is supplemented with information taken from Ernst Ludwig Theodor Henke, *Jakob Friedrich Fries: Aus Seinem Handschriftlichen Nachlasse dargestellt* (Leipzig: Brockhaus, 1867), 353.

VI. Hegel's Restoration, 1815-1818

a key figure in the so-called "Hegelian Right" after Hegel's death. These figures were also members of the conservative Prussian National Bible Society. For the reasons I will reveal shortly, I suspect strongly that Hegel had previously lobbied at least Nicolovius, if not both, for the Berlin post.

Hegel knew that the Berliners were taking his candidacy seriously but became increasingly anxious as the they dragged their feet. A few months earlier, he had a conflict with an administrator regarding the affairs of the gymnasium. In July, he sought Niethammer's permission to go to Munich and defend himself. "Apart from that, I hear that the plan for the universities is in fact to be presented this month. Kindly remember me, please, in this regard," he wrote.[12] Thus, Hegel was aware of the impending plan for the expansion and improvement of the universities under the new Restoration regime in Bavaria when he arrived in Munich in September. However, he was not about to leave the matter solely in Niethammer's hands, especially since, as we have seen in Chapter 4, the latter informed him previously that, under the new political circumstances, he himself was facing opposition in Munich, and so could not be of much help to Hegel.[13]

While in Munich, Hegel had met with Johann Kracker, the Royal Bavarian Commissioner in Nuremberg, and "others" with whom he certainly discussed the issue of his appointment to Erlangen. Kracker, he wrote to Niethammer upon returning from Munich to Nuremberg, "is very well disposed toward me." Via Niethammer, he also sent some "writings" to their mutual friend, "dear, most excellent Privy Councilor [Jacobi]," along with his "warmest regards" to the latter and "his sisters."[14] In other words, he also visited Jacobi in Munich and was now thanking him and his sisters for their hospitality.

With Niethammer's mediation, Hegel had already improved his personal relationship with Jacobi since 1812.[15] While in Munich, he asked Jacobi to contact Nicolovius, the latter's acquaintance, and to recommend him for the Berlin post. Hegel's targeted request suggests that he himself had contacted Nicolovius previously. Consequently, shortly after Hegel's visit, on October 21, 1815, Jacobi wrote a letter to Nicolovius. It should be noted that, despite their improved relationship, Jacobi was not exactly a Hegel admirer. Recently, he thanked Fries for his "excellent" critique of

---

[12] *Letters*, 317 (*Briefe II*, #249).
[13] *Briefe II*, #244.
[14] Ibid., 318-9 (#252).
[15] This was more of a strategic move on Hegel's part, and perhaps Jacobi's too, than the result of a philosophical agreement between them. The thawing in their relationship had begun after Niethammer and Jacobi befriended each other within the context of educational reform in Bavaria. In 1812, Hegel and Jacobi met in person when the latter visited Nuremberg. On July 19, Hegel wrote to Niethammer, thanking him for making his friendship with Jacobi possible. *Briefe I*, #207.

VI. Hegel's Restoration, 1815-1818

Hegel's *Logic*, that is, his "generous protection against [Hegel's] grobianism."[16] Thus, it is not surprising that, in his letter to Nicolovius, Jacobi first expressed his "great astonishment" at the news that some Berliners preferred "Professor [Gottlieb Ernst August] Mehmel" of the University of Erlangen to Fries. (In his youth, Mehmel had tutored Hardenberg's sons, and was consequently promoted by the latter, though I do not know if this had anything to do with his promising candidacy at Berlin University.) "How in the world," wondered Jacobi, "could such a mediocre subject be preferred to a Fries?" He then noted that Hegel "also applied for this position," and that he, Jacobi, "promised Hegel" to "mention his name" to Nicolovius in relation to this position. Hegel "is no longer who [i.e., the incoherent person] he was in Jena," said Jacobi unenthusiastically, but nevertheless gave Hegel's candidacy an "enthusiastic" endorsement. Clearly, Jacobi's recommendation of Hegel was based on his assumption that the opposition to Fries' candidacy in Berlin was too powerful to overcome.[17] Likely, his alliance and friendship with Niethammer had something to do with his support for Hegel's candidacy.

Jacobi's amazement with Berlin's disapproval of Fries' candidacy helps us evaluate Hegel's candidacy in relation to that of Fries: Why was the latter opposed by some powerful figures in Berlin? To recall, all this was taking place shortly after the Restoration and the Holy Alliance came into being. For this reason, it is not surprising that Fries', and Hegel's, candidacy was assessed in this *politicized* context. With this issue in mind, de Wette reported to Fries on October 20 that, influenced by Schmalz's "obnoxious writing about political associations," Count Friedrich von Schuckmann, the interior minister and Nicolovius' superior, was now increasingly "revealing himself as a narrow-minded royalist." This obviously did not bode well for the republican-liberal Fries.[18]

The Prussian regime was already cracking down on political opposition during this period. On June 15, 1815, "the king wrote to the liberal-minded governor of the Rhineland … that he would hold [him] personally responsible for any *Preßfrechheit* (subversive press) in that territory." He was now prepared to "muzzle troublesome journalists" more vigorously than he had done previously, he said. To the king's chagrin, Joseph Görres, the popular intellectual and publicist, doubled down on his criticism of the Prussian regime in his *Rheinischer Merkur*, provoking the king to turn over "the power of censorship" to Prince Wilhelm Sayn-Wittgenstein, the reactionary minister of police. For his part, Görres kept printing critical articles. In one of them, printed on December 8, he castigated Schmalz for

---

[16] *Berichten*, #170.
[17] Ibid., #172.
[18] Henke, *Jakob Friedrich Fries: Aus Seinem Handschriftlichen Nachlasse dargestellt*, 354.

VI. Hegel's Restoration, 1815-1818

the views he had expressed in his pamphlets. Also, in a four-part article entitled 'The Reaction in Prussia,' Görres condemned those officials who wished to snuff out the national spirit that had finally awakened in Germany ... [and was now] 'demanding its reward.'" His message was unambiguous: "the Prussian State, having encouraged the awakening national consciousness [during the war of liberation], could not now leave the people dissatisfied; nationalist demands for a constitution and German unity would not disappear, but had to be met." However, the king "had no desire to hear more of this kind of advice. On January 3, 1816, he signed an order, written by [Chancellor Karl August Fürst von] Hardenberg, commanding [Johann August] Sack to close down the *Rheinischer Merkur*."[19] Other such papers were also banned shortly thereafter, while some were converted into pro-government organs.[20] Schuckmann belonged to the Wittgenstein camp, and even Hardenberg, known for his earlier "liberal" sympathies, had to go along with the now-unfolding repression, whether he liked it or not.

By the end of March 1816, the pool of candidates also included Schelling and a few others. Briefly put, things did not go so well for either Schelling or Fries. By this time, Schelling was falling out of favor. Besides, Schuckmann despised his philosophy. More significantly for our purposes, Fries was accused of being "godless" during the faculty deliberations.[21] I strongly suspect that his recent publication, in which he called for a republican constitution, also worked against his candidacy.[22] Republicanism, liberalism, atheism, etc., meant the same sort of a dangerous thing in the eyes of the Holy rulers during this period. Regardless of the nature of the varying concerns the Berlin faculty might have had about the academic merits of the candidates, it was clear that Fries' appointment would not be approved by Schuckmann, Wittgenstein, and the king. As Leary succinctly puts it, given his philosophical accomplishments, "if Fries had not been politically censured, he very possibly would have received the appointment to the Berlin chair."[23]

Whether or not Hegel's political sympathies were known to the Prussian authorities and the Berlin faculty at the time is not clear. However, that he was Fries' philosophical archenemy was no secret, and this alone—independently of his political views—increased his chances. Indeed, some influential faculty members, such as Schleiermacher, supported Hegel's

---

[19] Heuvel, *A German Life in the Age of Revolution*, 212-13.
[20] Ibid., 222.
[21] *Berichten*, #174.
[22] Jakob Fries, *Von deutschem Bund und deutscher Staatsverfassung* (Heidelberg: Mohr und Winter, 1816).
[23] David E. Leary, "The Psychology of Jakob Friedrich Fries (1773-1843): Its Context, Nature, and Historical Significance," *Storia E Critica Della Psicologia* 3, no. 2 (1982): 217-48, 222.

VI. Hegel's Restoration, 1815-1818

candidacy (after initially voting for G. H. von Schubert) simply to block Fries' appointment, even though he was not very familiar with Hegel's philosophy.[24] "Schleiermacher's action was [undoubtedly] intended ... to head off Fries' chances."[25] In addition to their philosophical-theological differences, he feared that a de Wette-Fries alliance at Berlin would "eclipse his ... own views and sphere of influence."[26]

Soon thereafter, on April 1, the faculty senate informed Schuckmann of its decision to nominate Hegel as the top candidate for the chair of philosophy.[27] Schelling was ranked second, Schubert third, and Fries fourth. De Wette at once tried to bypass the senate's verdict by informing Schuckmann that Hegel is an advocate of Schelling's *Naturphilosophie*, toward which the minister had known aversion. Moreover, Hegel's *Logic* is muddled, and he himself is an incoherent lecturer, de Wette reported. He also described Schubert as a philosopher of the occult.[28] Perhaps not singlehandedly, he succeeded in making Schuckmann doubt Hegel's academic merits.

At any rate, the interior minister was not in a hurry to hire Hegel. He first had to investigate him to determine whether he was coherent enough to teach at a university, which is itself a remarkably low threshold. Oddly, and perhaps tellingly, Schuckmann did not bother to appoint anyone to evaluate Hegel's academic writings, which any objective academic would have found to be utterly incoherent at best. As for his political sympathies, Hegel had nothing to worry about. His earlier support for Napoleon and resentment of the Prussians were known only to his intimate friends. Besides, as we have seen in the previous chapter, and will further see in the ensuing section, he had already become a Restoration supporter.

3. Hegel's Other Campaigns and Triumph

Sometime in early 1816, Schelling declined a call from Jena. Having heard this news, Hegel contacted his bookseller friend, Karl Friedrich Frommann, who was well-acquainted with the academics and authorities in Jena. In his April 14 letter to Frommann, he wondered whether anyone has thought about him after Schelling declined the call, suggesting himself for the

---

[24] *Berichten*, #169.
[25] Richard Crouter, "Hegel and Schleiermacher at Berlin: A Many-Sided Debate," *Journal of the American Academy of Religion* 48, no. 1 (1980): 19- 43, 28-29.
[26] Thomas Albert Howard, *Religion and the Rise of Historicism: W. M. L. de Wette, Jacob Burckhardt, and the Theological Origins of Nineteenth-Century Historical Consciousness* (Cambridge: Cambridge University Press, 2000), 59.
[27] *Berichten*, # 175.
[28] *Briefe II*, Hoffmeister's note to #278, (page) 402.

VI. Hegel's Restoration, 1815-1818

position. He then reasoned that his reputation at Jena as a poor lecturer might have worked against him. However, he assured Frommann, his lecturing skills have improved significantly after many years of practice at the gymnasium.[29] Thus, Hegel was considering his options elsewhere while Schuckmann was dragging his feet. Alas, Fries, not Hegel, was called to Jena instead. Fries' departure from Heidelberg and the invitation he received from Jena were both politically motivated, as we establish in due course.

On May 2, 1816, Hegel requested Paulus' "assistance and advocacy" to fill Fries' now-vacant post at Heidelberg since, as he recently heard, "*Fries has been hired by Jena.*" But two longstanding obstacles—his well-known incoherence and enmity with Fries—might work against his candidacy, Hegel thought. Of the former obstacle, he falsely reassured his "dear friend," Paulus, as he did Frommann earlier, that "eight years practice in gymnasium instruction" has "helped" him become a better lecturer. In response to the latter problem, Hegel insincerely sent "to Professor *Fries* ... [his] compliments in reply to those sent to" him by Fries through Seebeck. "May he accept them just as warmly as I have accepted his," he hoped.[30]

As Hegel already knew, or would soon find out, Fries was now without influence at Heidelberg for political reasons. In fact, Paulus himself was also in a similar situation. "From what I hear," Hegel wrote to Niethammer on June 8, "Paulus has compromised himself, along with [Christoph Reinhard Dietrich] Martin and Fries, in the cause of freedom, and thus would only be allowed to tread softly" at Heidelberg.[31] With Paulus' situation in mind, Hegel realized that he had to also reach out to other influential faculty, such as Anton Friedrich Justus Thibaut and Karl Daub. Thus, a few days later, he visited his friend Sulpitz Boisserée, the wealthy and influential art-collector, and asked him to pull some strings on his behalf. The latter contacted his brother, Melchior, to see what could be done for Hegel in this regard. Based on the information he received from Hegel, Sulpitz informed Melchior that, because of his incoherent lectures, "Thibaut is said not to have spoken well of [Hegel] in Jena" while they were both teaching there. However, and this should be reported to Thibaut, Hegel has now abandoned these bad habits and that positive things are being said about his teaching skills in Nuremberg.[32]

It is interesting that, until 1816, the academic prospects of one of the most famous German philosophers of all times mainly depended on whether he could speak clearly or not. Equally interesting is the fact that no one,

---

[29] *Briefe II*, #262.
[30] *Letters*, 331 (*Briefe II*, #263).
[31] Ibid., 323, (#266).
[32] *Berichten*, #177.

VI. Hegel's Restoration, 1815-1818

including Hegel himself, had mentioned his published works as evidence of his qualifications.

In the meanwhile, the politics of the Restoration were affecting the careers of the pro-Napoleon officials negatively. "Niethammer was now encountering formidable obstacles ... in the Bavarian capital and was beginning to feel the displeasure of the King" and other officials.[33] In this context, on June 16, Niethammer informed Hegel that his educational reform efforts were now being undermined by the forces of "Reaction."[34] In his July 5 reply, Hegel maintained that the "Reaction" (Restoration) in Germany is the *apparently* irrational means by which the world spirit actualizes itself.

> I adhere to the view that the world spirit has given the age marching orders. These orders are being obeyed. The world spirit, this essential [power], proceeds irresistibly like a closely drawn armored phalanx advancing with imperceptible movement ... through thick and thin. Innumerable light troops flank it on all sides, throwing themselves into the balance for or against its progress, though most of them are entirely ignorant of what is at stake and merely take head blows as from an invisible hand. Yet no lingering lies or make-believe strokes in the air ... can achieve anything against it.[35]

Thus, all that has happened and was now happening could be understood as the work of the secretive and omnipotent rational Providence. Besides, he further reasoned, "all the fuss and paltry paper successes of human ants, fleas, and bugs," that is, "this most fearsome Reaction against Bonaparte," has not "changed so much, whether for good or evil." But the most telling aspect of Hegel's interpretation of the events was his conclusion: "If need be, what we can do, in light of this provident design, is to help these poor vermin [of the Reaction] along to their destiny."[36] However, Hegel likely suspected that Niethammer might not appreciate his metaphysical hocus-pocus. A week later, on July 12, he mailed another letter to assure him that he, Hegel, was on his side. At the same time, as if Niethammer did not have enough to worry about, Hegel asked: "have you heard nothing at all about my prospects at the University of Erlangen?"[37]

Hegel was thus simultaneously and rigorously running *at least* three campaigns (Berlin, Heidelberg, and Erlangen) to secure a post for himself.

---

[33] Horst Althaus, *Hegel: An Intellectual Biography*, trans. Michael Tarsh (Cambridge, UK: Polity Press, 2000), 124.
[34] *Briefe II*, #270.
[35] *Letters*, 324-25 (*Briefe II*, #271).
[36] Ibid.
[37] Ibid., 326-27 (#272).

VI. Hegel's Restoration, 1815-1818

Despite his attempt to appease Niethammer, he had by now firmly linked his own prospects to the "marching orders" of the world spirit. In other words, and stated more mundanely, Hegel knew that his career prospects, and those of others, were now in the hands of the forces of "Reaction."

Lo and behold, the news Hegel had been waiting for during the past sixteen years finally arrived from Heidelberg! Hegel's candidacy had initially faced some opposition from certain members of the faculty on the expected ground that he was incoherent. Daub, now the vice-rector at the university, argued against these charges, claiming, without any tangible evidence, that Hegel had become a competent lecturer at the gymnasium. Surely, he had received this misinformation from Hegel, via Paulus and Boisserée. Remarkably, although Daub claimed to admire Hegel's works in 1805,[38] it is evident that, up until 1816, he had understood very little of it. In fact, he would take Hegel's writings seriously only in 1817. By his own admission, it would take him three more years to fully appreciate them.[39] (Many Hegelians have since doubted whether Daub had ever truly understood Hegel.) There is no evidence to suggest that Thibaut had any interest in Hegel's works. At any rate, Daub formally offered the post to Hegel in a letter postmarked July 30, 1816.[40]

In the meanwhile, sometime in July 1816, and before Daub's letter reached Hegel, Friedrich von Raumer, a history professor at Berlin, was commissioned by the Prussian authorities to conduct surveys in Italy. On his way there, he stopped in Nuremberg and met with Hegel, likely at Schuckmann's urging. As Hegel's August 2 letter to Raumer indicates, Raumer asked Hegel to write a report on what we today call his "teaching philosophy." His letter contains this report.[41] Having done his own investigation, Raumer reported his generally positive impression of Hegel to Schuckmann on August 10. However, and ironically, the conclusion he drew on Hegel's incoherence was itself ambivalent. If one uses the "false sense" of what counts as an effective lecturing style, he wrote, then Hegel certainly is not a good lecturer. But he could not determine whether he was a good lecturer in the "true sense." This, he said, "ultimately depends on the contents of his philosophy" and the "curriculum" he might use to teach it, but the report Hegel provided contains insufficient information in this regard.[42]

---

[38] *Briefe I*, #58.
[39] *Briefe III*, #372.
[40] *Briefe II*, 277.
[41] *Letters*, 338 (*Briefe II*, #278).
[42] *Berichten*, #179. Upon reading Hegel's newly-published *Encyclopedia of Philosophical Sciences* (1817), Raumer bitterly complained to the same Solger in 1818 about the unclarity of Hegel's (and of other recent philosophers) language and thinking. *Berichten*, #269.

VI. Hegel's Restoration, 1815-1818

Several days after sending his report to Raumer, Hegel met with another Berlin professor in Nuremberg, namely, Niebuhr,[43] who is regarded as one of the first modern historians.[44] He was also well-known for his anti-revolutionary stance.[45] From his August 4 letters to Nicolovious and others, we learn that Niebuhr personally liked Hegel.[46] (I suspect that they also agreed on the merits of the Restoration politics.) It is likely that Schuckmann received Niebuhr's recommendation from Nicolovious. As we will see shortly, Niebuhr's report was instrumental in convincing Schuckmann to take Hegel's candidacy more seriously than he had done thus far. Hegel himself saw his meeting with Niebuhr as a clear sign that receiving an offer from Berlin was very likely.[47] However, Raumer's report only contributed to the minister's concerns about Hegel's incoherence, which he would reveal directly to Hegel himself soon.

Hegel met with Niebuhr after he received the offer from Heidelberg. In his August 6 reply to Daub, and perhaps encouraged by his prospects at Berlin, he requested a higher salary and additional perks than what he was initially offered:

> To the honorable inquiry as to whether I would be inclined to accept the position of titular Professor of Philosophy in Heidelberg with a salary of 1,300 florins and the indicated compensation in kind, I hasten to reply that my present salary consists of 1,560 florins. Yet, out of love for academic studies, I am inclined to accept the call at the indicated salary. But since I occupy an official residence here, which according to the local low rental rates is to be valued at 150 florins, I hope the advantage of the [free] lodging ... [provided to] the departing Privy Councilor Fries might likewise be granted to me.[48]

On August 8, Hegel informed Paulus of his negotiating tactics with Daub. His letter reveals that, like Daub, Thibaut also favored Hegel's appointment.[49] This information is also revealed in Hegel's letter to Boisserée, also sent on August 8, which concludes with the following line:

---

[43] *Briefe II*, #282.
[44] For useful discussion, see Peter Hanns Reill, "Barthold Georg Niebuhr and the Enlightenment Tradition," *German Studies Review* 3, no. 1 (1980): 9-26.
[45] Barthold G. Niebuhr, *Preussens Recht wider den Sächsischen Hof* (Berlin: Realschulbuchhandlung, 1814). For an informative biography, see Susanna Winkworth (ed.), *The Life and Letters of Barthold George Niebuhr* (London: Chapman and Hall, 1852).
[46] *Berichten*, #178, #180.
[47] *Briefe II*, #283.
[48] *Letters*, 342 (*Briefe II*, #279).
[49] *Briefe II*, #281.

VI. Hegel's Restoration, 1815-1818

"Please transmit my most cordial regards to Creuzer and Thibaut and assure them how much I will treasure their kind sentiments."[50]

Despite telling Boisserée and Paulus that he prefers Heidelberg, Hegel was still hoping to receive an offer from Berlin, which he clearly preferred over Heidelberg. This is indicated in his August 11 letter to Niethammer: "the [Berlin] post ... might perhaps even be the more excellent one— which it would be foolish to place behind Heidelberg." He was encouraged by his meeting with Niebuhr, he also noted. However, since he was hoping to receive an offer from Erlangen also, he instructed Niethammer "not to report anything of this to [the authorities in] Munich right away," and to "say in Berlin," where Niethammer would soon go on official business, "that there are designs upon ... [him] in Heidelberg."[51] In short, while negotiating the terms of his employment at Heidelberg, Hegel was still trying to get the best deal he could, Berlin being his top preference.

By now, Niethammer had received Hegel's previous letters also, including the one sent on June 16, in which he gave a vague metaphysical endorsement to the "vermin." In his August 21 reply, Niethammer took a swipe at Hegel's indifference to whether one's actions are good or bad in themselves, and then disparaged his desertion to the side of the "Reaction." "I cannot be indifferent to losing those with whom I had hoped to work in concert," he said. As disappointed as he was with Hegel's behavior, the good-natured Niethammer added that, when he goes to Berlin, he will act in accordance with Hegel's wishes, referring to the latter's instruction to him to inform the Prussians that Heidelberg is trying very hard to recruit him.[52] In fact, he informed Hegel on September 13 that, "in accordance" with his instructions, he had talked to some people in Berlin. However, Schuckmann did not make himself available, even though he had tried "diligently" to talk to him on Hegel's behalf.[53] Niethammer sent this letter to Hegel without knowing that the matter at hand had already been settled about three weeks earlier.

On August 13, a month prior to Niethammer's now-defunct report from Berlin, and two days after he informed him of his preference for Berlin, Hegel received another letter from Daub. The latter informed him of Heidelberg's willingness to pay him 1,500 florins per annum, that is, 200 florins more than the initial offer. However, his request for free lodging, which was previously granted to Fries, was not approved.[54] A week later, Hegel replied that the "reservations" he previously had about the initial

---

[50] *Letters*, 345 (*Briefe II*, #282).
[51] Ibid., 345-6 (#283).
[52] *Briefe II*, #288.
[53] Ibid., #301.
[54] Ibid., #285.

VI. Hegel's Restoration, 1815-1818

offer were now "entirely removed."[55] However, the increase of 200 florins, some of which was to be received in kind, did not bring his total annual salary to the level Hegel was hoping to receive. In fact, it was slightly less than his current salary at the gymnasium. Apparently, Hegel was not in as high demand at Heidelberg as he thought he was or wished to be.

On August 24, Hegel received a letter from Schuckmann, who claimed that he heard of his interest in the Berlin post from Niebuhr. Rather than directly calling him to Berlin, as it is often mistakenly supposed, Schuckmann asked Hegel to provide a self-evaluation of his problematic teaching skills and unimpressive academic accomplishments since his Jena days, explaining that this serious concern needs to be addressed before he could offer the position to Hegel. Briefly put, the minister wanted Hegel to convince him that he possesses the necessary "skill to teach" philosophy in a "lively" and "insightful" manner.[56] This request, so it seems, convinced Hegel that his prospects at Berlin stood on rather shaky grounds, forcing him to abandon his Berlin campaign immediately—at least for now. Besides, he must have reasoned that it would be unwise to keep Daub waiting after having accepted his offer.

The same day, with the official offer from Heidelberg at hand, Hegel sent a letter to the Interior Ministry of Bavaria to formally request his release from his duties at the gymnasium.[57] The next day, on August 25, he expressed his gratitude for the quick approval of his appointment by Duke Karl Ludwig Friedrich of Baden in another letter to Daub. (We will see shortly that the duke had recently cracked down on some of the radical professors at the university.) Perhaps fearing that his flirtation with Berlin, if heard, might complicate things at Heidelberg, Hegel revealed the Prussian minister's inquiry to Daub, but misleadingly presented it as if the minister left it entirely up to him, "as an honest man," to decide the issue of his Berlin appointment. "But, my main reply [to Schuckmann] will be that I already regard myself committed to Heidelberg," wrote Hegel.[58]

But this was not the end of the matter. On September 5, almost two weeks after he requested to be released from his gymnasium duties by the Bavarian authorities, the Nuremberg Royal Commissioner sent Hegel a letter, asking him whether he would prefer an appointment as professor of *philology* at Erlangen, rather than his release.[59] On September 7, Hegel replied with an unnecessarily elaborate and somewhat confusing

---

[55] Ibid., #286.
[56] Ibid., #284.
[57] Ibid., #290.
[58] *Letters*, 351 (*Briefe II*, #291).
[59] *Briefe II*, #295

VI. Hegel's Restoration, 1815-1818

explanation of why he preferred his release.[60] Hegel's reply urges the view that he had been negotiating with the Restoration authorities at the office of Nuremberg Royal Commissioner for a post at Erlangen. Indeed, as we know from his August 11 letter to Niethammer, he was expecting an offer from Erlangen. Moreover, he met with Johann Kracker, the Royal Bavarian Commissioner in Nuremberg, a year earlier in Munich, and thought the latter was "well disposed toward" him.[61] It is very likely that Hegel had kept in touch with Kracker and "others" since then. Differently put, the Erlangen appointment was undertaken by the bureaucratic elements of the Bavarian government, and with the king's authorization.[62] Evidently, the faculty senate was not consulted; it was simply ordered "to execute this royal command," as the senate itself informed Hegel with obvious resentment.[63] With this royal order, the Restoration authorities were able to quickly accomplish what Niethammer had failed to do for over a decade. More generally, it was now clear to all that academic careers were to be ultimately decided by government officials throughout Germany.

Moreover, without waiting for Hegel's reply, or perhaps thinking that he had already given his word, his appointment to Erlangen was announced in the official newspaper on September 4. Hegel saw the announcement three days later. On September 8, concerned that the announcement might cause some confusion and dismay at Heidelberg, he sent another letter to Daub. Interestingly, Hegel claimed that his "word of honor, which has already led ... [him] to decline an appointment to Berlin, simply obliged ... [him] to renew ... [his] petition for most gracious release."[64] This letter finally settled the complicated issue of Hegel's employment.

To recapitulate, 1816 represented a breakthrough in Hegel's career. The same person who had not been taken seriously for sixteen, if not twenty-eight, years was now in high demand. Indeed, the sudden interest in Hegel itself sufficed to significantly boost his reputation as a philosopher, proving that one's status often shapes how one is evaluated. While it is difficult to identify a single reason for his sudden triumph, it is safe to credit his inexhaustible lobbying efforts in making it possible. However, the sudden appeal for Hegel also had, directly and indirectly, much to do with the recent political changes in Germany. Somehow, if not his political sympathies, his well-known philosophical opposition to Fries, a known radical, had increased his appeal in Berlin. As we have seen, similar political considerations must have been at work with respect to the Erlangen post.

---

[60] Ibid., #297.
[61] Ibid., #252.
[62] Ibid., #299.
[63] Ibid., #302.
[64] *Letters*, 354-55 (*Briefe II*, #298).

VI. Hegel's Restoration, 1815-1818

As we are about to see, the Restoration politics provided the general context in which Heidelberg, with the duke's approval, hired Hegel.

Chapter Seven

VII. APOLOGIST-CAREERIST PROFESSOR OF HEIDELBERG

1. Restoration Politics and Academics in Baden

As we have seen, Hegel was hired to replace Fries, who followed Martin to Jena. They were both welcomed by the liberal-minded duke of Saxe-Weimar-Eisenach. Grand Duke Karl August was also one of the first to implement what was arguably the most liberal constitutions in Germany at the time on May 5, 1816. This move did not sit well with the rulers of Prussia and Austria. Consequently, he "quickly became a target of the reactionary [Holy] overseers during the years 1816–20, but [also] attained something of the status of a model for liberal and nationalist thinkers of the period."[1]

Martin and Fries left Heidelberg for the same political reasons that they chose Jena. About a year earlier, on January 12, 1815, the grand duke of Baden, Karl Ludwig Friedrich, repeated his promise to grant a *landständische* constitution. For various reasons, the duke dragged his feet. Much like the other Restoration rulers, he was concerned that a representative constitution would deprive him of the ability to rule his subjects in the way he saw fit. This postponement led to a growing impatience with the duke, shared by various key sectors of the Badenese society.

But the nobility and the "bourgeoisie" (very broadly conceived) had different sorts of constitutions in mind. The former demanded its old rights and privileges. Hailing mostly from the major municipalities, such as Heidelberg, the latter pushed for a liberal constitution and popular representation. Consequently, petitions were sent to the duke, urging him to fulfill his promise. The duke and his supporters, on the other hand, wanted a legislative scheme, based on the monarchical principle, in which he would have the upper hand. Moreover, following the sentiment generally shared by the Holy rulers, the duke thought that the petitions

---

[1] Thomas P. Saine, "The World Goethe Lived In: Germany and Europe, 1750–1830," in *The Cambridge Companion to Goethe*, ed. Leslie Sharpe, 6-22 (Cambridge: Cambridge University Press, 2002), 21.

VII. Apologist-Careerist Professor of Heidelberg

threatened his authority, urging him to act against the petitioners and to further justify delaying the promulgation of the constitution.[2]

Upon the request of the like-minded citizens of Heidelberg, Martin, a prominent professor of law at the university, had drafted and circulated the liberal petition. The Badenese police raided his home at night and ceased his papers.[3] "Deeply offended" by the actions the government had taken against him, Martin "requested his dismissal, which was granted to him by the government in January 1816 ...; he went to Jena."[4] His petition was signed by many members of the Heidelberg faculty, including Paulus and Fries. Fries, having vigorously defended Martin, found himself in a similar situation and followed him to Jena several months later. At the same time, Thibaut, Martin's and Fries' opponent, led the opposition to the petition at the university.[5] Martin and Fries now gone, Thibaut became "the undisputed head of the faculty until his death in 1840." In the words of Fries, "'since the fall of Napoleon,'" Thibaut had been possessed by "'all sorts of political phantoms,'" and constantly lived in "'the fear of revolution.'"[6]

It is obvious that neither Thibaut nor the duke had any inclination to hire another Martin or Fries to replace them. At a minimum, this means that they did not think Hegel was politically allied with the likes of these liberal activists. It does not necessarily mean, however, that they hired him to act as an apologist for the Badenese regime. It probably sufficed to know that he was Fries' philosophical archenemy and a friend of the influential brothers Boisserée.

Be that as it may, what matters more for out purposes is that Hegel was fully aware of the regime's actions against the trouble makers even before he came to Heidelberg. To step back several months, on December 12, 1815, Caroline Paulus informed him of the following news from Heidelberg:

> Our local Badenese [citizens] have likewise stretched their powerless hands out toward the provincial diets, pushing audacity to the point

---

[2] For a useful general discussion, see Markus J. Prutsch, *Making Sense of Constitutional Monarchism in Post-Napoleonic France and Germany* (Basingstoke, UK: Palgrave, 2013), 93 ff.

[3] For a more detailed discussion, see Robert Goldschmit, *Geschichte der Badischen Verfassungsurkunde: 1818-1918* (Karlsruhe i.B.: Braun, 1918), 12 ff.

[4] Peter Classen and Eike Wolgast, *Kleine Geschichte der Universität Heidelberg* (Berlin: Springer, 1983), 38.

[5] Ernst Ludwig Theodor Henke, *Jakob Friedrich Fries: Aus Seinem Handschriftlichen Nachlasse dargestellt* (Leipzig: Brockhaus, 1867), 152 ff; Karl Bartsch, *Ruperto-Carola: Illustrierte Fest-Chronik der V. Säcularfeier der Universität Heidelberg* (Heidelberg: O. Petters, 1886), 179 ff.

[6] Classen and Wolgast, *Kleine Geschichte der Universität Heidelberg*, 83.

VII. Apologist-Careerist Professor of Heidelberg

of presenting a humble petition on the subject, composed by Judicial Councilor Martin, to the Grand Duke. But the cause was nipped in the bud. The government sealed Martin's papers at 11:00 p.m. and sent a commission of inquiry from Karlsruhe [the capital]. Martin, offended by such a procedure, asked to be relieved of his functions ... Such are the fruits of this legendary German liberty conquered by arms ..., to which its champions have rightly assigned a [Iron] Cross as its symbol. The Crucifix will follow.[7]

With this context in mind, Hegel arrived in Heidelberg on October 19, 1816. His aim from the outset was to use his career at Heidelberg as a steppingstone to obtain higher posts and income. In fact, we know that he would start renegotiating with the Prussian authorities for the Berlin post just months after his arrival in Heidelberg.[8] Moreover, he understood well that his still-unsatisfied career ambitions were intimately linked to the political expectations of the rulers. Thus, on October 28, Hegel started his teaching career at Heidelberg with a politically-charged inaugural address, which was essentially an apology for the Restoration—plus some hyperbola and slander against the "false" philosophers.

Hegel began his address by lamenting how philosophy has been ignored, due to the turbulent recent history. More pretentiously put, "because the spirit of the world was thus occupied, it could not look within and withdraw into itself." But all this is about to change, Hegel heralded, "since the German ... nationality, the basis of all higher life, has been saved [during the war of liberation]," along with the new "German state," "which has swallowed up all other interests in its own." So, it is to be expected and hoped that "the Kingdom of God" (religion) and philosophy would now also receive their due. It turns out, "it is [only] in the German nation that [philosophy] has been retained as a peculiar possession."[9]

A strange remark appeared at this point in his address (as if Hegel had prepared his address for the Berlin post, forgetting that he was hired by Baden): "the Prussian State is a State constituted on principles of intelligence." He then repeated the same claim that the practical needs, stemming from the recent turbulent times, have undermined philosophical

---

[7] Clark Butler and Christiane Seiler (trans.), *Hegel: The Letters* (Bloomington: Indiana University Press, 1984), 324. Henceforth cited as *Letters*. Also see Johannes Hoffmeister (ed.), *Briefe von und an Hegel*, 4 volumes (Hamburg: Felix Meiner, 1952-1960), #256. Henceforth cited as *Briefe*, followed by the Latin numerical to indicate the volume number, in this case, *II*.

[8] *Briefe II*, #326. We will discuss this issue in some detail in due course.

[9] G. W. F Hegel, "Inaugural Address: Delivered at Heidelberg on the 28th October 1816," in *Lectures on the History of Philosophy*, vol. 1, trans. E. S. Haldane, xli-xliii (Lincoln: University of Nebraska Press, 1995).

thinking. After making this point, Hegel resorted to his old habit of slandering other philosophers:

> It has thus happened that, because vigorous natures [the ruling elite] turned to the practical [problems], insipidity and dullness [i.e., the false philosophers] appropriated to themselves the pre-eminence in Philosophy and flourished there. It may indeed be said that since Philosophy began to take a place in Germany, it has never looked so badly as at the present time—never have emptiness and shallowness overlaid it so completely, and never have they spoken and acted with such arrogance, as though all power were in their hands! To combat the shallowness, to strive with German earnestness and honesty, to draw Philosophy out of the solitude into which it has wandered—to do such work as this we may hope that we are called by the higher spirit of our time.[10]

It is rather obvious that Hegel's slander, supported by his "German earnestness and honesty," and urged by the call he has received from "the higher spirit," was directed against Martin and Fries, who had already "spoken and acted with such arrogance." They were to be held responsible for misleading the youth with their false philosophy.[11] Hegel was determined to fix all that.

In short, Hegel was no longer content with simply accusing his philosophical opponents with the usual charges of formalism or stupidity. They were now brought into the political context and declared to be the enemies of the German nation and state(s). Henceforth, Hegel would repeatedly declare his philosophical opponents the opponents of the state. Even if he was not hired to act as an apologist for the Restoration regimes, he took himself to be one as soon as he arrived in Heidelberg.

2. Making New Friends and Enemies

Hegel's Heidelberg inaugural address preceded his first lecture at the university, which was in his history of philosophy course. The next day, he wrote a letter to his wife, who was still in Nuremberg, to describe his initial teaching experience. "The number of students [who attended his lectures] certainly does not look as promising as I had been told and fooled into believing," lamented Hegel, adding that one of his "lecture courses ... had

---

[10] Ibid.
[11] As Hegel would recall several years later, "the greater number" of the students arrested after 1819 for "demagogic" activities "were in Heidelberg ... when Martin and Fries were there." *Letters*, 450 (*Briefe III*, #359).

VII. Apologist-Careerist Professor of Heidelberg

only four students." In other words, he was "fooled into believing" by Daub that his salary would be enhanced by high enrollment in his classes, as this would allow Hegel to collect additional fees from student exams, etc. However, reasoned Hegel, given time, his classes would attract more students,[12] which would turn out to be the case.

The initial low enrollment in Hegel's courses was likely, at least in part, related to the formidable opposition to his presence at Heidelberg from Martin's and, especially, Fries' supporters. As one of Fries' remaining faculty friends informed him from Heidelberg, Hegel was allied closely with Thibaut, Daub, and Creuzer, and appeared to be "too noble" to associate with "the younger professors,"[13] who tended to be Fries' allies. Relatedly, shortly after Hegel's arrival, Fries received another letter from H. Willy, his former student, who interpreted Hegel's presence at the university as an additional betrayal of Fries, a sentiment, he reasoned, Fries must have "heard from others already." Hegel, on the other hand, was expected to "please" Fries' opponents.[14] However, apart from his inaugural address, Hegel had not yet publicly demonstrated his political colors. This would happen in short order.

In 1813, the king of Württemberg, Friedrich I, ended his alliance with Napoleon and joined the Allies during "the war of liberation." As noted already, after defeating Napoleon, the thirty-nine German members (including Austria) of the alliance formed the German Confederation at the Vienna Congress (1814-1815). The Articles of the Confederation (1815) recognized each member as a "sovereign state," though it also stipulated their commitment to unity and common defense. In accordance with Article 13, each member of the confederation was expected to implement a "*landständische Verfassung.*" One of the first to implement Article 13 was King Friedrich I. On March 15, 1815, nine years after he suspended the old constitution and the Estates (assembly), he proposed a new constitution to his subjects.

The newly elected assembly at once attended the task of considering the king's constitution. As was the case in Baden, the delegates representing the old imperial nobility demanded the restoration of their traditional rights; the lawyer-delegates, who represented the "disenfranchised magistrates," called for greater representation for their towns; the more "radical" elements vehemently opposed the negligible powers the king's constitution granted to the unicameral assembly. A few delegates sided with the king. Certainly, the king's opponents were not all reactionaries, made of the same

---

[12] Ibid., 358 (*Briefe II*, #312).
[13] Günther Nicolin (ed.), *Hegel in Berichten seiner Zeitgenossen* (Hamburg: Felix Meiner, 1970), #196. Henceforth cited simply as Berichten.
[14] *Berichten*, #195.

VII. Apologist-Careerist Professor of Heidelberg

cloth. What united these politically diverse factions was their opposition to the king's proposed constitution, which they quickly rejected.[15] "In short, the estates believed that Friedrich's fundamental law signified a further dilution of their legislative powers, rather than a reestablishment of them. The subsequent negotiations ended when, on October 30, 1816, Friedrich I died."[16] In fact, anyone who consults the king's constitution would agree that it entailed a serious limitation of the legislative powers of the assembly.[17]

The king's successor-son, Wilhelm I, introduced his own constitution in March 1817, which is often regarded as "more liberal" than his father's. This constitution, which was also rejected, was conceived with the advice of his learned minister, Karl August von Wangenheim, who was previously the Chancellor of Tübingen University.[18] Before serving Wilhelm, Wangenheim had worked for Friedrich's government in various capacities. He was also appointed by him to a commission responsible for settling the differences between himself and the Estates. This move was chiefly occasioned by the publication of Wangenheim's *The Idea of a State Constitution* in 1815,[19] which was written with the aim of obtaining a "higher office."[20] Thus, it was naturally read by many as a king-friendly tract. His subsequent fourteen proposals to reconcile the differences between the king and the Estates also received negligible support from the latter. Indeed, regardless of what one thought about his politics, Wangenheim had quickly managed to earn the mistrust of many members of the Estates by revealing himself to be a devious lackey of the king, not the objective mediator he pretended to be. The articles he had anonymously (everyone knew he was the author) published in the Stuttgart *Allgemeine Zeitung* in late 1815 had helped crystallize this image of him.[21]

In short order, Paulus' criticism of Wangenheim would become a source of conflict between him and Hegel, two natives of Württemberg, now living and working in Baden. In a nutshell, Paulus submitted an essay to the *Heidelberg Yearbooks*, which disparaged Wangenheim for defending

---

[15] Eric Dorn Brose, *German History 1789–1871: From the Holy Roman Empire to the Bismarckian Reich* (Providence: Berghahn, 1997), 85.
[16] Bodie Ashton, *The Kingdom of Württemberg and the Making of Germany, 1815–1871* (London: Bloomsbury, 2017), 37.
[17] *Landständische Verfassung des Königreichs Württemberg vom 15. März 1815.* http://www.verfassungen.de/de/bw/wuerttemberg/verfassung1815-i.htm.
[18] For a useful discussion of Wangenheim's life and politics, see Heinrich von Treitschke, *Historische und Politische Aufsätze*, vol. 1 (Leipzig: S. Hirzel, 1903), 197-268.
[19] Karl August von Wangenheim, *Die Idee der Staatsverfassung in ihrer Anwendung auf Wirtembergs alte Landesverfassung und den Entwurf zu deren Erneuerung* (Frankfurt: Kröner, 1815).
[20] Daniel Moran, *Toward a Century of Words: Johann Cotta and the Politics of the Public Realm in Germany, 1795-1832* (Berkeley: University of California Press, 1990), 170.
[21] Ibid., 174-75.

VII. Apologist-Careerist Professor of Heidelberg

the despotic constitution of the king.[22] On April 19, 1817, Hegel informed Niethammer that, by this time, he had "taken over the editorship of several branches of the *Heidelberg Yearbooks*." In this capacity, "I have come to the point of written notification with Paulus," he said. This notification had to do with Hegel's rejection of Paulus' essay. It is important to note that what irked Hegel the most was Paulus' audacity to criticize the minister, Wangenheim, which Hegel called "disembowelment" of the latter. In other words, Paulus' essay treated Wangenheim "spitefully." Moreover, opined Hegel angrily, Paulus handled the whole thing "in a most philistine and crudely commonsensical manner—even though right on the title page ... [Paulus] calls himself ... a professor of philosophy." He even had the audacity "to send his product ... to the King [Wilhelm] and Queen of Württemberg." Paulus "thinks he is the God of our Provincial Diets."[23]

Why was Hegel so angry?

It is quite probable that, sometime during this period, Hegel was negotiating with Wangenheim, or people related to his office, about his appointment to Tübingen.[24] Even if this were not the case, Hegel was clearly trying to defend the minister (and the royal family) against criticism. This explains why he, as the editor of the *Yearbooks*, formally rejected Paulus' manuscript on the bogus ground that it was "too lengthy." Clearly, Hegel, the servile editor, could not have allowed the publication of a harsh critique of the minister in his journal, which would have likely also irked the Badenese authorities. In this endeavor, he was supported by Thibaut and (Friedrich) Wilken, the other two editors.[25] The most decisive issue in the present context is not what Hegel thought about the constitutional crisis in Württemberg. Rather, it is his willingness to silence Paulus, to ensure that the authorities were not criticized under his watch. With his "intrigue" against Paulus, who had helped him come to Heidelberg, Hegel thus revealed himself to be an apologist for the authorities.

In fact, he was now quite public about his royalism. According to Boisserée's diary entry of July 13, 1817, the Heidelberg faculty took a boat trip along the Neckar. During the trip, for some reason or another, Hegel

---

[22] Karl Alexander von Reichlin-Meldegg, *Heinrich Eberhard Gottlob Paulus und seine Zeit*, vol. 2 (Stuttgart: Magazin, 1853), 133 ff.
[23] *Letters*, 358-60 (*Briefe II*, #316).
[24] Hegel's negotiation with Wangenheim is reported by Haym. "For this information," he says, "I am relying on the verbal communication of a survivor involved in this matter." Rudolf Haym, *Hegel und seine Zeit: Vorlesungen über Entstehung und Entwicklung, Wesen und Wert der Hegelschen Philosophie* (Berlin: R. Gaertner, 1857), 350, 507 n. 13. Hegel's supporters vehemently deny the validity of this report. Given Hegel's past, as well as the fact that he would negotiate with the Württemberg authorities in early 1818, I find nothing shocking about it.
[25] *Briefe II*, #314.

VII. Apologist-Careerist Professor of Heidelberg

proposed a toast to the health of the Crown Prince Gustav of Sweden.[26] His proposal, which had political implications, angered Karl Welcker and several others, whom Boisserée disparagingly called a "disrespectful revolutionary pack." During the ensuing heated debate, which included Daub on Hegel's side, Welcker reportedly exclaimed: "German freedom— the Estates must live!"[27]

This boat incident was obviously informed by the contemporary political events and sentiments in Baden and elsewhere. After all, Welcker himself was a nationalist liberal,[28] who apparently decided to have nothing of Hegel's royalist toast. It is also likely that Hegel's intrigue against Paulus provided some pretext for the impatience of the "disrespectful revolutionary pack."

In the meanwhile, Hegel befriended Victor Cousin, the eclectic French philosopher. According to the latter's own testimony, he was in Germany to familiarize himself with the recent German philosophy. The specific philosopher he had in mind, as he would recall many years later, was Schelling. "The great name of Schelling" was talked about everywhere, "here celebrated, there almost cursed, everywhere exciting passionate interest." While in Heidelberg, he came across Hegel by pure "chance." Hegel, recalled Cousin, was at the time mainly known as a "disciple of Schelling," and his works were "little read." Cousin met Hegel soon after the latter's *Encyclopedia of Philosophical Sciences* was published in 1817. According to his own testimony, he found Hegel's book very obscure, and Hegel himself lacking in confidence, asocial, and not entirely lucid. The linguistic barriers between them also made their communication difficult. Yet, in a miraculous way, Cousin understood at the time that Hegel was his intellectual "superior" and his philosophy very profound.[29]

The young and curious Cousin was not in Heidelberg to find Schelling, however. Rather, as he himself would report in another memoir, he had spent some time with Fries before he met Hegel by chance. On October 15, Fries allegedly told Cousin in Jena that he was going to a political festival, adding that, there, he and others were to speak "against" the "petit" princes of Germany. "'The French Revolution had cut down some of them. I hope that the future will deliver us from the others,'" he told Cousin. Moreover,

---

[26] It is said that Hegel had given private lectures to the prince in Heidelberg. See Walter Jaeschke, *Hegel-Handbuch: Leben, Werk, Schule* (Stuttgart: J. B. Metzler, 2010), 38. Regretfully, I have neglected to further investigate this interesting detail.
[27] *Berichten*, #214.
[28] Welcker would later become a prominent liberal politician after his election to the Badanese diet in 1831. Friedrich von Weech, "Welcker, Karl Theodor," in *Allgemeine Deutsche Biographie*, vol. 41, 660–65 (Leipzig: Duncker & Humblot, 1896).
[29] Victor Cousin, *Oeuvres de Victor Cousin: Cours d'histoire de la philosophie morale. Fragments philosophiques*, vol. 2 (Bruxelles: Société Belge de Librairie, 1840), 20 ff.

VII. Apologist-Careerist Professor of Heidelberg

the rulers in Prussia and Austria would be reminded at the festival that "'it was the German people who ... saved them [from Napoleon], and that it is high time to give them the institutions promised to them.'"[30] We will have more to say on this impending festival, known as the Wartburg Festival, shortly.

Although he was invited to attend the festival On October 18, Cousin decided to move on. With pleasant thoughts in his heart toward Fries (Cousin must have been the only person who liked Fries, Schelling, and Hegel at the same time), he found his way to Heidelberg, where he met Hegel in late October. Likely, Cousin informed Hegel of his meeting with Fries, which would explain why the latter initially gave him a cold shoulder. We know that Hegel despised Fries and that he did not at all approve of the Wartburg Festival and the goals of its attendees.[31]

At any rate, one of Fries' friends reported to him from Heidelberg that Cousin, whom Fries "invited to attend" the Wartburg Festival, was now spending much time with Hegel and valuing this above all else. The friend interpreted Cousin's behavior as another betrayal of Fries in Heidelberg. What is more, he reported, there was now a general campaign against Fries at Heidelberg; the students there were told that he was crazy and deplorable. After all, it was being said, the book-burning event at the festival was an act of "highest intolerance," which no "educated" person would commit.[32] (Note: the book-burning incident was basically a minor bonfire, unrelated to the main festivities, which was readily exaggerated to discredit the organizers and attendees of the festival and their aims.[33])

Evidently, Hegel was also doing all he could to discredit both Fries and his followers. He was also preparing his *Proceedings of the Estates Assembly of the Kingdom of Württemberg, 1815–1816* for publication in the

---

[30] Victor Cousin, "Souvenirs D'Allemagne," *Revue des Deux Mondes* (1866): 594-619, 605-06.

[31] Hegel's brother-in-law, Gottlieb, was also an enthusiastic supporter of the *Burschenschaften*. The available evidence shows that Hegel strongly disapproved of Gottlieb's enthusiasm and designs to attend the festival. See Sussane von Tucher's September 22, 1817, letter to her daughter, Marie Hegel. *Berichten*, #233; also see #238.

[32] Henke, *Jakob Friedrich Fries: Aus Seinem Handschriftlichen Nachlasse dargestellt*, 193.

[33] It has been maintained ever since the occurrence of the festival that the demonstrators burned the "books" of some "reactionary" authors, the Napoleonic Code, and some works that do not quite fit under the category of "reactionary." However, the book-burning incident was a nonevent. Basically, about six individuals burnt bundles of paper in front of a handful of curious spectators and claimed that they were the books of their enemies. The ritual was staged some miles away from the castle after much of the crowd had already dispersed. See Steven Michael Press, "False Fire: The Wartburg Book-Burning of 1817," in *Central European History* 42, no. 4 (2009): 621-46; Sir Adolphus William Ward, *Germany, 1815-1890*, vol. 1 (Cambridge: Cambridge University Press, 1916), 157.

VII. Apologist-Careerist Professor of Heidelberg

Heidelberg Yearbooks.³⁴ Apart from it being an apologia for the regime, which claim we will establish in the next section, it is reasonable to assume that the Wartburg Festival had also influenced Hegel's thoughts while he was preparing his essay for publication.

3. Political Works, 1817-1818

3.1 On Württemberg's Constitutional Crisis

3.1.1 Justifying the Restoration State

This section discusses certain crucial aspects of Hegel's *Proceedings of the Estates Assembly of the Kingdom of Württemberg, 1815–1816* (henceforth *Proceedings*).³⁵ Its main aim is to show how Hegel defended the Restoration states in general and the one in Württemberg in particular.

Hegel notes from the outset that the debates on Friedrich's constitution must be interpreted as a process in which "a German government and a German people" have "engaged in spiritual labor." Their thoughts are now "occupied with the rebirth of an actuality [i.e., a state]" in Germany. To be sure, this spiritual labor is embedded in the trials and tribulations of the world spirit, not the motives of individuals, which has presented Württemberg with "the task of building ... a state." Therefore, Friedrich's "representative constitution" of 1815 must be seen as a valiant attempt to bring "to completion a German monarchy," in accordance with the dictates of the spirit.³⁶

Hegel contrasts this task very favorably in relation to "the absurd institution known as the German Empire." He now likes the way the state is shaping up in Germany. He is also delighted that, at last, Württemberg "threw off its subjection" from the previous conditions and, "with the monarchical dignity of a prince, stepped forward to claim its sovereignty and the status of a state."³⁷ Here, Hegel carefully avoids mentioning an inconvenient fact: this "monarchical dignity" was originally bestowed upon Friedrich by Napoleon. Another potentially embarrassing fact is also kept a secret: until recently, Hegel himself had supported the subjection of Germany, including Württemberg, by Napoleon. Another distinction from

---

³⁴ The original title of this essay is *Beurteilung der in Druck erschienenen Verhandlungen in der Versammlung der Landstände des Königreichs Württemberg im Jahre 1815 u. 1816*.
³⁵ G. W. F. Hegel, *Proceedings of the Estates Assembly of the Kingdom of Württemberg, 1815–1816*, in *Heidelberg Writings: Journal Publications*, trans. Brady Bowman and Allen Speight, 32-136 (Cambridge, UK: Cambridge University Press, 2009).
³⁶ Hegel, *Proceedings*, 33.
³⁷ Ibid., 33-34.

138

VII. Apologist-Careerist Professor of Heidelberg

his previous political sympathies also emerges here: Hegel now supports the sovereignty of the various Germanic states, whereas he had previously defended their subordination to the centralized authority of a single *"roi"* as late as 1814. Some scholars have assumed wrongly that his defense of the sovereignty of Württemberg was inconsistent with the Restoration agenda. To the contrary, it was the official position, enshrined in the Articles of the Confederation.

Once more, and in accordance with his metaphysical theory, Hegel attributes the emergence of this German state and its constitution to the spiritual development (*Geistesbildung*) of "the age," which has finally "produced the idea of a state and its essential unity." In addition to the "humiliating" experience of the "absurd" German Empire, "twenty-five years of a mostly terrifying actuality," that is, the wars and the irrational experiments following the French Revolution, including the Napoleonic order throughout Germany, "have afforded the rich and valuable experience of the diverse [but until now failed] attempts at grasping that idea." Overall, and in accordance with the marching orders of the world spirit, the time is now ripe for the "German realms" to assert their "sovereignty," and adopt "free [monarchical] constitutions." With the promulgation of the king's constitution, both "the *power* of the state" and "its *will* could be brought to life" freely.[38] Expectedly, Hegel does not utter even a single word on the power or right of the people to give itself a constitution. He believes, and would continue to believe hereafter, that this right belongs solely to the monarchs of the realm. By "free constitutions," he primarily means the constitutions freely promulgated by the monarchs of sovereign states.

3.1.2 The Ungrateful Estates and Scribes

Alas, the "temptation" to follow the wrong path is still present in Germany, notes Hegel. More specifically, some Germans want "the earlier republican forms to persist." This comment undermines the often-repeated claim that Hegel merely opposes the reactionary forces favoring the "old" arrangements, the so-called "good old law," in the *Proceedings*. According to Hegel, such "republican" forms are contrary to "the institutions of a rational" state, which must be built on the "monarchical" principle. Fortunately, "King Friedrich rose above the temptation of this [republican] deception." On March 15, 1815, he declared before the estates assembly that he was "laying the keystone of the edifice of the state by giving the people a [rational, monarchical] constitution," and urged those present to "unite the nation with the head of state" (hence "the monarchial principle")

---

[38] Ibid., 35.

VII. Apologist-Careerist Professor of Heidelberg

by approving the constitution.[39] As we will see in the next subsection, Hegel will gingerly and politely criticize the king's constitution for being too democratic-republican and generous-liberal.

Throughout *Proceedings*, Hegel complains that the estates (the king's opponents, especially the professional "scribes") were too unreasonable and selfish to have rejected the king's very generous and reasonable constitution. This situation reminds him of the olden days, which he had described in some detail, and with great dismay, fifteen years earlier in *The German Constitution*. Thus, Hegel revisits the lamentable "special history" of Germany, for which he once again blames the selfish estates. The latter, he says, "would rather have endured disgrace than make any decision of their own or undertake any action for the sake of honor. This inclination to neglect honor and refrain from [common] action in external affairs is bound up with a tendency to direct activity against the government rather than against external enemies." (Once again, that he himself supported these "external" enemies until recently is not mentioned.) The estates have looked upon every important occasion "merely as an opportunity to embarrass the government, an opportunity to prescribe conditions and acquire advantages for themselves against the government and for the efforts which the government made for the honor and well-being of the government and the people." Consequently, they had often brought "misfortune and an affront to the land [i.e., Germany], and ... [weakened] the government's power in the long term, thereby paving the way for internal and external destruction." In short, the German estates have historically been acting out of "a spirit of all-consuming private interest and indifference or indeed hostility to the very thought of national honor."[40] What we observe here is the reemergence of the illiberal and nationalist Hegel, who associates national honor with the power and interest of the state, and dishonor with the egotism of the estates and individuals, which are basically defined as opposition to the authority of the monarchical state.

The upshot for Hegel in the recent political situation is that the Estates Assembly of Württemberg has shown no "gratitude to a prince [Friedrich I], who was the first (and up to now ... the only) prince who has given his country such an open and liberal constitution." What the estates want from the king instead is to "bring back the old one." This is where Hegel switches, for the time being, from disparaging the "republican" enemies of the state to castigating its traditionalist opponents, with an exaggerated and ill-informed attack on the "scribes." These opponents are to be blamed for blocking the way to further negotiations and progress, not the king. Hegel goes on to admire the "rational basis" of the king's constitution, especially

---

[39] Ibid., 35-37.
[40] Ibid., 51.

VII. Apologist-Careerist Professor of Heidelberg

those paragraphs which define the rights and duties of the king's subjects, repeating once again that "only contrarian perversity or stubbornness or whatever one wants to call it could cause such an assembly" to reject the king's constitution.[41]

After tediously enumerating additional similar grievances against the Estates and estates, Hegel reminds them that what they demand is dead and that "the dead cannot come to life again."[42] What, then, is alive and rational? The "recently completed ... sovereign states," that is, the post-Congress Restoration states, which have more "powerful ... authority" than ever before, repeats Hegel.[43] If the Estates are to "retain their earlier authority," reasons he, "the state would cease to be a state," as it "would be destroyed by the [struggles of] two sovereign powers," namely, the Estates and the monarchical government.[44] In short, Hegel does not simply object to the demands to bring back the old arrangements in his essay. He also defends the augmentation of the powers of the monarchical government.

3.1.3 Hegel's Praise for the King's Constitution

As Hegel correctly informs us, the king's 1815 constitution is divided into two main parts.[45] The first part "bears the title 'The Constitution of the Estates' and the second part ... the title 'General Provisions in Relation to the Constitution of the Kingdom and the Rights and Duties of His Majesty's Subjects'." The first part proposes a single-chamber assembly, which is to consist of both representatives appointed by the king and those elected by their constituencies. The latter portion of the representatives is to be elected by various estates. However, the "crown officials, junior officers and soldiers, clergy, doctors, and surgeons" are not eligible to become representatives (due to their "emergency" related functions). Moreover, all members must be at least thirty years old, and belong to one of the three main "Christian confessions." "The Estates assemble only at the summons of the king and at least once every three years ... In the years when the Estates Assembly is not summoned, a committee of twelve members chosen from the Assembly for three years meets to complete pressing business." However, the assembly does not have the power to decide the issue of "taxes" or change "the laws." In these matters, "the king retains the initiative," though "the consent of the Estates is necessary." "The Estates have a similar part in legislation; without their approval, no new

---

[41] Ibid., 52-54.
[42] Ibid., 57.
[43] Ibid., 59.
[44] Ibid., 63.
[45] *Landständische Verfassung des Königreichs Württemberg vom 15. März 1815.*

VII. Apologist-Careerist Professor of Heidelberg

general law concerning personal freedom, property, or the constitution can be promulgated." The Estates "can present suggestions for laws," but the king does not have to accept them, though he must justify his refusal.[46]

In a nutshell, the king's constitution inverted the parliamentary system. Accordingly, if implemented, the king himself would appoint the cabinet, responsible to him alone. He would possess the power of legislation as well. The Estates would merely exercise the power of veto. However, as we are about to see, even this power was a sham since the king would have the right to appoint almost one-half of the representatives.

Despite all this, Hegel proceeds to exalt the generosity of the king. One must, he says, recognize "the infinite importance and liberality of the rights here allowed to the Estates." Moreover, if read "disinterestedly," the constitution "certainly honors the prince," who has managed to promulgate a rational constitution far superior to the formless, petty, and unclear "local [i.e., other German] and foreign [i.e., French, etc.] constitutions." He again admires the proposed abolition of the old constitutional "privileges and particularities" of the estates, which were simply "empty shams." Thus, asks Hegel rhetorically and confidently, must "not such constitutional foundations ... be recognized and taken up with nothing other than highest approval?"[47]

Obviously, this rhetorical question implies that those who did not approve it were being ungrateful, irrational, and selfish, for they wanted nothing less than the preservation of their old "privileges and particularities." This, once more, is a mischaracterization, or at best an oversimplification, of the opposition to the king's constitution, which Hegel tends to identify mainly with the lamentable "scribes."[48]

Hegel proceeds to claim that "whatever might be missing" from the king's proposals "cannot be anything that would be incompatible with such constitutional foundations." With this comment, he gingerly opens the door for his own suggestions for "more developed provisions as would accord with those universal truths of constitutional law."[49]

3.1.4 Hegel's Recommendations

First, Hegel supports the king's provision to retain "the [political] privilege of the aristocratic institution." This refers to the king's right to appoint a certain portion of the seats in the assembly from the ranks of the nobility.

---

[46] Hegel, *Proceedings*, 38-39.
[47] Ibid., 39.
[48] For an impressively rich and meticulously-researched account of the scribes, see Ian McNeely, *The Emancipation of Writing: German Civil Society in the Making, 1790s–1820s* (Berkeley: University of California Press, 2003).
[49] Ibid.

VII. Apologist-Careerist Professor of Heidelberg

Thus, our professor of constitutional law defends an old privilege while simultaneously admiring the "abolition" of the same. Friedrich's "aristocratic institution" is an improvement upon the "the democratic abstractions, which absolutely reject such an institution," he now claims. This "aristocratic institution" is also allegedly far removed from the irrational "feudal rights." To highlight the unreasonableness of the naysayers, he points out that "the king's Constitutional Charter grants only fifty votes to this [aristocratic] element, which has been united into one chamber with the elected deputies, while the elected representatives have seventy-three votes and thus a significant majority."[50]

Hegel fails to mention (perhaps deliberately) that the "Charter" reserves the "right" of the king to "increase the number" of the appointed members, provided that the elected representatives always remain the majority—at least by one vote, I surmise.[51] It does not take a constitutional genius to realize that this prerogative of the king, along with the unlimited right to dismiss the assembly and call for new elections,[52] if implemented, would have allowed him to easily obtain a friendly majority in the assembly, which was offered little legislative power in the first place. Perhaps, in rejecting his constitution, the king's opponents were not unreasonable after all. Only the likes of Hegel thought it was too generous or liberal.

Moreover, Hegel does not approve the single-assembly scheme proposed in the now-dead king's equally dead constitution. Instead, he prefers a "balance of power" scheme, based on "the dual-chamber system, whose considerable authority stems from its age-old and widespread acceptance."[53] What he wants is an assembly in which two chambers would "balance" each other, and thus pacify the "popular" part of the assembly with the help of the appointed representatives. This proposal, we should also note, is in line with Wangenheim's constitutional scheme,[54] which he recently, in September 1816, published in his essay, "On the Separation of the People's Assembly into Two Divisions."[55]

---

[50] Ibid., 39-40.
[51] *Landständische Verfassung*, §2.
[52] Ibid., §38.
[53] Hegel, *Proceedings*, 40.
[54] Rosenzweig famously objected to Haym's claim that Hegel's essay supports Wangenheim's proposals. One reason he gave for this was the rather nonchalant endorsement Hegel gave to the bicameral assembly. At the time he made this objection, Rosenzweig was unaware of Hegel's Heidelberg lectures on politics. In these lectures, which we will briefly discuss shortly, Hegel once again defended the bicameral model. Karl Rosenzweig, *Hegel und der Staat*, vol. 2 (Munich: Oldenbourg,1920), 50-60.
[55] Karl August Wangenheim, *Ueber die Trennung der Volksvertretung in zwei Abtheilungen und über landschaftliche Ausschüsse* (Stuttgart: [publisher unavailable], 1816). For a useful discussion, see Heinrich von Treitschke, *Historische und Politische Aufsätze*, vol. 1 (Leipzig: S. Hirzel, 1903), 211 ff.

VII. Apologist-Careerist Professor of Heidelberg

Having winked at Wangenheim, Hegel turns his critical gaze on "the wider scope and almost complete freedom given to the democratic principle by the mode of electing representatives, which allows this element [or principle] to enter into the order of the state in an almost completely unrestricted form." This is an exaggeration of "the democratic principle" entailed in the king's constitution. At any rate, Hegel wants to further restrict the "democratic principle." He complains in this regard that, in the king's constitution, this eligibility is "limited by very few conditions," such as the exclusion of "all civil servants and clergy, as well as doctors and surgeons."[56] Clearly, he wants to impose more restrictions, though he is about to also advocate removing the restrictions on the civil servants.

According to Hegel, due to their particularism, lawyers and the estate or class of "scribes" (*Schreiberstand*) are especially ill-suited for eligibility, and so should be deemed ineligible. This, of course, is an archaic refusal of the eligibility of individuals, based simply on their profession. His view of "the class of merchants, tradesmen, and other proprietors" shifts from one paragraph to the next, though it is likewise based on his unreformed and archaic idea that the political qualification of individuals is to be ultimately decided by their profession and estate. In the final analysis, he maintains that, although they "have an interest in maintaining civil order ..., their *immediate* purpose ... is [the defense of] what is *private* in their possession." Consequently, such people would "come into the Assembly with the will to give and do as little as possible for the universal. [i.e., the state].[57] Hegel does not offer a clear proposal on this issue. But he clearly wants to at least limit the political influence of the business class, if not eliminate it altogether.

To say this differently, Hegel wishes to see "more eligible" representatives in the assembly than the business class and infamous scribes. His main criterion for eligibility is consistent with his longstanding view that the state should be placed in the hands of those with "universal" aims and proclivities. Civil servants (the government employees) fall into this category of people, believes Hegel. Thus, he wants to remove the restriction in the king's constitution on the "civil servants." Indeed, he reminds his king-friendly audience, Friedrich himself had defended this view shortly before he proposed his constitution. "If civil servants are out of consideration," he further reasons, Württemberg will not have enough representatives "who possess sufficient insight and experience in universal matters—and even still fewer, in any case, who could be called statesmen." In short, and crucially so, with the exclusion of civil servants, the assembly would be deprived of representatives with the proper political ethos (*Gesinnung*) or "'sense of the state.'" Without their predominant presence

---

[56] Hegel, *Proceedings*, 40-41.
[57] Ibid., 42.

VII. Apologist-Careerist Professor of Heidelberg

in it, the estates assembly would "fall into the most dangerous evil" of private interests.[58] In a disorganized manner, Hegel returns to his argument for the inclusion of the "state officials" a few pages later, adding vaguely that, due to the recent developments, their inclusion is more "rational" today than ever before.[59] In short, Hegel proposes a system of representation in which the people are to be largely represented by civil servants and appointed aristocrats, perhaps each dominating one chamber of the proposed two-chamber assembly. Clearly, and in line with Wangenheim's views, he wants an assembly that would support the monarchical government.

Another group of people Hegel wants to see in the assembly are the veteran university students, who have fought to liberate Germany from the French yoke, that is, the very "liberators" he had castigated a few years ago (see Chapter 4). "The struggle for Germany's independence," argues he, has "imbued German youth in the universities with a higher interest than that of a mere focus on immediate future bread-winning and provision. Some of them have shed their own blood that German states might obtain free constitutions." They have returned from the "battlefield" with "the hope that they might further contribute to that cause and go on to play a role in the political life of the state." Along with "the entire educated class, who share this calling," such as Hegel himself, these veteran students should be eligible "to become members of the Estates and representatives of the people."[60] This odd proposal is clearly motivated by Hegel's desire to lure the students to his camp, away from the likes of Fries, and to urge them to work for the state, not against it.

Hegel also favors, with some reservations, the eligibility of the "magistrates." "Certainly, the position of a city magistrate is an appropriate school of preparation for Estates [Assembly] functions. Magistrates live, as do state officials, in the daily activity of handling the civil order and in the daily experience of how laws and institutions function, and of exactly which counter-forces of evil passions must be fought against or endured."[61]

In the next phase of his argument, Hegel complains about the "extreme" liberality of the king's constitution with respect to the *voting rights* of citizens. "The only requirement besides being 25 years old is ... [having] an income of 200 guilders from real estate." This flexibility "on voting eligibility has come into circulation [in Germany] only in more recent times," and mimics the dangerous French ideas, complains he. In such a system of voting, the "citizens appear as isolated atoms," as a "dissolved ...

---

[58] Ibid., 41-42.
[59] Ibid., 45-46.
[60] Ibid., 44.
[61] Ibid., 46.

VII. Apologist-Careerist Professor of Heidelberg

mass." This atomization is "the most unworthy" of the state's "essence and the most at odds with its concept, which is to be a spiritual [organic] order." Moreover, when a constitution makes the individual as such "a voter," it bestows upon "him a high political right without any connection to the rest of the roles he plays in his life." In this scenario, "an important constitutional matter is determined more by the democratic, even anarchical, principle of isolation than by the principle of an organic order." These "atomistic principles are—in science as in politics—death for every rational concept, articulation, and vitality." To avoid this predicament, "the French abstractions of pure number [i.e., age] and quanta of wealth must be left aside, or at least they must not be made the chief determination and represented as the only conditions of the most important political functions." Such qualifications are not the kinds of "qualities" that indicate "the worth of an individual in the civil order." The required sort of worthiness comes from an individual's "office, class, a civilly recognized occupational skill, and the qualifications for the same, for example, a master craftsman's diploma, title, etc."[62]

In the next few paragraphs, Hegel tries to undermine the importance of voting *tout court*. He haphazardly supposes that being a voter is "a completely isolated calling," without any real effect. It "chiefly" depends "on contingent conviction and momentary whim," which is exercised once in several years, and "expires with a single action" of voting. Moreover, given that an individual's vote is only one among many votes, and "the deputy whom he helps elect is himself only a member of a large assembly," the individual necessarily comes to realize that his vote is "quite insignificant." Consequently, "as experience shows," individuals quickly become "indifferent to their right" to vote. This is the proven outcome of "the atomistic method," claims Hegel. Above all, these atomistic "stipulations are not sufficient to eliminate the democratic formlessness from the people's share in universal concerns, and, more specifically, are not sufficient to eliminate contingency when it comes to finding competent deputies for an Estates Assembly."[63] Clearly, then, rather than simply desiring to make the eligibility to vote even more stringent than what the king's constitution allowed, Hegel wants to do away with popular, democratic elections altogether.

In opposition to this atomistic "French" institution, he proposes what he takes to be a German-corporatist solution to the problem of organizing the state, derived from "the great beginnings of internal legal relations in Germany, through which the formal development of a state has been [historically] prepared ..." When "the old monarchical government's power"

---

[62] Ibid., 47-48.
[63] Ibid., 48-49.

VII. Apologist-Careerist Professor of Heidelberg

disintegrated in the middle ages, "the knights, freed peasants, cloisters, the nobility, and those who run trade and industry formed themselves, against this state of disruption, into associations and corporations." However, since the "highest state power" was weak, the entities restricted themselves to the "formalism and guild-spirit," thus posing "an obstacle and a danger to the formation of state power." But this situation has changed with "the more complete development of the supreme powers of the state in more recent times." Initially, this development had led to the exclusion of "guild-circles and communities" from the "constitutional law," making them politically irrelevant. "Perhaps," adds Hegel, "it would again be time to bring ... [these] subordinate spheres back into political order and dignity and to lead them ... back into the state as an organic formation. A living connection lies only in an articulated whole, whose parts form the particular, subordinate circles."[64]

This idea of an organization of civil society via "corporations" was widely supported by the authorities and other intellectuals throughout Germany.[65] What distinguished them from each other was how much autonomy they were willing to grant the corporations. Hegel clearly wanted to "subordinate" them to the will of the state, to make them moments of the state in some "organic" manner.

In short, Hegel wanted Württemberg to have a more undemocratic state than even the one Friedrich I himself desired to have. This king, we should bear in mind, was widely known as a despot or "the Swabian tsar," though some historians refer to him more affectionately as an "enlightened despot."

3.2 Heidelberg Lectures on the State

Among other courses, Hegel taught natural right and political science at Heidelberg during the winter semester of 1817-1818. This brief section focuses on his lectures on the state, the third main part of his lectures, which have only recently been discovered and subsequently translated into English as *Lectures on Natural Rights and Political Science: The First Philosophy of Right* (henceforth *The First Philosophy of Right*).[66] One reason for the

---

[64] Ibid., 47-48. Translation slightly revised.
[65] For a useful comparison of Hegel's and List's views on corporations, see Günther Chaloupek, "Friedrich List on Local Autonomy in His Contributions to the Debate About the Constitution of Württemberg in 1816/1817," in *Two Centuries of Local Autonomy*, ed. Jürgen Backhaus, 3-12 (New York: Springer, 2011), 8-11.
[66] Hegel was in the habit of dictating the main claims of his unfinished "philosophy of right" to his students and then elaborating upon them during his lectures. Peter Wannenmann, one of Hegel's Heidelberg students, transcribed and polished Hegel's lectures, and titled the transcript *Naturrecht und Staatswissenschaft von Hegel*. His transcript was discovered in 1982 and subsequently translated into English in 1995 as G. W. F. Hegel, *Lectures on*

VII. Apologist-Careerist Professor of Heidelberg

brevity of our analysis is that the views Hegel defends in this text (or lectures) are repeated, without any significant philosophical or political changes, in his *Philosophy of Right* and Berlin lectures, which will be discussed in Chapter 10.

In Hegel's "philosophical" scheme, the individuals must have "absolute duty" toward the state. This duty stems from the "consciousness of freedom." In keeping with his old habits, Hegel defines this "freedom" as willing obedience ("disposition")."[67] Here is another illiberal thought: "The state is universal will, which is actual universal self-consciousness, the idea of God ...; that this idea should *be*, is the supreme right [or will of God]." "For this reason, ... the state has also been [rightly] worshipped by the nations as a god." The following sentence seals the deal on Hegel's alleged "liberalism:" "Substantial freedom [the God-given right and the will of the state] invests itself in the individual self-consciousness, which is devoid of rights over and against it." There is also the following bonus claim, just in case: "If individuals oppose this [divine] idea [a moniker for the state], they are devoid of rights, wholly lacking in dignity."[68] What we get here is a solid confirmation of Hegel's "notorious" deification of the state.[69] Hegel was no liberal—period.

According to Hegel, constitutions should not be made by the people, who are inherently ignorant; nor should a constitution be a contract between the people and the state. The "best educated ..., the wise," know that a rational constitution ought to be in "harmony with the national spirit" in its (God ordained) historical development, and that each nation must have its "individual" or specific constitution, appropriate to its unique spirit, to be determined by the Hegelian wisemen, such as kings, ministers, and possibly Hegel himself. "What is rational must *be*," or come into existence. As we will see later, Hegel assumes that the most rational constitution is already coming into existence in Germany. It is the German-style "*constitutional monarchy.*"[70]

"A people is rational only to the extent that its constitution is rational," says Hegel. By a "rational constitution," he mainly means a "*system of*

Natural Rights and Political Science: The First Philosophy of Right, trans. J. Michael Stewart and Peter C. Hodgson (Oxford University Press, 2012—first published in 1995). Henceforth cited as *First Philosophy of Right*.
[67] Hegel, *First Philosophy of Right*, §122.
[68] Ibid., §124.
[69] "Hegel's deification of the state is justifiably notorious," writes Ilting. However, after castigating Hegel for defying the state, he goes on to assure his readers of Hegel's "fidelity to liberal principles." K.-H. Ilting, "The Structure of Hegel's 'Philosophy of Right'," in *Hegel's Political Philosophy: Problems and Perspectives*, ed. Z. A. Pelczynski, 90-110 (Cambridge: Cambridge University Press, 1971), 102-03.
[70] Hegel, *First Philosophy of Right*, §§134-36.

VII. Apologist-Careerist Professor of Heidelberg

government" based on a specific organization or configuration of the powers of the state into an "organic whole."[71] He does not mean, nor does he attempt to construct, anything like the Bill of Rights or the Rights of Man and Citizen, or anything that says, "the government shall not …"

The first power Hegel discusses is the "sovereign" or "princely" power (which are used as synonyms), that is, the power of the monarch. The monarch must be a male and his title hereditary. Hegel imposes two meaningless limitations on the monarch's power: (1) "the constitution and the laws" constitute the basis of the decisions of the monarch, (2) who is also to receive the counsel of his ministers. However, the monarch has the power of "ultimate decision." Hegel's monarch also exercises ultimate and unhindered power "in the appointment [and dismissal] of state functionaries," including the ministers who counsel him, oversees foreign affairs, and has the right to "pardon criminals."[72] Thus, the monarch's legislative or executive power cannot be limited.

Next, Hegel considers the executive power (the government), led by the ministers, who are appointed solely by the monarch. The government supervises the provincial and local administrative units, which include an intractable medley of "estates or classes, guilds, corporations, provinces, cities, local communities," and, of course, the usual "etc." (i.e., "whatever has a determinate interest in common"). These corporations have the "right" of "self-administration." This right (freedom) is the "democratic principle in a monarchy." Based on this principle, each corporation has the right to choose *its own* "decision-making authorities." However, qualifies the double-speaking Hegel, these authorities must be subordinated to "senior [government] officials." Indeed, the elected officials, who run the corporations, "must be … confirmed by the senior officials," who are themselves to be appointed "by higher authority," namely, the ministers. In short, the whole system of administration must form a "pyramid, at the apex of which stand the ministries,"[73] who have their own "apex," namely, the monarch. Hegel's "democratic principle in a monarchy," then, is an "organic" sham.

Hegel now turns his attention to the (national) legislative power. Consistently with the constitutions proposed by the reactionary ruling kings and ministers throughout the Restoration-period Germany, Hegel claims that the representatives of the "rational" state "cannot make any [legislative] proposals"; they "must only have the right to present to the cabinet their wishes." In general, they must be "bound to foster the universal interest," the interest of the state, and not the particularistic interests of individuals,

---

[71] Ibid., §127.
[72] Ibid., §§138-40.
[73] Ibid., §§141-43.

VII. Apologist-Careerist Professor of Heidelberg

estates, or corporations they represent.[74] In other words, the assembly must be subservient and "subordinate to the government,"[75] to be appointed solely by the king.

Hegel proceeds to defend the virtues of bicameral assemblies. His two "logical" justifications for this model are unworthy of consideration.[76] The upper house is to be populated by the "*hereditary nobility*," the wealthy "*landowners*." Hegel assures himself that this class would naturally have "universal" aims.[77] He then proposes two "necessary qualifications" for the representatives of the lower house. First, they must be wealthy enough to sustain themselves independently of any income from the state or private business. Second, they must be experienced in the "business of government."[78] In short, Hegel wants the wealthy functionaries of the state to represent the people.[79]

Next, and quite absurdly, Hegel claims that, in accordance with its "concept," "there must be three parties in the assembly." One of these is "the party of the people" and the other "the party [that] is absolutely always on the side of the government." The third "sizable" party ought to be the "aristocratic party," which is also expected to take "the side of the government." In short, and once again, Hegel wants the majority in the assembly to support the "cabinet," which is to be appointed by the king.[80] Moreover, he wants the assembly to simply approve the legislation and other measures proposed by the monarch's cabinet, which are then to be approved by the monarch himself. The assembly's other responsibilities include "receiving and examining complaints by individuals concerning actions by officials and government authorities, for indicting ministers [who can only be dismissed by the monarch], and in particular for annually approving taxation." But these responsibilities, Hegel informs us, are generally superfluous in a "well-regulated state" in which "formal indictment of ministers" would be hardly necessary. As for "the approval of taxation," he takes it for granted that, in his scheme of things, the taxes demanded by the monarchical government would face no opposition from the assembly, since each party involved in this process would have "the political [or ethical] sense ... of having one's pride and honor in the greatness of the state and the great deeds it performs. There is nothing that must not be given up for the sake of this whole, whereby one's particular

---

[74] Ibid., §149.
[75] Ibid., §§146–47.
[76] Ibid., §151.
[77] Ibid., §152.
[78] Ibid., §150.
[79] Ibid., §153.
[80] Ibid., §156.

VII. Apologist-Careerist Professor of Heidelberg

interest is protected and furthered."[81] In the final analysis, then, Hegel's system of representation is also an organic sham.

In addition, he also favors limited freedom of the press, based on Wilhelm's 1817 constitution, which was conceived mostly by Wangenheim.[82]

Hegel has an additional plan to ensure that his state remains stable and "rational." This plan, which is consistent with his olden ideas, involves the indoctrination of the youth by means of education. "The wholly universal affairs of the state," proclaims the so-called "liberal" constitutional professor, "concern both the *training* and *education* of individuals to serve purposes of the state." Such an education should include the kind of philosophical training Hegel, an employee of the state *par excellence*, was hired to provide. In other words, "a people" must be "dedicated" to "the highest satisfaction of spirit, in which it recognizes the state," and this could be ensured by means of Hegelian education, which teaches that "the state is ethical spirit, spirit in and for itself, and constitutes the essence of all individuals."[83]

Through education, "children [must] become the children of the state," and so realize their inner essence and freedom by obeying it. Even if the ordinary individuals "cannot know it in this way, at least they [should] have [or be given] the impression that the state is something rational." Moreover, art, religion, and science must also be directed toward the satisfaction of this majestic, divine spirit. "There must accordingly [also] be a church in the state, [institutionally] independent of the state but one with it [in spirit]." In other words, the national church must endorse the state. But the "higher level" of consciousness of the state is achieved in "science," by which Hegel means his so-called *philosophy*. "There must be one class in the people that devotes itself to ... philosophical cognition," which should "comprehend the state ... as a temple of reason."[84] This simply means that philosophy, and education in general, must be at the service of the state. Would it be too harsh to say that Hegel worshipped the state?

---

[81] Ibid., §157.
[82] Ibid., §155. Hegel's comments in this paragraph basically repeat Section 7 of Wilhelm's constitution: "any attack on the honor of the head of state, his wife, and family, in books, writings and pictures" shall be considered a punishable libel. Section 8 of the same extends the prohibition to the libelous attacks on "the honor and the good name of private persons ..., the civil servants, as well as the estates assembly." The author and their accomplices are "liable to prosecution," according to section 15. Hegel's proposal to prosecute such transgressions in civil courts is also borrowed from Wilhelm's law (see sections 13 and 22). Wilhelm I, "*Gesetz über die Pressefreiheit vom 30. Januar 1817*," reprinted in Karl H. L. Pölitz, *Die Verfassungen des teutschen Staatenbundes seit dem Jahre* 1789, 373-77 (Leipzig: Brockhaus 1847).
[83] Hegel, *First Philosophy of Right*, §158.
[84] Ibid.

VII. Apologist-Careerist Professor of Heidelberg

With these comments, Hegel concludes his discussion of the "inner constitution" of the "rational" state, which is thoroughly illiberal and authoritarian, it now goes without saying.

The second subsection of "The State" deals with "international law." Succinctly put, Hegel denies both the legitimacy and efficacy of international law.[85] He also argues that each state consists of "a nation," which is based on the "anthropological principle." Furthermore, each nation has a "natural" and "absolute right to constitute a state." Hegel's olden ideas are recycled in the next set of claims he makes. Maintaining its independence is the "highest honor" of a nation. When this independence is at stake, all individuals have a "duty" to sacrifice their "life ..., property, and ... rights." According to Hegel, "individuals must feel the ethical substance, the spirit of the whole [i.e., the state]," which they come to do so during wars. This is because "what is demanded [in a war] is to sacrifice one-self to this substance willingly." Therefore, "there is a duty incumbent upon all to sacrifice themselves for the preservation of the state." Clearly, Hegel believes, as he had always believed, that wars are necessary and good for the ethical health of the state: "Wars are like winds upon the sea; without them the waters would become foul, and so it is with the state."[86] Once more: "without war, peoples sink into merely private life—the [false] security and weakness that make them an easy prey for other peoples." In short, and once again, "war is something ethically necessary."[87] Thus, the widespread assumptions that he did not justify war on ethical grounds, and even supported some version of Kant's "perpetual peace," are both flatly false.[88]

The very brief third subsection of "The State" deals with world history. The success or failure of a state in the sphere of international relations is ultimately decided by the *world spirit*, which oversees the "universal world history," asserts Hegel.[89] In other words, "the universal spirit ... exercises its absolute right" over nations and states in "*world history.*" As it turns out, in each historical epoch, the "divine" *Weltgeist* achieves its aims in "a single nation." Consequently, divines Hegel, the chosen nation becomes the "dominant" power of a given epoch; it has "absolute right of being the vehicle of this present highest stage in the development of world spirit." Against this right, "other peoples are without rights," since right is might.

---

[85] Ibid., §159.
[86] Ibid., §160.
[87] Ibid., §162.
[88] For a list of works that defend one or the other of these two claims, see Thom Brooks, *Hegel's Political Philosophy: A Systematic Reading of the* Philosophy of Right (Edinburgh: Edinburgh University Press, 2013), 226, n. 4.
[89] Hegel, *First Philosophy of Right*, §163.

VII. Apologist-Careerist Professor of Heidelberg

Moreover, world history exhibits "an advance to something higher."[90] The highest of all has been achieved in "the Germanic" world[91] of the "*Germanic peoples.*"[92] In other words, what we have here is the "actuality of developed reason," that is, the German "state as constitutional monarchy." This actuality finds its true knowledge in Hegel's philosophy of the state,[93] to which we have been exposed in this section. This thought concludes Hegel's Heidelberg lectures on "the science of the state," which concluded in March 1818.

In conclusion, we have sufficiently established in this chapter that, during his Heidelberg years, as before, Hegel had defended illiberal and authoritarian institutions. However, his political views had acquired a new twist during this "post-Napoleonic" period. He now believed—or pretended to believe—that the hitherto most rational state and ethical life, intended by the world spirit, was already taking shape in the Germanic territories, populated by the Restoration regimes. He also claimed that his "science of the state" basically explicated and justified the existing state, despite his own suggestions for its "improvement." He was now an apologist for the Restoration regimes, and this by his own admission.

---

[90] Ibid., §164.
[91] Ibid., §165. The widespread claim that Hegel used the word "Germanic" (*germanisch*) to mean "European" is indefensible.
[92] Ibid., §169.
[93] Ibid., §170.

Chapter Eight

VIII. THE INITIATION OF A PRUSSIAN STATE PHILOSOPHER, 1818-1820

1. Why Prussians Hired Hegel

The Wartburg Festival, held on October 18, 1817, brought together approximately 500 demonstrators, mostly delegates of the student fraternities of various universities (Berlin and Heidelberg included), some professors, such as Fries, Lorenz Oken, Dietrich Georg von Kieser, and Heinrich Luden, individuals from other walks of life, and likely some police spies. Their main slogan was "Honor, Freedom, and Fatherland." They sung radical and nationalistic songs, gave spirited speeches, and called for a liberal constitution, entailing popular representation, freedom of the press, and the unification of Germany.[1] Many participants, including Fries, were openly anti-Semitic,[2] though the student movement also counted some Jewish students among its ranks.[3] Only a few rulers, such as Karl August of Weimar, were sympathetic to the liberal-republican cause of the festival attendees. Indeed, it was organized within his realm and with his blessing. Overall, however, the gathering irked the most influential ones. Hegel's position coincided with that of the irked Holy rulers.

Metternich was aghast when he heard the embellished and sensationalized news about the "Jacobin" activities at the festival. Even George Rose, the British ambassador to Berlin, described the event as "a scandalous scene of revolutionary effervescence." The attendees gave "much countenance ... to persons of dangerous principles," Rose reported to his boss, Viscount Castlereagh.[4] On November 3, this rather inflated fear was conveyed to Friedrich Wilhelm III by his cousin and subordinate, Duke

---

[1] For Oken's eyewitness account, see Alexander Ecker, *Lorenz Oken: A Biographical Sketch*, trans. Alfred Tulk (London: Kegan Paul, 1883), 172-78.
[2] Their anti-Semitic views did not alarm the authorities, who were more concerned with their liberal and democratic views. Indeed, anti-Semitism was also rampant among the authorities themselves.
[3] For a good discussion of the Jewish membership in the *Burschenschaften*, see Keith Pickus, *Constructing Modern Identities: Jewish University Students in Germany, 1815-1914* (Detroit: Wayne State University Press, 1999), Ch. 2.
[4] Quoted in Sabine Freitag and Peter Wende, *British Envoys to Germany, 1816–1866*, vol. 1, *1816–1829* (Cambridge: Cambridge University Press, 2000), 76–77.

VIII. The Initiation of a Prussian State Philosopher, 1818-1820

Charles of Mecklenburg: "The mischief on the Wartburg assaults all sovereigns, great and small, promotes terrorism, intolerance, and demagogic despotism; from there it is only a few steps to outright revolutionary actions."[5]

On November 7, the Prussian king, having been spooked by his cousin, demanded answers and solutions from his subordinates. "Administrators scrambled to bring him local newspaper reports on the festival as police dispatched additional investigators to Eisenach. At the same time, the Prussian chief of police, Karl von Kamptz, acquired a list of persons involved in the Wartburg Festival and began to interrogate them privately."[6] The malleable chancellor, Karl von Hardenberg, joined the chorus by expressing the need to "suppress the revolutionary tendency ... and Jacobinism, which is almost everywhere raising its head." He thus urged "firm measures" to get rid of this "evil."[7] On December 27, the king issued a warning to Karl von Altenstein, his newly-appointed minister of culture and education: "It is the urgent duty of your ministry to counteract vigorously the highly dangerous and criminal state of mind which has gained ascendancy among the inexperienced youth in the German universities."[8]

Subsequently, Friedrich Wilhelm III and his subordinates decided to continue with, even intensify, quashing the efforts of the "demagogues." Thus, the king's cabinet order was followed by Hardenberg's memorandum to Altenstein, which ordered him to keep an eye on the radical scholars in Berlin. Among others, two influential figures, Ernst Moritz Arndt and Friedrich Ludwig Jahn, were now suspects. In his February 5, letter to Altenstein, Hardenberg described Jahn as "a highly dangerous man," and asked his subordinate minister to take appropriate measures against him.[9]

During the same period, several petitions to demand a constitution were being circulated in the Rhineland, now under Prussian rule. Görres,

---

[5] Quoted in Walter M. Simon, *The Failure of the Prussian Reform Movement, 1807–1819* (Ithaca, NY: Cornell University Press, 1955), 135.
[6] Steven Michael Press, "False Fire: The Wartburg Book-Burning of 1817," in *Central European History* 42, no. 4 (2009): 621-46, 632.
[7] Quoted in Matthew Levinger, *Enlightened Nationalism: The Transformation of Prussian Political Culture, 1806-1848* (Oxford: Oxford University Press, 2000), 139.
[8] Quoted in Simon, *The Failure of the Prussian Reform Movement, 1807–1819*, 135. Also see Eric Dorn Brose, *German History 1789-1871: From the Holy Roman Empire to the Bismarckian Reich* (New York: Berghahn, 2013), 89.
[9] Simon, *The Failure of the Prussian Reform Movement, 1807–1819*, 135. Arndt, a liberal-nationalist, was a historian, writer, and poet. Jahn, known as the "father of gymnastics" (*Turnvater Jahn*) also demanded a liberal and democratic constitution and the unification of Germany. Both were declared "demagogues" and punished in 1819 for their political influence on the youth. As far as I can tell, their punishment had nothing to do with their anti-Semitic views.

VIII. The Initiation of a Prussian State Philosopher, 1818-1820

whose newspaper was shut down in 1816, had played a leading role in this effort and even had his own petition. On January 18, 1818, he handed his petition, endorsed by more than 3,000 signatures, to Hardenberg.[10] The petition reminded the king of his promise to promulgate a constitution.[11] On January 30, Görres also published a pamphlet to disseminate the contents of the petition and to publicize his meeting with Hardenberg. The king interpreted the petition as an insult to his royal dignity and authority. His February 23 letter to Hardenberg described Görres' efforts as additional proof of the "utmost pernicious intrigues in the Rhine provinces." "It is impossible to permit and condone that one or several individuals collect signatures in such a manner, even if the petition itself is acceptable," he said.[12] Hardenberg agreed.

Although a commission, authorized by the king and led by Hardenberg, was still at work to devise a proper constitution for Prussia, the king's behavior basically signaled that the commission's efforts were done in vain. Moreover, his most trusted advisers, such as Jean Pierre Friedrich Ancillon, were warning him that granting a constitution would make him another Louis XVI. The latter's demise, Ancillon explained, resulted from making concessions to the "demagogues."[13] However, he could not simply declare his earlier promise null and void, and so appear to be a liar. Thus, he opted to postpone it indefinitely with his cabinet order of March 21, 1818:

> I will determine when the granting of an estates-based constitution shall be fulfilled, and I will not be disturbed in calm progress toward this goal ... The duty of my subjects is to trust my free will ... and to await that point in time that I, informed by my own view of the whole, deem suitable for its fulfilment.[14]

Hegel's recruitment by Altenstein coincided with the period extending from the Wartburg Festival to the day the king issued the March 21 cabinet order. We know that Altenstein had been preparing to formally offer the vacant chair of philosophy at Berlin to Hegel since December 15, 1817, as

---

[10] Jon Vanden Heuvel, *A German Life in the Age of Revolution: Joseph Görres, 1776-1848* (Washington DC: The Catholic University of America Press, 2001), 237 ff.

[11] Friedrich Wilhelm III issued a royal edict (*Verordnung über die zu bildende Repräsentation des Volkes*) on May 22, 1815, which promised his subjects a (virtually powerless) national representative assembly. The edict is reprinted in Wilhelm Altmann (ed.), *Ausgewählte Urkunden zur Brandenburg-Preussischen Verfassungs und Verwaltungsgeschichte* (Berlin: R. Geartners, 1897), 87-88. Also see Simon, *The Failure of the Prussian Reform Movement, 1807–1819*, 109 ff.

[12] Quoted in Levinger, *Enlightened Nationalism*, 139-40.

[13] Ibid.

[14] Quoted in Heuvel, *A German Life in the Age of Revolution*, 240, n. 92.

VIII. The Initiation of a Prussian State Philosopher, 1818-1820

the existence of various draft-letters to Hegel indicate.[15] As we will see shortly, he had been communicating with Hegel during the preceding few months, and even met him in Heidelberg during the summer of 1817. On December 26, he finally mailed the letter-of-offer to Hegel. As a member of the cabinet, Altenstein must have been expecting the king's cabinet order of December 27, which, to requote, read: "It is the urgent duty of your ministry to counteract vigorously the highly dangerous and criminal state of mind which has gained ascendancy among the inexperienced youth in the German universities." The king approved Hegel's appointment just a few days before he issued his March 21 cabinet order, declaring himself the sole decider on the fate of the constitution.

Given this context, the popular claim that Altenstein hired Hegel as a "liberal" ally is utterly implausible.[16] A much more plausible explanation is provided by Horst Althaus: Hegel's behavior in Heidelberg "suggested a future career as a political servant of the [Prussian] Crown ... The author of the essay on *The Estates Assembly of Württemberg* had publicly revealed himself admirably fitted for such a role." As the author of this essay, Hegel "could hardly fail to appeal to the government in Berlin. And the Prussia now entering upon a period of Restoration was undoubtedly looking for an appropriate philosopher."[17]

Given that they met during the summer of 1817 in Heidelberg, it is reasonable to assume that Altenstein knew about the kind of education Hegel was prepared to provide. It is also highly likely that they conversed about the current political developments in Germany, the growing radicalism of students and some professors, and even Hegel's censoring of the "disrespectful" Paulus. Their mutual friends must have also informed the minister about Hegel's political sympathies. After all, the minister was in town to express the Prussian state's interest in acquiring an art collection from the Boisserée brothers; Sulpitz Boisserée, Hegel's friend, had witnessed

---

[15] Johannes Hoffmeister (Ed.), *Briefe von und an Hegel*, 4 volumes (Hamburg: Felix Meiner, 1952-1960), the editor's note to #326, (page) 426. Henceforth cited as *Briefe*, followed by the Latin numerical to indicate the volume number, in this case, *II*.

[16] *Pace* Jacques D'Hondt, *Hegel In His Time*, trans. John Burbidge (Peterborough, Ontario: Broadview Press, 1988), 39 ff; Adriaan T. Peperzak, *Philosophy and Politics: A Commentary on the Preface to Hegel's Philosophy of Right* (Dordrecht: Martinus Nijhoff Publishers, 1987), 18. This claim is also repeated in other popular accounts, albeit less explicitly. For instance, see Shlomo Avineri, *Hegel's Theory of the Modern State* (Cambridge: Cambridge University Press, 1972). 116 ff; Terry Pinkard, *Hegel: A Biography* (Cambridge: Cambridge University Press, 2000), 412 ff.

[17] Horst Althaus, *Hegel: An Intellectual Biography*, trans. Michael Tarsh (Cambridge, UK: Polity Press, 2000), 145. For a very similar attempt to connect Hegel's essay to the Prussian interest in him, see Rudolf Haym, *Hegel und seine Zeit: Vorlesungen über Entstehung und Entwicklung, Wesen und Wert der Hegelschen Philosophie* (Berlin: R. Gaertner, 1857), 356.

VIII. The Initiation of a Prussian State Philosopher, 1818-1820

Hegel's altercation with the "disrespectful revolutionary pack" during a boat trip on the Neckar (see Chapter 7). Reversely and briefly put, it is very unlikely that Altenstein was uninterested in, and unaware of, Hegel's political views at a time when his own superiors were ordering him to keep an eye on the radical intellectuals and professors.

The impression that Hegel's *Proceedings*, which was published about a month before Altenstein called him to Berlin, was a royalist apology, as well as an attack against the king's opponents, including the republicans, was already wide-spread. As one antidemocratic reader privately put it at the time, despite being "irresponsibly one-sided" against the king's opponents, his essay was nevertheless an excellent portrayal of the "democratic *pudenda*" in Germany.[18] Niethammer, on the other hand, sarcastically congratulated Hegel for defending a "bad cause," that of "the rude and imperious authority," expressed from the standpoint of the "reigning reasons" of the regime.[19] Hegel's January 31, 1818, letter to Niethammer indicates that he had all along anticipated the negative reaction to his essay and that he remained defiant in the face of it. In it, he sarcastically referred to Paulus as "Estates advocate," and revealed that many (now unavailable) "anonymous or signed" negative responses to his own essay were produced, including one by Paulus.[20] Thus, and once more, Hegel's royalist sympathies were well-known.

However, such reactions against his royalism mattered little to Hegel. What really mattered to him was that he received a generous offer from the Prussians just a month after he published his essay. He must have also been pleased that, shortly thereafter, the government of Württemberg ordered its reprinting and wide distribution at a subsidized price.[21] (Paulus, on the other hand, was deported from Württemberg when he visited his terminally-ill son in 1819.[22]) The issue that needs to be addressed now is not whether Hegel was an apologist, which he clearly was. Rather, it is whether he was also a sycophant, that is, whether he had published his essay to advance his own career.

---

[18] Günther Nicolin (ed.), *Hegel in Berichten seiner Zeitgenossen* (Hamburg: Felix Meiner, 1970), #250.
[19] *Letters*, 361 (*Briefe II*, #327).
[20] Ibid., 362 (#329).
[21] There is a debate on which individuals were involved in making this possible. For an interesting treatment of this issue, see Paul Gehring, "Um Hegels Landständeschrift: Friedrich List im Spiel?"
[22] Reichlin-Meldegg, *Heinrich Eberhard Gottlob Paulus und seine Zeit*, 139 ff.

VIII. The Initiation of a Prussian State Philosopher, 1818-1820

2. Why Hegel Went to Prussia

Althaus makes another valid claim, which needs to be further justified: while in Heidelberg, "Hegel regarded his position as a professor ... [and author], we now know, merely as a transitional stage on the way to other and potentially higher things."[23] In other words, Hegel was an opportunistic figure, and not simply a state worshipper.

As his December 26 letter indicates, Altenstein was already aware of Hegel's career ambitions. Clearly, he was bent upon enticing Hegel to Berlin by offering him not only a significantly higher salary than what he was receiving at Heidelberg but also "a more extensive and more important sphere of action" in shaping the system of education. "You know what Berlin can procure for you in this respect," wrote Altenstein, adding that "it should surpass all your expectations if, as I hope, various projects to whose realization I am committed take more definite shape." For the time being, however, he was only able to offer Hegel a good salary and "the philosophy chair vacated by the death of Professor Fichte,"[24] which was prestigious enough in its own right.

The Prussian offer, which Hegel received on January 6, 1818, was indeed quite enticing. As his January 24 reply to Altenstein informs us, Hegel was offered "a guaranteed annual salary of 2,000 Thalers," which was significantly higher than his current salary at Heidelberg, and an "assurance of appropriate compensation for travel costs," as well as a ministerial promise to get him involved in "various projects." "In light of Your Excellency's" generous offer, Hegel replied, "there remains really very little for me still to wish." Still, Hegel could not resist the temptation to submit to his Excellency's "gracious consideration" additional "wishes."[25]

What needs to be reiterated here is that Altenstein's offer did not catch Hegel by surprise. As Altenstein recalled in his December 26 letter, Hegel had previously expressed his still-alive interest in Berlin University to him both in person (by "oral declaration," referring to their meeting in Heidelberg) and through their "common friends." This prior communication, said Altenstein, gave him the "hope" at the time "that it would still be possible to win ... [Hegel] for Berlin University" soon, and that Hegel's "previous view" in this respect "did not change."[26] This explains why Altenstein knew about Hegel's "expectations" and what would "exceed" them.

---

[23] Althaus, *Hegel: An Intellectual Biography*, 356.
[24] Clark Butler and Christiane Seiler (trans.), *Hegel: The Letters* (Bloomington: Indiana University Press, 1984), 378 (*Briefe II*, #326). Henceforth cited as *Letters*.
[25] *Letters*, 379-80 (*Briefe II*, #328).
[26] Ibid., 378, (#326). Some of the words quoted here are not included in *Letters*.

159

VIII. The Initiation of a Prussian State Philosopher, 1818-1820

Relatedly, as Altenstein noted in his February 20, 1818, letter to the king, Hegel had previously informed him of his willingness to leave his "cozy" post at Heidelberg "out of a fondness for the Prussian state and its scientific ambitions."[27] This comment indicates that Hegel's "fondness for the Prussian state" was known to Altenstein before he decided to hire him. Its "scientific ambitions," which coincided with his career ambitions, must have contributed to Hegel's "fondness for the Prussian state" since he had only recently acquired it. Thus, since his permission was needed, the king was also informed that the prospective philosopher admired his state. It took the king about three weeks to approve Hegel's appointment, which *suggests* that he ordered his police chief to further investigate Hegel's background.

On March 16, Altenstein relayed the good news to Hegel, indicating also that his additional "wishes" were granted, except his request for free housing. Thus, in addition to several other perks, Hegel was to receive 1,000 Thalers for his moving expenses, his salary payments were to resume several months before his arrival in Berlin, and his wife was to receive a widow's pension after his death. "The Ministry," concluded Altenstein, "appreciates ... deeply the advantage gained through such a profound thinker and academic teacher, steeped in solid science and moved by such earnest and proper zeal."[28] Along with this official, ministerial letter, Altenstein also sent a more personal letter in which, in a non-official manner, he repeated his earlier promise: "I am projecting a vast transformation of the Royal Academy of Sciences, and hope to have occasion to open up for you a very beautiful [field of] activity, augmenting your revenues in the future."[29]

We know, or everyone knew back then, that the naturally incoherent Hegel was not a good teacher at all.[30] Also, there is no evidence to suggest that Altenstein was sufficiently familiar with Hegel's "science." Indeed, he admitted at some point in his life that he was "'never able to advance beyond the philosophical teachings of Fichte,'" and that he found Hegel's philosophy too difficult to grasp.[31] Be these as they may, Hegel's *political* zeal must have counted among the main reasons why the Prussians wanted to recruit him. To be more specific, Hegel was hired to teach students to obey the state, and this is precisely what Altenstein meant by "proper zeal," as we will discover shortly. Apart from this, Hegel was hired to help

---

[27] Günther Nicolin (ed.), *Hegel in Berichten seiner Zeitgenossen* (Hamburg: Felix Meiner, 1970), #253. Henceforth cited as *Berichten*.
[28] Ibid., 380 (*Briefe II*, #331).
[29] Ibid. (#332).
[30] Hegel's lectures at Heidelberg were also largely incoherent. Berichten, #280.
[31] Robert M. Bigler, *The Politics of German Protestantism: The Rise of the Protestant Church Elite in Prussia, 1815-1848* (Berkeley: University of California Press, 1972), 79-80.

VIII. The Initiation of a Prussian State Philosopher, 1818-1820

Altenstein undermine the efforts of some of the influential Berlin faculty to prevent further state intervention in academic freedom.[32]

As noted earlier, Hegel's "fondness for the Prussian state" was an extension of his career ambitions. Having received an offer from Altenstein, the opportunistic Hegel went to Stuttgart, Württemberg, where he "spent a few days" in "spring."[33] It turns out, as he explained it to his sister, he was there for four days to discuss the "many advantageous offers" made to him by the government officials regarding his employment at Tübingen University (likely, to succeed Wangenheim as curator or chancellor of the university). However, although "inclined," he had already made a deal with Berlin, and so declined these offers, he said.[34] This was Hegel's way of explaining to his sister that he found the offer from the Württemberg authorities less appealing than the offer he received from the Prussians. Why else would he go to Stuttgart after receiving Altenstein's offer, if not to see whether he could negotiate a better deal for himself? Surely, he was not there to visit his sister, as his letter to her makes it abundantly clear.

It is rather undeniable that Hegel's essay made him attractive to the Württemberg regime. First, as noted earlier, the government facilitated the reprinting and distribution of his essay. Then, it offered him a job. Did Hegel write the essay to curry favor with the regime? What we know for certain is that, while in Heidelberg, Hegel was primarily interested in advancing his income and career. It was he who ultimately confessed to this. On April 21, he sent a letter to the Badenese Ministry of Interior to request his release from his obligations at Heidelberg. His letter included the following explanation: more than

> the considerable salary increase, which is of supreme importance to my family, it was above all the prospect of a greater opportunity" of advancing "from the precarious function of teaching philosophy at a university to another [higher] activity ... that led to the decision to renounce my present post.[35]

Subsequently, after fulfilling his remaining teaching obligations at Heidelberg during the summer semester of 1818, Hegel moved to Berlin with his family on October 6. With the promise of higher status and income in his sight, the ambitious and opportunistic Hegel was now more than willing to please the Prussian regime. In fact, he had rehearsed for this new role during the last two years in Heidelberg.

---

[32] Heinrich Leo, "Der Hegelianismus in Preussen," in ed. Helmut Diwald, *Zeitschrift für Religions- und Geistesgeschichte* 10, no. 1 (1958): 51-60.
[33] *Briefe II*, #344.
[34] Ibid., #347.
[35] Ibid., #334.

VIII. The Initiation of a Prussian State Philosopher, 1818-1820

3. Pledging Allegiance to the Prussian State

On October 22, Hegel delivered his inaugural address at Berlin University. It was an updated version of his Heidelberg address, made more palatable to a specifically Prussian audience. He began his address with the following statement:

> Since today marks my *first* appearance at this university in *that official capacity as a teacher of philosophy* to which I was graciously appointed by His Majesty the King, permit me to say ... that I considered it particularly desirable and gratifying to take up a position of wider *academic influence* both at this *particular moment* and in this *particular place* [all italics here and below are Hegel's].

The "*particular moment*," Hegel clarified, refers to "those circumstances" in which "*philosophy*" is once again valued. The "*particular place*" refers to Germany, especially Prussia, where the king and his ministers (read Altenstein) value philosophy. As was the case in his Heidelberg address, Hegel once again linked what he regarded as the recent debasement of philosophy and higher learning to "the *urgency of the times*," that is, the struggles to repel Napoleon. Due to this "*urgency*," the attempt to "restore and salvage the *political totality of national life and of the state*" naturally consumed the energies of the whole nation. At last, and fortunately, "the *German nation* at large had salvaged its *nationality, the basis of all vitality and life*." It is now high time to allow philosophy to "flourish independently [in its own right (*selbständig*)] within the *state*." "And," clarified Hegel, "it is this *state* [i.e., Prussia] in particular" in which philosophy ("the spiritual life") can, and ought to, regain its due importance.

> But it is not just spiritual [intellectual] life in general which constitutes a *basic moment* in the existence of *this state*; more particularly, that great struggle of the [Prussian] people, together with its ruler [Friedrich Wilhelm III], for independence, for the destruction of soulless foreign tyranny [of Napoleon], and for freedom, had its higher source in ... *the ethical power of the spirit*, which *felt its own energy*, raised *its banner*, and expressed this [ethical] *feeling* as a force and *power* in [the realm of] *actuality*.

This ethical "*soul*," Hegel noted, "is *also the true ground of [Hegelian, true] philosophy.*" In other words, the main task of true philosophy is to justify the ethical-political spirit that has, at last, prevailed in "*this state.*"

This sort of genuine philosophy, announced the new Prussian professor, belongs especially to "the *German* spirit." All "*other* nations" have "*debased*" it to such an extent that it is no longer recognizable as philosophy.

VIII. The Initiation of a Prussian State Philosopher, 1818-1820

What he meant to say was that only he possessed such a philosophy: "even in Germany ..., before the country's *rebirth* [in 1815]," philosophy succumbed to *"banality."* Especially detestable was the Kantian proclamation that "the eternal and the *divine*," that is, the absolute "truth," could not be known. This meant that the state itself could not be known as the existing actuality of the eternal and the divine spirit. This fake and dangerous philosophy naturally attracted to its ranks those with "superficial knowledge and ... superficial character." Alas, this banality, now advocated by the likes of Fries, Schleiermacher, and de Wette, "still holds the floor today." But behold! Hegel, who knew the absolute truth, was in Berlin to fix all that—as indicated in his frequent use of *"I"* in the ensuing sentences of his hyperbolic address.[36]

It is quite evident that his lofty and promising career at Berlin University had much to do with Hegel's newly-acquired admiration for, and allegiance to, the Prussian state. Differently put, his wife's alleged nightmares about the barbaric Prussians were now the forgotten relics of the past,[37] as were Hegel's sarcastic comments about them as "liberators" during "the war of liberation."[38] By the same token, the Napoleonic France was now declared the dead "enemy" of the divine *Weltgeist*, the rational actuality (the Prussian state), and Hegel himself. The world spirit, he told his Heidelberg students several months earlier, "strikes down the inferior spirits when they oppose it or stand in its way."[39] More such spirits would have to be struck down in short order. What would Hegel do?

4. Decrees, "Demagogues," and Non-Heroics

4.1 The Karlsbad Decrees

On October 18, 1818, just four days before Hegel delivered his inaugural address, Duke Karl August permitted the representatives from fourteen universities to meet at Jena University. The date tellingly coincided with the first anniversary of the Wartburg Festival. Their aim was to unite the *Burschenschaften* under an umbrella organization, namely, the General German Student Organization. Like the Wartburg Festival, this event confirmed the fears of the rulers that a revolution was in the works.

---

[36] G. W. F. Hegel, "Inaugural Address, Delivered at the University of Berlin (22 October 1818)," in *Political Writings*, eds. Laurence Dickey and H. B. Nisbet, 181-85 (Cambridge: Cambridge University Press, 1999).
[37] *Letters*, 306 (*Briefe II*, #233).
[38] Ibid., 199-200 (*Briefe I*, #148); 298-300 (*Briefe II*, #225); 305 (*Briefe II*, #230).
[39] G. W. F. Hegel, *Lectures on Natural Rights and Political Science: The First Philosophy of Right*, trans. J. Michael Stewart and Peter C. Hodgson (Oxford University Press, 2012—first published in 1995), §8.

VIII. The Initiation of a Prussian State Philosopher, 1818-1820

The foremost theorist of the Holy Alliance, Friedrich Gentz,[40] immediately issued a warning to all rulers of the realm:

> The *Allgemeine Burschenschaften* is based expressly and essentially upon the idea of German unity [a threat to the Holy Alliance and the Concert of Europe] ... It is also revolutionary in the highest and most frightful sense of the word ... [T]he unity towards which these Jacobins have been striving continuously for six years cannot be realized without the most turbulent of revolutions, without the overthrow of Europe.[41]

As if to confirm the fears of the Holy rulers, an assassination took place on March 23, 1819. Karl Sand, a confused and delusional theology student, murdered August Kotzebue, the *German* playwright, who was at the time serving as the *Russian* tsar's consul general in *Germany*. Sand shared the widely-held opinion that Kotzebue was a Russian spy, and so was a "traitor"—hence the main reason why he thought the playwright had to be killed.[42] Kotzebue's recently-published essay, in which he castigated liberal-republican nationalists and their demands for a constitution, only helped improve his ranking among the individuals most despised by the activists.

Kotzebue, in other words, represented just about everything the liberal nationalists opposed and the Holy rulers supported. The latter were not only opposed to the "Jacobinism" brewing in the background but also to the kind of nationalism these "demagogues" espoused. For many, nationalism meant, among other things, the unification of Germany under a single state and constitution. Such an arrangement was seen by many rulers as a threat to the European Concert or Vienna Settlement, devised by the Allies that defeated Napoleon. Within the German Confederation, some of the lesser rulers saw the single-state solution as a threat to their aspirations for independence. More crucially, the Prussian and Austrian rulers thought it would upset their alliance with each other and with the other two great powers, namely, England and Russia.[43]

---

[40] Friedrich Gentz was the confidant, assistant, and adviser to Metternich. He was also the main official theoretician of the Restoration era and had served as the secretary of the Vienna Congress. For a classic study on Gentz and his politics, see Paul Friedrich Reiff, *Friedrich Gentz, an Opponent of the French Revolution and Napoleon* (Urbana-Champaign, IL: The University of Illinois Press, 1912). Also see Paul Sweet, *Friedrich von Gentz: A Defender of the Old Order* (Westport, CT: Greenwood Press, 1970).
[41] Quoted in Lawrence J. Baack, *Christian Bernstorff and Prussia: Diplomacy and Reform Conservatism, 1818-1832* (New Brunswick, NJ: Rutgers University Press, 1980), 57.
[42] For a brief biography of Sand and a detailed discussion of the assassination, see Alexandre Dumas, *Celebrated Crimes*, vol. 3, trans. I. G. Burnham (Philadelphia: George Barrie & Son, 1895), 71-150.
[43] For a useful discussion, see Levinger, *Enlightened Nationalism*, 130-37.

VIII. The Initiation of a Prussian State Philosopher, 1818-1820

At any rate, the "traitor" Kotzebue was now dead. The Russian tsar demanded action. In May 1820, a court in Mannheim sentenced Sand to death. He was beheaded. In the meanwhile, Sand's deed was exactly the kind of excuse Metternich needed to orchestrate a concerted effort to crack down on the "demagogues" throughout the German Confederation. Now, even the duke of Weimar had to agree with his grand plan, he reasoned. As the shrewd Metternich informed Gentz on April 9, 1819, "in this instance some good will come out of evil, since poor Kotzebue stands as an *argumentum ad hominem* which not even the liberal duke of Weimar will undertake to defend. My concern is to turn the affair to good account."[44] Indeed, the duke would soon succumb to pressure to some extent, as we will see shortly.

In August, as a first step, Metternich convinced the king of Prussia to launch a coordinated effort to suppress the "revolutionary" tendencies in Germany. Such an effort was already implied in the agreed-upon principles of the Holy Alliance. However, the new plan also included putting an end to all efforts to promulgate a constitution in Prussia, especially the promised plan for a national representative assembly.[45] Earlier, in November 1818, Metternich warned Wittgenstein, the reactionary Prussian minister of police, that national representation "through deputies of the people means the dissolution of the Prussian state," suggesting that, at most, the king of Prussia should grant only provincial assemblies.[46]

Some historians blame Metternich and the likes of Wittgenstein for pushing the impressionable Prussian king to abandon his plan to set up a national representative assembly, forgetting that what the king himself promised in his edict of May 22, 1815, was a sham national representative assembly. "The effectiveness of the representatives," he clarified in his edict, "extends [only] to *advising* on all matters of legislation concerning the personal and property rights of citizens including taxation [emphasis added]."[47] To Metternich, even this sham arrangement of representation was too dangerous, as it would lead to the impression that the nation or the people had a right to make stately decisions. The rationale, now reinforced by Kotzebue's assassination, was that terror would surely ensue from allowing the people to have such an impression.

Thus, Gentz was tasked with the formulation of the official Confederation position on the question of acceptable constitutions in

---

[44] Quoted in Simon, *The Failure of the Prussian Reform Movement, 1807–1819*, 139.
[45] Heuvel, *A German Life in the Age of Revolution*, 242.
[46] Quoted in Levinger, *Enlightened Nationalism*, 151.
[47] Altmann (ed.), *Ausgewählte Urkunden zur Brandenburg-Preussischen Verfassungs und Verwaltungsgeschichte*, 87-8. Also see Simon, *The Failure of the Prussian Reform Movement, 1807–1819*, 109 ff.

VIII. The Initiation of a Prussian State Philosopher, 1818-1820

Germany, and to put it in writing. He regurgitated what he had been advocating all along. The "*landständische* constitutions," as required by Article 13 of the Acts of Confederation, he maintained, should preserve "the natural foundation of a well-ordered civil society." This was to be understood in terms of "*ständische* [estates] relationships and *ständische* rights" of particular "classes [estates] and corporations." In contrast, popular-representative constitutions, somehow, were founded on "the perverted concept of the *supreme sovereignty* of the *Volk.*" Such constitutions necessarily exhibited "the constant tendency to set the phantom of so-called *freedom of the people* (i.e., universal arbitrariness) in the place of civil order and subordination; and to set the *delusion* of *equality of rights*, or (what is no better) universal *equality before the law*, in the place of the ineradicable distinctions between the estates that were established by God Himself." Representative constitutions of this kind, moreover, would surely undermine monarchical authority. The best way to avoid this horrid outcome was to accept the monarch as the "supreme legislator," as well as the "recognized organ of the state." Moreover, the principle of "division of powers," demanded by the liberal advocates of freedom of the people, amounted to "an axiom which . . . always and everywhere must lead to the complete destruction of all power, and hence to pure *anarchy.*"[48]

Gentz's essay, which was distributed at the Karlsbad Congress, gained quick approval, especially for its defense of the "monarchical principle," if not for its defense of feudal inequalities. Hardenberg, for instance, unreservedly defended this principle in his vague constitutional proposal of August 1819.[49] Hegel was also an ardent defender of this principle, just as he was an opponent of such "dangerous" ideas as people's sovereignty and division of powers. He had expressed these views in Heidelberg, if not before, and would soon publish them in his *Philosophy of Right.*[50]

But the more urgent task of the dignitaries present at the Karlsbad Congress was to agree to Metternich's plan of action, already supported by the Prussians, against the "demagogues." This plan was accepted and formalized with the issuance of the Karlsbad Decrees.[51] One of the least discussed features of the Decrees in contemporary literature is the one that had a massive impact on the reorganization and regulation of the universities

---

[48] Quoted in Levinger, *Enlightened Nationalism*, 150-51.
[49] Ibid., 151.
[50] I do not maintain here that either Hardenberg or Hegel agreed with Gentz on every issue. We will return to this issue in Chapter 9, section 4.2.2.
[51] For a useful discussion, see Thomas Nipperdey, *Germany from Napoleon to Bismarck: 1800-1866*, trans. Daniel Nolan (Princeton: Princeton University Press, 1996), 247. Also see Heinrich von Treitschke, *History of Germany in the Nineteenth Century*, vol. 3, trans. Eden Paul and Cedar Paul (New York: McBride and Nast, 1917), Ch. 10.

VIII. The Initiation of a Prussian State Philosopher, 1818-1820

of the realm. This feature is articulated in some detail in the so-called "University Law," which is worth quoting in full.

> Sect. 1. The Sovereign shall make choice for each university of an extraordinary commissioner, furnished with suitable instructions and powers, residing in the place where the university is established; he may be either the actual curator, or any other person whom the government may think fit to appoint.
>
> The duty of this commissioner shall be to watch over the most rigorous observation of the laws and disciplinary regulations; to observe carefully the spirit with which the professors and tutors are guided in their public and private lectures; to endeavor, without interfering directly in the scientific courses, or in the method of instruction, to give the instruction a salutary direction, suited to the future destiny of the students, and to devote a constant attention to everything which may tend to the maintenance of morality, good order and decency among the youths.
>
> Sect. 2. The governments of the states, members of the confederation, reciprocally engage to remove from their universities and other establishments of instruction, the professors and other public teachers, against whom it may be proved, that in departing from their duty, in overstepping the bounds of their duty, in abusing their legitimate influence over the minds of youth, by the propagation of pernicious dogmas, hostile to order and public tranquility, or in sapping the foundation of existing establishments, they have shown themselves incapable of executing the important functions entrusted to them, without any obstacle whatever being allowed to impede the measure taken against them, so long as the present decree shall remain in force, and until definitive arrangements on this point be adopted.
>
> A professor or tutor thus excluded, cannot be admitted in any other state of the confederation to any other establishment of public instruction.
>
> Sect. 3. The laws long since made against secret or unauthorized associations at the universities, shall be maintained in all their force and rigor, and shall be particularly extended with so much the more severity against the well-known society formed some years ago under the name of the [*Allgemeine Burschenschaften*], as it has for its basis an idea, absolutely inadmissible, of community and continued correspondence between the different universities.
>
> The governments shall mutually engage to admit to no public employment any individuals who may continue or enter into any of those associations after the publication of the present decree.
>
> Sect. 4. No student who, by a decree of the Academic Senate confirmed by the government commissioner, or adopted on his

VIII. The Initiation of a Prussian State Philosopher, 1818-1820

application, shall be dismissed from a university, or who, in order to escape from such a sentence, shall withdraw himself, shall be received in any other university; and in general, no student shall be received at another university without a sufficient attestation of his good conduct at the university he has left.

The second decree severely limited freedom of the press, calling for rigid censorship. The third decree pertained to the coordinated investigation of agitators, to be overseen by a confederal central commission: "The object of this commission is to make careful and detailed inquiries respecting the facts, the origin and the multiplied ramifications of the secret revolutionary and demagogic associations ..."[52] In effect, such associations were now outlawed.

4.2 Decrees and "Demagogues" in Prussia

The Karlsbad Decrees were published, and so went into effect, on September 20, 1919. Shortly thereafter, a circular, issued by the Prussian king and his cabinet, was distributed to the ministers, ambassadors, and other diplomatic agents in foreign territories, instructing them to study and observe the Decrees. Although Sand likely acted on his own, the circular explained, it was clear that he was influenced by a "class" of agitators, bent upon destroying the existing law and order.

> Their object is, to dissolve society, to efface all the political differences which at present exist between the people of Germany, to substitute the real unity of that vast country for the union of its members, and to arrive, through the ruins of existing arrangements, at a new order of things. Their means are, to obtain a hold over the rising generation, by communicating the same spirit, the same sentiments, the same habits, in all the institutions for education, from the schools to the Universities. Their spirit is a spirit of independence and of pride, of subversive principles, founded on a system of abstruse metaphysics and mystic theology, for the purpose of fortifying political with religious fanaticism. Their sentiments are those of contempt for everything that exists, hatred against kings and governments, enthusiasm for the phantom which they call liberty, and love for things out of the ordinary course. Their habits are those of physical force and bodily address; and above all, a taste for secret and mysterious societies, as so many instruments that they may employ against the existing order of society.[53]

---

[52] "Appendix to Chronicle," in *The Annual Register, Or a View of the History, Politics, and Literature, for the Year 1819* (London: Baldwin, Cradock, and Joy, 1820), 158-62.
[53] Ibid., 162-69.

VIII. The Initiation of a Prussian State Philosopher, 1818-1820

Most members of the Prussian government went along with the intensified repression, with the notable exception of several liberals, such as Wilhelm von Humboldt. The latter had serious qualms about the Decrees. As a result, and in connection with the fact that he generally did not get along with Hardenberg, he was forced to resign from his ministerial post in December 1819, and this at Hardenberg's instigation.[54]

It is true that Hardenberg had sought to implement relatively liberal policies after he was appointed chancellor in 1810 to replace von Stein. Before that, he had even more "liberal" ideas about reforming Prussia, as his "Riga Memorandum" indicates.[55] However, his political sympathies were ultimately shaped by his career ambitions. "Indeed, some historians believe Hardenberg showed an alarming tendency to make concessions simply to cling to power."[56] Thus, it was not difficult for him to support and implement the Karlsbad Decrees. In fact, as noted earlier, he had by this time already ordered the arrests of several leading liberal-nationalists, such as Jahn and Arndt, the "malignant spirits."[57] This was yet another indication of Hardenberg's "tendency to make concessions," as he had previously promoted both men's careers.

As for Altenstein, he had always been, and still was, Hardenberg's lackey. As the minister of culture and education, he had already agreed to put Prussian universities under surveillance, suppress the *Burschenschaften*, and dismiss the "demagogue" professors even before the Decrees came into effect.[58] In a ministerial memorandum, addressed to his own subordinates, he noted that "the current [political] excesses" of the youth were due to "incomplete education in defective schools and in universities which have been afraid to tackle these phenomena." In April 1819, soon after Kotzebue's assassination, and with the ongoing political "agitation" in mind, he urged his subordinates to implement "severe punishment of every perversion ..., while at the same time respecting and encouraging as much as possible the pursuit of true learning." This "true learning," he advised, would lead to, or was the same as, avoiding unwelcome "excesses."[59]

---

[54] Levinger, *Enlightened Nationalism*, 145. Also see Leonard Krieger, *The German Idea of Freedom: History of a Political Tradition* (Chicago: University of Chicago Press, 1957), 222-3. For a detailed discussion of these circumstances, see Treitschke, *History of Germany in the Nineteenth Century*, 254 ff.
[55] For an English translation of the memorandum, see John Breuilly, *Austria, Prussia, and the Making of Germany, 1806-1871* (London: Routledge, 2011), 117-20.
[56] Mark Jarrett, *The Congress of Vienna and its Legacy: War and Great Power Diplomacy After Napoleon* (London: I.B. Tauris, 2014), 79. This belief is amply demonstrated throughout Simon's *The Failure of the Prussian Reform Movement, 1807-1819*.
[57] Simon, *The Failure of the Prussian Reform Movement, 1807-1819*, 207–11.
[58] Thomas Stamm-Kuhlmann, "Restoration Prussia," in ed. Philip G. Dwyer, *Modern Prussian History: 1830-1947*, 43-65 (London: Routledge, 2013), 58.
[59] Quoted in Simon, *The Failure of the Prussian Reform Movement, 1807–1819*, 136-37.

VIII. The Initiation of a Prussian State Philosopher, 1818-1820

As noted earlier, Altenstein hired Hegel to pursue an education of this kind, which the latter was more than willing to do. As we have seen in Chapter 7, Hegel instructed his students at Heidelberg University that "the wholly universal affairs of the state concern both the *training* and *education* of individuals to serve purposes of the state." Through education, "children [must] become the children of the state." Therefore, "there must be one class in the people that devotes itself to ... philosophical cognition," to "comprehend the state ... as a temple of reason," and pass this wisdom on to the youth.[60] Would it be too farfetched to assume that he told something like this to Altenstein when they met in Heidelberg in 1817?

At any rate, as Görres would soon find out, one could now be interrogated, even arrested, simply for criticizing the authorities. His recent essay, "Kotzebue, and What Murdered Him," irked the Prussian king, who was apparently still holding grudges against Görres for his previous misdeeds. In this essay, he basically interpreted Kotzebue's murder as an inevitable outcome of the general social malaise, to which both the authorities and the revolutionaries were blindly contributing. However, it was the publication of his *Germany and the Revolution*,[61] a rather lengthy book he had put together in short order, that finally urged the authorities to move against the popular icon, Görres, who was now treated as a dangerous iconoclast. His book criticized both the liberal "agitators" and the authorities. Some, including Gentz, were amused to find antirevolutionary sentiments in it, as Görres was known to be a rabid revolutionary during his younger years.[62] But the Prussian king was not amused, as he emphasized the "disrespect" Görres exhibited toward him and other sovereigns in his book. Consequently, he issued the following order to his relevant subordinates on September 30:

> [Görres,] ..., in his work committed to the press, entitled "Germany and the Revolution" ..., has not refrained from making use of the most disrespectful language towards his own and foreign sovereigns; and, under the appearance of warning the people against revolution and illegal violence, and recommending peace, has endeavored, by the most audacious censure of the measures of government, to fill the people with rage and discontent ... I hereby commission you to seize

---

[60] G. W. F. Hegel, *Lectures on Natural Rights and Political Science: The First Philosophy of Right*, trans. J. Michael Stewart and Peter C. Hodgson (Oxford University Press, 2012—first published in 1995), §158.
[61] Joseph Görres, *Germany and the Revolution*, trans. John Black (London: Longman, Hurst, Rees, Orme, and Brown, 1820).
[62] For a succinct but useful discussion of Görres' essays, see Heuvel, *A German Life in the Age of Revolution*, 242 ff.

VIII. The Initiation of a Prussian State Philosopher, 1818-1820

the whole of his papers, and to transmit them under seal to the minister [Friedrich] von Schuckmann.[63]

Görres escaped to France before the police could arrest him. Such arrests and interrogations of the opponents of the Restoration were not uncommon; nor were they limited to those who justified Sand's actions, as Görres' fate illustrates. In accordance with the Karlsbad Decrees, and under pressure from both Austria and Prussia, Fries was removed from his teaching post at Jena, as were other "demagogue" professors. Oken was given the option to either keep his periodical, *Isis*, in line with the Decrees or else resign from his teaching post. He chose the latter. They were all identified as the ringleaders of the "demagogues." Karl Follen, who was at the time a *privatdozent* at Jena, was arrested as a suspected accomplice of Sand. Due to lack of evidence, he regained his freedom, but not his teaching post. After a series of exiles, he immigrated to the United States. Jena University, in short, was gutted out, at least for the time being.

Purges of this kind would soon concern Hegel and his colleagues at Berlin University as well. De Wette, Hegel's colleague and opponent and Fries' friend and follower, sent a letter of sympathy to Sand's parents. In his letter, he explicitly disapproved of Sand's act, but exalted his "*conviction.*" Alas, the letter came to the attention of the Prussian police. Consequently, on September 30, 1819, the very same day the king issued his order against Görres, the authorities also dismissed de Wette from his post. This was done with Altenstein's endorsement, and it is said that Wittgenstein and Hardenberg played a crucial role in tipping the balance against de Wette.[64] On a related note, Karl Beck, de Wette's stepson, had to seek refuge in Switzerland for related reasons, and would subsequently move to the United States, together with Follen. While still living in Switzerland, he shared lodging with Görres, who went there after staying in France for a while. In 1822, de Wette would also join them.[65]

The Berlin faculty, though critical of his display of tenderness toward Sand's "conviction," *almost* unanimously opposed the government's dismissal of de Wette as an act against academic freedom. This opposition, which had no effect on the decision of the government, was spearheaded by Schleiermacher. Hegel, on the other hand, univocally supported the

---

[63] Görres, *Germany and the Revolution*, ix (editor's Preface).
[64] For a detailed and very informative discussion of de Wette's dismissal, see John W. Rogerson, *W. M. L. de Wette, Founder of Modern Biblical Criticism: An Intellectual Biography* (Sheffield, UK: Sheffield Academic Press, 1992), 155 ff.
[65] For an interesting account of de Wette's influence in the United States, see Siegfried B. Puknat, "De Wette in New England," in *Proceedings of the American Philosophical Society* 102, no. 4 (1958): 376-95.

VIII. The Initiation of a Prussian State Philosopher, 1818-1820

state's right to suspend de Wette.[66] After all, Altenstein had brought him to Berlin to help him implement this very right.[67] However, when the members of the faculty collected donations to support de Wette and his family, Hegel also contributed the non-negligible amount of twenty-five Thalers, one-half of Schleiermacher's fifty.[68] Schleiermacher and Hegel even had a heated altercation over the right of the government to dismiss de Wette.[69]

These events marked the beginning of a hostile relationship between Hegel and Schleiermacher, notwithstanding the fact that, despite de Wette's warnings, the latter had endorsed Hegel's appointment to Berlin University in 1816.[70] The Hegel-Schleiermacher conflict would soon have an important impact on the academic politics at Berlin University, as well as on the careers of the two belligerents. Also, to Hegel's delight, Schleiermacher would soon, if he was not already, come under police surveillance, and be reprimanded, much like Arndt, his brother-in-law.

4.3 Hegel's Non-Heroics

Many scholars claim that Hegel was both openly and secretly assisting many "demagogues," and so could not have been the servile apologist he is often said to be. Moreover, so the legend goes, Hegel had put himself in danger by engaging in such activities; to say the least, he himself had become a suspect.[71] Specifically, Gustav Asverus, Friedrich W. Carové, Leopold von Henning, and Friedrich Förster are mentioned as the beneficiaries of Hegel's daring and "clandestine" assistance during the philosopher's initial years in Berlin. The available facts, however, lend themselves to a very different story.

---

[66] See Hoffmeister's note to *Briefe II*, #361 (on page 450).
[67] Heinrich Leo, "Der Hegelianismus in Preussen," in ed. Helmut Diwald, *Zeitschrift für Religions- und Geistesgeschichte* 10, no. 1 (1958): 51-60.
[68] See Hoffmeister's note to *Briefe II*, #359, p. 447.
[69] See the letters they had exchanged with each other after the altercation to calm down the waters. *Briefe II*, #261 and #262. Also see Richard Crouter, *Friedrich Schleiermacher: Between Enlightenment and Romanticism* (Cambridge: Cambridge University Press, 2010), 86 ff.
[70] For a very interesting discussion of the conflict between Hegel and Schleiermacher, see Richard Crouter, "Hegel and Schleiermacher at Berlin: A Many-Sided Debate," in *Journal of the American Academy of Religion* 48, no. 1 (1980): 19-43.
[71] According to Butler, in the 1820s, Hegel was actively, but behind the scenes, supporting some "liberal 'demagogues' prosecuted by the Prussian police." See Butler's commentary in *Letters*, 16; also 445. For similar arguments, see Thomas M. Knox, "Hegel and Prussianism," in *Philosophy* 15, no. 57 (1940): 51-63, 56-7; Shlomo Avineri, *Hegel's Theory of the Modern State*, 130-1. The most exaggerated version of this legend is offered by D'Hondt, *Hegel in His Time*, 119-77.

VIII. The Initiation of a Prussian State Philosopher, 1818-1820

Gustav's father, Ludwig C. F. Asverus, was a lawyer in Jena. Hegel knew him while he was in Jena and had a long and amicable relationship with the Asverus family. Previously Hegel's student at Heidelberg, the son Asverus was now a student at Berlin. He was associated with the *Burschenschaft* of each university he had attended. On April 8, Gustav Asverus was detained and interrogated by the Berlin police for two weeks after one of his letters, which praised Sand's act, was intercepted. He was released after fourteen days. However, imprudently, the young Asverus kept writing similar letters in which he praised and suggested emulating Sand's action. Consequently, he was rearrested on the eve of July 14, 1819.[72] Upon his father's request, Hegel found himself obliged to help the young Asverus. Accordingly, on July 27, he wrote the following letter to Kamptz, the Berlin police chief:

> The Saxon Grand Ducal Judicial Councilor Dr. Asverus in Jena, an acquaintance of many years, has sent me the enclosed humble petition, with instructions that it be handed over to the appropriate bureau of the Royal Police. I believe these instructions to be best fulfilled by submitting it herewith to the Royal High Ministry of Police. To the humble request contained in this petition I believe myself permitted to add, for most gracious consideration, my own testimony that I came to know the student Asverus during his one-year stay at the University of Heidelberg and his almost equally long stay here in Berlin. I have come to know him to be a young man of upright character, in no way afflicted by introverted self-conceit and fanaticism but, on the contrary, open and modest, having increasingly turned away from the fomentation currently on the rise among a portion of the young. He has now shown himself to me at the local university [in Berlin] to be a student who has made [the] study of the sciences the earnest motive of his endeavor. It is also known to me in this regard that he has disassociated himself from the student association known as the *Burschenschaft,* and that during his stay here he has taken no part in this association.[73]

Hegel's letter proved ineffectual. In May 1820, he posted 500 Imperial Thalers as bail for Asverus. The next month, Asverus was released, though not cleared of the charges of being a "demagogue." He would be pardoned by the Prussian king six years later. Hegel's intervention on Asverus' behalf was simply an attempt to help the son of an old friend, who, Hegel mistakenly thought at the time, was no longer associated with the local

---

[72] See Hoffmeister's notes to *Briefe II,* #358 (432 *ff*).
[73] *Letters,* 449 (*Briefe II,* #358).

VIII. The Initiation of a Prussian State Philosopher, 1818-1820

Burschenschaft. Moreover, he himself did not become a suspect, or come under police surveillance, because of his association with Asverus.[74]

When Hegel came to Berlin from Heidelberg, he brought Carové with him, hoping that this, at the time very rare, Hegelian would serve as his teaching assistant. As was the case with many students at the time, Carové was also linked to the *Burschenschaft* in Heidelberg, though he seems to have had already abandoned his activism by the time he came to Berlin. However, his pamphlet on the murder of Kotzebue alerted the authorities.[75] His intention, so it seems, was to provide a Hegelian explanation for Kotzebue's assassination. Carové thus attacked the "Jacobin" notions of freedom and equality, but also gave Sand's action a dialectical justification, treating it as an irrational passion that cunningly served the interest and goal of the higher rational spirit. Dialectically put, Sand's deed demonstrated that the national spirit was not entirely corrupt, since it reflected the general sentiment against the corrupt Kotzebue. The same deed, as well as "the excuses and defenses offered for it," demonstrated the recent corruption of the same spirit. Thus, the deed should be understood as the unity of opposites. Carové was silly enough to send Altenstein a copy of his equally silly dialectical-Hegelian exercise in June 1819. Since Altenstein, despite admiring Hegel's philosophy, was not schooled in this sort of logic, he suspected that Carové's pamphlet might be a defense of Sand's deed, though he could not quite tell.

Carové's case was thus brought to Kamptz's attention. The police chief reported on December 24 that "there are no traces anywhere" of him belonging to a political association, demanding constitutional change, or having any revolutionary tendencies. Carové did not support Sand's act, he further concluded, though his obscure writing might lead one to conclude otherwise. "But," added the police chief, "this is not a fault of his convictions and principles." Rather, it stems from "the wretched mysticism of the new philosophy, especially the Hegelian one, to which Carové has dedicated himself." However, Wittgenstein would have nothing of this. Five days later, he issued his own report, claiming that Carové was indeed a subversive, who defended Sand's actions, and so should not be allowed to teach at the university. He received his wisdom from one Moritz Pauli, who not only attacked the likes of Carové but also noted that his "interpretation" of Sand's deed was "undoubtedly inspired by Hegel."[76]

---

[74] *Pace* Pinkard, *Hegel: A Biography*, 437-8. David DeGrood presents Hegel as a victim of Kamptz and others, to the extent that "Hegel seriously considered emigration to France." David H. DeGrood, *Dialectics and Revolution*, vol. 2, (Amsterdam: B. R. Grüner Publishing Co., 1979), 187.
[75] Friedrich W. Carové, *Ueber die Ermordung Kotzebue's* (Eisenach: Bärecke, 1819).
[76] *Briefe II*, Hoffmeister's note to #377, p. 460 ff.

VIII. The Initiation of a Prussian State Philosopher, 1818-1820

Having received these reports, Altenstein now thought that Carové might be innocent but decided to adopt a cautious settlement of his case. Thus, he told the accused to pursue his academic career in Breslau, rather than Berlin. Subsequently, further investigation of his case sufficed to convince Hardenberg, Altenstein, and other authorities that Carové could well be a "demagogue." In May 1820, he was permanently banned from obtaining an academic position but was not charged with the "crime" of being a "demagogue," due to lack of concrete evidence. As for Hegel, it is not true, or there is no evidence to prove, that his association with Carové "compromised him in the eyes of the police."[77] Altenstein knew better, and even Wittgenstein never demanded to investigate, not to mention fire, Hegel himself. Kamptz, on the other hand, simply blamed him for teaching "wretched mysticism," and not dangerous convictions.

As Hegel would recall two years later, in July 1819, Henning "was under arrest for ten weeks [other accounts say seven weeks] on suspicion of demagogy, with a gendarme guarding him—day and night in prison." Henning, a war veteran of aristocratic origins, was arrested simply on the strength of a vaguely-worded letter sent to him by his mother-in-law. He was released in September, which certainly depended on the conviction of the authorities that he was not a "demagogue." On November 13, Hegel asked Henning to join him at a gathering of the Lawless Society (*Gesetzlose Gesellschaft*), so named due to its lack of house rules. Highly likely, he wanted to introduce Henning to the authorities, with the aim of urging their approval of him as Hegel's assistant. After all, even Kamptz was a member of the Society.[78]

Soon thereafter, Christoph Ludwig Schultz, the government representative at the university and Hegel's friend, observed Henning's skills in reciting Hegel's philosophy and reported his favorable impression of him. Consequently, Altenstein informed Hardenberg that, according to Schultz's and Hegel's judgments, Henning was "not only harmless but also highly desirable." Such an assessment and confirmation were both required by the Karlsbad Decrees. Hardenberg approved Henning's appointment, and Altenstein informed Hegel on August 2, 1820, that he could now put him to work under close supervision, and that he should report back on his "effectiveness every six months."[79] By "effectiveness" was meant, primarily, his political convictions. In short, the Henning affair indicates that Hegel was a trusted insider, and not either a secret supporter of the "demagogues"

---

[77] *Pace* David MacGregor, *Hegel and Marx: After the Fall of Communism* (Cardiff: University of Wales Press, 2014), 101.
[78] See Hoffmeister's note to *Briefe II*, #360, p. 448.
[79] See the editor's notes in G. W. F. Hegel, *Berliner Schriften, 1818-1831*, ed. Johannes Hoffmeister (Hamburg: Felix Meiner, 1956), 598-99.

VIII. The Initiation of a Prussian State Philosopher, 1818-1820

or under police surveillance for his association with them.

Many scholars also mention Förster's relationship to Hegel to establish the latter's own "demagogic" credentials, as it were. Due to his political views, Förster was banned from state service in September 1819. At the time, he was a faculty member at the Royal Artillery and Engineering School. During this period, Hegel had nothing to do with Förster, though the latter was already beginning to follow Hegel's teaching. There is also no evidence to suggest that he had anything to do with Förster's reinstatement in 1823.

Be that as it may, "Förster's opposition to the existing regime ... was considerably mitigated when Altenstein and [Johannes] Schulze [Hegel's close friend and the minister's official representative at the university] succeeded in appointing him to a prestigious editorial position on the staff of the official Prussian state newspaper in 1823." Soon thereafter, he would be known as "the court demagogue." He earned this appellation "because of his fervent, often belligerent, defense of the Prussian bureaucratic monarchy as the actualization of the ethical community," obviously inspired by Hegel.[80] In other words, contrary to what some of Hegel's liberalizers claim, he did not earn it because he was a radical, anti-regime "demagogue," who was strangely employed by the court. At any rate, Förster entered Hegel's orbit as a staunch defender of the Prussian state, and not as a "demagogue," as we will see in the ensuing chapters.

Förster is responsible for the perpetuation of a related story about Hegel. According to what he publicized in 1861, he and others went to Dresden with Hegel in July 1820. While there, Hegel allegedly ordered expensive champagne for everyone at a local inn, filled his glass with it, and then announced, "this glass is for July 14, 1789—the storming of the Bastille."[81] Alas, there is a minor problem with this often-repeated story: it never happened. Hegel's own testimony indicates that he was in Dresden for "two weeks," and *for the first time*, in the "autumn" of 1820.[82] Hegel's testimony is corroborated by an entry found in Karl Förster's (Friedrich's brother) diary, which indicates that Hegel "arrived here [in Dresden] on August 26 [1820]." The next day, as Hegel reminded his hosts, it was his birthday; they had some "foaming champagne" to honor the guest's life, not the French Revolution.[83] Hegel left on September 11, as Karl's next entry indicates.[84] Friedrich Förster likely heard the 1820 visit to Dresden from his

---

[80] John E. Toews, *Hegelianism: The Path Toward Dialectical Humanism, 1805-1841* (London: Cambridge University Press, 1980), 120.
[81] *Berichten*, #323.
[82] *Letters*, 468 (*Briefe II*, #389).
[83] *Berichten*, #326.
[84] Ibid., #327.

VIII. The Initiation of a Prussian State Philosopher, 1818-1820

brother, and witnessed the toast-story in 1826,[85] and combined them into one story four decades later.

Hegel's own testimony clarifies that he had no patience with the "demagogues." By the end of October 1819, he came to resent their activities in Berlin, and elsewhere, more intensely than ever before. On October 30, he wrote a letter to convey this sentiment to Creuzer, his friend and former colleague at Heidelberg University. The letter was written at a time when Hegel was involved in the Asverus affair and exactly a month after de Wette's dismissal. After exalting the endowments of his wealthy university, Hegel noted that, "of course, the political agitation of the student association *[Burschenschaft]* and of de Wette's Friesianism have not won favor for the university [in the eyes of the rulers]," adding that "the greater number of those arrested were [previously] in Heidelberg" when "Martin and Fries were there." These "seeds of agitation" were sown "before" his time at Heidelberg, Hegel clarified, implying that the "demagogic" students were inspired by these false philosophers, not himself. He also reported the news of the "political and censorship measures" being implemented all over the "Confederation," anticipating many more arrests to come. All this trouble affected his "spirits" negatively, complained Hegel, adding that the last thirty years of his life has been spent in such "ever-unrestful times of hope and fear," which now seem to be "getting even worse."[86]

It is rather obvious that Hegel had mainly blamed the chief "agitators," such as de Wette, Fires, and Martin, for the ongoing troubles, and not so much their young followers, who could be reeducated. He feared because he thought, not unreasonably, that *anyone* could easily become a suspect under the current circumstances. As he would explain to a friend about a year or so later, "once one has been branded in a given place—no matter where and with no matter what label such as 'demagogy' or, ultimately, 'atheism'—one is a marked man everywhere in the German Empire [i.e., Confederation] and regions of the Holy Alliance."[87] However, Hegel was never a suspect precisely because he was not a "demagogue"—to the contrary.

Rather than commemorating the Bastille day in Dresden with the "demagogues," Hegel was preparing his *Philosophy of Right* for publication during the summer of 1820. As his June 9, 1820, letter to "Nicolai's Publishing House" indicates," the publication of his book was delayed, since it first had to go through "the censor,"[88] just like any other

---

[85] We will discuss the 1826 toast in Chapter 12.
[86] *Letters*, 449-51 (*Briefe II*, #359).
[87] Ibid., 467 (#389).
[88] Ibid., 451 (#368a).

VIII. The Initiation of a Prussian State Philosopher, 1818-1820

book intended for publication. He thus had to satisfy the censor's Karlsbadian gaze.

However, Hegel had nothing to worry about in this regard, as we will see in the next chapter. Indeed, circa June 21, he found out that he was promoted by Altenstein "to membership on the Royal Academic Board of Examiners," which was meant to boost both his status and income, as previously promised. On that day, he expressed his "most respectful thanks for the confidence shown" in him by the minister, as well as for "the gracious words which ... [the minister] deigned to add regarding ... [his] endeavors thus far by way of discharging ... [his] official teaching duties."[89] Hegel, as far he and the minster were concerned, was doing just fine at a time when the "demagogues" were either being arrested or fired.

---

[89] Ibid., 389 (#371).

Chapter Nine

IX. THE PHILOSOPHY OF RIGHT

1. The Infamous Preface

1.1 Exposing and Denouncing the "Demagogues"

Hegel completed writing the *Philosophy of Right* on June 25, 1820.[1] It was printed and circulated in October 1820. In the interest of brevity, I will mostly focus on Hegel's Preface and conception of the state in this chapter. This limited reading will prove to be more than enough to prove that he was a servile apologist, who espoused illiberal and antidemocratic ideas, consistent with the ideology of the Restoration authorities. We will also observe that he was *still* not much of a thinker from 1820 to 1825[2] and that he *still* attempted to justify his claims mainly by attacking others. This strategy frequently involved declaring them and their ideas dangerous to law and order.

Hegel's Preface is saturated with "true philosophy" of this slanderous kind. Thus, after clearing his throat in its first few pages, as it were, Hegel comes out swinging in what appears to be a vicious attack against certain victims of the Karlsbad Decrees. These "writers," he says at first, are responsible for the "shameful decay" of philosophy, especially since they have made "way for the arbitrary pronouncements of the heart, of fantasy, and of accidental intuition."[3] Furthermore, these "writers" think that the

---

[1] All citations from the Preface (without §) refer to the page numbers found in the widely-used G. W. F. Hegel, *Elements of the Philosophy of Right*, ed. Allen W. Wood, trans. H. B. Nisbet (Cambridge: Cambridge University Press, 1991). However, throughout this work, I use my own translation of G. W. F. Hegel, *Grundlinien der Philosophie des Rechts oder Naturrecht und Staatswissenschaft im Grundrisse*, ed. Eduard Gans (Berlin: Duncker und Humblot, 1833). In addition to the Nisbet translation, I have consulted, and borrowed from, the following translations: G. W. F. Hegel, *Philosophy of Right*, trans. S. W. Dyde (London: George Bell and Sons, 1896); G. W. F. Hegel, *Philosophy of Right*, trans. T. M. Knox (Oxford: Oxford University Press, 1952); G. W. F. Hegel, *The Philosophy of Right*, trans. Alan White (Newburyport: Focus Publishing, 2002).
[2] The *Philosophy of Right* we are about to examine contains the lecture notes of his disciples, Heinrich Gustav Hotho and Eduard Gans, which were taken during this five-year period.
[3] Hegel, *Philosophy of Right*, 10.

IX. The Philosophy of Right

world simply lacked "zealous disseminators of truths," such as themselves, to preach correct notions of "right, ethics, and the state." What is needed, says Hegel, is a "scientific" (i.e., Hegelian) comprehension of such eternal "truths,"[4] which instruct us to regulate our lives in accordance with "the substantial right [law], namely the commands of the ethical order and of the state."[5]

At this point, names are named: "Herr [Jakob] Fries" is "a ringleader of these superficial philosophers." "In fact," following Kant, "this self-styled philosophy has expressly stated the truth itself cannot be known, and that truth simply consists of what emerges from each person's heart, emotion, and enthusiasm about ethical institutions, especially the state, the government, and the constitution." This "false" teaching has, alas, corrupted "the young." What is worse, Fries did not even feel any shame to express, at the "notorious pubic festival [the Wartburg Festival],"

> the following idea in a speech on the subject of the state and the constitution: "In a people ruled by a genuine communal spirit, the life pertaining to the regulation of public affairs would emerge from below, from the people itself; living associations, steadfastly united by the sacred bond of friendship, would be dedicated to every single project of popular education and popular service"; and so on.[6]

Clearly, then, Hegel does not simply condemn Fries' "unscientific" subjectivism in his Preface. He also condemns his vision of a democratic, self-governing society, without at all mentioning his anti-Semitism.[7] This "superficial philosophy" of "feeling," he goes on to preach, "proves to be based on the utmost selfishness of empty arrogance" when it "refers to the 'people'." Apparently, its reference to the "people" proves this "superficial" philosophy's "hatred of law."[8]

Hegel now proceeds to egg the authorities on to punish the likes of Fries, or else to justify their punishment. This "arbitrary sophistry," he says,

---

[4] Ibid, 11.
[5] Ibid, 12.
[6] Ibid, 13-15.
[7] *Pace* Avineri, who, to be only slightly unfair, reduces Hegel's critique of Fries to a condemnation of the latter's and his followers' "violent anti-Semitic" views. Shlomo Avineri, *Hegel's Theory of the Modern State* (Cambridge: Cambridge University Press, 1972), 119-20. Others also repeat this line of reasoning, giving us the impression that the progressive Hegel attacked Fries for his anti-Semitism, along with his "false" philosophy. For instance, see Jacques D'Hondt, *Hegel In His Time*, trans. John Burbidge (Peterborough, Ontario: Broadview Press, 1988), 95-97; Allen W. Wood, *Hegel's Ethical Thought* (Cambridge: Cambridge University Press, 1990), 186 ff.; Paul Franco, *Hegel's Philosophy of Freedom* (New Haven, CT: Yale University Press, 1999), 122.
[8] Hegel, *Philosophy of Right*, 17.

warrants the "impatience" of the "right-minded men" toward its ideas about "the nature of the state," toward what it pretends to be "a philosophical science of the state." For some time now, governments have simply trusted their philosophers; or else, they remained indifferent to their activities. However, "their confidence has often been ill repaid" by the likes of Fries, who instigate disorder and lawlessness. One should not be fooled into thinking, warns Hegel, that their "superficial philosophy is ... compatible ... with public peace and order."[9]

According to Hegel, the superficial philosopher *par excellence*, the proof of this criminality lies in the fact that the likes of Fries "fear police intervention." Indeed, they should be fearful, for they teach "the [subjectivist] principles of the Sophists," which necessarily "lead to the destruction of inner ethical life and the good conscience, of love and right among private persons, as well as the destruction of public order and the laws of the state." "The state," insists he, should not "give free rein" to any of this or "permit" their "defiance, as if such defiance were entirely appropriate." Rather, the state should subject these "false" philosophers of subjective "conviction" to "police intervention."[10] Along with Fries, de Wette is also one of Hegel's targets here, since he praised Sand's "conviction."

Here, Hegel follows in the footsteps of the reactionary court bishop Rulemann Friedrich Eylert. While he was still writing his book, Eylert concluded that de Wette's view amounted to the claim that "murder is no longer a sin if he who commits it intends well by it." Eylert then went on to argue that, unless the likes of de Wette are stopped, all "*respect for authority and legal power will be undermined*," and all individuals will do as they wish in accordance with their "conviction."[11] The bishop also denounced all opposition to the government and called for its swift and decisive repression, lest "God's blessing would be withheld" from all.[12]

1.2 The Existing State (the Actual) is Rational

In the remaining few pages of the Preface, Hegel advances and defends one of his most well-known dictums: "What is rational is actual, and what is actual is rational."[13] His liberalizers have been claiming ever since his death

---

[9] Ibid., 17-19.
[10] Ibid.
[11] Both de Wette and Eylert are quoted in Matthew Bernard Levinger, *Enlightened Nationalism: The Transformation of Prussian Political Culture, 1806-1846* (Oxford: Oxford University Press, 2000), 142.
[12] Quoted in John W. Rogerson, *W. M. L. de Wette, Founder of Modern Biblical Criticism: An Intellectual Biography* (Sheffield, UK: Sheffield Academic Press, 1992), 157.
[13] Hegel, *Philosophy of Right*, 20.

IX. The Philosophy of Right

that this double dictum ("*doppelsatz*") has "been famously misunderstood" as a justification of the existing state.[14] Let me be abundantly clear: *there is no misunderstanding at all.*

Before brandishing the so-called "*doppelsatz*," Hegel tries to clarify the proper relationship of "philosophy to actuality." As it turns out, philosophy is simply "the grasping of the present and the actual." Negatively put, true philosophy is allegedly not involved in establishing a world "beyond" the existing one, "God knows where." Accordingly, his "treatise," informs us Hegel with unusual clarity, "in so far as it contains the science of the state [*Staatswissenschaft*], is ... nothing other than the attempt to conceive and present the [existing] state as inherently [*in sich*] rational."[15] It is thus abundantly clear (is it not?) that Hegel thinks the existing state is the "actual" mentioned in the *doppelsatz*.

Hegel will explain later that "modern" (read German) states may have some imperfections, though they are still "inherently" rational. The other side of this coin, and this is the main point of his "science of the state," is that the will of the state must be obeyed unconditionally, regardless of its external imperfections. Only in this way can individuals act rationally and claim to be truly free. This message is built into his claim that we must "dance here." By this, he means precisely that the rationality of the "here" (the "rose" or "Rhodes") must be recognized, accepted, and obeyed; we must reconcile ourselves to it. His following remark is also consistent with this accommodationist thought:

> To recognize reason as the rose in the cross of the present, and thereby to rejoice in [the present]—this rational insight is the reconciliation with actuality, which philosophy grants to those in whom the inner call has arisen to comprehend the substantial, and to maintain their subjective freedom [in it], thereby standing with their subjective

---

[14] Eduard Gans, Preface, xxx (1833); Knox, "Hegel and Prussianism," 55; Walter A. Kaufmann, "The Hegel Myth and Its Method," in *Hegel's Political Philosophy*, ed. Walter A. Kaufmann, 137-71 (New York: Atherton Press, 1970), 152; Avineri, *Hegel's Theory of the Modern State*, 123; Wood, "Editor's Introduction," vii, also 389-90, n. 22; Franco, *Hegel's Philosophy of Freedom*, 123. M. W. Jackson, "Hegel, the Real, and the Rational," in *The Hegel Myths and Legends*, ed. Jon Stewart, 19-25 (Evanston: Northwestern University Press, 1996); Yirmiahu Yovel, "Hegel's Dictum that the Rational is Actual and the Actual is Rational: Its Ontological Content and Its Function in Discourse," in *The Hegel Myths and Legends*, ed. Jon Stewart, 26-41 (Evanston: Northwestern University Press, 1996); Emil L. Fackenheim, "On the Actuality of the Rational and the Rationality of the Actual," in *The Hegel Myths and Legends*, ed. Jon Stewart, 42-49 (Evanston: Northwestern University Press, 1996). This list is by no means exhaustive of the existing attempts that try to reveal the real secret of Hegel's maxim.

[15] Hegel, *Philosophy of Right*, 20-21.

IX. The Philosophy of Right

[individual] freedom in what is in and for itself [i.e., the existing state], and not in something particular and contingent.[16]

With an appeal to Luther's and Francis Bacon's authority, Hegel clarifies (by paraphrasing Bacon) that "true philosophy leads to God," as it does, in the same way, to "the state." In other words, "reason," or true philosophy, "is not satisfied ... with that cold despair which claims that things in this temporal world are bad or at best mediocre." Rather, it is content with knowing that "nothing better can be had here," and that one should "make peace with actuality; [true] knowledge brings about a warmer peace with it."[17] The *doppelsatz*, it turns out, comes with this servile prescription (some call it "political quietism"). It comes with a motto as well: "*Hic* Rhodus, *hic* saltus."[18]

It is in the light of this quietism that we must also understand Hegel's other celebrated passage:

> A shape of life has already grown old when philosophy paints its grey in grey. It [i.e., this shape of life] cannot be rejuvenated by grey in grey [i.e., by philosophical thought]; it can only be recognized [or understood]. The Owl of Minerva begins its flight only with the falling of the dusk.[19]

2. Morality, Evil, and Revolutionary Disorder

One often gets lost in Hegel's "speculative" or "logical" jargon, and thus loses sight of the concrete political aims of his book. One of its concrete aims is to warn his readers, and the authorities, against the dangerous ideas of the individualist philosophers, who base their moral and political ideas on individual subjectivity. Frequently, he brings up the French Revolution, including the Reign of Terror, to scare people away from such ideas and philosophers. As we have seen, this scare-tactic permeates the Preface.

Thus, one quickly encounters the following reference to the French Revolution in his Introduction as well: the "arbitrary will," which is identical with the unrestricted will of the individual, typically manifests itself "in the active fanaticism of political and of religious life ... The Reign of Terror in the French Revolution" is an example of this "fanaticism." Since Hegel cannot explain how this deadly event *necessarily* issued from the "arbitrary will," he modifies it to mean the belief in the equality of the

---

[16] Ibid., 22.
[17] Ibid., 22-23.
[18] Ibid., 21.
[19] Ibid., 23.

IX. The Philosophy of Right

people and the rulers. This was a principle of the Revolution initially, as "all distinctions of talent and authority were expected to be suspended," and this is "the reason why, during the Revolution, the people destroyed the institutions they themselves had created [in 1789], since all institutions are contrary to the abstract self-consciousness of equality."[20]

Here, with this half-baked explanation of the Terror, Hegel basically agrees with the ideology of the Restoration authorities: popular sovereignty, declared Gentz, Metternich's reactionary secretary, "always and everywhere must lead to the complete destruction of all power, and hence to pure *anarchy.*"[21]

Once again, Hegel divines that "arbitrary will" is "the most common notion people have of freedom." It amounts to the view that freedom is "the ability to do as one pleases." When one hears people say this, he claims thoughtlessly, one immediately knows that such a notion is the product of ignorance. In this regard, Kant is partially and Fries fully ignorant: "In every philosophy of reflection, such as that of Kant, especially Kant's [philosophy] deprived of all its depth by Fries, freedom is nothing more than this formal self-activity" of the arbitrary will. Truly free will, adds the great philosopher of freedom, is "when I will what is rational," that is, when "I act not as a particular individual but in accordance with the concepts of ethics in general ... The rational [and ethical] is the high road where everyone travels, where no one is conspicuous."[22]

The illiberal, anti-individualistic message of Hegel's assertions is abundantly clear, as is the fact that these assertions contain little philosophical thought. All this is compounded by the fact that he thoughtlessly associates Kant's practical philosophy with dangerous, revolutionary ideas. As noted at the end of Chapter 3, Hegel's approach to the Revolution was informed by the views of the German conservatives, including their attempt to link both Rousseau's and Kant's doctrines to the destructive nature of the Revolution.[23] However, the "great" philosopher was not in the habit of acknowledging his sources.

Hegel goes on to reproach Kant once again. According to him, "the essential element in both the Kantian and the generally accepted definition of right is 'the limitation of my freedom or arbitrary will, so that it may coexist with the arbitrary will of everyone else in accordance with a universal law [i.e., the categorical imperative].'" The gist of his uninformed

---

[20] Ibid., §5.
[21] Quoted in Levinger, *Enlightened Nationalism,* 150-51.
[22] Hegel, *Philosophy of Right,* §15, R, A.
[23] For an excellent discussion of Kant's political views, especially within the context of the French Revolution, see Reidar Maliks, *Kant's Politics in Context* (Oxford: Oxford University Press, 2014).

IX. The Philosophy of Right

complaint becomes clearer when he identifies Kant's "definition of right [or will]" with Rousseau's definition of the general will, which Hegel misconstrues also. According to Rousseau, he says, "the substantial basis [of the rational will] ... is supposed to be the will of the particular individual."[24]

Hegel readily dismisses these allegedly subjectivist perspectives: the will of "the *particular* individual" cannot be truly rational, which further means that it cannot be truly free. Rather than explaining why this is so, he resorts to one of his already-familiar tactics, and so declares Rousseau's doctrine revolutionary, and so dangerous. It had "produced in [people's] heads and in actuality a phenomenon whose frightfulness has a parallel only with the shallowness of the thoughts on which they are based."[25] In the final analysis, in the *Philosophy of Right,* Hegel is more concerned with denouncing the allegedly subjectivist ideas of Rousseau, Kant, Fries than engaging with them philosophically.[26]

In the section titled "Morality," Hegel disparages Kant's moral doctrine on similar grounds. In this context, Hegel owns what he believes to be Kant's meritorious claim that "duty ... should be done for the sake of duty." The "merit" of "Kant's practical philosophy," says he, lies in the emphasis he puts on "this significance of duty." When duty is done for its sake, I am genuinely "with myself and free."[27] This misreading of Kant has a bearing on how Hegel converts the freedom implied in Kant's notion of acting *from* duty to the Hegelian sense of freedom as the duty to simply obey the law given by the state.

Moreover, adds Hegel, the "moral self-consciousness" of the Kantian individual "is abstract universality, whose determination is identity without content." By this, he (sometimes) means to say that Kant's moral point of view lacks any "criterion" to determine whether a given "content is a duty."[28] It is widely acknowledged by scholars, even those sympathetic to him, that Hegel's *emptiness charge* is problematic at best.[29] What is seldom acknowledged is that he borrowed (some would say "plagiarized") this charge from August W. Rehberg, a well-known conservative critic of Kant and the French Revolution.[30] Even worse than Hegel's insipid emptiness

---

[24] Hegel, *Philosophy of Right,* §29, R.
[25] Ibid.
[26] For a good discussion, somewhat gentler than mine, see Patrick Riley, *Will and Political Legitimacy: A Critical Exposition of Social Contract Theory in Hobbes, Locke, Rousseau, Kant, and Hegel* (Cambridge: Harvard University Press, 1982), Ch. 6.
[27] Hegel, *Philosophy of Right,* §133, A.
[28] Ibid., §135R.
[29] For a detailed analysis of Hegel's criticism of Kant, see Wood, *Hegel's Ethical Thought,* 154-73. In my view, at times against himself, Wood proves that Hegel did not understand even the most basic aspects of Kant's philosophy.
[30] For a discussion of Rehberg's own emptiness charge, see Maliks, *Kant's Politics in Context,* 57-59. Also see Frederick C. Beiser, *Enlightenment, Revolution, and*

IX. The Philosophy of Right

charge are his various attempts to find contradictions in what Kant takes to be noncontradictory, which are always embarrassingly silly.[31]

Willy-nilly, Hegel once again reaches the familiar point of declaring all shapes of subjective consciousness "evil" and dangerous. Although Kant's moral philosophy is also thrown into the mix once more, his primary targets now are the more recent "false" philosophers, Fries being one of them. According to Hegel, the latter defends the view that "the ethical nature of any action" is determined by one's "*conviction.*" This doctrine is also said to be devoid of content, which now readily means being devoid of Hegelian ethics. The following conclusion thus follows effortlessly: "Under these circumstances, any semblance of ethical objectivity has completely disappeared," since this false philosophy equates "the ethical with the distinctive outlook of the individual and his particular conviction."[32] De Wette is also one of his targets, as the following comment proves: "If, for example, an evil man [Kotzebue] is murdered, the positive side of the action may be presented [by such false philosophers] as the intention to resist evil or to diminish it."[33]

Hegel's next and final target is Friedrich Schlegel, who allegedly comprehends "subjectivity" in its "supreme form," and rests this

---

Romanticism: The Genesis of Modern German Political Thought, 1790-1800 (Cambridge: Harvard University Press, 1992), 307-08. Maliks mentions Hegel's link to Rehberg in this context.

[31] For instance, in the *Phenomenology*, which he generously references in the *Philosophy of Right*, Hegel attempts to take to task Kant's justification of private property. After making some confusing claims, he abruptly shifts his focus and attempts to show, with "logical" arguments, that the concept of property, "if resolved into its moments," is "an all-round contradiction." The first alleged contradiction is the following: "the single thing that is my property is held as such to be something universal, solidly established, and permanent; but this contradicts its nature, which consists in its being used and in *vanishing*." To wit, according to Hegel's "logic," the *solid* recognition of a loaf of bread by others as my property is contradicted by the fact that it exists for the sake of my consumption, and so exists as a *perishable*, non-solid (or non-absolute) thing. The second "contradiction" is that, as private property, a thing "is held to be [exclusively] *mine*, something which everyone else acknowledges, and lets alone. The fact, however, that I am acknowledged implies rather my equality, my identity, with everyone [as persons capable of property rights], and that is the opposite of exclusiveness." According to this logic, and for example, everyone's recognition of a loaf of bread as exclusively mine is contradicted by the fact that I am recognized by everyone as a person, which includes me within the community of persons. The third alleged "contradiction" runs as follows: the fact that "*I*," as an individual, "possess" a thing as *my* property "contradicts" its universality as a thing as such (i.e., its "thinghood" or *thingness*). Thus, reasons Mr. Speculative Logic, "property ... contains within it these two opposed, self-contradictory moments of individuality [mine] and universality [thingness]." Consequently, without any sense of embarrassment, he announces that property is "an all-round contradiction." Hegel, *Phenomenology*, §431.
[32] Hegel, *Philosophy of Right*, §140R.
[33] Ibid., §140A.

IX. The Philosophy of Right

comprehension on a specific sense of "'irony'." Hegel does not clearly express what Schlegel means by this term (likely because he did not understand it himself). His main aim is to argue that Schlegel's "subjectivity" is the basis of supreme evil, of the capacity to reject ethical objectivity altogether. This subjectivity is certainly aware of "the objective side of ethics." Without the necessary (Hegelian) preconditions for the attainment of ethical objectivity, that is, "without that self-forgetfulness [!]" and "self-renunciation [!]" of its subjectivity, Schlegel's subject winds up denouncing ethical objectivity, as it plunges into the worst kind of arbitrary will. Consequently, the issues of right and duty are determined in any way one wishes. This shape of subjectivity is "evil ... of a wholly universal kind)."[34]

3. Ethical, Patriotic Individual

Everything Hegel says in what follows must be understood through the prism of the following comment: "individuals are accidental" in relation to "the ethical powers that govern ... [their] lives." In other words,

> whether the individual exists or not is of no concern to the objective ethical order, which alone abides and is the power that governs their lives. Ethical order is therefore represented to nations [by Hegel, who speaks for the world spirit] as eternal justice, or as gods that are in and for themselves, and in relation to which the vain pursuits of individuals are merely a play of the waves.[35]

Thus, and for the nth time, the so-called "liberal" Hegel defines the ethical will (true freedom) of the individual as obedience to "laws and institutions" of the state.[36] Such an individual "is guided in its behavior" by the "absolute authority and power" of "the ethical substance [i.e., the state] and its laws."[37] These "powers and authority" of the state "are not something alien to the subject." "On the contrary, the [Hegelian-ethical] subject bears witness to them as to its own essence," in such a way that his/her essence becomes "identical with the powers and authority [or laws] of the state." Whereas, admits Hegel, it is true that self-consciousness may recognize this identity of ethical consciousness and the law through critical reflection, "the adequate cognition of this identity belongs to the thinking concept [*dem denkenden Begriffe*]."[38] Despite the cryptic meaning of

---

[34] Ibid., §140R.
[35] Ibid., §145, A.
[36] Ibid., §144, A.
[37] Ibid., §146, R.
[38] Ibid., §147, R.

IX. The Philosophy of Right

denkenden Begriffe, he is abundantly clear on the practical implications of his assertions: the laws and duties, which are given solely by the state, must be regarded as unquestionably "binding on the will of the individual."[39] By obeying the state unconditionally, that is, "in duty," "the individual finds his [substantial] freedom."[40] If the point is not clear enough yet, the following should do the trick: "All a man must do ... in an ethical community" is to simply obey what is "prescribed, expressly stated, and known to him within his situation,"[41] as if these were his "custom" ("habit") or "second nature."[42]

It turns out, this habitual obedience is also called the "ethical" or "political disposition" of individuals. In fact, claims the famous professor of Berlin, "patriotism" is simply this habitual obedience. "Political disposition" Hegel claims, means "patriotism in general," and this refers to "the will that has become habitual." "This disposition is in general one of trust," which stems from

> the consciousness that my substantial and particular interest is preserved and contained in the interest and end of another (in this case, the state), and in the latter's relation to me as an individual. In this way, this other is immediately not an other for me ... I am free in this consciousness.[43]

The "truth" about my patriotism, insists Hegel without any sense of embarrassment, does not issue from "subjective certainty," which is "merely an opinion."[44] Thus, and in keeping with what he told us earlier,[45] Hegel conceives patriotic or political disposition as an unreflective, habitual orientation toward the state, characterized by a "basic feeling of order that everyone has" as their "second nature."[46]

But our professor of ethics knows that "education [*Pädagogik*]" is also necessary for "making human beings ethical." With this sort of education, "the internal struggle of the subject is broken; to this extent [or in this sense], habit is part of ethics."[47] This was the sort of education Hegel was hired to provide. It is strange that his recent admirers have compared his approach to education to that of Wilhelm von Humboldt.

---

[39] Ibid., §148, R.
[40] Ibid., §149.
[41] Ibid., §150R.
[42] Ibid., §151, A.
[43] Ibid., §268R.
[44] Ibid.
[45] Ibid., §150, R.
[46] Ibid., §268, A.
[47] Ibid., §151A.

IX. The Philosophy of Right

It must have been known to his contemporary audience that Hegel's insipid definition of patriotism was an attempt to discredit Fries' understanding of the same. In his speech at the Wartburg Festival, Fries said the following:

> But if the spirit of a people were to attain to a genuinely common spirit, then justice, chastity, and self-sacrificing patriotism would rule in this people; then life in this people would come from beneath, from the people, in every business of public concern ... And in this people living societies would dedicate themselves to every individual work of popular education and service of the people, unbreakably united through the holy chain of friendship.[48]

With this in mind, we also realize that Hegel's scheme of patriotism is an anti-republican attempt to prevent "the people" from participating in the affairs of the "rational" state.

4. The Rational State

4.1 The State As "the March of God in the World"

The "rational" state, Hegel now says, should not be "confused with civil society." This "confusion" is imagined only by Hegel (who has ever confused civil society with the state?). What he means to say is that it is irrational to conceive the state essentially as an instrument to "secure and protect property and personal freedom." In this wrongheaded liberal scheme of things, the "ultimate goal" of the state is identified with "the interest of individuals as such."[49]

Unlike what some scholars claim, Hegel obviously *does not* keep the state of liberals intact. This does not mean that he wants to prevent individuals from having any private property or personal freedom whatsoever. Rather, it means that the state is not obligated to protect these, and that everything that belongs to individuals (the "accidents") is subordinate to the interests and aims of the state. "The right of the state," he says, "is superior" to the rights of the family and civil society. It is only "subordinate to the supreme absolute truth of the world spirit [a.k.a. God]."[50] Otherwise put, the right of the state trumps those of individuals in Hegel's illiberal scheme of things.

---

[48] Quoted in the editorial notes to Hegel, *Elements of the Philosophy of Right*, 385, n. 12.
[49] Hegel, *Philosophy of Right*, §258, R.
[50] Ibid., §33A.

IX. The Philosophy of Right

In his next move, by abusing Rousseau's political theory once more, Hegel opposes both the contractarian and democratic theories of the state in one and the same breath.[51] Allegedly, "as did Fichte later," Rousseau "considered the [political] will only in the determinate form of the individual will and regarded the universal will [the law] ... only as the common element issuing from this individual as a conscious will." Consequently, Rousseau reduced the state to a "contract," based on the "arbitrary will and opinions" of all individuals, "and on their explicit consent, based on their discretion, to enter [this social contract]."[52]

Hegel thus rejects both the democratic-republican and contractarian aspects of Rousseau's theory, in addition to his rejection of the liberal notion of the proper state as the instrument of protecting/pursuing the interest of individuals and civil society. However, he cannot quite explain why Rousseau's theory is faulty on philosophical grounds. Consequently, like a single-trick pony, he resorts to the same tactic with which we are already very familiar: if implemented, "the divine" will (of the state) and its "absolute authority and majesty" would be destroyed. This claim is supported by a factually inaccurate claim (copied from the *Phenomenology*): when *Rousseau's* ideas were "invested with power" during the French Revolution, "they induced, for the first time we know of in human history, the monstrous spectacle of the overthrow of all existing and given conditions of an actual great state," leading to "the most terrifying terror."[53]

What, then, is the rational and legitimate basis of the state? Hegel already answered this question in the previous paragraph: "the divine" will and its "absolute authority and majesty." In other words, "the state consists in the march of God in the world, and its [i.e., the state's] ground is the power of reason [i.e., God's plan] actualizing itself as will," he says.[54] So, it is true that Hegel deifies the state.

But what Hegel says next has provoked the contrary thought among some of his liberalizers: "In considering the idea of the state, we must not have our eyes on particular states or on particular institutions." Allegedly, this statement proves that Hegel does not deify any existing state at all. It

---

[51] I have already remarked on Hegel's chronic misunderstanding of Rousseau in Chapter 3. What remains to be said about it is that the various attempts to reconcile his political views with Rousseau's are necessarily flawed for a simple reason. As it is well known, Rousseau argued that freedom in a society is not possible unless the citizens obey self-given laws, made in accordance with his theory of the general will. As we see here, and will further see below, Hegel defends the very opposite view. Pace Frederick Neuhouser, *Foundations of Hegel's Social Theory: Actualizing Freedom* (Cambridge: Harvard University Press, 2000).
[52] Hegel, *Philosophy of Right*, §258R.
[53] Ibid.
[54] Ibid., §258A.

IX. The Philosophy of Right

does nothing of the sort. As he goes on to clarify, "in the light of some principle or another, any state may be pronounced bad; some sort of a defect may be found in it. However, provided it is one of the developed [*ausgebildeten*] states of our time, it has within itself the essential [or affirmative-rational] moments of its existence [*Existenz*]." In a nutshell, Hegel maintains here that all developed, modern states are intrinsically rational, even though some of their inessential aspects, or institutions, might be faulty in some sense, or might even be missing. What the true philosophy of the state considers is the rational, "affirmative aspect" or "the idea of the state," of "this actual God."[55] "The state," Hegel says some paragraphs later, "is the world which the [world] spirit has made for itself," and so expresses "the wisdom of God." For this reason, we "must revere [*verehren*] the state as an earthly divinity."[56]

4.2 Organic Constitution of the Monarchical State

4.2.1 The Rational and Irrational Political Constitutions

What is the (internal) "constitution" of the state? Hegel:

> The state ... is the development of the Idea into its distinctions and their objective actuality. These distinct aspects are thus the various powers [of the state] with their corresponding tasks and operations, through which the universal continually produces itself in a necessary way because these various powers are determined by the nature of the concept. It preserves itself in so doing because it is itself presupposed in its self-production. This organism is the political constitution.[57]

A few paragraphs later, Hegel claims once more that the constitution of the state "is rational within itself in so far as the state differentiates and determines its activity within itself in accordance with the nature of the concept."[58] This is the sort of gibberish with which most of the pages of the *Philosophy of Right* are generously filled. It is called "logic" or "dialectic," which allegedly explains the state (and everything else) "in accordance with the nature of the concept." If his superficial jargon is ignored, "the political constitution" Hegel has in mind simply refers to the three powers of the state (the three branches of government), which he wants to conceive as an "organic" whole.

---

[55] Ibid.
[56] Ibid., §272R.
[57] Ibid., §269.
[58] Ibid., §272.

IX. The Philosophy of Right

Since Hegel's jargon explains nothing, and Hegel has nothing else with which to justify his version of a "rational" political constitution in accordance with "the concept," he resorts to his other favorite method. Thus, with the "demagogues" ("recent times") in mind, Hegel launches a scolding attack against the "endless amount of chattering both about the constitution and about reason itself." Such "babble," says the babbler-in-chief himself, is uttered by those "who have persuaded themselves that all beliefs are irrefutably justified because they are allegedly based on religion and piety," or on the consideration of "ends, grounds ..., utilities ..., emotionality, love, and enthusiasm." They have even persuaded themselves that they know better than "all others," including "the government." These "superficial" figures simply fail to meet philosophical standards, claims Hegel.[59] Thus, we are back to the same thoughts he expressed in the Preface, and thereafter, though his defenders would have us believe that the Preface is an exception, designed to trick the censors.

Hegel goes on to also criticize the doctrine of "the necessary division [separation] of the powers of the state," which was defended by "Montesquieu," "Kant," and many others. He pretentiously admits that this is a "highly important" principle. It is so because it contains "rational determinacy," in the sense that it divides the whole into *three* different determinations. However, "the abstract understanding" of such philosophers offers a "false" view of the principle of the division of powers, based on "a general equilibrium rather than a living [organic] unity." In fact, their (liberal-republican) checks-and-balances scheme is dangerous: a "grand scale ... destruction of the state is immanently present" in it, as has "recently been seen" during the French Revolution.[60] If these powers "do exist independently and in abstraction," he repeats once more, "it is clear to see that ... [they] must certainly give rise to a struggle whereby either the whole [state] is destroyed or unity is restored by force," as was the case "during the French Revolution."[61] Hegel, I must repeat once again, was none of the following: a liberal, republican, progressive, or a supporter of the French Revolution.

Skipping some more jargon, we finally arrive at Hegel's three powers: princely (or sovereign), executive, and legislative.[62] Notice how his three powers are different from the more common version with which we are usually familiar. Hegel, in other words, subsumes the judiciary under the

---

[59] Ibid., §272R.
[60] Ibid.
[61] Ibid., §272A.
[62] Ibid., §273.

IX. The Philosophy of Right

executive power,[63] since, he says "logically," "the judiciary is not the third moment of the concept."[64] Imagine that!

Hegel's "organic unity" model is supposed to be understood as one in which each of the three powers contains the other two, in accordance with the *concept*. However, as we are about to see, the whole thing is basically a defense of "the monarchical principle," favored by the Restoration authorities.[65]

4.2.2 The Princely Power and the Monarchical Principle

Hegel begins his exposition with the princely power (*Die fürstliche Gewalt*), which is also the *sole* "sovereign." "We begin" with this princely power, this moment of "individuality," says Hegel, "for it [in accordance with its concept] contains within itself the three moments of the state as a totality." Why does this individuality "contain" within himself all three powers of the state? Because, answers the incorrigibly silly Hegel, this individual is essentially an "'I'," and so "is simultaneously the most individual and the most universal."[66] Hegel's nonsense reaches new heights when he tries to

---

[63] Ibid., §287.
[64] Ibid., §272A.
[65] "The monarchical principle" originated in France in 1814 and "was transmitted to Germany through the writings of French royalists, such as Louis de Bonald and Joseph de Maistre. The term received a formal definition in the Vienna Final Acts of June 1820. Article 57 of this document declared: 'The entire state power [*Staatsgewalt*] must remain united in the supreme head of the state. Only in the exercise of certain rights can the sovereign be bound to the participation of the Estates through a *landständische* constitution.'" Before that, a version of the principle "was first articulated in the Bavarian constitutional charter of 1818, and it was further elaborated the following year in an influential essay by Friedrich von Gentz, a renowned political theorist who was Metternich's closest adviser." Gentz's essay "was circulated at the opening of the Karlsbad Conference in August 1819." Levinger, *Enlightened Nationalism*, 149-50. As noted in Chapter 8, Gentz denounced the idea of "sovereignty of the people" and, like Hegel, linked it to the destruction of the state. Likewise, or relatedly, the principle of "division of powers," he claimed, amounts to "an axiom which . . . always and everywhere must lead to the complete destruction of all power, and hence to pure *anarchy*." Avoiding this horrid outcome required accepting the monarch as the "supreme legislator," as well as the "recognized organ of the state." Quoted in Levinger, *Enlightened Nationalism*, 150-51. Also see Michael Stolleis, *Public Law in Germany, 1800-1914* (New York: Berghahn Books, 2001), 43-44. The monarchical principle received approval in Hardenberg's brief and vague 1919 proposal for a "representative" constitution in Prussia: "All necessary steps must be taken to ensure that the monarchical principle shall be firmly established, that true freedom and security of person and property shall harmonize with that principle, and that in this way freedom and security may best and most enduringly persist in conjunction with order and energy." Karl August von Hardenberg, "Ideas for a Representative Constitution in Prussia," reprinted in Heinrich von Treitschke, *History of Germany in the Nineteenth Century*, vol. 3, trans. Eden Paul and Cedar Paul, 643-47 (New York: McBride and Nast, 1917), 647.
[66] Hegel, *Philosophy of Right*, §275, A.

IX. The Philosophy of Right

logically deduce "the monarch" from this "I."[67] (I skip his proof, the absurdity of which has justly enjoined the conclusion that "today" "virtually no one" takes it seriously, including many of Hegel's admirers.[68]

Of interest for our purposes is Hegel's argument against the "confused" demand for the "sovereignty of the people, of popular sovereignty." In the first place, says the speculative philosopher, we may legitimately speak of "popular sovereignty" only if we admit both that "popular" refers to "the whole in general" and "that sovereignty belongs to the state [the apex of which is the monarch]." Thus, the "confused ... notion of the people" ignores the fact that "without its monarch and the articulation of the whole that is necessarily and immediately associated with monarchy, the people are a formless mass and no longer a state."[69] "The 'confused notions' and 'the *wild* idea' are here exclusively Hegel's," notes the young Karl Marx, adding aptly that "all this is a tautology."[70]

We have not seen the best of Hegel's shenanigans yet. He now wants to prove, "logically" to be sure, that monarchy must be *hereditary*: "This ultimate self of the will of the state is simple in its abstraction and is therefore an immediate individuality; thus, in its very concept lies the determination of naturalness." In other words, the monarch is *immediately* an individual human being, and so must be a natural being. "Therefore," concludes Mr. Logic, "the monarch is essentially determined as this individual, in abstraction from every other content, and this individual is destined in an immediate natural way, i.e. through natural birth, to hold the dignity of the monarch." We are assured once again that "this [dialectical or logical] transition from the concept of pure self-determination to the immediacy of being, and hence to the natural realm, is of a purely speculative character; therefore, its cognition belongs to [the Hegelian] logical philosophy" alone. All objections to Hegel's absurd deduction are, of course, the work of "the understanding," and so are not philosophically valid.[71] In Marx's apt words, "Hegel has demonstrated that the monarch must be born, which no one doubted, but not that birth makes one a monarch."[72]

Hegel goes on to disparage various consequentialist justifications of hereditary monarchy. The upshot is that one can "deduce" the need for a hereditary monarchy from *endless* consequentialist arguments, which

---

[67] Ibid., §279.
[68] Michael O. Hardimon, *Hegel's Social Philosophy: The Project of Reconciliation* (Cambridge, UK: Cambridge University Press, 1994), 215.
[69] Hegel, *Philosophy of Right*, §279R.
[70] Karl Marx, *Contribution to the Critique of Hegel's Philosophy of Law,* in Karl Marx and Frederick Engels, *Collected Works*, vol. 3, 3-129 (New York: International Publishers, 1975), 28-29.
[71] Hegel, *Philosophy of Right*, §281, R.
[72] Marx, *Contribution to the Critique of Hegel's Philosophy of Law*, 33.

IX. The Philosophy of Right

proves to Hegel that the consequentialist method is arbitrary. But there is more at stake here. Such a method, or "rationalization," "debases" the "majesty" of the monarch. In other words, "every method of inquiry other than the speculative method of the infinite and self-grounded Idea abolishes the nature of majesty in and for itself."[73] Once again, I must agree with Marx's assessment: Hegel's argument amounts to a ludicrous attempt to present the monarch as "the true 'God-man', as the *actual incarnation* of the Idea."[74] Sidney Hook is even less charitable: "It is difficult to tell what is more nauseating in writing of this kind—its sycophancy or its obfuscation."[75] More recently, another author assessed Hegel's exercise as a "comical" exercise in futility.[76]

I cannot think of a good way to defend the "great" philosopher against these charges.[77] Hegel's friends, however, have come up with various creative ways to make him less of a monarchy-worshipper than he himself wanted to be. Thus, they have concocted a debate to determine whether he rendered monarchical power "merely" symbolic [78] or "primarily symbolic."[79] On similar grounds, others have declared Hegel's monarchical principle somewhat progressive, at least for his times.[80] There is also the claim that some passages permit a "soft" reading and others a "hard" reading of the monarch's powers.[81] All these views are fundamentally wrong; Hegel's monarch has unlimited powers; he just does not need to exercise

---

[73] Hegel, *Philosophy of Right*, §281R.
[74] Marx, *Contribution to the Critique of Hegel's Philosophy of Law*, 33.
[75] Sidney Hook, "Hegel and His Apologists," in *Hegel's Political Philosophy*, ed. Walter Kaufmann, 87-105 (New York: Atherton Press, 1970), 90.
[76] Dudley Knowles, *Hegel and the* Philosophy of Right, (London: Routledge, 2002), 327.
[77] Tunick defends Hegel by insisting that Hegel *also* offers a *political* justification, which could be useful for us "today." Mark Tunick, "Hegel's Justification of Hereditary Monarchy," *History of Political Thought* 12, no. 3 (1991): 481-96.
[78] According to Avineri, "Hegel divests the monarch himself of any real power by making the Crown into a symbol of self-determination. Avineri, *Hegel's Theory of the Modern State*, 186. Likewise, Pelczynski claims that Hegel's "preference was for an inactive monarch," though his times made him realize the need for a somewhat active monarch. Z. A. Pelczynski, "An Introductory Essay," in *Hegel's Political Writings*, trans. T. M. Knox, 3-137 (Oxford: Oxford University Press, 1964), 104.
[79] According to Franco, Hegel's monarchy is "primarily symbolic," not "merely symbolic." Franco, *Hegel's Philosophy of Freedom*, 314-16.
[80] Pace Bernard Yack, "Rationality of Hegel's Concept of Monarchy," *The American Political Science Review* 74, no. 3 (1980): 709-20, 70; Michael O. Hardimon, *Hegel's Social Philosophy: The Project of Reconciliation* (Cambridge, UK: Cambridge University Press, 1994), 215, 27; Franco, *Hegel's Philosophy of Freedom*, 314.
[81] Knowles, *Hegel and the* Philosophy of Right, 329-30. Also see Thom Brooks, *Hegel's Political Philosophy: A Systematic Reading of the* Philosophy of Right (Edinburgh: Edinburgh University Press, 2013), 96-113.

IX. The Philosophy of Right

them much in a well-ordered *ethical* whole.

Hegel bestows upon the monarch "the *right to* pardon criminals."[82] More significantly, "the highest advisory offices [i.e., the cabinet] and ... the individuals who hold them" should fall under the authority of the monarch. Furthermore, both "the selection [*Erwählung*] of individuals to this business and their removal fall under the monarch's unrestricted, arbitrary will."[83] Since, as we will see shortly, these "individuals" wield abundant political power in Hegel's scheme of things, "the unrestricted, arbitrary" right of the monarch to hire and fire them, it goes without saying, amounts to the monarch's absolute and arbitrary power to run the whole show as he sees fit.

> These individuals [ministers] bring before the monarch, for his decision, the content of current affairs of the state, or the legal determinations necessitated by present needs, along with their objective aspects (i.e., the grounds to be considered for his decision), relevant laws, circumstances, etc.[84]

Hegel does not here say anything else on this issue, though we know that his monarch makes the final, ultimate decision on these matters also. As we will see later, Hegel's bicameral assembly of representatives has no legislative power. This means that the legislative power is entirely bestowed upon the monarchial power, which includes the ultimate decision-maker monarch and his subordinate advisers.

Hegel goes on to make his monarch unaccountable. His justification for the monarch's unaccountability sheds some light on his attempts to make him an abstraction. In other words, the monarch is removed from the knowledge of the "objective" grounds for his decisions. For this reason, "the distinctive [*eigentümliche*] majesty of the monarch, as the ultimate subjectivity of decision, is raised above all accountability for the acts of government." By the same token, his ministers are to be held accountable, since they are the ones who supply the objective aspects of the subjective will of the monarch.[85] However, since only the unimpeachable monarch has the right to appoint and dismiss them, it follows that only he has the right to hold the ministers accountable. The monarch, it turns out, is both unaccountable and quite powerful.[86] As we will see later, he is also the commander-in-chief, and is fully in charge of the conduct of foreign

---

[82] Hegel, *Philosophy of Right*, §282.
[83] Ibid., §283.
[84] Ibid.
[85] Ibid., §284.
[86] *Pace* Franco, *Hegel's Philosophy of Freedom*, 317; Brooks, *Hegel's Political Philosophy*, 107.

IX. The Philosophy of Right

affairs.[87] To put this another way, not having much to do in a "rational" state does not limit the monarch's power: "if the constitution is firm, he often has nothing more to do than sign his name" on the laws.[88]

"The third element of the princely power concerns the universal in and for itself, which is present subjectively in the conscience of the monarch, [and] objectively in the whole constitution and in the laws." Therefore, "the princely power presupposes the other [two] moments [or powers of the state] insofar as they presuppose it."[89] In other words, the first moment of "the princely power" involves the making of "the constitution and the laws." Its second moment consists of the "counseling" provided to the monarch by his ministers. Its third moment entails "the ultimate decision as self-determination, into which everything else returns and from which ... [everything else] receives the beginning of its actuality." This is a fancy way of saying, everything that happens in the state receives its grounding and legitimacy from the will of the monarch. "This absolute self-determination," says Hegel, "constitutes the distinguishing principle of princely power as such."[90] Since it is "absolute," this power is also said to be the basis of the executive power, which is carried out by the monarch's ministers and their own subordinates.

4.2.3 The Executive Power

Apart from a brief "logical" mumbling about it, what Hegel offers in this brief subsection is a straightforward description of the activities of the bureaucracy in a "rational" state, which generally include "the execution and application of the princely decisions and ... the continued implementation and maintenance of earlier decisions, current laws, institutions, and arrangements to secure common ends, etc." The executive also exercises "the powers of the judiciary and the police," meaning that Hegel opposes the independence of the judiciary power. The powers of the judiciary and the police are more immediately related to "the particular affairs of civil society." This means to Hegel that the "universal interest" ultimately issues from the will of the monarch, which is then implemented in the regulation of civil society by the executive power.[91] Thus, Hegel's political state, rather than being separated from civil society, is deeply involved in its organization and affairs, and in an obviously top-down manner.

---

[87] Hegel, *Philosophy of Right*, §329.
[88] Ibid., §279A.
[89] Ibid., §285.
[90] Ibid., §275.
[91] Ibid., §287.

IX. The Philosophy of Right

Next, Hegel discusses how the government should manage the corporations. He does not here, or elsewhere, offer a meaningful definition of corporations. They "administer," he says vaguely, the "common interests" of specific private communities within civil society, which are distinct from the "universal interest of the state." These are the interests of "communities and other trades and estates and their authorities, supervisors, administrators, etc."[92] What we can say for certain is that Hegel's corporations are nothing like the civil-society institutions Tocqueville defends.[93] They are, instead, the subordinate organs of the Hegelian organic state, and so are to be controlled and regulated by the executive power at the behest of the monarch.

Corporations, Hegel thus urges, are to be subsumed under the authority of the government's authority (*Regierungsgewalt*), which is itself to be subsumed under the authority of the monarch. How all this is to be worked out in practice is given short shrift. We are told that corporations are to have their own administrators, who are chosen, with the "trust of their peers," to "look after the private property and interests of these particular spheres." However, "these circles must be subordinated to the higher interests of the state."[94] This subordination cannot be entrusted to the administrators of corporations, even though the administrators are "trusted" by their constituencies. Rather, it needs to be ensured by the "deputies of the government," who work together in advisory bodies, and remain in touch with "the monarch himself." Somehow, this oversight is expected to produce the happy result in which the "spirit of the corporation ... transforms itself into the spirit of the state, since the state provides the means of sustaining its particular ends." This outcome, in turn, is "the secret of the patriotism [political disposition] of the citizens." In other words, through the superior oversight provided by the government (the administrators of corporations are often "inept," he says), they come to recognize "the state as their substance, for it is the state which preserves their particular spheres ... as well as their welfare." This illiberal, authoritarian scheme of things allows the members of corporations some freedom to do as they see fit. However, Hegel clearly regards this freedom as insignificant and unworthy. "This sphere," he says, "can be seen" as the sphere in which "formal freedom, based on personal cognition, decision-making, and execution, as well as on petty passions and imaginations, can take place." The state may

---

[92] Ibid., §288.
[93] Pace Avineri, *Hegel's Theory of the Modern State*, 165; Steven B. Smith, *Hegel's Critique of Liberalism: Rights in Context* (Chicago: The University of Chicago Press, 1989), 144-45; Dana Villa, "Hegel, Tocqueville, and 'Individualism'," *The Review of Politics* 67, no. 4 (2005): 659-86. Hegel's corporations, claims Brooks, provide a "major" area of "democratic participation." Brooks, *Hegel's Political Philosophy*, 124.
[94] Hegel, *Philosophy of Right*, §288.

IX. The Philosophy of Right

accept or tolerate these to the extent that they do not affect the "universal interests of the state."[95]

Next, Hegel claims that "the division of labor is also found in the business of the government." Based on Nisbet's translation of this paragraph, many commentators have come to believe that Hegel here wants civil life to "be governed in a concrete manner from below." However, Hegel seems to be saying the following instead: as "difficult" as this may be, the government must ensure that "the below, where civil society is concrete, is governed in a concrete [organic] way." This rendition of the ambivalent original[96] is more consistent with what he says next: "this business" of governing the entire civil society must be "divided" into the "abstract branches" of the governmental (executive) power and put under the oversight of "particular authorities [*eigentümlichen Behörden*]." These branches and authorities would then serve as the "middle-points [*Mittelpunkten*]," or mediating moments, between the "below" and the "highest governmental power," thus "converging again in a concrete overview" of the organic whole.[97] Perhaps the best summary of these views is Marx's following, playful line: in Hegel's scheme of things, "the corporation is the bureaucracy of civil society; the bureaucracy is the corporation of the state."[98]

In the next paragraph, Hegel maintains that qualification, rather than "natural personality and birth," must be used in the appointment of lesser civil servants. Thus, these individuals must objectively demonstrate their "knowledge and ... ability." This method of appointment not only "secures the needs of the state" but also "ensures every citizen the possibility of dedicating themselves to the universal estate," the bureaucracy.[99] The bureaucrats are to be protected against the self-interested private persons. However, there is also a need to protect both "the state and the governed against the misuse of power on the part of the official bodies and their members." Hegel deals with these issues in some detail. The most crucial point he makes is that "the members of the government and civil servants make up the bulk of the middle class, in which the educated intelligence and the consciousness of right [*rechtliche Bewußtsein*] of the mass of the people are found." This somehow implies to Hegel that this class is less prone to corruption. The two institutions that check the power of this "middle" or "mediating" class of bureaucrats are "the sovereign [i.e., the

---

[95] Ibid., §289.
[96] "... daß von unten, wo das bürgerliche Leben konkret ist, dasselbe auf konkrete Weise regiert werde ..."
[97] Ibid., §290.
[98] Karl Marx, *Contribution to the Critique of Hegel's Philosophy of Law*, 45.
[99] Hegel, *Philosophy of Right*, §291.

monarch], who acts upon it from above, and the rights of the corporations, which act upon it from below."[100]

4.2.4 The Legislative Power

Hegel argues that the legislative power should simply revise the existing laws, as needed, creating a stable scenario in which the constitution (the existing laws) changes over time rather "imperceptibly."[101] Hence, he wants to preserve the status quo. Next, he discusses the benefits the state offers to its citizens and the services it expects from them in return. Basically, the nonobligatory benefits include law and order, and the services amount to paying taxes (the defense of the state in a war requires services of a different kind, as we will see later). This discussion is consistent with his notion of patriotism, discussed earlier, and anticipates the passive citizenship Hegel has in mind in relations to the legislative power.

Thus, Hegel asserts abruptly that "it is implicit in the organic unity of the powers of the state itself that one and the same spirit decrees the universal [i.e., the laws] and brings it to determinate actuality in implementing it."[102] In other words, "in the legislative power as a totality, the monarchical and the executive powers [as one power united under the monarch's will] ... are primarily effective." More specifically, based on the advice of his ministers, the monarch makes the "ultimate decision" regarding legislation. There is also the "element" of the "Estates [the national legislative assembly]" in this triadic totality. Hegel's aim here is to avoid the "fundamental error" of rendering each power independent of the others, for such a scenario "abolishes the unity of the state, which, above all, is to be demanded."[103] It takes very little thought to realize that he wants the third "element" to simply approve the decisions of the princely power, which includes the ministers.

"The Estates" is where "the moment of subjective formal freedom, [namely,] the public consciousness as empirical universality of the views and thoughts of the many, come to existence," says Hegel. This assertion is further explicated with self-serving word-mongering. You see, "the expression 'the many' denotes the empirical [atomistic] universality more correctly than the common term 'all'." He then proceeds to replace "the many" with "the people," which includes its "representatives." To the "scientific" Hegel, the concept of "the people" correctly denotes the ignorance of its atoms.[104] Differently put, "the people" refers to "a crowd,"

---

[100] Ibid., §§295-97.
[101] Ibid., §298, A.
[102] Ibid., §299, R, A.
[103] Ibid., §300, A.
[104] Ibid., §301R.

IX. The Philosophy of Right

which, by definition, is "a formless mass whose movement and action would only be elemental, irrational, savage [*wild*], and horrifying." All this can be deduced from the expression "the people," insists the famous philosopher once again.[105]

The "ordinary consciousness" fails to grasp this scientific definition of "the people," as it opines that the "representatives of the people, or even the people, understand best what serves their best [interests] and that it has the undoubtedly best will … [to pursue those] best [interests]." According to Mr. Logic, this is an absurd claim, for "it is rather the case that the people, insofar as this word signifies a particular part of the members of a state [i.e., the part that excludes the highest officials and the monarch], refers to the part which does not know what it wants." "To know what one wants," not to mention what "reason wants," is "the fruit of deep knowledge and insight," which the regular folk clearly lack, says Hegel.[106]

Therefore, concludes Hegel thoughtlessly, the determination of "universal welfare and public freedom" should not depend on the lowly "insight" of the representatives of the people, not to mention the people themselves. In fact, it is obvious to him that "the highest state officials necessarily have deeper and more comprehensive insight into the nature of the institutions and needs of the state, as well as greater skill" in dealing with such needs. With this move, he converts what is best for the people to what is best for the state and its institutions, which automatically produces the conclusion that only those with proven expertise in the affairs of its institutions know how to run the state and serve its needs. So, what is the purpose of having an assembly of people's representatives? In a nutshell, Hegel's representatives serve as the eyes and ears of the "highest officials" on the ground. They are expected to monitor "the activities of those officials who are more distant from the eyes of the higher authorities." They are also familiar with the "urgent needs and deficiencies" in their communities, and so can bring them to the attention of the ministers planted within the Estates. Apart from these functions, the people's representatives get to hear the legislative proposals of the ministers and express their own views about them.[107] In short, Hegel's representatives do not have any meaningful share in legislation.

Next, Hegel asserts that "the Estates" must adopt both the position of "the state and the government" and the "interests" of the people. In the first respect, the representatives must justify and legitimize the power of the monarch so that it "does not appear … as an arbitrary power of domination" to the irrational rabble, the people. In the second respect, which is

---

[105] Ibid., §303R.
[106] Ibid., §301R.
[107] Ibid.

IX. The Philosophy of Right

essentially the same as the first, they must harmonize the interests of "communities, corporations, and individuals" with those of the monarch and the government. Above all, Hegel warns, they must "ensure that individuals do not present themselves" to the state "as a crowd or heap" of "unorganized" "opinions and volitions," and thus as a "mass of power against the organic state."[108]

Dialectically put, the Estates must constitute a *mediating moment* within the organic whole, which amounts to pacifying any popular opposition to the monarchical state. And this, Hegel assures us, is "one of the most important insights of (speculative) logic," which teaches that the Estates must lose this "quality" of being a real "opposition" to the state. Somehow, speculative logic always adopts the position of the state. It stresses this very "important" point of view against "the frequent but highly dangerous prejudice, which conceives the Estates chiefly in terms of opposition to the monarchical government as if this were its essential position." This wonderful "logic" mediates the Estates (rather than the Estates mediating things) by reducing their "opposition" to the state to a mere "semblance" of an opposition. Speculative logic tirelessly warns that the state would face certain "destruction" if this opposition is not merely an apparent, "superficial opposition."[109] In reaction to Hegel's "logical" nonsense, Marx aptly notes that the Estates is a "luxury" Hegel wants "only for the sake of logic."[110] He should have added that Hegel also wants logic for the sake of the state.

Hegel proceeds to determine the denizens of the Estates with disconnected sentences and self-serving "logical" tautologies. We skip these and simply note that he wants the landed-nobility and the business class to be represented in the Estates as two separate estates.[111] It turns out, there must be a *mediating* moment *within* the Estates also. This is because the business estate and the party of the monarch (the members of the cabinet seated in the Estates) are two "extremes." Speculative logic teaches us (who would have thought?) that herein lies "only the possibility of agreement" between them, "and thus also the possibility of hostile opposition," and that this opposition must be mediated by another moment, a "middle point," if you will.[112]

Lo and behold, the nobility, by its very nature, is "capable" of functioning as this "political relation" or mediating "point," because it is based on "natural determination." In other words, it "includes the princely

---

[108] Ibid., §302R.
[109] Ibid.
[110] Marx, *Contribution to the Critique of Hegel's Philosophy of Law*, 64.
[111] Hegel, *Philosophy of Right*, §303.
[112] Ibid., §304.

IX. The Philosophy of Right

element" within its determination, since it is also *hereditary*.[113] To ensure the maintenance of this mediating estate, Hegel proposes the institution of "primogeniture." In his wording, "the [rational] ground of primogeniture lies in the fact that the state should be able to count on a [firm political] disposition ... as necessarily present," and the institution of primogeniture presumably ensures this outcome.[114] In short, "this estate ... is entitled to its political activity by birth, without the contingency of an election [*Wahl*]."[115]

It is "ridiculous," as Marx puts it, that the "rational" Hegel favors choosing a bulk of his representatives, as well as his monarch, by means of natural lottery, so that he can avoid their determination by means of "fortuitous" elections. Consequently, he "descends everywhere from his political spiritualism into the crassest *materialism*. At the summit of the political state, it is everywhere birth which makes certain individuals the incarnations of the supreme office of state."[116] Mundanely put, Hegel retains the nobility's political privileges, though he wants us to believe that this is dictated by the concept, and not the old, feudal requirements.

Civil society is to be represented in its own "section," meaning that Hegel wants a bicameral legislature. However, the "delegates" of civil society must represent their respective "associations, communities, and corporations," and not the *individuals* in their own community or, more generally, in civil society.[117] Their constituents must have "the confidence" (or trust) that the delegates "are better able to understand ... universal affairs" than they. Hegel also reasserts that these delegates are expected to subordinate the "the particular interest of their community or corporation" to the "the universal" interest, that is, the interest of the state. Thus, they are in effect to be representatives of the state, not their constituents. However, in the final analysis, none of this really matters, as Hegel's assembly is simply a debating club, where the delegates mainly "instruct and convince one another."[118]

In the "rational" system of "representation," Hegel now maintains, "consent is not given directly by everyone but only by plenipotentiaries [*Bevollmächtigte*]." Moreover, these "electors" express their consent as "trust," not as a "vote."[119] The delegates receive this trust because they have proven to be competent, "above all, in the disposition, skill, and knowledge [*Kenntnis*] of the institutions and interests of the state and civil society,

---

[113] Ibid., §305.
[114] Ibid., §306, A.
[115] Ibid., §307.
[116] Marx, *Contribution to the Critique of Hegel's Philosophy of Law*, 105.
[117] Hegel, *Philosophy of Right.*, §308.
[118] Ibid., §309.
[119] Ibid., §309A.

IX. The Philosophy of Right

which they have acquired through the actual conduct of business in the magistracies [*obrigkeitlichen*] or offices of the state [*Staatsämtern*]." It now appears to be the case that Hegel wants the experienced civil servants to represent civil society, since they are apt to have proper "political sense" or disposition toward the state, in addition to possessing the required knowledge of how the state works and what it needs.[120]

Thus, as Marx again observes, "Hegel seems to be rather inclined to turn the Lower House into a chamber of civil service *pensioners*. He demands not only 'political sense', but also 'administrative', bureaucratic sense."[121] Moreover, Hegel's "thoughtless inconsistency" is now becoming "*repulsive*." The "guarantee for the electors has secretly been developed into a guarantee against the electors." Rather than representing what their electors want, the delegates must satisfy what the state wants, which are "recognizable" and "tested" qualities, derived from their commitment to their prior political service.

> All that is missing is for Hegel to demand that the ... [members of the lower house] should pass an *examination* set by their worshipful government. Hegel here descends almost to servility. We see him infected through and through with the miserable arrogance of the *Prussian* civil service which in its bureaucratic stupidity grandly looks down on the 'self-confidence' of the 'people's own subjective opinion'.[122]

It is now high time to provide a "logical" justification for the bicameral parliament:

> Each of the two sections contained in the Estates (see §§305 and 308) contributes a particular modification to the process of deliberation. Since ... one of the moments in question also has the specific function of mediation ... between [two distinct] existents [*Existierenden*], this moment must likewise take on a separate existence [*Existenz*]. The assembly of the estates will thus be divided into two chambers.[123]

"Good Lord!" was Marx's proper response to this magnificent piece of reasoning.[124] It basically states that the representatives of the nobility must have their own distinct chamber since they perform an essentially different function than the representatives of the corporations.

---

[120] Ibid., §310.
[121] Marx, *Contribution to the Critique of Hegel's Philosophy of Law*, 124.
[122] Ibid., 126-27.
[123] Hegel, *Philosophy of Right*, §312.
[124] Marx, *Contribution to the Critique of Hegel's Philosophy of Law*, 129.

IX. The Philosophy of Right

Hegel concludes his discussion of the legislative power without saying anything about the processes of legislation. However, he has told us enough to conclude that the Estates do not legislate at all; they simply debate things and, ideally, defend the interests of the state. The legislative power, he told us previously, belongs solely to the monarch and his ministers. This utterly undemocratic scheme of legislation sheds further light on Hegel's scheme of individual rights. Since he identifies rights with the laws, and since neither individuals nor their representatives make these laws, their rights simply consist of what the princely power wills. Moreover, as we have seen, Hegel's monarchical state is not obligated to protect the rights of its subjects, though his theory obligates the latter to subordinate their interests and rights to those of the state. For these reasons alone, it cannot be said that Hegel was a liberal.[125] That he was no democrat is not much disputed nowadays.

4.2.5 Freedom of the Press and Speech

After disparaging public opinion in his typically muddled (dialectical) manner,[126] Hegel discusses freedom of expression. According to him, "freedom of public communication," of the printed "press [and] the spoken word," which he links to "the tingling urge to say one's opinion and to have said it, is directly secured by the police and laws and ordinances, which hinder or punish its excesses."[127]

Clearly, Hegel is unenthusiastic about this punishable freedom. For instance, he adds immediately that it is also secured when it is rendered relatively "harmless" in a stable state.[128] In other words, Hegel's defense of this freedom is predicated upon the strength and stability of the state; it is less likely to be harmed by "freedom of public communication" when it is sufficiently stable. This line of reasoning occurs throughout the *Philosophy of Right*: the rights and freedoms of individuals and minority groups may be tolerated, concludes Hegel at some point, when "the state is otherwise strong."[129]

---

[125] According to Siep, "Hegel's state is liberal in the sense that the protection of individual rights, including a great part of what belongs to modern human and civil rights, is a necessary task of any legitimate state." Yet, Hegel's "state is not liberal in the sense that these rights have no basis beyond the states' legislation, neither on an international level nor as constitutional rights that citizens could refer to before a constitutional court. State sovereignty is not dependent on fulfilling the 'responsibility to protect' those rights." Ludwig Siep, "Hegel's Liberal, Social, and 'Ethical' State," in ed. Dean Moyar, *The Oxford Handbook of Hegel*, 515-34 (Oxford: Oxford University Press, 2017), 530-31. Siep's verdict on why Hegel's state is "not liberal," which is correct, renders his verdict on why it is liberal virtually meaningless.
[126] Hegel, *Philosophy of Right*, §§316-17.
[127] Ibid., §319.
[128] Ibid.
[129] Ibid., §274R (Hegel's note).

IX. The Philosophy of Right

Hegel's unenthusiastic endorsement of freedom of the press is manifest in his next comment, which also exhibits his usual thoughtlessness: "To define freedom of the press as the freedom to say and write whatever one wants is parallel to saying that freedom in general means freedom to do whatever one wants." "Such talk," maintains the omniscient Mr. Logic, "belongs to the crudity and superficiality of utterly uneducated imagination." A quick reflection on his equation of "freedom to say and write whatever one wants" with "freedom to do whatever one wants" would indicate that it is Hegel who deserves this vituperation. Does my right to write whatever I want about Hegel really imply that I also have the right to torch his house on fire? (This is a rhetorical question.) At any rate, his aim here is to argue that freedom of the press must be restricted. For instance, "injury to the honor of individuals, slander, abuse, [and] contempt for the government, its officials ..., and, especially, the person of the prince, contempt for the laws, incitement to rebellion, etc., are crimes and misdemeanors of widely varying degrees of gravity." If so, they ought to face either preventive "police" action (censorship) or "actual punishment."[130] Thus, on the issue of free press, Hegel basically agrees with the Karlsbad Decrees.

However, the genuine "sciences" do not belong "in the sphere of opinion and subjective views," claims Hegel. If so, scientific works (such as the *Philosophy of Right*) should not only be exempt from censorship but also safeguarded against the vicious "contempt" (the "legally punishable" ones) they receive from the inferior minds, which feel "oppressed by the superior talents and virtues"—of Hegel and the like, if you will.[131] Thus, *critiques* of "scientific" works should also be censored. As we will see in the next chapter, Hegel would soon ask the ministry of his master, Altenstein, to punish a journal for publishing a scathing review of his "scientific" book.

4.3 External Sovereignty, War, and the Military Class

Hegel presents "external sovereignty" as the second major aspect of sovereignty, the first aspect being its "internal constitution." Based on some "logical" hocus-pocus, which I must here ignore, he then arrives at the conclusion that the state exists "as an actual and immediate individual," which is "exclusive" of, or excludes, other individuals like itself.[132] He also reaches the conclusion that the "independence" of their state is "the primary freedom and the highest honor of a people." He then disparages "those who speak of the desires of an ... independent state to ... form a whole with another state." These ignoramuses "know little about the nature

---
[130] Ibid., §319, R.
[131] Ibid., §319R.
[132] Ibid., §321.

IX. The Philosophy of Right

of a totality and of the pride [*Selbstgefühl*] a people has in its independence."[133] Once again, Hegel's targets here are the "demagogues," many of whom called for the unification of Germany, which the Restoration authorities opposed.

Hegel's main aim in this context is to further justify the absolute power of the state over its own subjects. As he puts it, the absolute independence of the state requires its "absolute power" "against everything individual and particular, that is, against life, property … rights, and even against the wider circles [of civil society, such as corporations]." The other side of this coin is the absolute ethical duty of individuals to preserve "the independence and sovereignty of the state," even if this requires them to "endanger and sacrifice" everything the "concept of life" implies. This argument is further justified with the typical castigation of those (i.e., liberals) who identify the essential aim of the state with the protection of the "life and property" of its citizens.[134]

Hegel does not simply make it the absolute duty of individuals to defend their states against the invaders at any cost. He also claims that war is "not to be regarded as an absolute evil and as a purely external contingency," as something "that ought not to be." While these sentences suggest that he might regard it as evil in some sense, Hegel has nothing to say on what makes war evil. Instead, he perversely emphasizes its ethicality and necessity. The gist of his argument, which he had repeated in his earlier works many times, is that war urges individuals to become ethical, since "war is that condition in which the vanity of temporal things and temporal goods" is proven. To further articulate his point, Hegel proudly quotes what he himself

> expressed elsewhere [i.e., in his *Natural Law* essay]: "the ethical health of peoples is preserved in their indifference to the solidity [*Festwerden*] of finite determinacies [such as life, property, etc.]; just as the movement of the winds preserves the sea from the decay, which would be caused by lasting calm, so would a lasting, let alone "perpetual," peace would produce [ethical decay] in peoples."[135]

To complete Hegel's thought, wars are necessary to prevent the corruption of peoples, and so serve ethical ends for this reason. If so, the claim that Hegel neither glorified nor promoted war is false.[136]

---

[133] Ibid., §322, R.
[134] Ibid., §323, R.
[135] Ibid., §323R.
[136] For various attempts to save Hegel from himself in this regard, see Thomas. M. Knox, "Hegel and Prussianism," in *Philosophy* 15, no. 57 (1940): 51-63, 62; Donald P. Verene, "Hegel's Account of War," in *Hegel's Political Philosophy: Problems and Perspectives*, ed. Z. A. Pelczynski, 168-80 (Cambridge, UK: Cambridge University Press, 1971), 179-80;

IX. The Philosophy of Right

Hegel goes on to argue for the necessity of a standing army, which he calls "the estate of courage."[137] He plunges into further absurdities when he attempts to express this as a "logical" necessity, which is allegedly given by "the concept of the thing [*Sache*]."[138] Skipping all these, we encounter a dialectical move in which Hegel reduces courage to absolute obedience. What is "important here," he says, is the complete subordination of the individual to the command of the universal, and "not personal courage."[139] If so, "true" courage, like true patriotism and freedom, is "complete obedience, renunciation of one's opinions and rationalizations—in fact, complete absence of mind [*des Geistes*], coupled with the most intense and comprehensive presence of mind and determination [*Entschlossenheit*]" to carry out orders from above. This turns out to be the highest shape of "freedom" an individual can exercise.[140]

Hegel has, at last, discovered the truly ethical and free individuality he has been looking for all along, and this in the persona of a completely dehumanized, robotic soldier.

We now encounter another "logical" explanation of the monarch's absolute right over the foreign affairs of his state:

> The external orientation of the state derives from it being an individual subject. Therefore, its relationship with other [states] falls to the princely power [because the prince is also an absolute, independent, individual subject], which therefore has direct and sole authority to command the armed forces, to conduct relations with other states through ambassadors etc., to make war and peace, and to conclude treaties of other kinds.[141]

Common sense, I dare say, was not Hegel's strong suit. If we ignore his unwarranted *therefores*, what remains is a defense of the absolute power of the monarch to run the foreign affairs of the state as he sees fit. This sort of a power, we must now note, becomes particularly worrisome when it is understood in relation to Hegel's other relevant claims: wars are ethically

---

Avineri, *Hegel's Theory of the Modern State*, 194-207; Errol E. Harris, "Hegel's Theory of Sovereignty, International Relations, and War," in ed. Donald P. Verene, *Hegel's Social and Political Thought: The Philosophy of Objective Spirit*, (Atlantic Highlands, N.J.: Humanities Press, 1980), 146; Wood, *Hegel's Ethical Thought*, 28-29; Smith, *Hegel's Critique of Liberalism*, 160; Robert R. Williams, *Hegel's Ethics of Recognition* (Berkeley, CA: University of California Press, 1997), 342-48; Brooks, *Hegel's Political Philosophy*, 133-47.
[137] Hegel, *Philosophy of Right*, §325.
[138] Ibid., §326R.
[139] Ibid., §327, A.
[140] Ibid., §328.
[141] Ibid., §329.

necessary and must be waged periodically; individuals have absolute duty to sacrifice all they have for the sake of the state; and, they have virtually no say in legislation. This picture looks even gloomier when we consider his Karlsbadian approach to freedom of the press, which essentially prohibits any criticism of the monarch and his government.

Hegel goes on to evaluate the rationality of the state within the context of world history. I discuss his brief account in Chapter 13, along with his lectures on the philosophy of history. To anticipate, we will discover there that his account amounts to deification and glorification of the state and makes it abundantly clear that the "rational" state of the Hegelian kind exists only in Germany, especially in Prussia.

Chapter Ten

X. MAKING FRIENDS AND ENEMIES

1. Receptions of the *Philosophy of Right*

As noted previously, the *Philosophy of Right* was released in October 1820, despite its official printing date of 1821. We know this because Hegel hastened to send copies of it to Altenstein and Hardenberg on October 10, together with letters to assure them that his book and teaching coincide with his official duties. In his letter to Altenstein, Hegel wrote the following:

> In presenting this writing, it is above all my deepest wish that Your Excellency may most graciously accept and regard it as evidence of my official activity, and as an attempt to return the content of teaching to [the] recognition of the concept. The printing of this text at once gives [an] account of the scope of the principles I teach in my lectures on the subject. I consider myself duty-bound as a publicly appointed professor at the Royal University to render such an account to you in view of the genuine freedom of philosophizing enjoyed in the Royal lands under the fair protection and admirable support provided by Your Excellency's high leadership.[1]

What we have of Hegel's letter to Altenstein is a draft with missing parts. Based on Altenstein's reply, which will be quoted later, it is very likely that Hegel's letter to him included something like the following passage he included in his letter to Hardenberg:

> My scientific endeavors aim to extirpate from philosophy all that falsely usurps this title and, even more importantly, to demonstrate the harmony of philosophy with those principles generally required by the nature of the state. But most immediately they aim at showing agreement with the principle which the Prussian state—belonging to

---

[1] Clark Butler and Christiane Seiler (trans.), *Hegel: The Letters* (Bloomington: Indiana University Press, 1984), 459-59. Henceforth cited as *Letters*. Also, Johannes Hoffmeister (ed.), *Briefe von und an Hegel*, 4 volumes (Hamburg: Felix Meiner, 1952-1960), #374. Henceforth cited as *Briefe*, followed by the Latin numerical to indicate the volume number, in this case, *II*.

X. Making Friends and Enemies

which necessarily gives me great satisfaction—has had the good fortune of having upheld and of still upholding under the enlightened Government of His Majesty the King and Your Highness' wise leadership. My treatise is thus intended as an attempt to grasp in its principal characteristics what lies before us to such great effect, the fruit of which we enjoy.[2]

Hegel's letter to Hardenberg speaks for itself. It also documents how Hegel himself was the very first person to regard his *Philosophy of Right*, and his post-1818 "scientific endeavors" in general, as an apology for the Prussian state. We will see in due course that he expected to be, and would be, rewarded for his servile "scientific endeavors."

The likes of de Wette, on the other hand, were punished for their unruly behavior, as we have seen in Chapter 8. When Hegel's book went into circulation, de Wette was residing in Weimar, where the liberal duke implemented the Karslbad Decrees as little as he could under the pressure from the Austrian and Prussian Holy rulers. By December 30, as his letter to Schleiermacher indicates, de Wette had read at least the Preface of Hegel's book and rightly interpreted it as an apologist slander. Thus, he was not at all surprised to learn that Hegel himself "reads and hears terrible things about" him (many of which have not been preserved). The "slander" in the Preface against him and Fries "could not be more malicious," wrote de Wette.[3] Indeed, in one of his letters to Daub, Hegel himself agreed with this assessment: "Preface and the explosive statements in it tried to strike a blow at this indigent though arrogant sect [of professors]."[4]

As we have seen in Chapter 9, the *Philosophy of Right* as a whole, and not simply its Preface, indeed contains much malicious slander, declaring the likes of de Wette and Fries dangerous "criminals." Hegel did not have to go this far in order to keep his teaching post and/or avoid censorship. But it is telling that he did. In a way, too, malicious slander had always been his main means to advance his career. As we have seen in Chapter 2, he founded the *Critical Journal* with Schelling in 1801, with the intention to "put an end and limit to unphilosophical rubbish." "One may call … the weapons" the journal will use "cudgels, whips, and bats. It is all for the good cause and glory of God," he informed a friend back then.[5] As Jacobi saw it, "most violent anger [prevailed in the *Critical Journal*], so it seems."[6] In October 1807, Hegel anonymously published an advertisement for his

---

[2] *Letters*, 459 (*Briefe II*, #376).
[3] Günther Nicolin (ed.), *Hegel in Berichten seiner Zeitgenossen* (Hamburg: Felix Meiner, 1970), #332. Henceforth cited as *Berichten*.
[4] *Letters*, 460-61 (*Briefe II*, #387).
[5] Ibid., 89 (*Briefe I*, #32).
[6] *Berichten*, #58

X. Making Friends and Enemies

Phenomenology of Spirit, which pointedly informed his readers that "the author, in "the Preface," disparages "the presumption and mischief of the philosophic formulas that are currently degrading philosophy."[7] In 1808, while working in Bamberg as the editor of a provincial newspaper, he advised Niethammer to found something like the *Le Moniteur* (the official organ of Napoleon's state at the time) in Bavaria and to put him in charge of it. "The advantage of the *French Moniteur*," he told Niethammer, "is that it has the authority to put adolescent insolence in its place, to tame and shut up impudent mouths."[8] In 1817, he became one of the chief editors of the *Heidelberg Yearbooks*. In this capacity, he refused to publish Paulus' essay because of its "spiteful" criticism of the authorities in Württemberg, from whom Hegel was hoping to receive a prestigious employment offer.[9] Thus, the *Philosophy of Right* was not Hegel's first rodeo; nor would it be his last, as we will see in the ensuing chapters.

Shortly after its publication, and given Hegel's history, Paulus had no qualms about giving his book its due. In a very scathing review, he deemed Hegel's cryptic language "unfit for communication." He also observed aptly how Hegel often resorts to vituperation to discredit the views of his philosophical and political opponents, highlighting specifically Hegel's frequent use of the word "shallowness" to describe the views of "all German philosophers," excepting, of course, himself. He also noted accurately that Hegel mingles philosophy with a police-function and exalted the "statesmen." After a quick summary of the contents of the *Philosophy of Right*, Paulus pointed out, again correctly, that Hegel identifies the state with the "whole ethical world." Indeed, he concluded, Hegel's book preaches obedience.[10]

With the *Philosophy of Right* in mind, Fries, who was very familiar with Hegel's activities since his Jena years, summed up Hegel's political progression quite accurately in his January 6, 1821, letter to one Ludwig Rödiger: Hegel's "metaphysical mushroom grew not in the gardens of science but on the dung-heap of servility. He had French metaphysics until 1813, then it became ... [the royalist metaphysics] of Württemberg; he is now kissing the horsewhip of Herr von Kamptz,"[11] the police chief in Berlin.

---

[7] G. W. F. Hegel, "Hegel's Advertisement for the Publication of *The Phenomenology of Spirit*," in *Miscellaneous Writings of G. W. F. Hegel*, ed. Jon Stewart, 281-82 (Evanston, IL: Northwestern University Press, 2002).
[8] *Letters*, 155-57 (*Briefe I*, #112).
[9] Ibid., 358-60 (*Briefe II*, #316).
[10] Heinrich Paulus, "Hegels Philosophie des Rechts," *Heidelberger Jahrbücher für Literatur*, no. 25 (1821): 392-400.
[11] *Berichten*, #334.

X. Making Friends and Enemies

Thaden, who had previously admired Hegel's *Logic* and advised him to write books on the state (see Chapter 5), was utterly disappointed with Hegel's new book on the state. In his letter to Hegel, he noted with much dismay how Hegel's "new campaign shocked and wounded friend and foe alike." "You are decried by turns as a 'royalist philosopher' and a 'philosophical royalist'," wrote Thaden. After all, Hegel argues in his book that "all is right and legitimate" in Prussia and, under the guise of logical deduction, dogmatically deduces "an actual constitution ... out of zeal for Princes."[12]

In the meanwhile, in October 1820, while Hegel was busy sending complimentary copies of the *Philosophy of Right* to Altenstein, Hardenberg, and others, a fellow named C. W. Fenner appeared at Berlin University and requested to lecture on the philosophy of nature. To make the long story short, Hegel, who was soon to assume the post of the dean of the philosophical faculty in 1821, was asked to examine his documents. He discovered that Fenner's documents were forged. On May 8, after his application was rejected, Fenner advertised in a local newspaper that he would hold private lectures on Oken's philosophy of nature "for ladies." This irked the authorities not only because Fenner had tried to cheat his way into the lecture halls but also because Oken was a known "demagogue" and, allegedly, an "atheist." Consequently, following the king's orders, Altenstein banned the teaching of Oken's philosophy throughout Prussia.[13]

On June 9, Hegel reported the news to Niethammer: "There is now a new peril which I hope will leave me equally untouched. In response to the petition of a useless fool [Fenner], a few weeks ago the King issued a cabinet order instructing the Minister to prohibit the teaching in Prussian universities of Oken's philosophy of nature and similar doctrines *leading to atheism* and misleading youth." Being the timid soul that he was, Hegel briefly entertained the thought that he might also be accused of preaching atheism. However, he hastened to add, "I am lecturing on the philosophy of religion this summer and am doing so in good conscience." This is because being in the middle of everything affords him with "more accurate knowledge of what is *likely* so that one can be more assured of one's interest and situation." In short, clarified Hegel,

> I have withstood the peril of demagogy without personal risk—but not indeed without concern in the face of those casting suspicion, slander, and so forth. Or at least I was concerned until I read *de Wette*'s letter [to the king] and got to know better both a few demagogical

---

[12] *Letters*, 463 (*Briefe II*, #394).
[13] G. W. F. Hegel, *Berliner Schriften, 1818-1831*, ed. Johannes Hoffmeister (Hamburg: Felix Meiner, 1956), 595-97.

X. Making Friends and Enemies

individuals and a few [authorities] who had to take action against them. I then realized the wretchedness and well-deserved fate of the demagogues.[14]

What Hegel meant, but did not report to Niethammer, was that he had already assured Schultz, another representative of the government at the university, that his own philosophy had nothing to do with atheism. Not only that—Schultz instructed Hegel on May 31, 1821 (nine days *before* Hegel's letter to Niethammer, in which he confessed to being in the middle of things) to find out if anyone taught any dangerous ideas and to "occasionally, but only orally and confidentially," report his findings to him.[15] I have little doubt that Hegel took his marching orders very seriously.

This story informs the context in which Hegel, his book, and his teaching were evaluated. Accordingly, on August 24, 1821, Altenstein finally replied to Hegel's letter of October 10, 1820, with the following evaluation:

> In putting stress in this work [i.e., the *Philosophy of Right*] as in your lectures generally, with the earnestness that becomes philosophy, on the need to grasp what is present and actual, to conceive the rational in nature and history, it seems to me that you assign to philosophy the only position that is correct with regard to what is actual. In this way, you will most assuredly succeed in preserving your students from the pernicious presumption which repudiates what exists [i.e., the present actuality] without having come to know it, and which, with respect to the state in particular, indulges in the self-flattery of arbitrarily postulating empty ideals.[16]

Clearly, Altenstein was very pleased with his hireling. In the final analysis, the minster's approval of his loyalty to the state was what really mattered to Hegel. After all, he understood quite well that his career ambitions could not be realized without the minister's approval and support. In fact, this was a clear sign, if one was still needed, that Altenstein would support him so long as he used his pen and lectures to attack the enemies of the state and cure the "demagogic" ailments of students.

Still, Hegel was not happy to see more, but by now dwindling, critical reviews of his *Philosophy of Right* appear in journals. In February 1822, someone anonymously published a negative review of his book in the *Hallesche Allgemeine Literatur-Zeitung*. Given that the Karlsbad Decrees were still being implemented with full force, the reviewer wisely refrained

---

[14] *Letters*, 470 (*Briefe* II, #390).
[15] Hegel, *Berliner Schriften*, 597.
[16] *Letters*, 458 (*Briefe* II, #397).

from explicitly criticizing Hegel for defending the repressive regime. Instead, he/she took issue with some of Hegel's pretentious claims and noted his indulgence in "very vague," even "strange," sentences. The reviewer concluded by chastising Hegel's unfair treatment of Fries' philosophy. However, what bothered the reviewer the most, so it seems, was Hegel's willingness to attack a man (Fries) who was already in despair. (Fries was recently, but temporarily, removed from his professorial post at Jena.) Such a "behavior is not noble," remarked the reviewer, but left it up to the "thoughtful reader" to give the proper appellation to Hegel's behavior, implying that his character deserves a harsh condemnation.[17]

According to Rosenkranz, incensed by this "insult," Hegel wrote to Altenstein's ministry, asking for governmental action against the *Hallesche Allgemeine Literatur-Zeitung* for publishing such a review. He reasoned that it was unacceptable for a journal supported by the Prussian government to publish such a denunciation of a Prussian civil servant, namely, Hegel himself. He then linked this issue to too much freedom of the press (at a time when the Karlsbad Decrees were still in full effect!). Hegel's demand was utterly unreasonable. Thus, Altenstein found a compromise solution to his request. He instructed the journal to impose more stringent censorship on the contents of its publications but refrained from slapping a journal supported by his own government with a lawsuit on Hegel's behalf. In his reply to Hegel, Altenstein gingerly noted that his ministry "'completely recognizes the rightness of [his] conviction.'" However, the ministry could not press charges on his behalf, and that he should do so himself; or else, he should issue a public notice in response to the review.[18] This incident helped further galvanize Hegel's image as a lackey and favorite of the minister.

2. Requesting the Promised Rewards

On April 12, 1822, the king of Prussia issued a cabinet order, instructing his ministers, specifically the minister of culture and education, Altenstein, to "discipline" the "demagogically predisposed lecturers and professors," and to report back after three months on the results of the measures taken in this regard.[19] On July 18, soon after the expiration of the given deadline, Hegel informed Niethammer that the results of this cabinet order were not as harsh as expected (likely because most "demagogues" had already been silenced or sought refuge in other places). "All I hear," he said, "is that it is

---

[17] Anonymous, *Hallesche Allgemeine Literatur-Zeitung* 40 (1822): 313-17 (columns).
[18] Karl Rosenkranz, *Georg Wilhelm Friedrich Hegels Leben* (Berlin: Duncker und Humblot, 1844), 336-37.
[19] See Hoffmeister's note to *Briefe II*, #421, on page 498.

X. Making Friends and Enemies

to be proposed that the situation is to be defused by means of a circular to the universities—admonishing, praising, recalling, and so forth, except perhaps for one individual [i.e., Schleiermacher], who has not been found praiseworthy." Hegel's letter also included his preface to Hermann F. W. Hinrichs' book, on which we will have more to say shortly. He also squeezed in the following comment: "One has the least success of all [in the eyes of the opponents of the regime] ... with concepts and reason regarding matters touching on the state. Yet I have ... already explicitly disclaimed wanting any greater success with our rabble of 'liberty-minded' militants,"[20] namely, the "demagogues."

As we have seen in the previous section, while the king's cabinet order was still in effect, Hegel received very high praise from Altenstein for his book and teaching. It was now high time, Hegel thought, to convert such praises into actual rewards. Thus, on June 6, he respectfully reminded Altenstein of his earlier promise: "Your Excellency was gracious enough at the time of my appointment to the local university to give me hope that your developing plans for scientific establishments would enable you to open up a more extensive [field of] activity for me and increase my income in the future." Hegel was now hard-pressed to issue this reminder, given the financial difficulties he was currently having, due to his increasing familial expenses. The supplementary income of 200 Thalers he had received for his work at "the local Royal Scientific Board of Examiners," to which he was appointed by Altenstein, was all but gone, he said. Given that he has "totally sacrificed what means [he] possessed to acquire the training which I now place in the Royal service," he now expected more compensation.[21]

In his reply to Hegel, Altenstein explained that, due to the "'demagogy' scare," he could neither "press forward quickly" on Hegel's behalf nor "execute ... [his own] project too quickly." Still, he was able to procure a 600-Thaler travel fund (about one-third of his annual salary) for Hegel, half of which was meant as a payment for the previous year.[22]

Of course, Altenstein had to receive Hardenberg's approval for this grant, and so had to convince the chancellor of Hegel's usefulness (or "effectiveness," as he used to call it) to the state. He did so with the following message, written on June 10:

> He is probably the most profound and dignified philosopher Germany has. Even more decisive, however, is his value as a human being and as a university teacher. He has been infinitely beneficial

---

[20] *Letters*, 473-74 (*Briefe II*, #421).
[21] Ibid., 576 (#413).
[22] *Briefe II*, #417.

to the youth. With courage, earnestness and expert knowledge, he has opposed solid philosophizing to spreading degeneration and has broken through the conceit of young people. He is to be highly honored for his convictions, which, along with his beneficial effectiveness, will generally be recognized even by those who are filled with mistrust of all philosophy [i.e., those authorities who are suspicious of all philosophy].[23]

Hardenberg, who would die a few months later, approved the request. Hegel thanked Altenstein for the grant in July. It freed him "from the various urgent economic burdens." He was also grateful, "all the more deeply," for the minister's "satisfaction thus far" with his "public activity" as a philosophy professor. This, he said, "encourages and strengthens me in this difficult profession of mine." Particularly important to "me," he told Altenstein, are "the various unmistakable signs," such as the travel grant and the minster's compliments, which

> have instilled the heartening conviction in me that possible anxieties on the part of the highest authorities, which can easily be caused by wrongheaded endeavors in philosophy, have left my public efficacy as a professor untouched. *I have, on the contrary, been persuaded that my work as well has not gone without recognition and success in helping young minds studying here attain correct concepts, and in making me worthy of the trust of Your Excellency and of the Royal Government* [emphasis added].[24]

The trust Altenstein had shown in Hegel's ability to stray the "young minds" away from "demagogic" inclinations would yield more benefits, in addition to the generous travel grant and verbal compliments. As we will see throughout the remainder of this book, Altenstein would continue to support Hegel's activities and bestow upon him increasingly more authority to shape the academic landscape in Prussia.

3. Overshadowing Schleiermacher (and Savigny)

Hegel's growing influence was also aided by others. Indeed, in 1819, he befriended Johannes Schulze, a high-ranking administrator of universities and high schools in Altenstein's ministry.[25] His friendship with Schulze was correctly perceived by others both as a sign of Hegel's growing influence

---

[23] *Berichten*, #376.
[24] *Letters*, 577 (*Briefe II*, #418).
[25] *Berichten*, #317.

X. Making Friends and Enemies

and, relatedly, as Altenstein's growing and unwelcomed interference in academic affairs.[26]

Moreover, already in the early 1820s, "there was a formal Hegelian school" at Berlin University, thanks in no small measure to the help Hegel was receiving from the likes of Marheineke, Henning, and Heinrich Gustav Hotho (Eduard Gans and others would join them soon). These figures had significantly "contributed to the dissemination of his teaching."[27] In return, they were supported by Hegel and his own handlers.

Naturally, Hegel's growing influence did not please everyone. For instance, Friedrich Karl von Savigny found it "increasingly worrisome."[28] Savigny's annoyance with Hegel's growing influence had mainly to do with their academic differences, not to mention the earthly struggles for power at the university, in which Hegel was now beginning to have the upper hand.

Savigny was no spring chicken. He had gained his bearings at the university long before Hegel arrived there in 1818. In 1810, soon after the university was (re)founded, Savigny was appointed the chair of the law faculty with the support of Wilhelm von Humboldt, one of the main founders of the new university. He was hired because of his much-acclaimed achievements in the study of Roman law, which were regarded as important contributions to the new school of thought known as the Historical School. He had also served as the rector of the university for a year. Subsequently, he was appointed by the government to work with the commission for organizing the Prussian provincial estates in 1817. Two years later, in 1819, he became a member of the supreme court of appeal for the Rhine Provinces and a member of the commission for revising the Prussian legal code in 1820. In 1822, a mental breakdown caused him to slow down and even to retreat from his formidable functions and accomplishments.[29] In short, as far as Savigny was concerned, an ambitious and obnoxious sycophant suddenly appeared at the university and was now beginning to call the shots, pushing aside the founding fathers, as it were, of the university.

However, Hegel's main opponent at the university was the very influential Schleiermacher, who is still regarded as one of the most respected Protestant theologians today.[30] Hegel's main problem with him was that he

---

[26] Horst Althaus, *Hegel: An Intellectual Biography*, trans. Michael Tarsh (Cambridge, UK: Polity Press, 2000), 155-56.
[27] *Berichten*, #385.
[28] Ibid., #336.
[29] For a brief but useful biography, see John MacDonell and Edward Manson (eds.), *The Great Jurists of the World* (Boston: Little, Brown, and Company, 1914), 561-89.
[30] See Jacqueline Mariña (ed.), *The Cambridge Companion to Friedrich Schleiermacher* (Cambridge: Cambridge University Press, 2005).

X. Making Friends and Enemies

had too much influence at the university. This meant that, if the situation remained unaltered, Hegel would have less of it than what he intended to acquire—total power. Moreover, the struggle between them was linked to Altenstein's struggle against the established faculty.

As Goethe noted when Hegel was hired, "Minister Altenstein seems to want to acquire a scientific bodyguard for himself"[31] against the likes of Schleiermacher. Some years later, Heinrich Leo, the historian, who was a Hegel groupie at the time, approvingly recalled that Altenstein (and Hardenberg) recruited Hegel to pacify the likes of Niebuhr, Savigny, Süwern, Schleiermacher, and Humboldt, who were jealously guarding academic freedom against state intervention. Hegel understood immediately that "he would procure for himself the most important position [at the university] if he made himself the tool ... [of the minister against the formidable] influence of this circle" of recalcitrant academics.[32]

Initially, only de Wette, who knew Hegel since their mutual Jena years, fully understood Hegel's aims. For this reason, among other reasons, he was the foremost opponent of Hegel's appointment at Berlin in 1816 (see Chapter 6). He was clearly shocked when Altenstein hired him in 1818, though he was able to muster enough optimism to believe, with some trepidation, that Hegel was destined to fail in achieving his aims. He expressed this optimism to Fries with the following words: "Hegel is coming here. I am not afraid of him. I now have too much influence among the students of my faculty, and Schleiermacher certainly eclipses him too much."[33] For the reasons provided in Chapter 8, things did not go so well for de Wette. Of course, Hegel was not responsible for his dismissal, though he was one of its chief advocates among the Berlin faculty.

More pertinent to our present story in this context is the confrontation Hegel and Schleiermacher had over de Wette's dismissal at the end of 1819, which officially inaugurated their decade-long struggle. It is said with reasonable plausibility that Hegel decided to lecture on the philosophy of religion, for the first time in 1821, to undermine Schleiermacher's influence, since this was the latter's field of specialization.[34]

It is also widely claimed in the existing literature that Schleiermacher himself was responsible for fueling Hegel's reaction to him with his (and Savigny's) successful effort to block Hegel's membership in the very prestigious Prussian Academy of Sciences. There is some truth to this claim,

---

[31] *Berichten*, #264.
[32] Heinrich Leo, "Der Hegelianismus in Preussen," in *Zeitschrift für Religions- und Geistesgeschichte* 10, no. 1 (1958): 51-60.
[33] *Berichten*, #262.
[34] Richard Crouter, "Hegel and Schleiermacher at Berlin: A Many-Sided Debate," *Journal of the American Academy of Religion* 48, no. 1 (1980): 19-43, 35-36.

X. Making Friends and Enemies

though it is important to note two things in this regard. First, as noted earlier, Altenstein brought Hegel to Berlin to undermine the likes of Schleiermacher, which means that the latter's opposition to Hegel's membership originally stemmed from the hostile acts of Hegel toward him. Second, Schleiermacher's opposition to Hegel's membership was linked to an earlier policy of the Academy, which had been in effect since 1812. In other words, it is more accurate to say that Schleiermacher had continued to adhere to the policy "in order to keep Hegel away from the Academy"[35] after it became clear to him that Hegel was precisely the kind of fellow the policy was meant to keep away from this institution in the first place.

The Academy's policy was established in relation to Fichte, it is said, who was also denied membership. It rested on the conviction that speculative philosophy was too doctrinaire and partisan, and so too exclusive to deserve representation in such an enterprise. Otherwise put, the policy was meant, not without some irony, to urge collaborative effort and a collective spirit both within and among the prevailing academic sciences, even if this meant excluding some scholars. However, and this is important, the policy was also at odds with Altenstein's ambitions.

In his October 1819 report to Hardenberg, Altenstein took issue with the Academy's policy, arguing that it constituted an impediment to the development of sciences within the Prussian state. The Academy had to be reformed, he reported.[36] Evidently, his report was inspired by his desire to have more control over the Academy, which included the plan to make Hegel one of its members. After all, he promised just such a membership to Hegel when he recruited him in 1818. This was a rare struggle in which Altenstein, and Hegel by extension, would fail to prevail. Even after Schleiermacher ended his opposition to Hegel's membership a decade later, the (real) natural scientists opposed it on the grounds that he preached false science and was too partisan.

However, Altenstein found another way to significantly empower his "scientific bodyguard." Hegel was now deputized to decide academic appointments throughout Prussia. Hinrichs, Hegel's former student at Heidelberg, was one of the first to benefit from Hegel's new authority. The prepayment for this benefit was the "Hegelian" book he had written, in some measure, against Schleiermacher. His publisher agreed to publish it on the condition that Hegel contribute a preface to it, which Hinrichs requested from his master on March 14, 1821.[37] After merely skimming

---

[35] Adolf Harnack, *Geschichte der Königlich preussischen akademie der wissenschaften zu Berlin*, vol. 1 (Berlin: Reichsdruckerei, 1900), 691-93, n. 1.
[36] Altenstein report is reprinted in Harnack, *Geschichte der Königlich preussischen akademie der wissenschaften zu Berlin*, 417-19.
[37] *Briefe II*, #382.

X. Making Friends and Enemies

through his manuscript (by his own admission), Hegel agreed to write the preface on April 7.[38] Hinrichs' book was published in May.

On August 13, 1822, Hegel informed Hinrichs that he recently spoke with "the Minister of Education," Altenstein, about his employment. Tellingly, the authorities were not checking to see whether the applicant had grasped the true significance of the master's philosophy. "A main factor in being able to come to a decision is the receipt of assurance from the police that you are not known for demagogical intrigues and opinions," clarified Hegel to Hinrichs. But Hegel was convinced, and must have told this to his own master, that the young academic was nothing of the sort: "Since I am convinced that your entire intellectual orientation, as well as your character, have left you wholly untouched by such twaddle, commotion, and baseness, at least no obstacle will be put in your way from this [the minister's] quarter."[39] As Hegel correctly anticipated, Hinrichs was appointed to a post in the Prussian city of Breslau in short order.

In the same letter, Hegel also hastened to add, gleefully, that "Schleiermacher has been refused a leave of absence for travel during the present vacation period. Rumor has it that he faces an investigation." Schleiermacher, a famed theologian and philosopher, as well as an original founding-faculty at Berlin, was suspected of having "demagogical" sympathies. Consequently, his lectures and sermons were monitored by police spies and other informants. Very likely, Hegel heard the "rumor" from Altenstein during the conversation he mentioned to Hinrichs. He also had a chat with "the Minister" about his preface to Hinrichs' book.[40] The preface had little to say on Hinrichs' book, which it was supposed to introduce to the public. In other words, the aspiring academic's book was eclipsed by Hegel's infamous attack against Schleiermacher in its preface.

As I have been at pains to show throughout this work, Hegel had excelled in superficial jargon and vituperation, not philosophical thinking, and it was now high time to utilize this *modus operandi* against Schleiermacher in someone else's book. Accordingly, in his preface, he first took Schleiermacher's theology to task with pretentious metaphysics. Then, he resorted to his well-known tactic of basically declaring his opponent stupid. According to Hegel, the latter's understanding of religion as essentially a *feeling* of dependence on God implied that dogs were the best Christians:

> If religion in man is based only on feeling, then he really has no further determination other than the feeling of his dependence, and so a dog

---

[38] Ibid., #383.
[39] *Letters*, 488-89, (*Briefe*, #425).
[40] Ibid.

X. Making Friends and Enemies

would be the best Christian, for it carries this [feeling of dependence] in itself most intensely and lives primarily in this feeling. A dog even has feelings of salvation when its hunger is satisfied by a bone.[41]

"To compare the consciousness of absolute dependence to an animal feeling," comments an informed author, "seems manifestly unfair as an interpretation of the introductory paragraphs of *The Christian Faith*. Any careful reader of Schleiermacher knows that the feeling in question presupposes a capacity for self-consciousness that is possessed only by humans." [42] My claim is that Hegel was not only ignorant of Schleiermacher's theology but also tried to cover his ignorance with deliberately vicious slander, intended to harm him. This is more evident in what Hegel says in a less-cited passage, in which he attempts to establish a link between the philosophers of "feeling" and "evils of the time."[43]

The much more mature Schleiermacher apparently took all this with a grain of salt. On December 28, he wrote to his friend, Karl H. Sack, about his preference to respond to Hegel's slander "with silence."[44] It turns out, Hegel, proud of his silly dog-analogy, continued to use it in his lectures. As Schleiermacher informed de Wette during the summer of 1823, "Hegel, as he has already done in the preface to Hinrich's *Religionsphilosophie*, continues in his lectures to rant about my animal-like ignorance of God, and to exclusively recommend Marheineke's [Hegelian] theology. I take no notice of it, but it is not pleasant."[45]

Apparently, Schleiermacher was unaware of the fact that Hegel was bent upon destroying him with more serious denunciations than making offensive and unwarranted allusions to his theology. On March 6, Varnhagen von Ense noted in his diary that, during a lecture, Hegel likened Thersites (form the *Iliad*)—likely because of his appearance as a disobedient agitator—to the contemporary "demagogic" philosophers and provided "definite" signs to clarify that Schleiermacher was his target. Some "students," added Varnhagen, "stomped their feet" to demonstrate "their displeasure" with Hegel's insinuation.[46] To be sure, unlike what a recent biographer would have us believe, these were not merely "sarcastic" jibes. They were very malicious accusations at a time when the "demagogues" were facing police action.

As H. W. A, Stieglitz, one of his students and incorrigible admirers (he used to send platonic love poems to Hegel), reported on August 15, 1824,

---

[41] Hegel, *Berliner Schriften*, 74.
[42] Crouter, "Hegel and Schleiermacher at Berlin: A Many-Sided Debate," 36.
[43] Hegel, *Berliner Schriften*, 77.
[44] *Berichten*, #383.
[45] Ibid., #391.
[46] Ibid., #388

Hegel's repeated "bitter polemic" against others, parroted by his "followers," was earning him many "enemies."[47] In fact, Hegel's lectures, especially on the philosophy of right, were frequently interrupted with denunciations of his opponents either as insipid figures or dangerous "demagogues" or both, as we have seen in Chapter 9 (note: the version of the *Philosophy of Right* we have examined contains the lecture notes [1822-1825] of Hotho and Gans). Apparently, he was exercising the same strategy in his lecture on the philosophy of religion.

Despite his growing influence, however, Hegel's "party," on which we will have more to say in the next chapter, remained a minority within the faculty, though it was more powerful than the majority in terms of its influence. One reason for this superior influence was the "party" itself, which included militant disciples, spreading his gospel. Another advantage he had over his opponents, on which just about all else depended, was the uncheckered support he was receiving from Altenstein and his ministry. As noted earlier, Hegel had by now become the deputized decision-maker on who could and could not procure a teaching post in the philosophy and related departments of Prussian universities. On December 16, 1822, Savigny lamented that Hegel "enjoys such unconditional trust from Minister Altenstein that the most vigorous [*wackersten*] philosophy teachers cannot find a job unless they belong to his school."[48]

If Savigny was exaggerating, it was not by much. Several months later, Schleiermacher also reported to a friend that a very gifted lecturer "is completely repudiated by the ministry [of Altenstein] because he is not Hegel's follower."[49] Another report stated more generally, and perhaps also with only slight exaggeration, that "the ministry continued to favor" Hegel's clique or "party" to such an extent that "Hegelian philosophy became the royal Prussian political philosophy," and that all it took was "a little" Hegelian "speculative logic" and "theology ... to become a full professor."[50]

4. Victor Cousin: Hegel's "Demagogue" Friend

"It is praised that the Berlin University is now free of the [demagogic] machinations; [it is said that] Hegel has induced this better spirit among the students," observed Varnhagen on February 24.[51] As we will see in due course, this was a common evaluation of Hegel's services to the state until

---

[47] Ibid., #411.
[48] Ibid., #382.
[49] Ibid., #390.
[50] "Die Universität Berlin," 22.
[51] *Berichten*, #399.

X. Making Friends and Enemies

his death in 1831. It was also the main reason why he kept receiving governmental support. This image of Hegel has been increasingly questioned during the second half of the twentieth century and remains a largely disputed image today (see Epilogue). One reason given for this unwarranted revisionism is Hegel's involvement in the liberal Cousin's entanglement with the Prussian authorities. However, this involvement does nothing to undermine the double-image of Hegel as the sworn enemy of the "demagogues" and a philosopher of the Prussian state. Indeed, it helps reinforce it, but rather indirectly.

On October 14, 1824, at the instigation of the French secret police, Cousin was arrested in Dresden. He was suspected of conspiring with some German radicals, such as Follen, to foment a revolution in Germany. Cousin certainly knew Follen through Lafayette, their mutual friend. However, Follen was *en route* to the United States from France, not in Dresden, when Cousin was arrested.[52] Still, in accordance with the Karlsbad Decrees, and with the coordination of the Mainz Commission, Cousin was imprisoned in Berlin while his case was being investigated. Shortly before his arrest, and by coincidence, Hegel ran into Cousin in Dresden. When he heard of Cousin's arrest and imprisonment in Berlin, he resolved at once to write a letter to Schuckmann, the Prussian minister of interior, requesting to visit the incarcerated Cousin.

It is important to note that Hegel's November 4 petition was carefully composed and delivered to avoid any indication of defiance on his part. He thus consulted Kamptz, the police chief, about the permissibility of sending his petition to Schuckmann and then submitted the petition to Kamptz, asking him to determine "the propriety and admissibility of delivering it to His Excellency [i.e., Schuckmann]."[53] In short, Hegel had taken some necessary steps to avoid putting himself at risk by requesting to visit the inmate. The widespread assumption that he acted very "courageously" by petitioning to visit Cousin is thus a great exaggeration.

In his petition, Hegel first explained how he met Cousin in Heidelberg in 1817 and ran into him once more in 1818.[54] Based on these limited encounters, he "came to know him as a man with very serious interest in the sciences in general, and in his own special field in particular." However, and to distance himself from Cousin's well-known liberal politics, Hegel felt the need to "add that it was in this [strictly academic] capacity alone

---

[52] Eliza Cabot Follen, *Life of Charles Follen* (Cambridge: Thomas H. Webb, 1844), 67, 80.
[53] *Letters,* 634-35 (*Briefe III,* #486).
[54] For Cousin's accounts of their first encounter, see Victor Cousin, *Oeuvres de Victor Cousin: Cours d'histoire de la philosophie morale. Fragments philosophiques,* vol. 2 (Bruxelles: Société Belge de Librairie, 1840), 20 ff.; Victor Cousin, "Souvenirs D'Allemagne," in *Revue des Deux Mondes* (1866): 594-619, 605-06.

that I then came to know him." In the remaining portion of the letter, Hegel continued to describe Cousin's "ardent" interest in German philosophy and activities "at the University of Paris" favorably. He also mentioned, admiringly, Cousin's "large-scale literary endeavors," such as his translations of Plato's dialogues. However, clarified Hegel once again, his own interest in Cousin's literary endeavors has been pursued without any personal contact with him during the last "six years that have now gone by." In other words, and this could not be overemphasized, they have not had any direct contact during the last six years, implying that he is not privy to Cousin's other activities. Wisely so, Hegel proceeded to explain that he "ran into [Cousin] in transit through Dresden" by pure coincidence and that their conversation simply consisted of Cousin's "various assurances of his continued kind sentiments toward" Hegel. He was also careful enough not to vouch for Cousin's innocence, for he had no way of knowing for certain what Cousin had been up to since their last encounter in 1818, or why he was in Dresden shortly before his arrest. Since he has not thus far thought of him as an agitator, he reasoned in his petition, Hegel was now "all the more surprised to have to conclude from his present arrest that ... [the minister] must hold very grave circumstantial evidence against" Cousin. However, since Cousin has not yet been "pronounced guilty, and in as much as nothing has yet been decided on his guilt," Hegel is inclined to retain his prior "respect" for him. Based on this prior conviction, he explained, he desires to visit him. Hegel concluded the letter by emphasizing that his request is not based on "any further motives" than the one just stated, adding: "I will not fail to consider most respectfully all the conditions which it may please Your Excellency, in the interest of the police, to place upon this visit [with Cousin], should it be permitted, in order to assure that my visit reflects honorably on myself."[55]

Hegel's request was denied, likely in accordance with the general policy to keep those suspected of "demagogic" activity in isolation while their investigation was still ongoing. In fact, Hegel himself must have known that his petition would not be approved for this well-known reason, though he pretended to be "uncertain as to the permissibility" of visiting Cousin in his petition. But this observation does not explain why he requested it in the first place. It is possible that he really thought he owed Cousin a visit out of personal friendship (certainly not because he was a liberal). However, this hypothesis is made rather implausible by the fact that Hegel, who had not met or communicated with Cousin for six years, did not in 1824 regard him as a close friend. If so, there was something quite strange about his petition.

---

[55] *Letters,* 634-35 (*Briefe III,* #486).

X. Making Friends and Enemies

In my view, Hegel's petition was mainly a ploy to clear his own name, since he could have been put under investigation merely for talking to him in Dresden, if not also for having met him six years ago. After all, the police had been questioning everyone who knew Cousin and had some information about his previous visits to Germany. Schelling, who was also questioned, attested to his innocence. The naturally anxious Hegel, I suspect, thought it wise to clarify the nature of his relationship to Cousin to the authorities before they learned about it from others.

Be that as it may, as Varnhagen observed, Hegel's "good standing with the government" explained why he had not risked becoming a "suspect" in the eyes of the police by requesting to see Cousin.[56] More minimally put, his good standing with the government was not in any way tarnished by his petition. Cousin himself was released from Prussian custody in February 1825, due to lack of evidence to convict him, though he was ordered to stay in Berlin until the completion of the investigation. There is no evidence whatsoever to validate the claim that Hegel had played an important role in securing his release by urging public protest against Cousin's arrest.[57]

As Varnhagen noted in his diary entry of February 12, 1825, Cousin was released after his arrest was "recognized as a mistake." Oddly, he noted, Cousin initially praised the local authorities the most for securing his release, especially Schuckmann and Kamptz—the very people in charge of investigating his case. He also visited Hegel, Schleiermacher, Ancillon, and Niebuhr.[58] The latter was a conservative academic (historian) and a state official; Ancillon was a well-known lackey of the king of Prussia and, some say more so, of Metternich. On February 16, Varnhagen himself was introduced to Cousin by Hegel. He noted in his diary that Cousin was eagerly visiting with many prominent scholars, including Hegel, Schleiermacher, Bekker, and Savigny. This mixture of friends was itself strange enough, though not as strange as the fact that Cousin had the most intimate relationship with Niebuhr. Thus, Varnhagen understandably found Cousin's friendships quite bizarre.[59] Niebuhr, on the other hand, told his wife on March 18 that Cousin was having "great intimacy" with Hegel, largely due to the latter's concern about his "imprisonment," and that Hegel was giving the Frenchmen all sorts of strange ideas about the history of Christianity. Even "Christ himself knew very little about Christianity," Hegel allegedly told Cousin.[60]

---

[56] *Berichten*, #419.
[57] *Pace* Pinkard, *Hegel: A Biography*, 526-27.
[58] *Berichten*, #423.
[59] Ibid., #424.
[60] Ibid., #426.

X. Making Friends and Enemies

For his part, Hegel was not as enamored with Cousin as the latter was with him. This can be observed in the fact that he refrained from replying to Cousin's letters for a year after the latter's departure from Berlin. Hegel's first letter to Cousin was mailed on April 5, 1826, and mainly consisted of an elaborate apology for not replying earlier, expressing gratitude for the literary material Cousin had sent to him and praising the latter's scholarly endeavors. Even though Cousin's last letter informed him that he still spent his time "regretting" his unjust imprisonment in Prussia, Hegel's letter barely went into this topic, merely commenting that Cousin's youth might account for his "somberness." In other words, unlike Hegel, he was "not yet so hardened in the habit of renunciation." However, he refrained from clarifying that he had been renounced for attacking the "demagogues," whereas Cousin was renounced for being one. He also made some general comments about the current French and Prussian politics.[61]

However, Cousin was not about to forget either his lamentable experience or the sentimental debt he owed Hegel. In one of his subsequent letters, he included his 1826 translation of Plato's *Gorgias*, which he dedicated to Hegel. The dedication included the following comment: "When, as I was recently traveling again in Germany, the extravagant police ... dared attack my liberty, making the most atrocious accusations, declaring me proven guilty and convicted in advance, you [Hegel] spontaneously rushed forward to tell my judges that I was your friend."[62]

Hegel once again refrained from replying to the several letters Cousin had sent him subsequently. On July 1, 1827, he finally replied. Apart from the usual apologies and pleasantries, Hegel's letter mentioned the dedication and Cousin's experience at the hands of the Prussian police in a lighthearted manner: "This dedication, a monument of your friendly sentiments in my regard, contains at last your manifesto against our police—for whose omniscience Plato, I may add, is probably an obscure corner into which it has not likely penetrated." This vague statement about the unphilosophical police, I suspect, was Hegel's way of refraining from rehashing the issue of Cousin's arrest. The more important news Hegel reported, which was likely the main reason why he decided to reply belatedly, was that he was now ready to accept Cousin's invitation to visit Paris.[63]

After a long journey in August, Hegel arrived in Paris on September 3, 1827. As his multiple reports to his wife suggest, he was generally impressed by what he had seen and experienced in Paris. As for his reunion with Cousin, he reported in one of his letters that they "get on well together,

---

[61] *Letters*, 636-38 (*Briefe III*, #508).
[62] Ibid., 639 (#530). For the dedication, see Hoffmeister's note to #530, pages 404-05.
[63] Ibid., 640-41 (#547).

X. Making Friends and Enemies

enjoying a warmly cordial relationship."[64] On October 2, as previously planned, he left Paris with Cousin for Cologne. Of key interest for our purposes in this book is a conversation Hegel had with Cousin on the relationship of philosophy and religion during their visit to Cologne. As Cousin would later remember it, they agreed that "religion is absolutely indispensable, and that one must not give oneself over to the fatal chimera of trying to replace religion with philosophy." However, "Hegel believed that only in Protestantism is the reconciliation between religion and philosophy possible." "As soon as the question of Catholicism was brought up," remembered Cousin, Hegel "forgot the principles" they "shared in common and lost himself in thoughts quite unworthy of a philosopher."[65]

Clearly, the French philosopher had all along misunderstood Hegel's principles, and so was now shocked to hear him castigate his, Cousin's, own religion. In fact, his memory must have failed him, since he was informed by Hotho a year earlier that, on one occasion, Hegel offended his Catholic students by demeaning their faith. We will discuss this issue in the next chapter.

---

[64] Ibid., 650 (#559).
[65] *Berichten*, #528.

Chapter Eleven

XI. RECEPTIONS OF HEGEL'S LECTURES

1. Incoherent Genius and Mystic

> Hegel's philosophy is so odd that one would not have expected him to be able to get sane men to accept it, but he did. He set it out with so much obscurity that people thought it must be profound.[1]

Hegel was little noticed during his initial days in Berlin. "Nobody talks about him," complained his friend Karl Solger on November 22, 1818.[2] Unfortunately, Solger died about a year later without witnessing how his friend had quickly become a popular subject of conversations in Berlin.

Heinrich Heine, the famed poet, journalist, essayist, satirist, and literary critic, had many encounters with Hegel from 1821 to 1823. Based on his observations, he reported the following satirical observation of the popular philosopher to a friend:

> I saw how Hegel, with his almost comically earnest countenance, sat on the fatal eggs like a brood-hen and heard him cackle. To tell the truth, I seldom understood him, and only contrived to comprehend him by subsequent reflection. I believe he did not want to be understood, which accounts for his parenthetical style, and perhaps for his predilection for people who, as he knew, could not understand him, and whom he, therefore, honored the more willingly with his intimacy. Everyone in Berlin wondered at the close relations between the contemplative Hegel and the late Heinrich Beer ..., [who] was a very foolish fellow ... [He] was the philosopher's most intimate friend, his Pylades, and followed him like his shadow ... I believe that ... Hegel was persuaded that Beer understood nothing he heard him say, and so could give vent to all sorts of fanciful ideas in his presence. Hegel's talk, moreover, was a sort of monologue, delivered by jerks in a monotonous

---

[1] Bertrand Russell, *Philosophy and Politics* (London: Cambridge University Press, 1947), 16.
[2] Günther Nicolin (ed.), *Hegel in Berichten seiner Zeitgenossen* (Hamburg: Felix Meiner, 1970), #290. Henceforth cited simply as *Berichten*.

XI. Receptions of Hegel's Lectures

voice; and the strangeness of his expressions often struck me, and many remain in my memory.³

If Heine speculated that Hegel did not want to be understood, a Polish student, Mickiewicz, concluded that anyone "who spoke so unclearly, and who had to spend an hour trying to develop the meaning of just two terms [*understanding* and *reason* in this case], probably did not understand himself." The intriguing idea that even Hegel could not understand what he was saying was questioned by another student, who wondered whether such a psychological state was even possible at all.⁴

Another account, a later reminiscence (1841), noted that Hegel's incoherence had initially repelled many people away from his lectures. "It was thought [at the time] that he was perhaps even more incomprehensible [jargon-wise] than Fichte," and even lacked "the strong, manly personality, and eloquence" of the latter to compensate for his "grandiose incomprehensibility." However, the same attribute of the philosopher would become one of his attractive features, as the Berlin socialites (lectures were open to the public), government officials, and his regular students alike began disputing the meaning of Hegel's unusual nomenclature, such as "being in-itself, for-itself, and in-and-for-itself." Some were even "pleased" to have finally gasped "the great [Hegelian] paradox of the identity of being [*sein*] and nothing [*nichts*]," which was thought to be "the key to his system."⁵

Heinrich Gustav Hotho also portrayed a similar image of him. When he first met him, this future disciple was repelled by Hegel's external appearance and thought that the philosopher looked as good as dead. His lectures were not any better:

> Exhausted, he sat there morosely as if he had collapsed into himself, his head bent down. While lecturing, he kept turning the pages of his long folio notebooks ... The ceaseless clearing of his throat and coughing interrupted his flow of speech. Every sentence remained isolated and came out with much effort, cut in pieces and jumbled. Every word, every syllable was released only reluctantly so as to receive a strangely pronounced emphasis from the metallic and empty voice, expressed in his heavy Swabian dialect, as if each were the most important.⁶

---

³ Gustav Karpeles (ed.), *Heinrich Heine's Life Told in His Own Words*, trans. Arthur Dexter (New York: Henry Holt and Company, 1893), 111-12.
⁴ *Berichten*, #600.
⁵ Anonymous, "Die Universität Berlin," in *Hallische Jahrbücher für deutsche Wissenschaft und Kunst* (Leipzig: Otto Wigand, 1841): 21-23.
⁶ *Berichten*, #385.

XI. Receptions of Hegel's Lectures

Yet, in retrospect, Hotho was able to give a dialectical twist to this unfortunate appearance and performance of his master. After describing "eloquence" in public speech as a sign of superficiality, he concluded that "this man [Hegel] had to produce the most powerful thoughts from the deepest ground of things, and if they were to have a living effect then … they had to regenerate themselves in him in an ever living present." Thus, as an ideal-type acolyte, Hotho was able to grasp and appreciate the "inner merits" of Hegel's incomprehensible lectures and would soon follow him with the zeal and earnestness expected of him.[7]

Another student, Gustav Parthey, the philologist and art historian, who had fond memories of his encounters with the Hegel crowd at Berlin, recalled later that Hegel's all-encompassing "dialectic" was impressive enough to attract a formidable and devoted following. Soon after his arrival in Berlin, Hegel "gathered around a circle of disciples, who repeated his words and fanatically made propaganda for him." Parthey himself was impressed with Hegel's logic, but was dismayed by the "most incomplete lecture" he attended one day (likely, the only one he attended). "After the lecture, I asked the philosophical friend who had taken me along, and who was one of Hegel's enthusiastic followers, what the following sentence meant: 'essence is the negation of the negation.' To my great astonishment, he did not know what it meant," even though he had been following Hegel's lectures on logic all along and advertising his wisdom to others.[8]

According to another eye-witness report from 1828, the philosopher looked ghostly and sounded ghastly. His eyes often closed, he appeared to have a monologue with himself, repeating his sentences with slight alterations; he frequently paused to think hard about the most correct word he wanted to use, and interrupted all this awkwardness with frequent coughs. He was fond of using the word "therefore," often when it was not warranted. His unimpressive physical presence was enhanced with the awkward movement of his hands, resembling those of a swimmer struggling in rough waters. He was also in the habit of slandering other academics. Many opined that all these were but various symptoms of his greatness.[9]

Some took this opinion to even higher levels, believing that Hegel was a higher being of some kind, to be worshipped. Indeed, as we have seen in Chapter 2, he had the same effect on a small group of his students at Jena as well. To repeat Gabler's account, "the new philosophy," the philosophy of "the Absolute," "was still … garbled chaos," which was expressed in a "strange and unfamiliar … language and terminology," leading many students to declare the whole thing "'nonsense.'" Still, a few of them, the

---

[7] ibid.
[8] Ibid., #693.
[9] Ibid., #558.

XI. Receptions of Hegel's Lectures

true disciples ..., had the greatest esteem for the Master. They exhibited almost idolatrous worship for everything that emanated from him. He was to them a higher being ... This worship extended to everything, even the least of what one could learn from the man's life and deeds, every move, every manner of conduct and behavior, every utterance. Behind every word that one could catch [from his mouth] was [assumed to be] a deep meaning, implying a [profound] truth.[10]

A similar phenomenon was unfolding at Berlin University, apparently at a larger scale. Some of his devoted students had even experienced miraculous transfigurations. Hotho was one of them. In "a thinly disguised autobiographical novel published in 1835," he "made the Hegelian conversion the nodal point of his protagonist's spiritual pilgrimage:"

> Inwardly exhausted and spiritually dead, without hope and without faith, I threw myself into the arms of philosophy and she alone embraced me with generous consoling grace. I can no longer describe the specific stages of this process—the emotionally moving days of learning and striving, the glimmerings of the first comprehension, the expanses that opened up to me ... the riches that flowed toward me daily without interruption, until I was overcome by an unhoped-for blessedness—but the remembrance of this happiness still rests in my soul with the echo of an attained peace, as when doubters are delighted when, forgetting all earthly dissensions, they suddenly feel themselves elevated to a pure heavenly activity. Hardly a year had passed, and I discovered myself again as a totally new person.[11]

After his encounters with the teaching of the master, Wilhelm Vatke was also transfigured in his own way, so he thought. He now "knows with certainty," he told his brother, "the eternal beings as they are; the longing is satisfied."

> You will find it insane if I tell you that I am seeing God face to face; yet, it is true. The beyond [or the transcendent] has become this world [to me]. Man himself is a point of light in the infinite light, and the like recognizes the like. Because I am all essence [*Wesenheit*], I know all essence; and insofar as I rest in the great heart of God, I am blessed already. Oh, only if I could tell you how blessed I am! All sciences are

---

[10] Ibid., #92.
[11] Quoted in John E. Toews, *Hegelianism: The Path Toward Dialectical Humanism, 1805-1841* (London: Cambridge University Press, 1980), 91.

XI. Receptions of Hegel's Lectures

clear and transparent to me: I know what history wills [or wants] …, how art forms itself …, how religion creates itself.[12]

For his part, Karl Ludwig Michelet, another committed acolyte, explained to his father that Hegel's philosophy is "'a science that exalts man and teaches him his highest calling," because it elevates "the individual to a state of complete identification with the divine spirit. In the activity of philosophical comprehension man 'carries the consciousness of God within himself,' Michelet insisted, and 'is thus elevated above the limitations of the world and lives eternally in the realm of truth.'"[13]

An incident captures well the dilemma entailed in Hegel's incomprehensibility, though the verdict reached was more negative than the ones reached by his transfigured acolytes. On October 16, 1827, Hegel visited Goethe in Weimar. Goethe, Hegel's boss during his Jena years, was pleased to see him and to learn that he was doing quite well for himself in Berlin. As we have seen in Chapter 2, he was also quite concerned about Hegel's incoherence. Perhaps, one can only guess, he wondered about this when Hegel showed up for lunch, invited. Ottilie, Goethe's daughter-in-law, and several others were also present. As Ottilie noted, Goethe was in the habit of inviting people over without introducing them, so that she and others had no idea who the guest was. Thus, the lunch started with the reciprocated "silent bows" of Hegel and Goethe's entourage.

> During the meal, Goethe mostly abstained from talking, probably in order not to disrupt the speech of the very talkative and logically astute guest, who [expressed himself with] oddly formulated sentences. An entirely novel nomenclature, a mode of expression mentally transgressing itself, the peculiarly-employed philosophical formulas of the ever more enlivened man in the course of his demonstrations finally sufficed to reduce Goethe to complete silence without the guest even noticing it … After the … guest departed, Goethe asked: "Well, how did you like the man?" "Strange! replied [Ottilie's sister,] I cannot tell whether he is intelligent or confused. He gave me the impression of an unclear thinker." Goethe smiled ironically, and said: "Well, well, we have just been eating with the most famous modern philosopher—with Georg Wilhelm Friedrich Hegel."[14]

Thus, not everyone was impressed with the incoherent master's transformative abilities.

---

[12] Quoted in Heinrich Benecke, *Wilhelm Vatke in seinem Leben und seinen Schriften* (Bonn, Emil Strauß, 1883), 47-48.
[13] Toews, *Hegelianism: The Path Toward Dialectical Humanism*, 91.
[14] *Berichten*, #525.

2. "Mystifying Charlatan"

As was the case with his earlier career, Hegel had quickly earned the reputation of being a slanderous charlatan in the eyes of many. An early example of this was his "harassment" of Immanuel Hermann Fichte (the famous philosopher's son). In attempting to take Fichte's dissertation to task, Hegel "embarrassed himself with his [poor] Latin, and so spoiled his philological and learned fame among the local scholars."[15] This news was reported to Fries by Rödiger, who, it should be disclosed, disliked Hegel.

Arguably, Hegel's nature-philosophy was the most ridiculed aspect of his "system" as it often came into conflict with the observational sciences and their discoveries. As we have seen in Chapter 2, the ridiculing of Hegel's knowledge of natural sciences dates to the beginning of his teaching career in 1801. His *Dissertatio philosophica de Orbitis Planetarum* was ridiculed by both Duke Ernst II and Baron Franz Xaver von Zach, two of the foremost astronomers in Germany at the time. Leaping forward two decades, Arthur Schopenhauer, who famously despised Hegel, was among the first philosophers to openly question Hegel's scientific wisdom in Berlin.

Schopenhauer's only known *direct* encounter with Hegel took place on March 23, 1820.[16] This encounter had to do with Schopenhauer's dissertation defense to acquire his teaching license (*habilitation*) at Berlin University. His dissertation focused on the three causes (mechanical, physical, and chemical), which explain the stimuli and motives involved in "animal functions." Apparently, Hegel took himself to be an expert in this field of science as well. During the cross-examination, he first requested additional clarification on "the motive" of a horse lying down on the street. Schopenhauer replied that the earth as its resting place, coupled with its need to rest, counted as the *causes* in this example since the horse would not lie down in the absence of either. However, his response was not an answer to Hegel's question, which was about the *motive* behind the animal's behavior. Hegel sought further clarification by asking confusing, if not confused, questions: "Do you also consider animal functions as motives? That is, do the stroke of the heart, blood circulation, etc., result from motives?" Schopenhauer likely and understandably thought Hegel was asking one question—whether he called such bodily functions as "animal functions." Accordingly, he clarified that in the science of physiology, only "the conscious movements of the animal body" are called "animal functions," citing Albrecht Haller as the authority on this matter. Hegel retorted that such movements could not be called animal functions. At this point, Martin H. K. Lichtenstein, a zoologist by training, confirmed that

---

[15] *Berichten.*, #310.
[16] It is likely that Schopenhauer had attended some of Hegel's lectures.

XI. Receptions of Hegel's Lectures

Schopenhauer's definition of the term was correct. This intervention ended the rather abortive debate, and the interlocutors, including Hegel, declared Schopenhauer qualified to teach.[17] He could now teach as a *privatdozent* at Berlin University.

Schopenhauer went on to tell one of his friends, Karl Bähr, that "'Monsieur know-nothing [*Monsieur Nichtswisser*]'" was exposed during the disputation. "In fact, the *summus philosophus* revealed his lack of scientific knowledge on this issue [of animal functions]," reasoned Bähr in his own version of what Schopenhauer narrated to him shortly after his defense.[18]

Despite his bloated self-confidence, Schopenhauer's career at Berlin would soon falter. It is well-known that he deliberately scheduled his course at a time that was simultaneous with Hegel's lectures. Apparently, and to his dismay, very few students chose to hear him while Hegel's auditorium filled.

The related claim that Schopenhauer despised Hegel because he thought the latter was responsible for his failed career misses the point that he despised Hegel even before his teaching career at Berlin began, and that he would have despised him anyway. This claim rings even truer when we consider the fact that Schopenhauer was also hostile to Fichte and Schelling, who had nothing to do with his career. In fact, he thought the entire post-Kant German philosophy was unclear twaddle, Hegel's philosophy being the worst of all. Simply put, whatever else might have been his motive, Schopenhauer was just repelled by Hegel's character and teaching, and had repeatedly regarded him as a charlatan, who corrupted the minds of his students and followers.

At the close of 1829, Schopenhauer expressed how he felt about Hegel in a letter (written in English) to Francis Haywood:

> ... so much did by and by degenerate our German philosophy that we now see a mere swaggerer and charlatan, without a shadow of merit, I mean Hegel, with a compound of bombastic nonsense and positions bordering on madness, humbug about a part of German public, though but the more silly and untaught part, to be sure, yet by personal means and connections he contrived to get a philosopher's name and fame.[19]

After Hegel's death, Schopenhauer would frequently make similar comments about Hegel.[20] Such comments are usually regarded as mere

---

[17] Hegel, *Berliner Schriften*, 587-92. Also see *Berichten*, #321.
[18] *Berichten*, #321.
[19] Ibid., #621.
[20] The following is a well-known one:

XI. Receptions of Hegel's Lectures

"diatribes," not to be taken seriously, by Hegel's supporters. What is seldom noted is the fact that he had read Hegel's works, and some of his criticisms were well-founded reflections on Hegel's so-called "nature-philosophy." An example of this is found in the Preface to his *The Two Fundamental Problems of Ethics* (1841). Here, he once again calls Hegel a "very ordinary mind but extraordinary charlatan." "The so-called philosophy of *Hegel*," one also reads in his Preface, "was a colossal mystification," as he "scrawled nonsense as no mortal ever did before him."[21] To demonstrate his claim, Schopenhauer provides three examples from Hegel's *Encyclopedia of the Philosophical Sciences* (second edition, 1827).

> So in that book, in the section called 'Physics, §293, [Hegel] is dealing with specific gravity ..., and contests the assumption that it rests upon difference in porosity, using the following argument: 'An example of the *existent* specification of gravity is furnished by the following phenomenon: when a bar of iron, evenly balanced on its fulcrum, is magnetized, it loses its equilibrium and shows itself to be heavier at one pole than at the other. Here the one part is so affected that without changing its volume it becomes heavier; the matter, without [an] increase in its mass, has thus become specifically heavier.' Here, then, the ... [so-called] 'distinguished philosopher' makes the following inference: 'If a bar supported at its center of gravity subsequently becomes heavier on one side, then it falls to that side; but an iron bar falls to one side once it has been magnetized: therefore, it has become heavier in that place.' A worthy analogue to the inference: 'All geese have two legs, you have two legs, therefore you are a goose.' For, put into categorical form, the Hegelian syllogism reads: 'Everything that becomes heavier on one side falls to that side; this magnetized bar falls to one side: therefore, it has become heavier in that place.' [This] is the syllogistic reasoning of this 'distinguished philosopher' and reformer of logic ... [L]ikely ..., a textbook containing arguments of this sort and speaking of bodies becoming heavier without increase in mass will

---

The public had been forced to see [in Kant's philosophy] that what is obscure is not always without meaning; what was senseless and without meaning at once took refuge in obscure exposition and language. Fichte was the first to grasp and make vigorous use of this privilege; Schelling at least equaled him in this ... But the greatest effrontery in serving up sheer nonsense, in scrabbling together senseless and maddening webs of words, such as had previously been heard only in madhouses, finally appeared in Hegel. It became the instrument of the most ponderous and general mystification that has ever existed ...

Arthur Schopenhauer, *The World as Will and Representation*, vol. 1, trans. E. F. J. Payne (New York: Dover, 1966), 429.
[21] Arthur Schopenhauer, *The Two Fundamental Problems of Ethics*, trans. Christopher Janaway (Cambridge: Cambridge University Press, 2009), 15-16.

XI. Receptions of Hegel's Lectures

render the straightforward understanding of young people crooked and bent ...

The second example of the lack of common human understanding in ... [Hegel] is put on record by §269 of the same ... work ..., in the sentence: 'Gravitation directly contradicts the law of inertia; for, by virtue of the former, matter strives to get away *out of itself* to an Other.' What? [Here follows a brief correction of Hegel's silly claim and more insults, followed by an explanation of how Hegel's uneducated claim of contradiction rejects the fundamental law of causality.]

The ... [so-called] 'distinguished philosopher' ... [also makes the following claim] in §298 of the same master-work, where, polemicizing against the explanation of elasticity by means of pores, he says: 'True, it is admitted in the abstract that matter is perishable, not absolute, yet in practice this admission is resisted, ... so that in point of fact, matter is regarded as *absolutely self-subsistent, eternal.* This error springs from the general error of the understanding, that etc.'—What fool has ever conceded that *matter* is *perishable*? And which one [or a fool (i.e., Hegel)] calls the opposite an error? [Here follows an explanation of how the imperishability of matter, or the constancy of its "quantum," is a "cognition *a priori*, as firm and certain as any mathematical one."] ...

[In sum,] ... [the so-called] 'distinguished philosopher' teaches explicitly that bodies can become heavier without [an] increase in their mass, and that this is particularly the case with a magnetized iron bar; likewise, that gravitation contradicts the law of inertia; and finally, that matter is perishable. These three examples will certainly suffice to show what sticks out a mile when an opening is left for once in that thick cloak of nonsensical gibberish that scorns all human reason, in which the 'distinguished philosopher' is wont to be enveloped as he strides in and impresses the intellectual rabble.[22]

Schopenhauer goes on to cite more examples from Hegel's textbook to further justify why he thinks Hegel deserves his harsh language. He also disparages "the infinite loftiness with which this sinner looks down upon *Newton's* [principle of] universal attraction and *Kant's* metaphysical principles of natural science." Hegel, he goes on to say,

> gives a distorted portrayal of the Kantian philosophy and then, unable to gauge the magnitude of Kant's achievements and placed too low by nature to be able to rejoice at the appearance—so unspeakably rare—of a truly great mind, instead looks down loftily on this great, great man from the height of self-assured, infinite superiority ... True, this affectation of superiority towards genuine achievements is a well-

---

[22] Ibid., 16-19.

XI. Receptions of Hegel's Lectures

known trick of all charlatans on foot and on horseback, yet when presented to imbeciles it does not readily fail in its effect.[23]

Schopenhauer had said all these things without being privy to what his nemesis was telling his students in his courses verbally. Hegel had taught courses related to what he dubbed "the philosophy of nature" and, at times, "rational physics." They were among the least popular of his courses, though popular enough to attract about sixty (a rough average) students per semester.[24] Hegel's editors later polished and added the lecture notes (*Zusätze*) of his students to his *Encyclopedia of the Philosophical Sciences* (and other works). Michelet, a devoted disciple of the master, was the editor of its second part, *The Philosophy of Nature*. Michelet (and other disciple-editors) has been harshly judged for taking too many liberties with what Hegel himself might have had said, forgetting that Hegel's original *Encyclopedia* is largely unreadable and uninterpretable without the *Zusätze*. As Ludwig Boumann, the editor of the third part of the *Encyclopedia*, explained,

> I worked on the view that it was my absolute duty to bring the more or less raw material of the planned lectures into the artistic form rightly demanded of a scientific work. Without such a reworking, there would, in the present case, have been a repugnant lack of harmony between the work to be illuminated and the additions made for this purpose. Hard work was needed to achieve such a harmony. Hegel lectured with great freedom, and what he said had all the enchanting freshness of a new thought-world created at the moment, but such more or less total improvisation unfortunately led to unwitting repetitions, vaguenesses, divagations, and sudden jumps [i.e. leaps of thought]. These defects had to be carefully avoided in my revision. [Moreover, these (revised) lectures could not be omitted, since] in the printed text ... extreme comprehension often gave an impression of externality and asseveration.[25]

In sum, what we have, at least with respect to his *Encyclopedia*, is a philosopher who published, and sold, unintelligible material, claiming that it would be made intelligible in his lectures. Alas, as we have seen in the previous section, and now in Boumann's testimony, his "listeners" showed

---

[23] Ibid., 20.
[24] For a list of the courses Hegel had taught in Belin, the number of "listeners" attended to each course, and other related information, see Hoffmeister's table in Hegel, *Berliner Schriften*, 743-49.
[25] Quoted in J. N. Findlay, "Foreword," in G. W. F. Hegel, *The Philosophy of Mind*, trans. William Wallace and A. V. Miller, v-xix (Oxford: Oxford University Press, 1971), vi.

XI. Receptions of Hegel's Lectures

up only to discover a lecturer whose speech was barely intelligible. This begs the following questions: How did his disciple-editors manage to understand what he meant? Was Hegel's philosophical "system," as well as his assumed greatness, largely invented by his followers? What we can say for certain is that all that revising, editing, and supplementing could not make Hegel's nature-philosophy palatable and/or fully intelligible.

Consider, for instance, his following comment on the matter:

> Matter, *qua heavy*, is at first only *in itself* (*an sich*) the totality of the Notion [*Begriff*]; as such it is without intrinsic form; the Notion posited in it with its particular determinations, at first manifests the finite individuality whose particular moments fall asunder. The totality of the Notion being now *posited*, the center of gravity is no longer a subjectivity merely *sought* by matter, but a subjectivity immanent in it as the ideality of those form-determinations which were at first immediate and conditioned, but which are from now on moments developed from within outwards. Material individuality, being thus identical with itself in its development, is infinitely *for itself*, but is at the same time conditioned: it is the subjective totality, but at first only in immediate fashion. Therefore, though infinitely for itself, it involves relationship to *another*; only as it develops are this externality and this conditionedness posited as self-sublating. Individuality thus becomes the existent totality of material being-for-self, which is then Life in principle, and in the Notion passes over into Life."[26]

Likely, his students had no idea what this passage meant. This is Hegel's explanation (edited by Michelet) of it to his students:

> The two moments of real physical body—form as an abstract whole and determinable matter confronting it—are in themselves identical; therein lies their transition into one another in conformity with the Notion. For just as form is the pure, physical self-related identity-with-self which lacks determinate being, so matter, too, as fluid, is this universal identical existent which offers no resistance. Matter, like form, is without internal distinction, and is thus itself form. As universal, matter's destiny is to become inwardly determinate and this is precisely what form, whose 'in-itself' (*Ansich*) matter is, is obliged to be.[27]

"The distinguished philosopher" filled his *Encyclopedia* and the minds of his listeners with "science" of this kind, which certainly impressed some

---

[26] G. W. F. Hegel, *Philosophy of Nature, Part Two the Encyclopaedia of the Philosophical Sciences*, trans. A. V. Miller (Oxford: Oxford University Press, 1970), 158-59.
[27] Ibid., 159.

XI. Receptions of Hegel's Lectures

and repelled the likes of Schopenhauer. However, he also had occasional down-to-earth epiphanies. One of my personal favorites is the following: "The Moon is the waterless crystal, which strives, as it were, to unite itself with our sea and so to quench the thirst of its rigid, immobile nature, and which so produces the ebb and flow of the tides [on our planet]."[28] He was also unsatisfied with the current explanation of rain, which held that water molecules ("particles") are retained in the air and then "turn into water again" under favorable conditions. According to Hegel, the "fact" that sometimes "the rain comes ... from dry air" debunks this theory. Relatedly, he maintained, water is not "a mere *compositum*" of oxygen and hydrogen plus "an electric spark." "More correctly, it must be said that oxygen and hydrogen are only different forms assumed by water."[29]

The famous philosopher was perplexed by those species that seemed irrational to him (or opposed "the concept"), such as "*reptiles*, or *amphibians* ..., the duck-billed platypus (*ornithorhynchus*) ..., vampires and bats ..., the flying fish," and more. According to him, "these [are] imperfect products of Nature, which are only mixtures of such [ambivalent or intermediary] determinations."[30] They are the sorts of "imperfections" that urged the emergence of the theory of evolution, which Hegel flatly rejected. Rather than pointing toward the theory of evolution, Hegel absurdly regarded these "imperfect," "intermediate" forms of life merely as the "impotence of Nature to remain true to the Concept," which allegedly proved that nature in some respects fails "to adhere to thought determinations [i.e., Hegelian logical categories] in their purity."[31]

More generally, Hegel divined that the theory of evolution "does not explain anything at all." "A thinking consideration must reject such nebulous, at bottom, sensuous ideas, as in particular the so-called *origination*, for example, of plants and animals from water, and then the *origination* of the more highly developed animal organisms from the lower, and so on," he said.[32] Consistently with his rejection of the theory of evolution, he preached that all qualitative changes in nature occurred in leaps. For example, "water, in cooling, does not gradually harden as if it thickened like porridge, gradually solidifying until it reached the consistency of ice; it suddenly solidifies, all at once."[33]

Despite his growing influence, and fortunately for the Prussian system of education, Hegel was unable to control the faculty of natural sciences. In

---

[28] Ibid., 101.
[29] Ibid., 116-17.
[30] Ibid., 425.
[31] Ibid., 423.
[32] Ibid., 22.
[33] G. W. F. Hegel, *Science of Logic*, trans. A. V. Miller (London: George Allen & Unwin, 1969), 368-71.

fact, as time passed, a real scientist, Alexander von Humboldt (Wilhelm's brother), managed to acquire the support and interest of the Prussian king and even became more popular lecturer than Hegel himself. Unlike Hegel, Humboldt was a genuine polymath and had contributed significantly to the formation of several scientific fields.[34] In one of his very popular Berlin lectures on physical geography, delivered during the Winter semester of 1827-1828, he cautioned against the kind of "metaphysics" that is "devoid of knowledge and experience [or facts]." It is not surprising that many of his listeners thought he was targeting Hegel, though he clarified later that he had in mind Schelling also.[35] Thus, Humboldt thought they were both *charlatans*.

3. Obnoxious Philosopher

Hegel, on the other hand, thought that this appellation, *charlatan*, was appropriate for Schelling, not himself. In his first comment to his students on *Naturphilosophie*, he lamented that this branch of science "is in considerable disfavor." This was to be expected, he continued in his typically cryptic manner, because it has recently been proposed in the shape of a "fantastic" and "pretentious" doctrine, which

> made a chaotic mixture of crude empiricism and uncomprehended thoughts, of a purely capricious exercise of the imagination and the most commonplace way of reasoning by superficial analogy, and which passed off such a hotchpotch as the Idea, Reason, philosophical science, divine knowledge, and pretended that the complete lack of method and scientific procedure [i.e., Hegelian dialectic] was the acme of scientific procedure.

Then, he announced the main culprit: "It is on account of such charlatanism that the Philosophy of Nature, especially Schelling's, has become discredited."[36]

Despite his attacks against Schelling and growing fame, Hegel was not able to fully dispense with the rumors that he was little more than Schelling's philosophical offspring, perhaps a misbegotten one. As Ancillon,

---

[34] For an excellent biography, see Nicolaas A. Rupke, *Alexander von Humboldt: A Metabiography* (Chicago: The University of Chicago Press, 2008).

[35] Johannes Hoffmeister (ed.), *Briefe von und an Hegel*, 4 volumes (Hamburg: Felix Meiner, 1952-1960), the editor's notes to volume 3, #570, pp. 424-26. Humboldt managed to trick Hegel into believing that he was not his target. Hegel was very pleased to learn this. Clark Butler and Christiane Seiler (trans.), *Hegel: The Letters* (Bloomington: Indiana University Press, 1984), 530-31 (*Briefe III*, #570).

[36] Hegel, *Philosophy of Nature*, 1.

XI. Receptions of Hegel's Lectures

who did not like Hegel's philosophy, was supposed to have said during this period, Hegel's philosophy "is the *caput mortuum* of Schelling's philosophy."[37] Indeed, Schelling himself was now beginning to come out of the woodworks, making similar claims and expressing his desire to expel the "Usurpator Hegel" from what rightly belonged to him.[38] This man of a "limited mind," he told Cousin, has killed the "living principle" of his, Schelling's, philosophy.[39] In another context, he referred to Hegel as "the cuckoo who sat down in his nest," claiming that Hegel's jargon-laden "pure thinking" was "essentially empty thought."[40]

At any rate, the obnoxious Hegel himself was in the habit of slandering everyone, including Newton. To mention a few of such slanders, he referred to Newton's mathematical "proofs" of Kepler's laws in his *Principia* as "*the illusion of a scaffolding of proof,*" which, Hegel claimed, is "nothing more than sleight of hand and logical charlatanism."[41] Of his theory of color (or light) in *Optiks*, Hegel spoke of Newton's "conceptual barbarism ..., ineptitude ..., incorrectness ..., stupidity*, and as Goethe has even shown ..., *dishonesty.*"[42] Elsewhere, he mistook (or, charitably read, self-servingly misinterpreted) Newton's maxim, "Physics, beware of metaphysics," to mean, "Science, beware of thought," and went on to advise that physics could not accomplish anything without (speculative) thought. He then condemned his observational method, from which Newton allegedly "made bad observations and drew worse conclusions." "In this way, Newton is so complete a barbarian ... This Newton, like all the Physicists, indeed, never learned; he did not know that he thought in, and had to deal with Notions [Concepts], while he imagined he was dealing with physical facts ..."[43] It takes a *bona fide* charlatan to say such things as these about the scientific achievements of Newton.

The obnoxious Hegel was also becoming increasingly more intolerant of Catholicism. As Varnhagen, who was in the habit of recording the daily news in his diary, noted on March 26, 1826, "some Catholic students" had complained to "the Ministry of Culture" that Hegel was attacking "the

---

[37] *Berichten*, #514.
[38] Ibid., #520.
[39] Ibid., #585.
[40] Ibid., #552.
[41] Here, I use Giovanni's translation. G. W. F. Hegel, *The Science of Logic*, trans. George di Giovanni (Cambridge: Cambridge University Press, 2010), 234.
[42] Hegel, *Philosophy of Nature*, 198.
[43] G. W. F. Hegel, *Lectures on the History of Philosophy*, vol. 3, trans. E. S. Haldane (Lincoln: University of Nebraska Press, 1995), 323. For a rehabilitative collection of essays on Hegel's treatment of Newton, see Michael J. Petry (ed.), *Hegel and Newtonianism* (Dordrecht: Kluwer Academic Publishers, 1993). For a similarly charitable collection of essays on his philosophy of nature, see Stephen Houlgate (ed.), *Hegel and the Philosophy of Nature*, (Albany, NY: SUNY Press, 1998).

XI. Receptions of Hegel's Lectures

Catholic religion in his lectures. However, the ministry has rejected their complaint without even informing Hegel."[44]

Hotho, who was likely an eye-witness, sent the following, more detailed report of the incident to Cousin on April 1:

> In his history of philosophy course, our friend [Hegel] spoke about the philosophy of the Middle Ages and Catholicism. He said that the Catholic cult [with its doctrine of the Eucharist] represents God as being present in a thing, and so, for example, if a mouse were to eat that thing, God would be present in the mouse and even in its excrement. Offended by these words, the disciples of Catholicism complained to the ministry [of Altenstein] ..., which then reported it to our friend ... [Hegel] simply replied that, as a Protestant professor and as a professor of philosophy, he had the right to ... [examine] the nature of Catholicism [as he saw fit], and that Catholics who did not want to hear such things did not need to attend his classes.[45]

It is not difficult to sense a tone of resentment toward his master's behavior in Hotho's report to the Catholic Cousin, though he was not about to cause a raucous. Hegel, on the other hand, was spewing out his venom whenever he could. Indeed, his defense of his right to speak his mind was more vicious then what Hotho reported to Cousin. As Varnhagen noted, Altenstein had dismissed the complaints against Hegel's bigotry rather quietly, though he had no idea that the minister had informed Hegel, via Schulze, his emissary at the university and Hegel's close friend. For his part, rather than letting the ordeal pass away quietly, the obnoxious Hegel at once resolved to further clarify what happened to Altenstein on April 3.

First, Hegel noted that "the disclosure" was "made confidentially to" him "by Privy Councilor Schulze," who acted "on behalf of the Minister" himself. Likely, Altenstein intended to discreetly advise Hegel to exercise more caution, which only urged Hegel to become more defiant. He replied to Altenstein with a six-fold explanation, much of which is barely cogent. It is important to note that, by his own admission, Hegel "had already publicly addressed" the contents of his self-defense to his "listeners [students] from the lectern," which admission is also confirmed in Hotho's report to Cousin. Thus, Hegel also brought the issue back to his Catholic students, as if to rub it in. His explanation to Altenstein speaks for itself:

> 1) As Professor of Philosophy at a Royal Prussian University in Berlin, and as a Lutheran Christian, I am expected to speak in such ...

---

[44] *Berichten*, #440.
[45] Ibid., #442.

XI. Receptions of Hegel's Lectures

[critical] terms about the teachings and spirit of Catholicism ... I would have to consider any other expectation as a personal affront, indeed as an insult to the esteemed Government itself, which not only tolerates the Evangelical Church but has also taken the sublime position of being at the helm of the Evangelical German states, and to which all Protestants always turn their eyes, seeing in it their mainstay and firm attitude.

2) ... [In accordance] with my lectures on the history of philosophy ..., I had to speak of the Catholic religion since the scholastic philosophy moves within and is based in and has its basis in it.

3) In the interest of science, which I keep in mind in my lectures, I ... had to interpret the Catholic doctrine through its central idea, the Host, ... and had to speak of it with scientific certainty. [In contrast to this doctrine, and in the interest of science,] I have explained and expressed Luther's teaching as [the] true [religion], and as recognized by philosophy as true ...

4) ...

5) ... [A]mong the claims I have been accused of, I find much that I could simply deny and describe as misunderstanding urged by enfeeble minds ... [Another portion of the accusations must simply be declared] false, drawn from false premises ... [Yet another portion must be taken simply as] malicious disparagement.

6 ... Catholic students ..., [if they are disturbed by my comments should] blame only themselves for attending philosophical lectures at a Protestant university under a professor, who is proud of having been baptized and raised a Lutheran, which he still is and shall remain. Otherwise, they ... [should] blame their [Catholic] superiors for failing to warn them against, or ... prohibiting them [from, attending a Lutheran professor's courses].[46]

Here you have it: Hegel insulted his Catholic students and claimed afterward that their complaints were "malicious" attacks both against himself and the government. As we will see in due course, this was not the end of Hegel's anti-Catholic crusade.[47]

Hegel's obnoxious behavior could also be observed in social settings, which is not to say that he was always and everywhere annoying everyone. In March 1829, Karl Friedrich Zelter, the famed musician, who was Goethe's close friend and Hegel's acquaintance, decided to help two of his protégés put together a performance in Berlin. These were the up-and-coming Felix Mendelssohn and the singer Eduard Devrient, who had

---

[46] Hegel, *Berliner Schriften*, 572-75.
[47] For an accessible and informative review of Hegel's hostility toward Catholicism, see Lawrence S. Stepelevich, "Hegel and Roman Catholicism," *Journal of the American Academy of Religion* 60, no. 4 (1992): 673-691.

XI. Receptions of Hegel's Lectures

conspired together to perform Bach's *Saint Matthew Passion*. As Therese Devrient, the singer's wife, later remembered, the second performance of the *Passion*, staged on March 21, "succeeded just as well as the first performance, and excited the same enthusiasm from the public." Zelter invited a good number of his friends and acquaintances to have dinner with the performers. Eduard and Therese arrived somewhat late. As the former was ushered to his seat, the latter was directed to hers, which happened to be in between the seats of Mendelssohn and another fellow, whom she did not know. When she approached her seat, both men stood up to allow her to access her seat. As she conversed with Mendelssohn, the man on the other side kept insisting to assist her in various ways, repeatedly attempting to fill her glass with wine, despite her objections. "He also wanted to keep talking to me" she recalled. "In short, he annoyed me with his gallantry so much that I asked Felix, 'Tell me, who is the stupid fellow next to me?' Felix held his handkerchief over his mouth for a moment and then whispered: 'The stupid fellow next to you is the famous philosopher, Hegel.'"[48]

---

[48] *Berichten*, #593.

Chapter Twelve

XII. THE MOST POWERFUL PHILOSOPHER AND HIS VANGUARD PARTY

1. Hegel's Society

Hegel was now directing a cult. The nuisance at the university was no longer simply Hegel but "the Hegelians" or "the Hegel party," some were saying. This situation bothered Savigny immensely, who kept complaining about it to no avail. On April 6, 1826, he informed Creuzer that "the Hegelians" are openly seeking "exclusive dominance," and are "strongly supported in this endeavor by some very influential persons," such as Altenstein and Schulze.[1] About three weeks later, he told another friend that "there are all sorts of strange tendencies at our local university. The Hegelians have passionately united in their sectarian [*sektenartig*] ways and are my formidable adversaries."[2] To the chagrin of the likes of Savigny, Hegel would soon organize a formal vanguard party of sorts.[3]

As Varnhagen noted on May 29, 1826, Hegel formed a "philosophical club with his friends."[4] This "club" would soon develop into the Society for Scientific Criticism, and go on to publish its own journal, the *Berlin Yearbooks for Scientific Criticism*. The founding meeting of the *Yearbooks* took place on July 23 at Hegel's residence. Two days later, Hegel reported to his vacationing wife the following news: "On Sunday morning I had a meeting with fifteen gentlemen here at my place—with sweet drinks, though they had no time to drink even a glass. Our grand literary venture has now been founded."[5] About a month later, he also reported to her

---

[1] Günther Nicolin (ed.), *Hegel in Berichten seiner Zeitgenossen* (Hamburg: Felix Meiner, 1970), #443. Henceforth cited as *Berichten*.
[2] *Berichten*, #448.
[3] For a detailed study of the membership in the Hegelian "school" or "party," see John E. Toews, *Hegelianism: The Path Toward Dialectical Humanism, 1805-1841* (Cambridge: Cambridge University Press, 1980), 71-94.
[4] *Berichten*, #451.
[5] Clark Butler and Christiane Seiler (trans.), *Hegel: The Letters* (Bloomington: Indiana University Press, 1984), 505. Henceforth cited simply as *Letters*. Also, Johannes Hoffmeister (ed.), *Briefe von und an Hegel*, 4 volumes (Hamburg: Felix Meiner, 1952-1960), #515. Henceforth cited as *Briefe*, followed by the Latin numerical to indicate the volume number, in this case, *III*.

XII. The Most Powerful Philosopher and His Vanguard Party

about how he had been working hard on preparing the second edition of the *Encyclopedia* for publication. This endeavor has forced him to lead a "quiet life," which involves having, on occasion, "a really good time" with Hotho and Gans. With Hegel's help, the former had just received his doctorate,[6] and would soon start to teach at Berlin. A year earlier, Hegel recruited Gans to take over his course on the philosophy of right. He was to use Hegel's *Philosophy of Right* and remain true to the master's method. In the meanwhile, Hotho and Gans were dispatched to various places to recruit famed contributors to the *Yearbooks*. Indeed, Gans was deputized to oversee all the logistics involved in the publication of the *Yearbooks*. Hegel was now running an organized operation with his followers.

Things were going well for Hegel. His fifty-sixth birthday (August 27, 1826) was approaching, and it was now high time for a formidable celebration of the life of the beloved leader. As Varnhagen noted, "Hegel's birthday was celebrated splendidly by his friends and students. Many poems and speeches were given."[7] The next day, Hegel gleefully reported the news to his still-vacationing wife. The celebration of his birthday began the night before. Hegel was caught up in a prolonged game of whist with his friends that had lasted until midnight, at which time the participants drank to the philosopher's life and health, as the ringing bells reminded them that it was now August 27. The next morning, wrote Hegel gleefully, "there were various well-wishers, dear loyal souls and friends, plus several letters with poems. Then a business meeting during which I received a visit from his Excellency Privy Councilor von Kamptz [the head of the Prussian police] himself in person!" (Kamptz's visit debunks the rumors that he was holding grudges against Hegel, due to Cousin's recent homage to Hegel and condemnation of the Prussian authorities.) In the evening, "in a new restaurant, *Unter den Linden* ..., about twenty persons" showed up to celebrate his birthday, though this number increased when "a deputation of students arrived, presenting [him] with an exquisite silver cup." Other birthday paraphernalia were also presented, followed by recitations of poems, written and read to honor the great philosopher. "At midnight we linked my birthday with Goethe's on the 28th," reported Hegel.[8]

Three days later, *Vossische Zeitung*, a local newspaper, reported the event in great detail and even printed some of the poems recited in Hegel's honor.[9] No one could have anticipated during that night that the celebration of Hegel's (and Goethe's) birthday would soon become a cause of concern for the authorities. "Hegel's opponents," Varnhagen noted,

---

[6] *Letters.*, 505-06 (*Briefe III*, #520).
[7] *Berichten*, #466.
[8] *Letters*, 644-5 (*Briefe III*, #524).
[9] *Berichten*, #463.

XII. The Most Powerful Philosopher and His Vanguard Party

were immensely "annoyed" by the glorifying description of the event in the newspaper, and so "raised a great deal of fuss" about it. Apparently, it was reasoned that newspapers should not treat "private celebrations" as if they were "royal family celebrations." So, more than Hegel and his friends, the blame was put squarely on the newspaper. Consequently, some figures in his cabinet convinced the king to prohibit the printing of "such essays on private celebrations" in the future.[10]

However, Hegel was not in any way harmed or undermined because of this absurd cabinet order, which was itself a symptom of a time and place in which a figure like Hegel could be worshipped. Indeed, the birthday celebration itself was a manifestation of this master-worship, which was reinforced by the support he had been receiving from Altenstein and Schulze. In fact, much of the Hegel worshipping was, via Hegelian indoctrination, translated into the glorification of the Prussian state. This is revealed in the metamorphosis of Friedrich Förster from a punished "demagogue" in 1819 to a paid "court demagogue" several years later, after Altenstein and Schulze appointed him to a prestigious editorial position at the official Prussian state newspaper in 1823. He was now called the "'court demagogue' because of his fervent, often belligerent, defense of the Prussian bureaucratic monarchy as the actualization of the ethical community he had formerly [as another kind of a 'demagogue'] sought in the popular consciousness of the *Volk*." At Hegel's birthday celebration, "Förster praised Hegel for helping him recognize that the communal 'home' he had sought so long was already there in the present, real world of the Prussian state."[11] Surely, he had been studying the master's teaching well.

With his influence and party growing, it was now time to realize the idea of the *Yearbooks*. Initially, there were some disagreements on some crucial aspects of the journal, such as who was to be excluded from it and whether it should be sponsored by the government. As we will see shortly, it would soon be sponsored by Altenstein's ministry. On the former issue, it was clear from the outset that the "Hegelian party," under the master's direction, was to dominate the journal.[12] However, several individuals, who did not belong to Hegel's immediate circle, were also invited to participate, for this was necessary to increase the influence of the Society.

August Boeckh, a classicist at Berlin, had to do much soul-searching before and after he decided to accept Hegel's invitation to join the Society. "For many years," he wrote to Niebuhr, "I have been in a rather pronounced tension with Hegel; his whole endeavor, his intolerable

---

[10] Ibid., #472.
[11] Toews, *Hegelianism: The Path Toward Dialectical Humanism*, 120. Also see *Berichten*, #463.
[12] For a more detailed account, see Gans' recollections in *Berichten*, #486.

XII. The Most Powerful Philosopher and His Vanguard Party

partisanship ..., the supreme favor his followers receive from above, and even the unpleasant nature of his personality, have continually repulsed me; and he, too, disliked me." Despite all this, he had reasons, he said, to participate in Hegel's endeavor.[13] Perhaps he had calculated that this would allow him to avoid the wrath of the "party," or even have a piece of Hegel's growing pie for himself.

About a month later, on November 29, Boeckh once more reported to Niebuhr about the first meeting of the Society he himself attended. During this meeting, he "demanded that ... the Society should invite Schleiermacher and Savigny" to join it. Or else, he explained to the other attendees at the meeting, the whole thing would appear to "serve a party and embrace a particular," Hegelian persuasion. In other words, as per impossible, he wanted to implement something like the non-partisanship policy of the Prussian Academy of Sciences in an organization that was avowedly partisan. It is not clear whether Boeckh was too naïve to anticipate Hegel's response to his proposal or proposed it to simply make a point. The leader clarified this ambiguity by causing a "tremendous storm." "Because this Hegel is really a cursed person," concluded Boeckh, he always found himself in the opposite pole of every issue he discussed with him. His own participation in the activities of the Society would not last very long, he anticipated.[14]

That Hegel's reaction to the proposal to invite Schleiermacher and Savigny to join the Society was quite stormy is also confirmed by Gans' later recollection of what had transpired during that meeting. Apparently, upon hearing it, Hegel bolted out of his chair in great anger and warned, while pacing the room, that their membership would result in his own resignation from the Society. Even Gans interpreted Hegel's behavior as an unreasonable reaction, based strictly on personal grudges, rather than philosophical differences, though he kept this assessment to himself during this incident.[15]

Gans could not have done otherwise, even if he wanted to, since his own promotion rested squarely in Hegel's hands. Indeed,

> it was their skill as Hegelian apologists and their importance as academic representatives of Hegel's position in disciplines dominated by members of the Historical School [such as Ranke and Savigny] that brought ... Gans [and others] the attention, favor, and support of Hegel, Schulze, and Altenstein; and the same factors were

---

[13] Ibid., #474.
[14] Ibid., #477.
[15] Ibid., #486.

XII. The Most Powerful Philosopher and His Vanguard Party

instrumental in their appointments and rapid promotions within the Prussian university system.[16]

At any rate, Hegel ultimately triumphed at the contentious meeting, proving that the Society was his own show, and so had to abide by his wishes.

This scolding of the members of the Society was not an isolated incident. Referring to this period (1826), Karl Rosenkranz recalled in his memoirs how he was recently recruited to the Society. During one of its meetings, the participants were discussing a certain work on "the war of liberation." Their discussion rapidly turned into a heated debate between Hegel and Varnhagen about the (undisclosed) facts of the war. The latter, "who had been an officer" during the war in question, and so could be justly regarded as "an expert," "strongly objected to Hegel's views." But Hegel would have nothing of it, and so "tirelessly" adduced reasons to vindicate his own opinions. When this failed, he resorted to scolding and insulting everyone involved in the debate, so much so that his behavior became "embarrassing" to watch. Henning, "a war veteran himself," finally stepped in and, by utilizing his "gift" to calm people down, brought the disputants to a peaceful conclusion. Rosenkranz remembered having later reminded Varnhagen of this awful "scene" on several occasions, and was informed by the latter that, on that day, Rosenkranz had only witnessed "a small degree" of how "dreadful [Hegel's] anger and scolding could be."[17] Based on events of this kind, Varnhagen himself recalled some years later that Hegel had increasingly become "more and more difficult, more tyrannical, and behaved so strangely in the sessions that the whole Society felt that things could not go on, and that the whole thing had to eventually falter."[18] This, of course, did not happen—not while Hegel was still alive.

On December 26, 1826, Varnhagen penned down several related observations in his diary. "Hegel's reputation and influence are still growing," he first noted, adding that he is supported by the government, as "the ministries" believe that his servile philosophy legitimizes the Prussian regime, despite his (according to Varnhagen's own misjudgment) preference for the constitution of England. Hegel had no such preference, as we will see in due course. Be that as it may, what is more relevant to our present purposes is Varnhagen's second observation, which, in a way, contradicts his first: Hegel is mainly interested in building a "faction" by exercising power, based on personal connections, rather than philosophical convictions, and this is becoming more and more visible in the proceedings

---

[16] Toews, *Hegelianism: The Path Toward Dialectical Humanism*, 122.
[17] *Berichten*, #622.
[18] Ibid., #489.

XII. The Most Powerful Philosopher and His Vanguard Party

of the Society.[19] Varnhagen, despite his reservations about Hegel's behavior, remained on very friendly terms with him. Apparently, he had a forgiving heart, which often allowed him to give Hegel's obnoxious behavior a positive spin.

The *Yearbooks* itself was as good as the philosophical virtues of its "tyrannical" overseer and his epigones. For this reason, it failed to attract enough readership to financially sustain itself. The famous publisher of the journal, Johann Friedrich von Cotta, recorded financial losses from the outset, due to the lackluster sales and subscriptions. Consequently, Hegel convinced Altenstein to fund his journal, which gave it a new lease on life. As Varnhagen noted on January 25, 1827, the minister had convinced the king to grant 400 Thalers per annum to Hegel's enterprise. However, Varnhagen was irked by the fact that Altenstein would now attempt to "subordinate the whole enterprise to his official influence," and that he even, "without any reason, flatters himself by stating that he is indeed the very founder of the thing [*sache*]."[20] Varnhagen, I am forced to say, was somewhat naïve, thinking that Hegel was not fully at the service of the minister and that the latter had no reason to think he had something to do with the founding and running of the *Yearbooks*.

Alas, to Varnhagen's dismay, the view that the *Yearbooks* was ultimately an organ of the Prussian state, which was already widely-held, received a new boost shortly thereafter: "Dr. [Ludwig] Börne ..., [in] a small pamphlet printed in Heidelberg against the [*Yearbooks*] ..., warns all German scholars of the official influence of Berlin, of the anti-liberal tendencies that are to be feared!"[21] A month later, Varnhagen also registered Wilhelm von Humboldt's following, related, personally-expressed warning to him in his diary: if the Society wants to avoid Altenstein's influence, then it has to fund itself. In this regard, Humboldt's reasoning was sound as justly he expected Altenstein to attach strings to the fund.[22]

To Hegel, on the other hand, the stately grant was nothing short of an all-around blessing, rather than an intrusion to his and his colleagues' academic liberties. Indeed, Hegel's philosophy denied the very possibility of such an intrusion. As Humboldt opined during this period, Hegel had strong illiberal tendencies, and so "inclined towards despotism." Varnhagen, who chronicled this piece of information also, privately disagreed with Humboldt's assessment of Hegel's political sympathies, noting in his diary that, to the contrary, Hegel "is thoroughly constitutional, Protestant, liberal,

---

[19] Ibid., #481.
[20] Ibid., #494. There is some ambiguity on the delivery of the fund Altenstein promised Hegel.
[21] Ibid.
[22] Ibid., #495.

fully sympathetic to the French Revolution, and [is also] for English life of freedom."²³ In a few years, our chronicler would disabuse himself of this misinformation, reaching the same verdict as Humboldt on Hegel's political sympathies, as we will see in due course.

Varnhagen heard of Hegel's alleged sympathies for the Revolution from Hegel's mouth several months earlier. In the company of "mostly young people," wrote Varnhagen in his diary, Hegel remembered that that day was July 14 (1826) and drank to commemorate the seizure and destruction of Bastille, claiming that he had been doing this every year. He then reminded his drinking partners that the storming of the Bastille was a very joyous event for all at the time it had occurred.²⁴ There is no way to conclusively dispute or confirm Hegel's claim.²⁵ However, given what we know about his life and writings, his claim about celebrating the Bastille Day every year strikes me as incredible. My guess is that this was a one-time celebration, perhaps urged by high levels of alcohol in his blood. Indeed, all his lectures and works from this period reveal Hegel's continued support for despotism, not the liberal-republican ideals of the French Revolution. As Wilhelm Traugott Krug correctly noted in his critique of the second (1827) edition of Hegel's *Encyclopedia*, Hegel defended a state in which individuals could not be differentiated from the subjects of "a despotic sultan." He also described Hegel's entire philosophical "system" as little more than "a game of ideas that is not very far from being a fantasy of reason."²⁶

2. More Tantrums before the Calm

In the meanwhile, just about everyone knew that the *Yearbooks* and the Society were now under the exclusive sway of the Hegelian "clique," funded and endorsed by the Prussian state.²⁷ As some opined rather justly, "the deification of Hegel" was constantly increasing in the journal.²⁸ Boeckh, who had by now stopped participating in the activities of the Society, reported to a friend in early August 1827 that the glorification of Hegel in the journal was out of control. However, he also lamented that Hegel himself "was being attacked from all sides in a crude and unjust manner, just when he is now beginning to" refrain from attacking others.

---

[23] Ibid., #535.
[24] Ibid., #457.
[25] As we have seen in Chapter 8, Förster's allegation that Hegel had done the same thing in Dresden in 1820 is false.
[26] See Hoffmeister's notes to *Briefe III*, #579, p. 430.
[27] *Berichten*, #496.
[28] Ibid., #509.

XII. The Most Powerful Philosopher and His Vanguard Party

Boeckh found these attacks "repugnant."[29] He was wrong, however, to think that Hegel had initiated a permanent ceasefire of sorts.

In fact, Hegel went on to publish a review of Wilhelm von Humboldt's *On the Episode of the Mahabharata Known as the Bhagavad-Gita* (1816)[30] in the *Yearbooks*.[31] Hegel's well-known bigoted attitude towards non-European cultures is manifest in this review, as is his propensity to present himself as the foremost expert on virtually *everything*.[32] Unlike what Humboldt (and Schlegel) would have their readers believe, claimed the self-declared expert, the secrets of Indian philosophy could be revealed, and successfully translated into, German (or else into European languages) by appeal to the system of categories found in his speculative philosophy. This was an odd suggestion in the sense that he also thought the "inferior" Indian spirit was essentially different from the advanced European one, which originated in Greece, not India. The "solution" to this dilemma was to render the former a lower spiritual and historical category and declare it pre-philosophy in the history of philosophy.

On March 1, 1828, Humboldt privately complained about Hegel's critique of his essay to Gentz, who was still his friend from their earlier years, despite their political differences. Hegel's review (which was longer than Humboldt's essay), noted Humboldt, "conflates [or confuses] philosophy and fable, the real [*Echtes*] and the unreal, the ancient and the modern." He could not help but conclude that, despite appearing otherwise in some respects, "the whole review is … against me …, and clearly stems from the conviction that I am anything but a philosopher." Humboldt also lamented Hegel's obscurity and lack of ease in speaking and writing even about ordinary things. "It is as if the author could not penetrate the language," he said, adding that this "may be due to a great lack of imagination" on Hegel's part. Yet, Humboldt thought it was proper to endorse, with due caution and reluctance, Hegel's Society and the *Yearbooks*, reasoning that it was senseless to be rigidly either for or against him. He even admitted that a few articles published in the *Yearbooks* (not the ones written by Hegel) were quite decent, but this could not be said of the whole journal. He had serious qualms about Hegel's philosophy, for instance, which was glorified in the journal by his epigones. "I do not think this kind of a philosophy should

---

[29] Ibid., #513.
[30] Originally published as *Über die unter dem Namen Bhagavad-Gítá bekannte Episode des Mahá-Bhárata* (Berlin: Königliche Akademie der Wissenschaften, 1826).
[31] G. W. F. Hegel, *On the Episode of the Mahabharata Known by the Name Bhagavad Gita by Wilhelm Von Humboldt,* trans. Herbert Herring, 1-151 (New Delhi: Indian Council of Philosophical Research, 1995).
[32] For a very informed and much more charitable discussion of Hegel's familiarity with this topic, see Jon Stewart, *Hegel's Interpretation of the Religions of the World: The Logic of the Gods* (Oxford: Oxford University Press, 2018), 109-44.

XII. The Most Powerful Philosopher and His Vanguard Party

take root; to say the least, I have not been able to make friends with it thus far," he said.[33]

In late 1827, Hegel was powerful enough to request private meetings with Altenstein, the minister fully in charge of education and cultural affairs in Prussia.[34] However, Schleiermacher still thought that Hegel would ultimately fail to fully control the university. On February 7, 1828, he reported to a friend that there were reasons to "not have anything to fear from the Hegelian party for now because he [Altenstein] does not have enough money to establish a Hegelian majority, even though he would otherwise be more than willing to do so." What occasioned this remark was the nomination of Gans to full professorship (he had been an assistant professor since 1826) at the law faculty with Hegel's urging and to the chagrin of Schleiermacher, Savigny, and others. Schleiermacher anticipated that this "imprudent" decision would likely undermine the Hegel party and its sponsors, Altenstein and Schulze. The latter yelled at Gans' opponents for disputing his Christian faith (Gans, a Jew, converted to Christianity in 1825), and Gans himself had allegedly insulted Savigny. At any rate, it seems that Schleiermacher was the only real loser in this recent debacle. With Altenstein's blessing, Schulze "has finally, but only ... for a year, dispensed me from faculty and university matters," he added.[35]

Obviously, his critics had qualms about Gans' Jewish origins and the sincerity of his conversion. After all, their letter to the ministry regarding his promotion concluded with the following statement:

> In conclusion we would venture to point out that we do not know if Dr. Gans, who stems from a well-known Jewish family, has personally converted to the Christian faith, and whether, therefore, there may not be an obstacle to his appointment to a position of public service from this side [in addition to his academic virtues] as well.[36]

However, it cannot be said that Altenstein, Schulze, and Hegel defended Gans' right to remain a Jew and work as a Jewish professor since the issue at hand had to do with whether he was a genuine Christian. In the final analysis, they supported his candidacy, and the others opposed it, precisely because he was known to be a reputable member of Hegel's party. Shortly thereafter, Gans' became a full professor.

In the meanwhile, Hegel was also troubled by the political developments taking shape in France. In March 1828, fearful of another

---

[33] *Berichten*, #559.
[34] *Briefe III*, #545.
[35] *Berichten*, #555.
[36] Quoted in Toews, *Hegelianism: The Path Toward Dialectical Humanism*, 111.

XII. The Most Powerful Philosopher and His Vanguard Party

revolution in France, Hegel, Varnhagen's "liberal" friend, sent a letter to Cousin, in which he expressed vague views on Cousin's anticipated defense of "the rude roaring of ... liberal energy with which Paris, all France, and Europe resound."[37] In his reply, dated April 7, Cousin assured Hegel that both he himself and the French people will be prudent and that Hegel had no reason to fear:

> I insist strongly on the necessity of being wise, measured, conciliatory, to prove finally that the liberal opinion should not frighten anyone, neither individuals nor governments and that it can hold the reins of business ... Suffice it to know ... that, finally, the future of France has nothing that can frighten anyone. Rest assured that we will be prudent. Be calm about France, regardless of what you are told and whatever appears to be the case to you from afar.[38]

As these two letters suggest, Hegel and Cousin were now becoming increasingly more aware of their philosophical and political differences, even though Cousin wanted to iron them out. It seems that Hegel himself did not want to be associated with Cousin's liberalism, "prudent" or otherwise, and so refrained from corresponding with him for two years, despite the contrary efforts of Cousin to keep the line of communication between them open.

About the same time as he received Cousin's letter, Hegel launched a new attack on his opponents. As the recognized "expert" of all things, he assumed the responsibility of publishing a review of Solger's posthumously-published writings in the *Yearbooks*. Unsurprisingly, his review contained a critique of the lesser spirits, and so caused some "stir." More specifically, it contained attacks against Friedrich von Schlegel and Ludwig Tieck.[39] As Johann Wilhelm Loebell informed Tieck on May 9, he could not find anything but "a clumsy and malicious attack" against the latter in Hegel's review.[40] This attack was mainly a defense of Goethe against what he, Hegel, regarded as Tieck's unwarranted and misinformed criticisms of Goethe. Schlegel fared even worse as Hegel basically disputed his philosophical credentials *tout court*.[41]

Evidently, much of academic practice at Berlin University, if not in entire Prussia, was now turning into an unpleasant experience. Clearly, being at the center of it all, Hegel had much to do with this outcome,

---

[37] *Letters,* 650 (*Briefe III*, #575).
[38] *Briefe III*, #577.
[39] *Berichten*, #569.
[40] Ibid., #571.
[41] G. W. F. Hegel, *Berliner Schriften, 1818-1831*, ed. Johannes Hoffmeister (Hamburg: Felix Meiner, 1956), 155-220.

XII. The Most Powerful Philosopher and His Vanguard Party

though Altenstein and his sidekick, Schulze, also deserve at least as much credit. This problem was aptly captured by Vatke in September 1828. He observed that the Berlin faculty was now divided into two hostile camps, which despised each other. On one side stood the party of Hegel. This "minority" party was led by Hegel and his lieutenant, Marheineke. This clique, noted Vatke, was fully supported by Altenstein. Schleiermacher was the acknowledged leader of the powerless majority. "You see how dangerous it is to work as a teacher," told Vatke to his brother, adding that "if one is Hegelian, then one has the ministry supporting and almost the entire faculty against him, and vice versa."[42] Such was the situation surrounding Hegel at the close of 1828. As for Vatke, he would soon choose to become a devoted Hegelian, and subsequently a teacher.

On May 16, 1829, Hegel notified Altenstein, his golden goose, that his enduring chest pain "has not sufficiently abated in its consequences ... As the most effective remedy my doctor has advised and prescribed a trip to a spa," he said. Alas, noted Hegel,

> I ... find myself in such unfavorable economic circumstances that I cannot afford such a trip on my own—all the more so because, due to my weakened health and the needed leisure to revise my *Science of Logic* for a new edition, I am giving only one private lecture course this semester, resulting already in a significant loss of income considering my limited means.

In short, Hegel requested additional funds to pay for his "trip to a spa for treatment and recuperation."[43] Eleven days later, Altenstein approved Hegel's request with the usual 300-Thaler travel grant.[44] He was to visit Karlsbad, famous for its spas, three months later.

In the meanwhile, however, something unusual happened. On August 16, "all feud" seemed to suddenly disappear from the Berlin campus as Hegel, Schleiermacher, and other professors were spotted together, having a good time. They "came together, talked, and treated each other honorably" during the festivities commemorating the twentieth anniversary of the (re)founding of Berlin University. "It is good that humanity drives out rudeness, and that different views and directions develop side-by-side," wrote Raumer to Tieck.[45]

It seems that Hegel left Berlin for Karlsbad in friendly spirits at the end of August, perhaps because he now felt invincible and thus quite content.

---

[42] *Berichten*, #584.
[43] *Letters*, 396-97 (*Briefe III*, #599).
[44] *Briefe III*, #601.
[45] *Berichten*, #606.

XII. The Most Powerful Philosopher and His Vanguard Party

He seemed uncharacteristically peaceful and calm. Likely, he was informed by Altenstein and/or Schulze that a major reward would soon be bestowed upon him after his Karlsbad trip.

Via Prague, Hegel arrived there on September 3 and checked into his inn. After some sightseeing, someone informed him that one of his old acquaintances was also in town, whereupon Hegel proceeded to find the acquaintance at his own inn. "Imagine," wrote the acquaintance to his wife, "while I am sitting in the bath, I hear a somewhat unpleasant, half-familiar voice asking for me. Then the unknown person calls his name: it is Hegel from Berlin." The acquaintance was Schelling, who was obviously somewhat annoyed, especially since Hegel showed up later to see him again, "very eager and unusually friendly," pretending that nothing had happened between them.[46]

Hegel, on the other hand, reported to his own wife from Karlsbad that they "are both pleased about meeting again," treating each other "as cordial friends of old." "Schelling," he added, "arrived here alone ... a few days ago to take a cure like myself, though I am not taking one. He is, by the way, very healthy and robust, the use of spring water being only a preservative in his case." This was the first time Hegel and Schelling had seen each other in twenty-six years and would be the very last. There was also a miracle of sorts to report: "After only two or three days, I no longer felt any of my chest pains," due to "my mineral water cure [i.e., drinking mineral water]."[47]

Another miracle, this time not imagined, occurred upon Hegel's return to Berlin, which, I suspect, he had known all along, explaining his recently-acquired friendly behavior toward his archenemies. On September 15, Altenstein appointed Hegel to two posts simultaneously: Rector and State Plenipotentiary for the Control of the University. The latter appointment meant that Hegel would now govern the university in accordance with the dictates and wishes of the government. Hegel's double appointment went against one of the rules of the Karlsbad Decrees, which required that the representative of the government should not be a member of the faculty.[48] In a way, however, the new arrangement was compatible with the spirit of the Decrees, since Hegel was Altenstein's lackey, and so would not offer any resistance to the government's control over the university—to the contrary.

---

[46] Ibid., #609.
[47] *Letters*, 397-98 (*Briefe III*, #607).
[48] *Berichten*, #611.

XII. The Most Powerful Philosopher and His Vanguard Party

3. Long Live the King, the Prussian State, and Hegel!
In the meanwhile, just before resuming his new duties, Hegel kept working on his usual double-task of supporting his followers and combatting his opponents. As he wrote to Daub on September 27, 1829,

> in the critical *Yearbooks* I have—unfortunately I must say—begun to take on opponents, a number of whom came out against my philosophy last year ... Much in these writings is indeed all too base. *Letters Against Hegel's Encyclopedia* [1829], vol. I, is said to be by Schleiermacher. *Doubts concerning Being, Nothing, and Becoming* [i.e., *A Few Doubts Regarding Professor Hegel's Teaching*, 1829] was sent to me by the author himself, my colleague and friend Schmalz.[49]

However, the main purpose of Hegel's letter was to urge Daub's support for the candidacy of one of his earliest students for the philosophy chair at Heidelberg. The former student was, who was Hegel's student at Jena, and was now the rector of the gymnasium in Bayreuth. Gabler had gained Hegel's support after publishing, as Hegel noted, "his *Propaedeutic to Philosophy*."[50]

The *Propaedeutic* (1827) was Gabler's first publication. It basically paraphrased certain parts of the *Phenomenology* and exalted its virtues. It also disparaged three of Hegel's chief opponents: Fries, Krug, and Johann Friedrich Herbart. Consequently, Hegel praised Gabler to the skies. In fact, he also tried to help Gabler procure a professorship at Berlin, though thought the prospects for this outcome were not very promising, given the limited budget at Altenstein's disposal.[51] Apparently, Gabler could not publish the second part of his book, due to lack of interest in the first part.[52] It was even disliked by some of Hegel's other acolytes.

Another Hegelian book was published in 1829 by Karl Friedrich Ferdinand Sietze, one of Hegel's former students at Berlin, and now a professor of law at Königsberg. Sietze described the Prussian state as "a giant harp tuned in God's garden to guide the world's chorale," as anyone with a genuine "living feeling" would surely attest. "The first chords of this harp," he added in a Hegelian manner, "have shattered the shackles of spiritual slavery as they reverberate in the soul of every free German."[53] After taking a swipe at the Historical School's approach to law, led by Savigny, he went

---

[49] *Letters*, 536-37 (*Briefe III*, #609).
[50] Ibid.
[51] Ibid., 534-35 (#576).
[52] *Berichten*, #758.
[53] Karl Friedrich Ferdinand Sietze, *Grund-Begriff Preußischer Staats- und Rechts Geschichte als Einleitung in die Wissenschaft des Preußischen Rechts* (Berlin: Fr. Laue, 1829), xvi.

XII. The Most Powerful Philosopher and His Vanguard Party

on to argue that, even in advanced Europe, the laws and customs of the Prussian state stood above all others. The true philosophy of history reveals that none of this is accidental and that the Prussian state, its laws, and customs have divine status.[54] As we will see in the next chapter, Sietze had learned all this from his master's lectures on the philosophy of history. His work also received little attention, likely because, unlike the master's works, it could be read and understood with relative ease, revealing its superficiality.

On October 16, 1829, with his new promotion in mind, Hegel sent a letter to Altenstein, profusely expressing his gratitude and "deeply deferential" devotion to the authority of the minister. He also asked to visit him to express all this in person, though it is likely that he also wanted to discuss his impending inauguration address, to be delivered two days later, with which his new duties would formally begin.[55] Varnhagen noted that Hegel's inaugural speech, delivered in Latin, was "beautiful."[56] He forgot to mention, or perhaps was unable to discern in his Latinized metaphysical words, that Hegel's address was ultimately an apology for the God-ordained Protestant king, calling upon all his subjects to work for the "salvation of the state." This duty was tantamount to serving the "common good," which included, for the academics, the taming of the youth, helping them avoid "wantonness."[57] This, one is apt to conclude, was his education policy as the new rector and government official.

Hegel's services were deemed worthy of a stately medal and honor. Thus, Altenstein "proposed Professor Hegel … to the Order of the Red Eagle, Third Class," an honorary medal (and title) given to individuals in various professions in recognition of their services to the state. This information was reported by Varnhagen, who also added that Altenstein's effort was unsuccessful. In other words, the king followed Alexander von Humboldt's recommendation instead, and allotted the same title/medal to "professors [Johann Franz] Encke and [Eilhard] Mitscherlich." The former was an astronomer and the latter a chemist, each with important scientific discoveries in their respective fields. Thus, it is difficult to see their recognition as an undeserved reward to simply rebuff either Altenstein or Hegel. Yet, according to Varnhagen, some people were lamenting: "we saw that there is a kind of sub-ministry [i.e., Humboldt] that has more favor [with the king] than the real one [i.e., Altenstein]."[58] Likely, this unreasonable chatter issued from the mouths of Hegel's epigones, who thought the whole universe revolved around their master. But, as we will

---

[54] Ibid., 97–100.
[55] *Briefe III*, #620.
[56] *Berichten*, #613.
[57] Hegel, *Berliner Schriften*, 25–29.
[58] *Berichten*, #624.

XII. The Most Powerful Philosopher and His Vanguard Party

see in due course, this was not the end of Altenstein's campaign to have the king reward Hegel with the Order of the Red Eagle; he was simply waitlisted for a year.

Soon thereafter, Altenstein designated Hegel to address the public on the tercentenary of the Augsburg Confession, which he delivered on June 25, 1830. The central theme Hegel exercised in his address was *freedom* which, of course, was realized only in the Lutheran realm—mainly in the Prussian state. According to Hegel, "it was the princes and civil magistrates who solemnly concluded the business at Augsburg," and this was "accomplished by public debate and volition [of the princes], not through the pressure of the multitude." In other words, the *confession* did not contravene "the majesty and authority of the laws and of the princes." Rather, "the latter held sway over law-governed states [*civitates*] and obedient peoples."[59] This, he clearly implied, was the true source of these peoples' freedom.

Hegel went on to assert that the Protestant rulers have now become *one* with the Lutheran doctrine, which truly expressed the will of God. Thus, the state and its rulers (especially the king) expressed "the divine will" on earth.

> We now understand [he preached] that the commonwealth, by divine authority, should be internally one, and that the laws [*iura*] pertaining to the state [*civitas*] and citizens and the precepts of virtue are divinely sanctioned. Princely power has been reconciled with the Church, and while the former is now at one with the divine will, the latter renounces all unjust authority.[60]

Therefore, in the case of the Protestant Germans, "divine providence ensured that the precepts of the religion we profess are in accord with what the state regards as just." For this reason, what the princes set in motion "three hundred years ago" has finally developed into "the free concord of the state and religion, and particularly that evangelical religion of which ... this concord is characteristic." As importantly, unlike what had transpired in the Catholic, revolutionary France, "all these things were accomplished peacefully, without internal convulsions and crimes, through the discernment and goodwill of those [rulers] in whom supreme power is invested," he said.[61]

---

[59] G. W. F. Hegel, "Address on the Tercentenary of the Submission of the Augsburg Confession," in *Hegel: Political Writings*, eds. Laurence Dickey and H. B. Nisbet, 186-96 (Cambridge, UK: Cambridge University Press, 1999), 189.
[60] Ibid., 191.
[61] Ibid., 195.

XII. The Most Powerful Philosopher and His Vanguard Party

The address ended with an unabashed exaltation of King Frederick Wilhelm (William) III:

[T]he piety of our princes fills us with confidence and security and assures them of our love. And whereas on the birthday of our most gracious King Frederick William [to be celebrated three weeks later], we turn our eyes every year to the image of his virtues and remind ourselves of the benefits which he so richly bestows on this his university, let us today joyfully praise his exceptional piety, which is the source of all his virtues. And since this directly concerns his subjects, let us cherish it, venerate it, and rejoice in it. Our joy and reverence gain considerable extra significance from the fact that the whole Protestant [*evangelicus*] world, both within Germany and beyond its frontiers, knows that our cause is an important one, and the admiration, trust, and pious wishes of all those good people who rejoice in this freedom join with us in turning to that person whom they recognize as the sure defender of the evangelical doctrine and of the freedom which goes with it. We have prayed, pray now, and shall not cease to pray to almighty God that he may favor our most gracious King and his whole illustrious house by preserving and increasing those blessings with which he eternally rewards piety, justice, and mercy.[62]

Hegel's address received much praise, and this for the very message he intended to deliver. For instance, touched by Hegel's speech, Karl Gottlob Zumpt, a professor of classical philology at Berlin, wished to obtain a printed copy of it, for it debunked the Catholic unfreedom "much more powerfully" than the contemporary theologians were able to do in their sermons.[63] Zumpt expressed this sentiment to a friend on July 12, 1830. Some of Hegel's epigones were also touched by his address, which inspired them to commission a local artist to create a copper engraving to commemorate the address and honor the speaker. Other similar paraphernalia were also produced, including a bust, a sketched portrait, and a medal. The latter two items were produced in (unknown) quantities. Hegel, demonstrably exhilarated, proudly encouraged their distribution. Complimentary copies of the medal were sent to various dignitaries, including Altenstein and Goethe.

Hegel's rather unflattering profile is imprinted on one side of the medal. On its other side, there is an allegorical image. A naked, angelic, male youth, with his oversized wings, unassuming penis, and all, stands in the middle. His right hand is placed on the shoulder of what appears to be an ancient philosopher, immersed in a gigantic book under the gaze of the Owl of

---

[62] Ibid., 196.
[63] *Berichten*, #633.

XII. The Most Powerful Philosopher and His Vanguard Party

Minerva. The boy's left arm stretches out to hold the cross, presented to him by a burly woman, connecting, as it were, philosophical wisdom and religion.

Not everyone was pleased with this medal business, at least not with all of it. Upon receiving two of the medals directly from Hegel himself, one of which was meant for Goethe, Zelter informed the latter that the "head" on the medal was a fair representation of Hegel, but the image on the back was not to his liking.[64] Having received his own complimentary medal from Zelter, Goethe was taken aback by the allegorical image: "how much of the reverse side of the medallion displeases me," he replied. Although, a glorifier and beautifier of the cross in his own works, Goethe could not take any "comfort from the fact that a philosopher has led his students along the darkest pathways and byways of being and non-being [sarcasm meant] to such an arid conclusion as this."[65]

Altenstein, by contrast, was thrilled to see the medal. "It is well-balanced and presents the picture of a great man in a grand manner," he said. He was particularly pleased that "the efficacy of the man, who so earnestly teaches" wonderful things to his students, received its due token of appreciation from them. "I regard [Hegel] as worthy of any distinction in relation to knowledge, conviction, and efficacy," he said.[66] Hegel's "conviction and efficacy" were the buzzwords Altenstein had often chewed in his mouth like a piece of cheap bubble gum. Clearly, in his dual capacity as the rector and the government's deputy at the university, Hegel had efficaciously prevented the ongoing revolutionary agitation from spreading among the students at Berlin, so Altenstein thought. Now, there was a medal in circulation to confirm his conviction.

The agitation in question had issued from the July Revolution in France a month after Hegel's address. We will discuss the July Revolution briefly in the next chapter and in more detail in Chapter 14. The next chapter focuses on some key aspects of Hegel's popular lectures on world history. One of its main aims is to illustrate why Altenstein admired his "conviction and efficacy."

---

[64] Ibid., #652.
[65] Quoted in Horst Althaus, *Hegel: An Intellectual Biography*, trans. Michael Tarsh (Cambridge, UK: Polity Press, 2000), 269.
[66] *Berichten*, #653.

Chapter Thirteen

XIII. THE PHILOSOPHY OF HISTORY

1. Preliminaries

> (An apocryphal story:) When Hegel was lecturing on the philosophy of history, a ... student in the class interrupted to say, "But Herr Professor, the facts are different,' to which Hegel, unruffled, replied, "So much the worse for the facts."[1]

The first edition of *The Philosophy of History* (henceforth *History*) was posthumously-published by Gans in 1837. With the assistance of Hegel's other disciples, a second edition was published by Karl Hegel, the philosopher's son, in 1840, a year after Gans died at the young age of forty-two. This edition was subsequently translated by J. Sibree. Other editions and translations also exist, but the widely-available Sibree translation, with occasional revisions, will do for our purposes.[2] What we have before us is a combination of Hegel's own manuscripts and the various transcriptions of his lectures, authored by multiple students and largely modeled after his 1830-1831 lectures.[3]

The main aim of this chapter is to illustrate how Hegel's lectures on world history, which were among his most popular, and which he had repeated until the end of his life (1831), ultimately amount to yet another apology for the Restoration-period Germanic states, especially the Prussian one. For this reason, and by also drawing from the ending of his *Philosophy of Right*, this chapter focuses mostly on the "last" stage of history described by Hegel, where his apology is most visible. However, certain other parts of his lectures need to be discussed beforehand, albeit briefly, since they crucially inform his belief in the superiority of Germans.

---

[1] Andrew Collier, *Marx: A Beginner's Guide* (Oxford: Oneworld, 2004), 132. There exist many different versions of this story, though they all tell the same basic message.
[2] G. W. F. Hegel, *The Philosophy of History*, trans. J. Sibree (New York: Dover, 1956).
[3] For a more detailed discussion, see Joseph McCarney, *Routledge Philosophy Guidebook to Hegel on History* (London: Routledge, 2000), 7-10.

XIII. The Philosophy of History

2. The Cunning of Hegel

Hegel asserts in the *Philosophy of Right* that "the universal spirit, the [unrestricted] spirit of the world, which ... produces itself as that which asserts its right—and its right is the highest of all [rights]—over ... [the states or nations] in world history, which is the world's court of judgement."[4] This sentence captures the main point of his doctrine of history. Thus, he states at the outset of *History* that "speculative philosophy" contemplates history from the standpoint of a simple principle (or presupposition, *we* might say), "that Reason [or the manifestation of the Divine Being in the spiritual world] is the Sovereign of the World; that the history of the world, therefore, presents us with a rational process." "This 'Idea' or 'Reason'," he adds, "is the True, the Eternal, the absolutely powerful essence; ... it reveals itself in the World, and that in that World nothing else is revealed but this and its honor and glory."[5]

On the one hand, these preliminary formulations already suggest that his philosophy of history is based on superficially grandiose statements. On the other hand, they suggest at least two things: a hierarch of rights, which we will discuss later, and a vision of world history in which "the universal spirit" (a.k.a. God, the Idea, Reason, Substance, Divine Being, Providence, the world spirit, etc.) judges and determines all that happens. In *History*, the latter presupposition is explained with the use of such clever expressions as "the *cunning of reason*."

You see, reason, or the Reason, is not "implicated in opposition and combat, and ... exposed to danger. It remains in the background, untouched and uninjured. This may be called the *cunning of reason*—that it [Reason] sets the passions to work for itself, while that which develops its existence through such impulsion pays the penalty and suffers loss." This loss is of no importance to Hegel, the spokesperson for the Reason, also known as the Idea, since the "particular is for the most part of too trifling value as compared with the general [or universal]: individuals are sacrificed and abandoned. The Idea pays the penalty of determinate existence and of corruptibility, not from itself, but from the passions of individuals."[6] Thus, Hegel's so-called "philosophy" of history, despite the protestations of his recent advocates, *does* indeed justify all the horrible things that have happened in history as a part of the Idea's cunning plan.

In some passages, Hegel claims that the world spirit mainly utilizes the states or nations to carry out its major plans. In others, he says that "all

---

[4] G. W. F. Hegel, *Grundlinien der Philosophie des Rechts oder Naturrecht und Staatswissenschaft im Grundrisse*, ed. Eduard Gans (Berlin: Duncker und Humblot, 1833), §340. Henceforth cited as *Philosophy of Right*.
[5] Hegel, *Philosophy of History*, 9-10.
[6] Ibid., 33.

XIII. The Philosophy of History

significant actions in the theater of world history," especially the "world-historical" ones, are led by world-historical individuals, who are the "living expressions [or instruments] of the substantial deed of the world spirit and are identical with it." Alas, this is "hidden from them," meaning that they do not recognize the plan of the world spirit as their own "object and purpose." We must thus surmise that only Hegel (and perhaps his disciples) knows this, for he also claims that neither the "contemporaries" nor the "posteriority" of these great men acknowledges their deeds as the deeds of the world spirit. Instead, such men are recognized by all (except Hegel) merely as "formal subjectivities" with "immortal fame."[7] In this manner, and once more, the world spirit lurks in the back ground, secretly puppeteering the great men, or the great states, to carry out its deeds.

In fact, we the mortals might think, the word spirit is mean-spirted. Once it is done with the great men, it casts them aside, and even makes them miserable. "When their object is attained, they fall off like empty hulls from the kernel. They die early, like Alexander; they are murdered, like Caesar; transported to St. Helena, like Napoleon." Thanks to Hegel, we now know the real reason behind the early demise of these world-historical individuals. Anyone who denies these profound truths automatically proves to be ignorant of how the world spirit operates.[8]

Moreover, those who regard the actions of such men as immoral are equally ignorant for the same reason since they fail to realize that such men are ultimately set in motion by the world spirit. Admittedly, Hegel says, the world-historical "men may treat other great, even sacred interests, inconsiderately—conduct which is indeed obnoxious to moral [and so subjective] reprehension. But, as it proceeds, such a mighty figure must trample many an innocent flower underfoot and destroy many things in its path."[9] Gee!

A similar combination of grandeur and ill-fate is bestowed upon the great nations as well, claims Hegel. Once the world spirit is done with each great nation (and there can only be one of these at a time), it abandons it, and chooses another nation. The former inevitably declines, at least in relation to the newly chosen nation.[10] For this reason, "world history is … divine tragedy … World spirit is unsparing and pitiless." However, according to its own standpoint, which is the *substantial* standpoint, "no people ever suffered wrong; what it suffered, it had merited."[11]

---

[7] Hegel, *Philosophy of Right*, §348.
[8] Hegel, *Philosophy of History*, 31-32. Translation revised.
[9] Ibid.
[10] Hegel, *Philosophy of Right*, §347R.
[11] G. W. F. Hegel, *Lectures on Natural Rights and Political Science: The First Philosophy of Right*, trans. J. Michael Stewart and Peter C. Hodgson (Oxford University Press, 2012), 306-07.

XIII. The Philosophy of History

Thus, and once more, everything that has happened in history is rational and justified from the higher standpoint of the *Weltgeist*, now revealed to us by the Hegelian speculative philosophy. After all, the right of the world spirit is superior to the right of the states, nations, and individuals.[12]

3. Ranking Races and Nations

The world spirit, says Hegel, progressively actualizes itself at a "stage higher than that at which it stood in its earlier" historical stages.[13] "The spirit [itself] ... prepares and works out the transition to its next, higher stage,"[14] which, we now assume, it does so cunningly. Hegel knows all about this because "what powers ... [the world spirit] inherently possess we learn from the variety of products and formations [such as states] which it originates."[15] One way our great sage knows about the plan of the world spirit to "transition to its next, higher stage" is that its new, chosen products (nations or states) are mightier, and so possess a higher right over the forsaken ones. In his wording, "against this its absolute right," which the chosen nation derives from the world spirit, "the spirits of other nations are without rights, and they, like those whose epoch is already over, no longer count in world history."[16]

Hegel's readymade, self-serving calculus comes into play in yet another way: "On the basis of the same determination, civilized nations [*Nationen*] are [right] to regard and treat as barbarians those who lag them in the substantial moments of the state."[17] This is not to say that the more powerful "civilized nations" recognize and respect the rights and independence of the lesser ones; they do not.[18]

The question now becomes, which nations have been chosen as the dominant ones throughout history? In a speculative move, which makes his foregoing, silly comments relatively reasonable, Hegel assures us that the world spirit has four principles—the latest being the most advanced, which it has assigned to four nations (or cultures). Hegel's epiphany on this issue runs as follows:

> As spirit, it [i.e., the world spirit] is simply the movement of its own activity of knowing itself absolutely, of liberating its consciousness

---

[12] Hegel, *Philosophy of Right*, §33, §340.
[13] Ibid., §343, R.
[14] Ibid., §344.
[15] Hegel, *Philosophy of History*, 73.
[16] Hegel, *Philosophy of Right*, §347.
[17] Ibid., §351.
[18] Ibid., §§330-40.

XIII. The Philosophy of History

from the form of natural immediacy, and so of returning to itself. Therefore, in the process of its liberation, the principles ... of this self-consciousness ... are four in number.[19]

This claim, which speaks ill of his logical powers, is an example of Hegel's frequent and unwarranted use of the word "thus" or "therefore." But there is more of this "logical" nonsense where it came from: "In accordance with these four principles," or *therefore*, "the world-historical realms are [also] four in number: 1) the Oriental, 2) the Greek, 3) the Roman, 4) the Germanic."[20]

Other nations or cultures or races barely, if at all, count in Hegel's historical scale of stages. "Africa proper, as far as History goes back," says the ignorant philosopher, "has remained ... the land of childhood, which lying beyond the day of self-conscious history, is enveloped in the dark mantle of Night." "In Negro life," adds he, "the characteristic point is the fact that consciousness has not yet attained to the realization of any substantial objective existence." The "Negro" is "natural man in his completely wild and untamed state." For this reason, "among the Negroes moral sentiments are quite weak, or more strictly speaking, non-existent."[21] Hegel spews out more racist garbage of this kind elsewhere.[22] He even justifies the enslavement of "the Negro," but is willing to grant that they should be freed gradually under the tutelage of their owners in America, who seem to civilize them to a limited extent by enslaving them under civilized conditions. At any rate, our expert ignoramus excludes Africa from world history, "for it is no historical part of the World; it has no movement or development to exhibit."[23]

Hegel shared both the racism of many of his contemporaries and their justification of slavery. However, in this regard, he was far behind the likes of Rousseau and many abolitionists, including the Jacobins. Indeed, and to bring the point home, Follen, one of the organizers of the Wartburg Festival, who was forced into multiple exiles, wounded up in the United States where he became a committed abolitionist, even if this meant losing his job at Harvard University. He was also an ordained minister and, at the opening of his new church, prayed that his

> church might never be desecrated by intolerance, or bigotry, or party spirit; that more especially its doors might never be closed against any

---

[19] Ibid., §352.
[20] Ibid., §354.
[21] Hegel, *Philosophy of Right*, 91, 93, 96.
[22] G. W. F. Hegel, *Philosophy of Mind*, trans. William Wallace and A. V. Miller (Oxford: Oxford University Press, 1971), 42-43.
[23] Hegel, *History of Philosophy*, 99.

XIII. The Philosophy of History

one, who would plead in it the cause of oppressed humanity; that within its walls all unjust and cruel distinctions might cease, and that there all men might meet as brethren.[24]

In short, Hegel was frequently in the camp of the reactionary elements of his times. Amazingly, countless sophisticated academic tricks have been utilized by his admirers to prove that he was really a progressive, non-racist thinker—if understood "correctly."[25]

"The Negros," however, fare better than the native Americans in Hegel's scale:[26]

> A mild and passionless disposition, lack of spirit, and crouching submissiveness towards a Creole, and still more towards a European, are the chief characteristics of the native Americans; and it will be long before the Europeans succeed in producing any independence of feeling in them. The inferiority of these individuals in all respects, even in regard to size, is very manifest; only the quite southern races in Patagonia are more vigorous natures, but still abiding in their natural condition of rudeness and barbarism ... [T]he negroes are far more susceptible to European culture than the Indians.[27]

This nonsense is embellished with additional idiotic claims, such as: Catholic priests need to ring a bell at midnight to remind the Paraguayan Indians of their matrimonial duties.[28] It takes a silly person, and not simply a racist, to believe that they could not figure out such "duties" on their own.

In the overall scheme of things, then, Hegel's lectures on world history may be summarized as an attempt to create a hierarchy of races and cultures. In this hierarchy, the European-Caucasian race is held to be superior to the rest. With the Caucasian race, claims he, the spirit

---

[24] Eliza Cabot Follen, *Life of Charles Follen* (Cambridge: Thomas H. Webb, 1844), 425-26.
[25] For an attempt, among many, to absolve Hegel of his racism, see Stephen Houlgate, *An Introduction to Hegel: Freedom, Truth, and History* (London: Blackwell, 2005). For a sound exposition of Hegel's racist attitude toward the peoples of Africa, see Robert Bernasconi, "Hegel at the Court of the Ashanti," in *Hegel after Derrida*, ed. Stuart Barnett, 41-63 (London: Routledge, 1998). For two more recent and comprehensive treatments of Hegel's Eurocentric racism, see Teshale Tibebu, *Hegel and the Third World: The Making of Eurocentrism in World History* (Syracuse: Syracuse University Press, 2011); M. A. R. Habib, *Hegel and Empire: From Postcolonialism to Globalism* (New York: Palgrave, 2017).
[26] For a good exposition of Hegel's racist treatment of American Indians, see Michael H. Hoffheimer, "Hegel, Race, Genocide," in *The Southern Journal of Philosophy* 39 (2001): 35-61.
[27] Hegel, *History of Philosophy*, 81-82.
[28] Ibid., 82.

XIII. The Philosophy of History

first attains to absolute unity with itself. Here for the first time ... [the spirit] enters into complete opposition to the life of Nature, apprehends itself in its absolute self-dependence, wrests itself free from the fluctuation between one extreme and the other, achieves self-determination, self-development, and, in doing so, creates world-history.[29]

This is yet another Hegelian gibberish, which nevertheless underscores the relevance of race (or nation) to his home-made categorization of world history into periods and scales of hierarchy: only (a portion of) the Caucasian race has been, and still is, capable of making history.

Thus, despite listing it among the four stages of the world spirit, Hegel in fact keeps the Asian peoples outside of it, at least from the one that counts as significant to him. This works much better in the calculus of a speculator, who was obsessed with triadic divisions and other mental tics. Consequently, he believes, or pretends to believe, that there are only *three* historical stages in world history and *three* European peoples or nations that have made it. These are, once again, "the Greek, the Roman, [and] the Germanic" nations. Of course, he also counts four, but then hesitates to include "the Orientals." Ultimately, he settles on a silly expression, "unhistorical History," which applies to the "stable" China.[30] "On the other side," there are the less stable states of Asia, which are "in ceaseless conflict." "This history, too ..., is, for the most part, really *unhistorical*."[31]

It would be an exercise in futility to take seriously, or attempt to make sense of, a vision of history that smacks of ignorance and charlatanism, embellished with silly buzzwords. But a brief clarification is in order. Hegel's division of world history, as noted earlier, is based on the presupposition that history is essentially the self-realization and development of the world spirit in different places, times, and peoples. The hierarchy is decided by the compliance of each epoch/people with the Hegelian principle of *freedom*. Many people understandably interpret Hegel's formulation as the *progressive* realization of higher shapes of *freedom*. Unthinkingly, they even celebrate him as a freedom-loving progressive, without realizing that the "substantial" freedom he advocates is blind obedience to the state.

Quantitatively put, and here we get a different triadic division, we first have "the Orientals," who "have not attained the knowledge that Spirit—Man as such—is free; and because they do not know this, they are not free. They only know [or recognize] that *one is free*," and since this one is a

---

[29] Hegel, *Philosophy of Mind*, 44.
[30] Hegel, *History of Philosophy*, 106.
[31] Ibid., 107.

"despot," and a despot is not free, no one is really free. Thus, according to Hegel's freedom-scale, "the Orientals" do not really count. Then comes the second category, which now encompasses both the Greeks and the Romans. They were free, says Hegel, but "knew that only some are free." Then emerged the third principle among the Germans. "Under the influence of Christianity," they were the first to attain the "consciousness that man, as man [i.e., *all* men], is free: that it is the freedom of Spirit which constitutes its essence."[32] These "three" stages are said to coincide with the following political forms: "[1] *Despotism* [one is free] ..., [2] *Democracy* and *Aristocracy* [some are free] ... [and, 3] *Monarchy* [all are free]."[33]

I will not refute Hegel's "classification of historical data" by counting the free and unfree Orientals, Greeks, Romans, and Germans. Suffice it to say that, unwittingly, and at least in the present context, Hegel himself does not think that all human beings are inherently free. Otherwise put, he thinks only the Germans of his time are truly free, though he attributes this verdict to the consciousness of the Protestant Germans themselves. Others, especially the non-European races, are inherently unfree and subhuman in some speculative sense, according to the most famous philosopher of Germany.

Be that as it may, the question we must now answer is this: What does Hegel's conception of political freedom in a hereditary monarchy entail? "It must ... be understood," he answers initially, "that all the worth which the human being possesses—all spiritual reality, he possesses only through the State," which "is the Divine Idea as it exists on Earth." Evidently, Hegel here prescribes state-worship. Therefore, one is truly human and free when one worships the state. Expectedly, he proceeds to identify this praxis with passive obedience, claiming that "only that will which obeys [the] law is free." However, and here comes another speculative trick, rather than its obedient subjects, it is the modern (German) monarchical state that is truly free. This form of state itself, says the famous philosopher of freedom, is "the realization of Freedom" since "it exists for its own sake."[34]

In short, "all are free" in a Hegelian monarchy in the sense that they are the obedient subjects of the modern (German) monarchical state, which "is the Divine Idea as it exists on Earth." We will have more to say on this Hegelian "freedom" in the next section.

---

[32] Ibid., 18.
[33] Ibid., 104.
[34] Ibid., 39-40.

XIII. The Philosophy of History

4. The Emergence of the Divine, Rational State in Germany

> [F]or Hegel the apex and terminus of world history coincided in his own Berlin existence.[35]

After reading 400-plus pages of insufferable "history," we realize that the superior, freest European nations are the ones that "adopted the Reformation" and, it goes without saying, the Catholic, "*Romanic nations*" are excluded from this list. Hegel also draws some distinctions between German and English characteristics in this context to highlight the superiority of the former.[36]

In the next phase of his consideration, Hegel points out the significance of "the political development" in modern times to the actualization of the world spirit. Here, he mentions the emergence of "the monarchical principle" as the hitherto, and forever, the most rational political principle on which the "free" state is based. This state is none other than the kind of hereditary monarchy in which the monarch "must have a final decisive will."[37] This comment, like the related ones we are about encounter, strongly suggests that Hegel equates the "rational" state he "logically" formulates in the *Philosophy of Right* with the historical "rational" state, which, as we are about to find out, exists in the post-Napoleonic Germany, especially in Prussia.

What needs to be reiterated in the present context is that Hegel puts this "rational" state at the end of *recent history* (and, arguably, all history), which, in his account, began with the French Revolution and reached its apex in the post-Napoleonic period in Germany, coinciding with "his own Berlin existence."

Those who wish to portray the "mature" Hegel as a supporter of the French Revolution often underscore only the following words found in his *History*: The Revolution was a "glorious mental dawn." This selective use of "evidence" distorts what the cryptic Hegel wants to say in this context. Let us first quote the entire passage in which these words are uttered:

> Never since the sun had stood in the firmament and the planets revolved around him had it been perceived that man's existence centers in his head, i.e., in Thought, inspired by which he builds up the world of reality. Anaxagoras had been the first to say that *nous* [the cosmic mind]

---

[35] Friedrich Nietzsche, *On the Advantage and Disadvantage of History for Life*, trans. Peter Preuss (Indianapolis: Hackett, 1980), 47.
[36] Hegel, *Philosophy of History*, 420-21.
[37] Ibid., 427.

XIII. The Philosophy of History

governs the [physical] World; but not until now had man advanced to the recognition of the principle that Thought ought to govern spiritual [human] reality. This was accordingly a glorious mental dawn. All thinking beings shared in the jubilation of this epoch. Emotions of a lofty character stirred men's minds at that time; a spiritual enthusiasm thrilled through the world, as if the reconciliation between the Divine and the Secular was now first accomplished.[38]

To begin with, it is not clear to me that "glorious mental dawn" expresses Hegel's own sentiment about the Revolution. More importantly, and be that as it may, it does not refer to anything that had happened *during* and *after* the storming of the Bastille. In other words, as is the case in the *Phenomenology* (see Chapter 3), he depicts "the course the French Revolution in France took" entirely negatively, and this includes *all* institutions and ideals that came into being after 1789, as we are about to see.

However, first, Hegel abruptly goes on to describe the "rational" state. Among other things, he maintains that, in a rational state, the "ultimate decision is the prerogative of the monarch." Yet, since "the State is based on Liberty, the many wills of individuals also desire to have a share in political decisions." According to the supremely "rational" Hegel, this "share" is to be avoided entirely, for the will of the many is irrational. Rather than having a meaningful say in political decisions, Hegel maintains once more that the true freedom of the citizens consists in their "disposition" toward the monarchical state. By *disposition* he means (as he had always meant) "an *ex animo* acquiescence in the laws ... and the Constitution as in principle fixed and immutable, and of the supreme obligation of individuals to subject their particular wills to them." Thus "the citizens" must regard their own "opinions as subordinate to the substantial interest of the State, and to insist upon them no further than that interest will allow; moreover, nothing must be considered higher and more sacred than good will [i.e., *ex animo* disposition] towards the State."[39] This already-familiar, servile rhetoric serves a specific purpose here: it is meant to clarify beforehand that, from its very outset, the French Revolution proceeded in the wrong direction by straying away from the Hegelian sort of political freedom and rational state.

Why was this the case? Hegel: "Here it must be frankly stated that with the Catholic Religion no rational constitution is possible." This certainly means that the predominantly Catholic French people are incapable of a "rational" constitution. In other words, they lack the Protestant sort of

---

[38] Ibid., 447.
[39] Ibid., 447–49.

XIII. The Philosophy of History

"disposition," as defined above by Hegel, which is a "Religion that is not opposed to a rational political constitution," also as defined above.[40] These thoughtless assertions, which amount to pedestrian tautologies, basically predetermine the "course the French Revolution took" in Hegel's ensuing account. They also confirm that, in the same account, "the glorious mental dawn" would turn quite inglorious *with* the inception of the Revolution in the Catholic and Romanic France, precisely because neither its principles nor its institutions nor the disposition of its proponents were of the required, glorious kind.

Hegel traces "the course of the French Revolution" in the ensuing three pages, in which all major developments that had happened during the past forty-one years (1789-1830) are lined up as inevitable results. The constitutional monarchy, established during the Revolution, was bound to fail since "the legislature absorbed the whole power of the administration," controlling "the budget, affairs of war and peace, and the levying of the armed force ... The government was thus transferred to the Legislative Chamber, as in England to the Parliament." What is even worse, "this constitution was also vitiated by the existence of absolute mistrust" (i.e., lack of Hegelian disposition) in "the dynasty." Thus, both the "government" and the "constitution" inevitably collapsed. Then followed the Reign of Terror, which is described (in the language of Robespierre himself) as the reign of "Virtue." Again inevitably, things quickly fell apart, as the intrinsically irrational actors, or rather actors with merely subjective disposition, succumbed to all-around "suspicion" (a reference to the law of suspects, issued by The Committee of Public Safety in 1793), which then translated into the rule of the guillotine. This ruinous regime was succeeded by the "Directory of Five." Suspicion remained in great doses, however. Also, the incorrigible French had learned nothing from their initial experiences, and so left the government "in the hands of the legislative assemblies." Expectedly, things did not improve, as more disorder ensued. "Napoleon," who "knew how to rule," restored order, making himself the sole leader of the state. "He then ... subjected all Europe and diffused his liberal institutions in every quarter." But his "great victories" were ultimately powerless, as the "disposition of the [conquered] peoples [mainly Germans], i.e. their religious disposition and that of their nationality, ultimately precipitated this colossus [i.e., the Napoleonic Empire]."[41]

Then followed the restoration of the Bourbon "constitutional monarchy, with the '*Charte*' as its basis." However, the Catholic French remained what they had been previously. Consequently, a "fifteen years' farce was played" as the French merely pretended to have the proper

---

[40] Ibid., 449.
[41] Ibid., 449-51.

XIII. The Philosophy of History

disposition toward their monarch. Alas, in reality, "the ruling disposition was a Catholic one, which regarded it as a matter of conscience to destroy the existing institutions," giving way to the lamentable July Revolution of 1830. Despite paying lip service to other factors, Hegel ultimately holds the Catholicism and individualism ("the subjective will") of the French responsible for the "forty years of war and confusion." The "Catholic principle," he says, "inevitably occasions" such destruction, though the reliance on "men's subjective will" (i.e., liberalism) also necessarily contributed to it. Consequently, and to Hegel's chagrin, "liberalism" has once again emerged in France during the July Revolution of 1830.

> 'Liberalism' sets up in opposition to all this the atomistic principle, which insists upon the sway of individual wills, maintaining that all government should emanate from their express power, and have their express sanction. Asserting this formal side of Freedom—this abstraction—the [liberal] party in question allows no political organization to be firmly established ... Thus, agitation and unrest are perpetuated. This collision, this nodus, this problem is that with which history is now occupied, and whose solution it has to work out in the future.[42]

To clarify, unlike what some scholars maintain, Hegel *does not* claim here that the present history is *entirely* preoccupied with "this problem," and that the future will entail the realization of the "liberal" ideals of the Revolution. As we will see shortly, he thinks the Protestant Germany has already solved this "problem." Thus, the "problem" only persists in the Catholic-Romanic world, without any clear signs of its resolution in the horizon.

Accordingly, the liberal "principle" of the Revolution, he goes on to argue, "has gained access to almost all modern states, either through [the French] conquest or by express introduction into their political life." In particular, "the Roman Catholic World," especially "France, Italy, [and] Spain," were "subjected to the dominion of Liberalism." Thus, "as an abstraction emanating from France," liberalism "traversed the Roman World." However, it "became bankrupt everywhere," as "these countries" have now (1830) "sank back into their old [wretched] condition" of "slavery."[43] We will return to Hegel's treatment of, and vehement opposition to, the July Revolution in the next chapter.

"Contrasted with these Romanic nations, we observe the other powers of Europe, and especially the Protestant nations," which "were not drawn

---

[42] Ibid., 451-52.
[43] Ibid., 452-53.

XIII. The Philosophy of History

within the vortex of internal agitation [caused by liberalism], and exhibited great, immense proofs of their internal solidity."[44] Thus, the "problem" of Revolution, or liberalism, is inapplicable to "the Protestant nations." In Hegel's view, "internal solidity" is one of the main indicators of being rational and free. However, he also has other reasons and indicators in mind, which lead him to further narrow down his list of the "contrasted" nations.

Austria, for instance, is stable. But it is an empire, not a kingdom (i.e., not a monarchical state of a single people). This makes it an admixture of "many political organizations," which is not a good thing for undisclosed reasons. Moreover, Austria is "not German in origin and in character and has [for this reason?] remained unaffected by 'ideas.'" Another negative aspect of Austria (and this both at once!) is that it has kept "the lower classes in some districts ... in a condition of serfdom," and suppressed "the nobility" in others. For these and other reasons, Austria has no essential connection to Germany; properly speaking, it is not German.[45] Thus, Hegel excludes Austria from his list of most "rational," "free," and (genuinely) Germanic states.

(Hegel downgrades England below Germany for different reasons. I skip his treatment of England[46] since his similar critique of it in his "The English Reform Bill" will be discussed in Chapter 14.)

According to Hegel, the most advanced (rational) states are found in Germany proper. Germany has reached this position when its "nationality delivered it from" the "yoke" of the French. An important aspect of the German states "is that code of Rights [laws] which was certainly occasioned by French oppression." Hegel here has in mind the (Napoleonic) Code and constitution, the introduction of which, he says, was the "especial [cunning] means of bringing to light the deficiencies of the old system" of the German Empire.

> The fiction of an Empire has utterly vanished. It is broken up into sovereign states. Feudal obligations are abolished, for freedom of property and of person have been recognized as fundamental principles. Offices of State are open to every citizen, talent and adaptation being ... the necessary conditions. The government rests with the official world, and the personal decision of the monarch constitutes its apex ... Yet with firmly established laws, and a settled organization of the State, what is left to the sole arbitrament of the monarch is, in point of substance, no great matter. It is certainly a very fortunate circumstance for a nation, when a sovereign of noble character [e.g., Friedrich

---

[44] Ibid., 453.
[45] Ibid.
[46] Ibid., 453-55.

Wilhelm III of Prussia] falls to its lot; yet in a great state even this is of small moment, since its strength lies in the Reason incorporated in it. Minor [German] states have their existence and tranquility secured to them ... by their neighbors: they are therefore, properly speaking, not independent, and have not the fiery trial of war to endure. As has been remarked, a share in the government [i.e., bureaucracy] may be obtained by everyone who has a competent knowledge, experience, and a morally regulated will. Those who know ought to [or do] govern, not ignorance and the presumptuous conceit of "knowing better." Lastly, as to Disposition, we have already remarked that in the Protestant Church the reconciliation of Religion with Legal Right [of the state] has taken place. In the Protestant world there is no sacred, no religious conscience in a state of separation from, or perhaps even hostility to Secular Right [of the state].[47]

Otherwise put, "the History of the World," preached by Hegel to be sure, "is nothing but the development of the Idea of Freedom," which is, at last, realized in Germany, especially Prussia. Hegel pretentiously calls this "Objective Freedom" or "real Freedom," which demands "the subjugation of the mere contingent Will," that is, the subjective wills of individuals, to the will of the state. This does not eliminate "subjective [personal] freedom," he insists, which is also realized when individuals' political "insight and conviction" corresponds with the laws of the state. Of course, this philosophical achievement cannot be wrapped up without fireworks, which come next:

> The History of the World ... is this process of development and the realization of Spirit," and so "is the true *Theodicaea*, the justification of God in History. Only this insight can reconcile Spirit with the History of the World—viz., that what has happened, and is happening every day, is not only not 'without God,' but is essentially His Work.[48]

This last statement confirms the main claim with which this chapter began: Hegel believes that everything that has ever happened is justified as God's intention and doing. This also applies, *especially*, to the rise and fall of states-nations. Relatedly, he maintains that the post-Restoration German states, especially Prussia, are not only the most rational of all but are also, in one and the same respect, divine in some sense. This conclusion dovetails Hegel's following claim, found in the *Philosophy of Right*: "The state

---

[47] Ibid., 455-56.
[48] Ibid., 456-57.

XIII. The Philosophy of History

consists in the march of God in the world, and its basis is the power of reason [or God] actualizing itself as will"[49]

Clearly, then, Hegel was in the business of glorifying and justifying the Prussian state. Moreover, he thought the period in which he had lived was the end of history, meaning that God was finally done with state-building and bestowing freedom upon his chosen people. In "the German World," he assured his listeners from his professorial pulpit, the "contradictions" between "the church and the state," between the spiritual and secular, have vanished. "Freedom has found the means of realizing its concept, as well as its truth." "This is the goal of world history," which has now been accomplished.[50]

---

[49] Hegel, *Philosophy of Right*, §258A.
[50] Here, I use the original German. G. W. F. Hegel, *Vorlesungen über die Philosophie der Geschichte* (Berlin: Duncker und Humblot, 1848), 134-35.

Chapter Fourteen

XIV. HEGEL'S FINAL STRUGGLES

1. Hegel's Reaction to the July Revolution

> With horror, my father saw in it a catastrophe that seemed to make the safe ground of the rational state wavering ...[1]

Hegel had served as both the rector and the deputy of the government at Berlin University from October 1829 to September 1830. As we have seen in Chapter 12, Altenstein chose him to address the public on the 300th anniversary of the Augsburg Confession, which he did on June 25, 1830. This choice reiterated the fact that the government thought of Hegel as its foremost ideolog. Hegel's address did not disappoint in this regard. Soon thereafter, his acolytes had produced various objects, including a widely-distributed medal, to celebrate their beloved leader. He was now at the height of his power, basking in glory.

However, his confidence was suddenly undermined by the July Revolution, which seemed to challenge both his history of philosophy and increasingly cozy existence. This fact is not readily revealed in his 1830-1831 lectures on world history, during which Hegel appeared confident that the revolutionary upheaval was mainly a liberal-Catholic-Romantic malaise, which had no appeal in the "solid" Germany, not to mention Prussia, the latest and most blessed product of the *Weltgeist*.

The July Revolution, as its other name ("Three Glorious Days") suggests, was a brief episode.[2] On July 25, 1830, Charles X signed the July Ordinances. The next day, the Parisians (and others) awoke to learn from the newspapers that the newly elected Chamber of Deputies was summarily dismissed, freedom of the press suspended, and the bourgeoisie banned from

---

[1] Günther Nicolin (ed.), *Hegel in Berichten seiner Zeitgenossen* (Hamburg: Felix Meiner, 1970), #637. Henceforth cited simply as *Berichten*.
[2] For informative accounts, see David H. Pinkney, *The French Revolution of 1830* (Princeton: Princeton University Press, 1972); Pamela Pilbeam, *The 1830 Revolution in France* (New York: St. Martin's Press, 1991); Jill Harsin, *Barricades: The War of the Streets in Revolutionary Paris, 1830-1848* (New York: Palgrave, 2002).

running as candidates for the Chamber of Deputies in the future. The bourgeoisie quickly went on what we might call a general strike, paralyzing the economy. The first victims of all this were the workers, many of whom involuntarily joined the already-swelling ranks of the unemployed, thus providing more available bodies to protest the ordinances and, more generally, the reign of the Bourbon monarchy. Many journalists also joined the protest in defiance of the ordinances, only to see the police raid some of the presses, which then urged even more revolutionary fervor against the regime. On July 27, Tuesday, the July Revolution began in earnest, as the growing crowds in the streets came to blows with the soldiers in the evening, resulting in the deaths of twenty-one protestors. Fighting in Paris continued throughout that night and into the next day, urging one of the commanders to clarify the terms of the ongoing struggle to the king: "Sire, it is no longer a riot, it is a revolution."[3] As the revolutionaries gained more strength, the king and his ministers succumbed to inaction and fear. On July 29, the reign of Charles X practically ended, though he formally abdicated on August 2 and set sail for England with his family shortly thereafter. The provisional government installed Louis Philippe of the House of Orléans to the vacant throne under a new scheme of constitutional monarchy. The new constitution was too illiberal to please the Left and too liberal for the likes of Hegel. It would be overthrown in 1848.

When the Revolution broke out, Gans was in France, hanging out with Cousin. From there, he sent a report to Hegel on August 5:

> 1. Peace has been restored in Paris. 2. The National Guard has assembled, with Lafayette at its head. 3. The old Royal Guard was asked to declare itself either for or against the Ordinance, and to remove itself from Paris should it be for it; it has marched out of Paris. 4. Where the King and [Jules Armand] Polignac are no one knows. 5. The Lords and Chamber of Deputies have assembled. 6. A provisional government has been appointed.[4]

Although Gans was enthusiastic about these developments, it seems that he knew well enough not to openly reveal this to Hegel in his letter. However, Hegel had been following the news closely and was quickly becoming more and more irritated. One reason for this was that the July Revolution in France had encouraged uprisings in Belgium, Italy, and

---

[3] Philip Mansel, *Paris Between Empires* (New York: St. Martin Press, 2001), 247.
[4] Clark Butler and Christiane Seiler (trans.), *Hegel: The Letters* (Bloomington: Indiana University Press, 1984), 669. Henceforth cited as *Letters*. Also, Johannes Hoffmeister (ed.), *Briefe von und an Hegel*, 4 volumes (Hamburg: Felix Meiner, 1952-1960), #644. Henceforth cited as *Briefe*, followed by the Latin numerical to indicate the volume number, in this case, *III*.

XIV. Hegel's Final Struggles

Poland between August and November. The fear of more revolutions erupting elsewhere, and perhaps even another Europe-wide war, had struck all reactionaries, large and small, with fear, as French intervention to support these uprisings now seemed quite probable.

Hegel was one such reactionary. With the Revolution in mind, in his December 13, 1830, letter to Karl Friedrich Göschel (one of his epigones), he claimed that "the [current] immense interest in politics has drowned all others. It is a crisis in which everything that formerly was valid appears to be made problematic." He also lamented that the "shallow ... political theorists and orators [i.e., his opponents] ... accuse those who defend the rights of magistrates and the state [such as himself] of servility, and of seeking to bring such [shallow] theorists and orators under the suspicion of governments and bring the vengeance of these governments upon them." Thus, Hegel was once again urging the authorities to punish the "shallow ... orators," and consequently facing the charges of being a servile lackey of the reactionary state (it was claimed that he was a "philosopher of the Restoration"). Moreover, he had come to believe now that philosophy, his own to be sure, could not tame the people and avoid irrational, revolutionary uproars: "As little as philosophy is able to oppose ignorance, violence, and the evil passions of this loud uproar, I scarcely believe that it could penetrate those circles that have settled in so comfortably," he said, adding that "philosophy may come to realize that it is destined for only a few."[5]

Hegel's letter to Göschel confirms Karl Hegel's observation: "Suddenly, in 1830, the political silence was interrupted by the July Revolution in France and its consequences in Poland and Belgium. With horror, my father saw in it a catastrophe that seemed to make the safe ground of the rational state wavering."[6]

As he recalled in 1886 (!), Michelet was allegedly caught by surprise when he observed Hegel's vehement objection to the revolutionary upheaval: "diversity of our political views ... emerged" in 1830, when Hegel refused to "approve the July Revolution." According to Michelet, he tried on one occasion to counter Hegel's opposition with a Hegelian argument, retorting that history progresses and that the July Revolution implies its next stage. Apparently, Hegel was not humored. "That's exactly how Gans talks," he replied wryly. Clearly, his disciple had misunderstood both his political philosophy and philosophy of history, which preached that the spirit had already cast liberalism and revolutionary ideas into the dustbin of history. Michelet proved his misunderstanding once again by pointing out, in the master's own vernacular, that the July Revolution is an

---

[5] *Letters*, 544 (*Briefe III*, #659).
[6] *Berichten*, #637.

XIV. Hegel's Final Struggles

expression of the "substance," which he identified with the "spirit of the French people," and so is stable and trustworthy. The master "replied swiftly": "one only negotiates with persons, and not with the substance."[7]

As Varnhagen also recalled some years later, he had political disagreements with Hegel in the aftermath of the July Revolution. "You know," he reminded Rosenkranz, Hegel had become "quite absolutist" during this period, adding that "he especially hated the Belgian disturbances" and the failure of the Dutch to crush the Belgian uprising. Hegel's absolutism, he added, brought him into conflict with Gans, who "stood completely on the opposite side."[8]

On January 18, with some bravado, Hegel informed his sister, Christiane, that the "copper engraving" of himself, which she wished to obtain, "can no longer be found. But since I have not only been engraved and sculpted but now imprinted on a medal as well, I shall send you two such medals instead." He also hastened to express his ongoing worries about the unfolding political turmoil: "We are presently and—we hope—forever safe from all the [current] unrest. But these are still anxious times, in which everything that previously was taken to be solid and secure seems to totter."[9] Clearly, Hegel saw in the current upheaval a rejection of what he had been preaching until recently: the rational actuality, the Restoration states, were not as permanently and stably established as he had thought, and taught, they were.

As noted earlier, Hegel was also perturbed by the "fervor" taking place in Poland. In a letter to his editor and publisher, Cotta, dated January 22, 1831, he sarcastically referred to this fervor as "the great carnival."[10] A week later, Hegel sent a letter to Christoph Ludwig Friedrich Schultz, a former government official and Altenstein ally, to inform him, among other things, of his efforts to secure appointments for some of his acolytes at various universities. But he was also compelled to comment on the recent political events. Referring to the Revolution-inspired, anti-Prussian sentiment in Poland, which raised the specter of a French intervention on behalf of the Poles, Hegel disparaged the "ever so loudly proclaimed French attitudes," which still exhibit both bitterness "over just humiliation and thirst for glory and conquest."[11]

While disparaging these events, Hegel was rewarded with the medal and honor of the Order of the Red Eagle, Third Class, for which Altenstein

---

[7] Ibid., #638.
[8] Ibid., #489.
[9] *Letters*, 422 (*Briefe III*, #664).
[10] Ibid., 671 (#665).
[11] Ibid., 672 (#669).

was the first to congratulate him.[12] Why Hegel was decorated with this medal should be abundantly clear by now. But, as Hegel well understood, this was a give-and-take relationship, and so more benefits and services could be reciprocated. It was now time for another public statement about the virtues of the Prussian state, as well as a warning to the youth that the liberal-republican path was a path to disorder and destruction. The reform bill, currently debated in England, conveniently provided Hegel with the opportunity to make such a statement. In April 1831, he published "The English Reform Bill" to achieve this end, and in a manner that calls to mind the servile and opportunistic aims of the *Proceedings* and the *Philosophy of Right*.

2. Hegel's Last Apologia: "The English Reform Bill"

Hegel thinks, or rather laments, in his essay that "those who promoted the Bill" in the parliament were driven by "a sense which was greatly reinforced by the disquieting impression produced among ... [them] by the example of neighboring France." He wants the English to avoid the French ideas, which he associates with the "liberal" insistence that private interests should be promoted in politics. In his exaggerated words,

> It is probably a fairly unanimous view among pragmatic historians that, if private interest and squalid financial advantage become the predominant factor in the election of heads of government within a given nation [*Volk*], this condition can be regarded as a prelude to the inevitable loss of that nation's political freedom [in the Hegelian sense], the downfall of its constitution and of the state itself.

In other words, he opines, "the right way to seek improvement" cannot be based on "such moral means as representations, admonitions, or associations of isolated individuals designed to counteract the system of corruption and to avoid becoming indebted to it, but to change the institutions [themselves]."[13] As we are about to see, "the right way" exists in Germany.

However, Hegel first wants to set the record straight on a misperception about the existing English system. "The peoples of the Continent," he says in this regard, "have allowed themselves to be impressed for so long by declamations about English freedom and by that nation's pride in its own legislation." The contrary is the case, claims he. In fact, "this inherently incoherent aggregate of positive determinations has not yet undergone the

---

[12] *Briefe III*, #666.
[13] G.W. F. Hegel, "On the English Reform Bill," in *Hegel: Political Writings*, eds. Laurence Dickey and H. B. Nisbet, 234-70 (Cambridge: Cambridge University Press, 1999), 235-37.

XIV. Hegel's Final Struggles

development and transformation which has been accomplished in the civilized states of the Continent, and which the German territories, for example, have enjoyed for a longer or shorter period of time." "England," in other words, "has hitherto lacked those elements which have played the greatest part in these glorious and auspicious advances. Foremost among these elements is the scientific [read Hegelian] treatment of law [*Recht*]." But the servile apologist must give "even more important" credit to "the broad vision of [the German] princes in making such principles as the welfare of the state, the happiness of their subjects, and general prosperity." Even more importantly, these princes possess "the sense of a justice which has being in and for itself." On the other hand, and once more,

> England has lagged so conspicuously behind the other civilized states of Europe in institutions based on genuine right, for the simple reason that the power of government lies in the hands of those who possess so many privileges which contradict a rational constitutional law and a genuine legislation.[14]

Hegel now returns to what the main theme of his essay was supposed to be: "the proposed Reform Bill." He warns that, if implemented, it will further weaken "the power of the [already weak] monarchic element of the constitution [of England]." Relatedly, the proponents of the bill are wrong to assume that giving more power to the parliament to decide the issue of taxes will reduce both the tax burden of the people and the wasteful spending of the government. "Indeed, the examples of England and France might lead to the induction that countries in which the political administration relies on the approval of assemblies elected by the people bear the heaviest burden of taxes."[15]

The Church of England receives a swipe for the "odious" practice of "*tithes*," which have long ago been, luckily, either abolished or significantly altered in the Protestant countries, especially "in the Prussian territories." What is worse, the English clergymen use these taxes to support themselves without even performing religious services. They are often occupied with "hunting" and "other kinds of idleness."[16] Furthermore, the English have confiscated the property of the Irish (Catholic) Church. "Even the Turks" have fared better than the English in this regard. Here, Hegel forgets his own hostility toward the Catholics.

The exploitation and pauperization of the peasant class in England are also quite awful, though not as bad as the situation of the dispossessed poor

---

[14] Ibid., 238-39.
[15] Ibid., 242.
[16] Ibid., 244.

XIV. Hegel's Final Struggles

in Ireland. Hegel does not propose any solutions to alleviate poverty; nor is this his aim. Rather, the main task at hand is to make the German "freedom" look better than the English one: "the English law of property, in ... many ... respects, is too far removed from the freedom enjoyed in this area by the continental countries." Hegel cannot see any way out of this predicament in England, where "the monarchy is too weak" and the rights and privileges of private interests are too strong.[17]

"The rambling confusion of English *civil law*" is Hegel's next target. You see, "the English nation has not yet achieved through [its] popular representation what several centuries of quiet work in the cultivation of science and of princely wisdom and love of justice have accomplished in Germany." The most famous philosopher of Germany is also certain that the proposed bill reflects "the crass ignorance of the fox-hunters and rural gentry," who have been schooled in such unworthy institutions and practices as "social contracts, newspapers ..., parliamentary debates," and lawyering. What is even worse, "the Bill ... sanctions the principle that a free income of £10 derived from landed property fully qualifies an individual for the task of judging and deciding [i.e., voting] on [a person's] capacity for the business of government and political administration with which Parliament is concerned." What Hegel prefers is a good-old German bureaucracy, appointed, not elected by popular vote, to run the government under the monarch's direction. This is unlikely to occur in England, where

> the pomp and circumstance surrounding the formal [and s worthless] freedom to debate the affairs of state in Parliament and other assemblies of all classes and estates, and to resolve such issues in Parliament, together with the unqualified right to exercise this freedom, prevent the English from grasping the essence of legislation and government through quiet reflection.[18]

Hegel now wants to tackle the issue of "the need for the various major interests of the nation to be represented in Parliament, and the changes which this representation would suffer as a result of the present Bill." This was the crux of the proposed bill, which would be enacted in 1832 as the Representation of the People Act (more commonly and informally known as the 1832 Reform Act). One main aim of the bill was to enlarge the scope of the electorate; its other aim was to restructure the electoral districts in order to make representation more balanced with respect to the population size of the growing cities, due to industrialization and expansion of

---

[17] Ibid., 245-49.
[18] Ibid., 249-50.

XIV. Hegel's Final Struggles

commerce. In Hegel's own wording, the bill expresses the "view that the various major interests of the nation should be represented in its main deliberative body." This view, Hegel says, "runs counter to the modern principle [advocated by Hegel], according to which only the abstract will of individuals as such should be represented."[19] More mundanely put, there should be no popular representation.

Accordingly, Hegel maintains next that representation in England, including those of the nobility, is currently based on "the subjective and arbitrary will" of the representatives, and so is necessarily "left to chance." Such a system of representation, he further opines, necessarily leads to corruption. If implemented, the bill, expected to enhance popular representation, will most likely make things worse. Above all, it is self-defeating since the expansion of "the right to vote," as "experience" shows, does not enhance popular interest and participation in politics. Rather, it produces "a great indifference" among "the electors [voters]." However, the voters should not be very harshly criticized for this "lukewarmness," for the atomistic system of voting itself urges it. The "obvious factor" in this regard "is the feeling that the individual vote is really of no consequence among the many thousands which contribute to an election." Therefore,

> while those great political bodies [both in England and France] which are currently making decisions on the franchise believe they are fulfilling a duty of supreme justice by relaxing the external qualifications for this entitlement and granting it to a larger number of people, it may well escape their notice that they are thereby reducing the influence of the individual, weakening his impression of its importance and hence also his interest in exercising this right.[20]

One might get the wrong impression here that Hegel would like to enhance the political influence of the voters and to reduce apathy. This is certainly not the case. In other words, and this is one of his original ideas, Hegel's solution to apathy is to eliminate popular participation in politics. Overall, the ordinary folks are characterized by their political "ignorance and limited ability to judge the talents, business experience, skill, and education required for high offices of state."[21]

Although it was just linked to political apathy, the famous philosopher now worries that the expansion of the franchise would certainly encourage political violence. Proof? That is what happened in "France," where "such ideas" have produced "those outbreaks of violence with which we are all

---

[19] Ibid., 251-52.
[20] Ibid., 253-59.
[21] Ibid., 259.

XIV. Hegel's Final Struggles

familiar." In response, Hegel has nothing else to offer but another praise for Germany: "In Germany, an actual transformation—peaceful, gradual, and lawful—of the old legal relationships" has occurred, thanks to the strong "inner conviction," that is, proper political disposition or trust in authority, with which the Germans are guided. "Thus, we have already made great progress here with the institutions of real freedom; we have now finished work on the most essential of them and enjoy their fruits."[22]

The English, according to Hegel, have the bad habit of allowing the majority party in the parliament to form the government (the executive power). If the proposed bill is enacted, more "new men" (the bourgeoisie or "shopkeepers") will be elected to the parliament. Given their large number in England, they will surely have a major say in the formation of the government. Having run out of ideas, of which he did not have many in the first place, Hegel once again refers to "the dangerous ... French abstractions" to explain this probable outcome, suggesting that the "new men" will destroy the English state.[23] In a nutshell, enhanced popular representation will put the lamentable principle of *people's sovereignty* to practice.

What is even worse, the French principle of "*droits de l'homme et du citoyen*" might follow suit. Quite unthoughtfully, Hegel asserts that people's sovereignty necessarily creates the following, unresolvable dilemma: it implies the "equality" of the rulers and the ruled, and this principle is "incompatible" with the governmental "authority to issue commands." Consequently, when the authorities seek to govern the "indeterminate mass," called "the people," they will, as they frequently do in France, "appear to be in the wrong [*Unrecht*] for having rejected equality and taken a stance opposed to the people, which has the infinite advantage of being recognized as the sovereign will."[24]

Based on the foregoing analysis, which falsely assumes that (liberal) individual and political rights deny political authority, Hegel issues the following warning to the English parliamentarians: If the main principle of the bill is accepted, the ensuing "conflict would threaten to become increasingly dangerous," bringing the old (feudal) privileges into sharp conflict with the new (bourgeois) ones within the government. This is to be expected in England where "the monarchic element" is too weak and the German-style "legislation," "based on principles of real freedom," is lacking. Consequently, if approved, the bill will urge a dangerous "opposition" in the English parliament between the old privileges and the part (i.e., the bourgeoisie) that derives its source from "the people." It is

---

[22] Ibid., 264.
[23] Ibid., 264-65.
[24] Ibid., 265-69.

XIV. Hegel's Final Struggles

very probable, reasons Hegel, that the latter interests will be "misguided enough to look to the people for its strength, and so to inaugurate not a reform but a revolution."[25]

To recapitulate, Hegel makes three general arguments in his essay. First, the German states are the most rational, and their denizens are the freest, of all nations in the world. In this sense, his essay is an apology for the Restoration regimes in Germany, especially Prussia. Second, he believes that the English system, as it currently exists, is quite corrupt and irrational. Third, what England needs is something like the monarchical principle of the Germans, though he seems to suggest that the English might not be able to implement it. What it does not need is the kind of reform proposed in the bill, for this will lead to an utterly unwelcomed revolution. It turns out, we should add, everything worked out in the opposite way: the bill passed in 1832 and the English system arguably remained the most stable system in Europe.

3. Hegel's Last Foe

The first three parts of Hegel's essay were published in the official *Prussian State Newspaper* in April 1831.[26] This fact is significant enough in its own right: Hegel clearly wanted to give his apologia the appearance of an official doctrine. However, following the advice of his subordinates, the king ordered the editors of the paper to not publish the last part of his essay.[27]

In our times, some scholars have attempted to explain Hegel's motive behind publishing "The English Reform Bill." Many speculations abound, including the widely-held claim that he wanted to explain, "indirectly" it is said, why Prussia itself needs political reform. This allegation is certainly false for at least two related reasons. First, as we have seen, the contents of the essay do not at all endorse it. Second, Hegel himself explained his motivation for publishing it in his May 21 letter to Karl von Beyme, a government official, who praised Hegel's essay very highly. As Hegel confirmed to Beyme, his essay was an attempt to defend "the Prussian constitution and legislative process," the "principles" of which "have been a constant source of misunderstanding and defamation." Relatedly, "the pretension and admitted renown of English liberty are allowed to count as valid against that [Prussian] constitution and process." The essay, then, also aimed to show how that the "English liberty" is bogus, and so is no match

---

[25] Ibid, 269-70.
[26] G. W. F. Hegel, "Über die Englische Reformbill," *Allgemeine Preußische Staatszeitung*, nos. 115-118 (1831).
[27] G. W. F Hegel, *Berliner Schriften, 1818-1831*, ed Johannes Hoffmeister (Hamburg: Felix Meiner, 1956), 785-86 (the editor's notes).

to the Prussian one.[28] In short, the claim that Hegel's essay was censured because of its suggestive criticisms of the Prussian state is simply false.[29]

Why, then, was the last part censured? As Hegel gingerly explained it in the same letter, the published parts of his essay urged the Prussian authorities to conclude that "the English political constitution was being attacked. And this, being unseemly for the Prussian *State Newspaper,* is said to have prevented the conclusion of the article from being printed."[30] In other words, as other existing documents also prove, what was published thus far put the authorities, including the king, into an uncomfortable situation as they rightly read Hegel's essay as an insult to the English regime, a Prussian ally at the time. Thus, the king, through his personal secretary, ordered the editors of the paper to not publish the last part of Hegel's essay, even though the king himself took "no exception to the article" itself.[31] Likewise, according to Hegel's wife's testimony, "His Majesty had nothing against it," and even ordered (might have even funded), *sotto voce,* the publication of the last part in a private journal.[32] In short, the king in fact approved of Hegel's essay.

Although safe in Berlin, Hegel was still preoccupied with the aftershocks of the July Revolution elsewhere. On May 29, 1831, he mailed a letter to his publisher, Cotta, the main purpose of which was to discuss the impending publication of the second edition of his *Science of Logic.* After discussing this issue in some detail, Hegel abruptly added a paragraph to lament the political developments taking place in various parts of Germany. Since Cotta was in Munich, Bavaria, at the time, Hegel reasoned that he must be "witnessing ... closely the deliberations of the estates on important issues of the day now being dragged out on the carpet: freedom of the press, the answerability of ministers, Catholic difficulties regarding

---

[28] *Letters,* 673 (*Briefe IV,* 675b).
[29] Harris maintains that "the last installment" of this essay was "suppressed by the Prussian censorship because it expressed approval of the genuinely democratic aspect of the advocated reforms." Errol E. Harris, "Hegel's Theory of Sovereignty, International Relations, and War," in ed. Jon Stewart, *The Hegel Myths and Legends* 154-66 (Evanston, IL: Northwestern University Press, 1996), 159. Harris' source for this misinformation is Avineri, *Hegel's Theory of the Modern State,* 208-09. There are many more inexplicably wrong treatments of Hegel's essay in circulation. Petry, on the other hand, provides one of the most informed analyses of Hegel's article, or "apologia [and propaganda] for the Prussia of 1831," especially on Hegel's sources. Michael J. Petry, "Propaganda and Analysis: The Background to Hegel's Article on the English Reform Bill," in *The State and Civil Society: Studies in Hegel's Political Philosophy,* ed. Z. A. Pelczynski, 137-58 (Cambridge: Cambridge University Press, 1984).
[30] *Letters,* 673 (*Briefe IV,* 675b).
[31] Hegel, *Berliner Schriften,* 785-86 (the editor's notes).
[32] *Berichten,* #739. A printed (published) copy of the last part of Hegel's article does not seem to exist, and I have not been able to determine where it was published.

marriage." "It seems," he reasoned, that in Munich, "as elsewhere, German imitations of French freedom fetishes—indeed imitations introduced by German Princes—have straightaway begun to cause trouble and interference for a few governments and ministries." In Berlin, on the other hand, "things are [politically] quite." What he meant was that "the *people*" (a derogatory term in Hegel's vocabulary) behaved subserviently toward the king. "A few days ago," he reported to prove his point,

> the King could scarcely prevent those who happened to be about him as he rode away from a spectacle of trick riders—i.e., the *people,* to use the official term for them—from unharnessing the horses and pulling ... [his carriage] home themselves. His admonition to them not to sink to the level of animals, coupled with his assurance that he would otherwise be obliged to go home on foot, allowed him to ride away to loud applause.[33]

Clearly, the philosopher despised "the people," though he was happy that, in Berlin, they were not infatuated with "French freedom fetishes."

Hegel mailed this letter to Cotta from Kreuzberg, a suburb of Berlin. He and his family had rented a house there to escape the cholera endemic, now plaguing Berlin. As Rosenkranz recalled, this was the upper floor of a garden house, which the Hegels affectionately called the "little palace." Hegel had regularly entertained visitors during these few months and seemed to be enjoying his life. There was even a jubilant celebration of his sixty-first birthday on August 27, despite the fear of cholera hovering above everyone's head. However, he could not refrain from cursing the "small uprisings" in various German cities.[34]

Sometime during this period, Hegel was invited to dine with the crown prince of Prussia, who would become King Friedrich Wilhelm IV in 1840. According to Arnold Ruge's report, which I find generally reliable, "'it is a scandal,'" said the prince to Hegel, "'that Professor Gans makes all our students republicans'" in his lectures on "'your philosophy of right.'" The prince found it particularly worrisome that hundreds of people attended Gans' lectures, and that the latter was giving Hegel's political philosophy "a perfectly liberal, even republican, coloring." Given these grave concerns, the prince suggested that Hegel himself should teach the course. Hegel did not attempt to dispute the prince's account of Gans' activities. He simply apologized for not knowing what his own lieutenant was preaching to his own students and promised to teach the course during the winter of 1831.[35]

---

[33] *Letters*, 674-75 (*Briefe III*, #677).
[34] *Berichten*, #676.
[35] Ibid., #682.

XIV. Hegel's Final Struggles

When exactly Hegel became aware of Gans' liberal-republican politics is not clear. My *guess* is that this was a recent revelation to him, and perhaps even to Gans himself. One reason why this might be the case is that all mentions of the political split between Hegel and Gans (by Varnhagen, Michelet, and Ruge) refer to the 1830-1831 period, even though Karl Hegel's account suggests that Gans had been interested in French politics at least since 1828 and that this was known to Hegel.[36] Another reason is that Gans himself became more visibly radical *after* the July Revolution, and this was a *volte-face* of sorts. "[Gans' and Leo's] opposition to the existing order," explains John E. Toews, "was moderate, reform-oriented, and basically 'loyal'" to the regime. In the final analysis, "no one appeared to notice that their defense of Hegel implicitly contained a specific, critical interpretation of the Hegelian doctrine of the realization of Reason in history."[37] Likely, what was not noticed, especially during a period in which the police spies were watching everyone carefully, did not exist.[38] Differently put, it is highly unlikely that Hegel knowingly had been sheltering a radical since the mid-1820s. More importantly, it is *evident* that he did not at all share Gans' liberal republicanism and sympathies for the July Revolution.

At any rate, perhaps thinking that cholera was no longer a threat, Hegel returned to Berlin in October to resume his teaching activities. In addition to philosophy of history, and as promised to the prince, he announced his course on political philosophy ("philosophy of right"). Unaware of Hegel's new teaching plan, Gans also announced that he would be teaching the same course. As a result, "four or five" students enrolled in Hegel's course, while Gans reported "several hundred." Hegel was not amused. He at once wrote to Gans, rather than speaking to him in person, informing him that they should not teach the same course on *his own* philosophy, which would lend itself to the unwelcome conclusion that opposing views could be attributed to it. Clearly, he returned to the university after the break to assert his authority, as instructed to do so by the crown prince. Gans was now proving to be an obstacle, and the master wanted him out of his way. Gans, however, had no intention of upsetting or disrespecting Hegel. In accordance with Hegel's wishes, so he thought, he posted a notice at the university, informing his students that he would teach a course on "legal

---

[36] Ibid., #708.
[37] John E. Toews, *Hegelianism: The Path Toward Dialectical Humanism, 1805-1841* (London: Cambridge University Press, 1980), 121-22.
[38] Relatedly, "neither Gans nor Hegel ever explicitly addressed their differences; the two colleagues were either unaware of such differences, chose to ignore them, or considered them to be entirely compatible with Gans's eminent role as a proponent of Hegelian philosophy." Michael H. Hoffheimer, *Eduard Gans and the Hegelian Philosophy of Law* (Dordrecht: Kluwer Academic Publishers, 1995), 11. Hoffheimer provides a useful account of their differences.

history," instead of the previously-announced course on the "philosophy of right," and urged them to enroll in Hegel's course. Alas, Gans' recommendation was largely ignored: "Hegel's auditorium ... did not fill up, and it was clear that the students wanted to wait until Gans would ... [teach the course on the philosophy of right] again," since, they thought, he "was not only more liberal but also much more understandable" than the incoherent and reactionary Hegel. Hegel thus "found his embarrassing situation very painful." This was not because he thought his political sympathies were misunderstood by the prince. Rather, in his capacity as a philosopher of the Prussian state, he was instructed by the latter "to assert his authority, but it turned out that he had none."[39]

Immensely disturbed by all this, Hegel sent another letter to Gans on November 12 (soon after he gave his first lectures), this time to scold him for advising the students to take his course:

> [B]y posting a notice in which you both inform the students of a circumstance of rivalry ..., and permitting yourself to recommend my lectures to the students, it might well seem I owed it to myself to post a public notice of my own to counter the obvious appearance of placing me in a foolish light with colleagues and students, as if such a notice on your part together with a recommendation of my lectures had been made at my bidding and instigation ... Both my hope that at least those who know me will not [falsely] credit me with such a procedure and my concern not to give you an opening for further awkwardness lead me to declare my view of your notice, not by a public notice of my own, but merely by these [private] lines.[40]

This was Hegel's last struggle against his and the regime's opponents, which now included Gans. His foremost disciple was his last foe.

4. Two Deaths, One Funeral

4.1 First Death

On November 14, Hegel's wife, dispatched an urgent note to Schulze: "My Hegel is very sick ... Come, dear friend, before it is too late."[41] Schulze, who lived next door, received the message at 4:45 pm. Shortly thereafter, he reported to Altenstein, who was away, that Hegel died at "five o'clock," just before Schulze entered his room. Schulze was certain that cholera was

---

[39] *Berichten*, #682.
[40] *Letters*, 677 (*Briefe III*, #687).
[41] *Berichten*, #710.

the cause of Hegel's death. However, he could not dare tell this to Hegel's wife and two sons since cholera came with certain stigmas at the time. "The sad certainty that our friend had died of the most intense cholera" was announced by the three doctors who arrived at the scene soon thereafter, Schulze reported.[42]

At the same time, visibly shaken by the news he just heard, Gans burst into Michelet's residence and "breathlessly" announced: "Hegel is dead."[43] Hegel's son, Immanuel, immediately reported the same news to a friend, adding that Hegel's struggled with his illness was very brief (less than two days).[44] All eye-witnesses (his wife and two sons) agreed that he died peacefully.

Soon after Hegel's death, many started to speculate that his recent debacle with Gans had weakened his immune system, making him vulnerable to cholera.[45] Other speculations were in the air as well, though it was generally accepted that cholera was ultimately responsible for his death. However, Hegel's wife reported to her own mother, Hegel's sister, and Niethammer that her husband did not show "any of the common symptoms" of cholera, even though, in her letters to them, she described certain symptoms that suggested otherwise. Certain of the cause of his death, the doctors isolated his body in the living room, where he died, and "smoked and disinfected everything."[46]

4.2 Second Death

Upon his arrival at the Hegel residence, Schulze found Marie, Karl, and Immanuel at the deceased philosopher's bedside, shocked and in much grief.[47] Where was the third son, whom no one had mentioned?

As noted in Chapter 2, Ludwig Fischer was born on February 5, 1807, as an "illegitimate" son, during Hegel's last days in Jena. His mother was Christiana Charlotte Johanna Burkhardt, Hegel's landlady and housekeeper. Hegel abandoned them both. Ludwig had spent the first ten years of his life

---

[42] Ibid., #711.
[43] Ibid., #713.
[44] Ibid., #712.
[45] Ibid., #682.
[46] Ibid., #714, #727, #739. Following his wife's objections, some biographers have recently disputed the validity of the doctors' verdict on the cause of Hegel's death. See, for instance, Horst Althaus, *Hegel: An Intellectual Biography*, 273; Terry Pinkard, *Hegel: A Biography*, 659. The latter is more adamant on this issue than the former. However, a recent expert-analysis has reaffirmed the verdict of Hegel's doctors. See Dr. Helmut Döll, "Hegels Tod," in *Zeitschrift für ärztliche Fortbildung* 79 (1985): 217-19. For a general discussion, see Barbara Dettke, *Die asiatische Hydra: Die Cholera von 1830/31 in Berlin und den preußischen Provinzen Posen, Preußen und Schleisen* (Berlin: Walter De Gruyter, 1995), 185-88.
[47] *Berichten*, #711.

XIV. Hegel's Final Struggles

in a foster home. In August 1816, after his mother's death, Hegel begrudgingly agreed to take him into his home.[48] Ludwig was brought to Hegel's home in Heidelberg by one of his friends sometime in April 1817.[49] By then, Hegel had been married to Marie for five years and had begotten two more sons with her. Ludwig was treated poorly; at best, he was of secondary status in the Hegel household. On August 29, 1819, Hegel sent some "picture-sheets" to his sons in Berlin. "One of them is for Manuel [Immanuel]" and the other for "you," he told Karl. "I also send grapes for mother and for the two of you," he added—as if to make a point.[50]

Ludwig was a very successful student at the French gymnasium; he wanted to study medicine. Hegel refused to pay for his education. The money was needed for Karl's and Immanuel's higher education, perhaps he and his wife thought. In 1822, against Ludwig's wishes, Hegel sent him to Stuttgart. He was fifteen years old. "It is preferable," Hegel instructed a friend in Stuttgart, "to make him a forester or agriculturalist. However, given the circumstances … [he must be dedicated] to the merchant class."[51] This was not to the liking of Ludwig. Without the financial support to do anything else, he decided to join the Dutch army in 1825.

On July 11, before his departure to the East Indies, Ludwig sent a letter to Dr. S. H. Ebert, his sister's foster father. It contained his own testimony of dashed hopes: "When I left Jena for Heidelberg, I hoped to receive the fruits of an education and to be reared in love. I was mightily disappointed." His father and stepmother, he told the good doctor, "always put me last," favoring the other two sons. "I always lived in fear, never in a relationship of love to them," he wrote, adding that he had contemplated to run away many times while living in Berlin with them. He also recalled being "drawn to the study of languages" and ranking "first" in his "Latin and Greek" class. "How gladly I would have studied medicine! However, it was made clear to me that there could be no thought of that: I was to become a merchant." Ludwig then explained how he found his apprenticeship in Stuttgart unbearable and how he had managed to secure his release with some difficulty. After learning this, "Herr Hegel *formally severed relations with me, and did so through my superior*—he did not even bother to write *directly to me.*" These were among the reasons why Ludwig decided to call Herr Hegel "my father" no longer. But Ludwig was more concerned about the wellbeing of his sister, Theresa (Auguste Theresia Burkhardt), then his own. "Now, my dear Doctor," he wrote before his departure, "my heart bears a heavy burden—what else could it be but cares concerning my one

---

[48] *Briefe II*, #293.
[49] Ibid., #317.
[50] *Briefe IV*, #358b.
[51] *Briefe II*, #419.

and only, my beloved sister." He expressed immense gratitude for the "parental" care the doctor had thus far given her. "Greet my dear sister and comfort her," he said, adding that he would have his guitar sent to the Ebert household from Stuttgart.[52]

Ludwig's August 27 farewell letter to his sister was shorter. He was still in Ghent but would soon be shipped off to the East Indies in a ship filled with other recruits. "Fare ye well, forget me not, and keep me in your love—this all I can cry out to you, weeping—never worry about me! … Haste prevents me from writing more. Farewell! Your brother who loves you unto death." His letter also included a P.S. in which he explained that sixty Guilders were set aside for her, should he never return. He also asked her to arrange for the delivery of his guitar to her address, likely hoping that he would be able to play it again one day.[53] He enlisted in the Dutch army for six years, though he clearly suspected that this might mean until the end of his life for the obvious reasons. Six years later, on August 28, 1831, one day after Hegel celebrated his last birthday, Ludwig died of a fever in a military hospital in Jakarta. He was buried unceremoniously, we must assume.

4.3 Hegel's Funeral

Hegel died on November 14, unaware of Ludwig's death. His funeral was much more glorious. Ironically, his eulogists likened Ludwig's mean-spirited father to Jesus, as we are about to see. One of them, Marheineke, specifically referred to the sorrowed widow and the "two sons" of the deceased. No one thought about the third son, so it seems.

However, a proper funeral could not be arranged for the deceased philosopher without state intervention, as the Prussian law demanded that all cholera victims, which Hegel was believed to be, be buried very quickly under the cover of the night, and in a cemetery especially designated for such victims. Schulze and other friends managed to get permission to bury him ceremoniously on November 16 at the Dorothea Cemetery, near Fichte and not so far away from Solger, in accordance with Hegel's own wishes.[54] This arrangement was also not without some irony as Hegel had spent much of his academic life disparaging Fichte.

A sizeable funeral procession took place on November 16. Marheineke and Förster were designated as the funeral orators. Tellingly, Gans, who had been in a more intimate relationship with Hegel than they,[55] at least until

---

[52] Ludwig Fischer's letter to Dr. Ebert is translated and reprinted in David Farrell Krell, *Son of Spirit: A Novel* (Albany, NY: SUNY Press, 1997), 140-42.
[53] Ibid., 144.
[54] *Berichten*, #716.
[55] See *Letters*, 506 (*Briefe III*, #520).

XIV. Hegel's Final Struggles

Hegel's last days, was not one of them. As if to suggest a natural succession of philosophical sovereignty, Marheineke, who was now the rector of the university, was to deliver the first speech at the Great Hall on campus. He belonged to the theological branch of the Hegel party, and so chose to contextualize the master's life and death from this vantage point. Hegel, he said, was immersed in "the work of the eternal Spirit," which operates "behind all the contradictory phenomena of life in nature and history." His bodily death has only freed his spirit "from all sensuous appearance," securing his "imperishable" presence in the "hearts and minds of all," especially his followers. A comparison to Christ was now inevitable:

> Like our Savior, whose name he always glorified in his thought and activity, in whose divine teaching he recognized the deepest essence of the human spirit, and who, as the son of God, gave himself over to suffering and death in order to return to his community eternally as spirit, he too has now returned to his true home and attained glory through his death and resurrection.

Perhaps even more surprising than casting him in the image of Christ was Marheineke's exaltation of Hegel's "gentleness and patience …, his humbleness and modesty," to be emulated by his followers.[56]

Förster, the "court demagogue," was to deliver his eulogy at Hegel's grave. His speech on Hegel's birthday in 1826 must have counted among his qualifications for being chosen to speak at Hegel's funeral. During that birthday speech, "Förster praised Hegel for helping him recognize that the communal 'home' he had sought so long was already there in the present, real world of the Prussian state."[57] What would he say now?

Is this grave, "this handful of dust," supposed to bury "the one who revealed to us the secrets of the Spirit, the wonders of God, and the world?" he first asked. "No, my friends," he answered expectedly, "let the dead bury the dead; the living belongs to us, who, having discarded the earthly bonds, celebrate his transfiguration …" "Yes," concluded the self-proclaimed "disciple" after listing Hegel's great achievements, "he was a helper, savior, and deliverer from every need and affliction, for he redeemed us from the bonds of delusion and selfishness." As if to confirm the theory that Hegel was a "demagogue proselytizer,"[58] Förster also praised the "savior's" ability to disabuse the perplexed of their ill-conceived political ideas, to help them regain their trust in the fatherland's virtues, to abandon foreign ideas and

---

[56] *Berichten*, #723.
[57] Toews, *Hegelianism: The Path Toward Dialectical Humanism*. Also see *Berichten*, #463.
[58] According to Rosenkranz, Hegel was thought to be a "*Demagogenbekehrer.*" Karl Rosenkranz, *Georg Wilhelm Friedrich Hegels Leben* (Berlin: Duncker und Humblot, 1844), 338.

XIV. Hegel's Final Struggles

influences. Hegel's "German science," he continued, is already a beacon for his disciples and would continue to spread "without [any real] resistance." To say the least, his name deserves to be included among those who "made Prussia famous," such as Friedrich the Great, Leibniz, Kant, and Fichte. "Although he was born in southern Germany," Hegel found "his true home here" in Prussia, much like Fichte. In the name of all his followers, Förster then vowed to "defend [Hegel's] glory and honor" against the "Pharisees and scribes," who "arrogantly and ignorantly misunderstood and defamed him." "Foolishness, insanity, cowardice, apostasy, hypocrisy, fanaticism, narrow-mindedness, and obscurantism—we are not afraid of you, for his spirit will be our guide," he said.[59]

These two funeral orations suggest that Schopenhauer was perhaps right: "The extensive field of spiritual influence with which Hegel was furnished by those in power has enabled him to achieve the intellectual corruption of a whole generation."[60] However, "those in power," especially Altenstein and Schulze, thought that Hegel prevented the corruption of the Prussian youth by directing them away from "demagogic" inclinations. But they did not deny that they had enabled him to become influential and serve the Prussian state. Thus, in his November 15 letter to Schulze, Altenstein appeared to be shocked by the unexpected passing of the philosopher and contemplated what a great loss his sudden passing must be to his family, friends, and "the Prussian State."[61] Another private eulogy was equally telling, but Hegel was not its only object. In his reply to the minister the next day, Schulze thanked God for giving "the Prussian state ... a minister to guide its most sacred interests," which he has thus far carried out successfully, not least because he brought Hegel to Berlin in 1818.[62]

---

[59] *Berichten*, #724.
[60] Schopenhauer quoted in Karl R. Popper, *The Open Society and Its Enemies, vol. 2: The High Tide of Prophecy: Hegel, Marx*, and the *Aftermath*, (Princeton, NJ: Princeton University Press, 1971—first published in 1945), 32-33.
[61] *Berichten*, #717.
[62] Ibid., #726.

EPILOGUE: "THE CONSENSUS VIEW"

As noted earlier, Gabler was Hegel's student at Jena. He then became a gymnasium rector, much like Hegel. He was virtually unknown in the academic circles of Germany until he published his book on Hegel's *Phenomenology* in 1827. No one took it seriously except Hegel, who decided that Gabler could be a good acolyte. Subsequently, he tried to bring him to Berlin to teach philosophy. This plan did not materialize, but Hegel thought at the time that Altenstein, clearly at Hegel's urging, praised Gabler's book very highly.[1] It turns out, to the chagrin of the master's other disciples, and to the surprise of everyone else, Altenstein and Schulze hired Gabler to succeed him in 1835. It was rumored throughout Germany that Hegel once said only one person understood him, but he too misunderstood him.[2] Lo and behold, it was also speculated that Altenstein and Schulze took this "myth" seriously, thinking that Hegel had Gabler in mind.[3]

At any rate, by 1835, the Hegel party was already in great disarray; his main disciples not only started to attack each other but also imitated Hegel's dogmatism and intolerance for disagreement.[4] Although there is no agreement on when this exactly happened (after all, it was a gradual process), Hegel's philosophy fell out of favor very quickly during the first decade after his death. To quote a succinct but apt explanation, his "system was discredited from a scientific point of view by formal logicians, from a political viewpoint by the July Revolution, and from a religious viewpoint by the advent of Left Hegelians,"[5] many of whom were very critical of Hegel's philosophy. Also, his "nature-philosophy ... was generally regarded as a horrible example of the aberrations of philosophical speculation" by the scientific community.[6]

However, in too many ways to be enumerated here, Hegel's philosophy was subsequently both admired and despised by some influential thinkers, though it never became more than a fringe philosophy. Moreover, it remained a mysterious puzzle, intriguing many generations of scholars. Tellingly, there still exist major disagreements on what his "system" is all about and, to use Benedetto Croce's popular title, on *What Is Living and What Is Dead of the Philosophy of Hegel*.

---

[1] *Letters*, 535 (*Briefe III*, #576).
[2] The earliest printing of this legend I was able to find is Heinrich Heine, *Der Salon*, vol. 2 (Hamburg: Hoffmann und Campe, 1834), 221.
[3] *Berichten*, #758.
[4] Ibid.
[5] Andries Sarlemijn, *Hegel's Dialectic*, trans. Peter Kirschemann (Dordrecht: R. Reidel, 1975), 6.
[6] Herbert Schnädelbach, *Philosophy in Germany 1831-1933*, trans. Eric Matthews (Cambridge: Cambridge University Press, 1984), 76.

Epilogue: "The Consensus View"

Obviously, the legacy of Hegel's political views is of much relevance to the present study. As we have seen, during the last thirteen years of his life, Hegel was widely known as an apologist for the repressive, authoritarian Prussian regime. He himself had made no secret of this fact. The distortion of this original, factually accurate image of Hegel began soon after his death, as two of his admirers, Gans (1833) and, especially, Rosenkranz (1844) tried to erase from collective memory the fact that Hegel was a servile apologist.[7] A corrective response to this distortion was issued by Haym in 1857.[8]

To skip a few decades and many interpretations of Hegel's political views, Croce himself suggested, albeit ambiguously, that Hegel might have indeed been "the special philosopher of the Prussian Restoration, the philosopher of the secret council of government and of the bureaucratic ruling of the state." However, he insisted, this was the Hegel of "the biographer and the political historian," who should not be confused with "Hegel the philosopher." *This* Hegel's "conception of life was so philosophical," he opined, "that conservatism, revolution, and restoration, each in turn, finds its justification in it."[9] Although shared by some others as well, this uninteresting explanation has failed to gain much traction.

During the 1930s, if not before, the original view, ambivalently accepted and rejected by Croce, came to be known as Hegel's "Prussianism." Edgar F. Carritt was one of its renown defenders.[10] However, Carritt and others had also distorted Hegel's political views by anachronistically linking them to totalitarianism. In 1939, another well-known author, Sidney Hook, reiterated an aspect of the original view, namely, Hegel's political accommodationism, claiming that Hegel's mature political philosophy was essentially a servile apology for the reactionary Prussian state.[11] For the record, Hook wisely refrained from associating Hegel's views with totalitarianism.

In 1940, Thomas M. Knox challenged the views of both Carritt and Hook (and the similar views held by others) in a wholesale manner. While admitting that some of Hegel's views were illiberal, Knox argued rather

---

[7] Eduard Gans, "Preface to Hegel's *Philosophy of Law*," translated and reprinted in Michael H. Hoffheimer, *Eduard Gans and the Hegelian Philosophy of Law*, 87-92 (Dordrecht: Kluwer Academic Publishers, 1995—Gans' Preface was published in 1833); Rosenkranz, *Georg Wilhelm Friedrich Hegel's Leben*.

[8] Rudolf Haym, *Hegel und seine Zeit: Vorlesungen über Entstehung und Entwicklung, Wesen und Wert der Hegelschen Philosophie* (Berlin: R. Gaertner, 1857).

[9] Benedetto Croce, *What Is Living and What Is Dead of the Philosophy of Hegel*, trans. Douglas Ainslie (London: Macmillan, 1915) 65 ff.

[10] Edgar F. Carritt, *Morals and Politics: Theories of Their Relation from Hobbes and Spinoza to Marx and Bosanquet* (Oxford: Clarendon Press, 1935).

[11] Sidney Hook, *From Hegel to Marx* (New York: Columbia University Press, 1994—originally published in 1939), 19-20.

inconclusively that they were more liberal than totalitarian. As crucially for our purposes, he also rejected the view that Hegel was a servile apologist for the Prussian regime. In his own wording, Hegel did not construct "his philosophy of the State with an eye to pleasing the reactionary and conservative rulers of Prussia in his day."[12] Thusly was born the most basic premises of what would later be called the "consensus view." Knox is still regarded as one of the founding fathers of this view.

Herbert Marcuse also weighed in on this issue a year later: "The ... [*Philosophy of Right*] is reactionary in so far as the social order it reflects is so, and progressive in so far as it is progressive."[13] To oversimplify, Marcuse thus left the issue at hand largely unsettled, though he did reject the interpretations that identified Hegel's political theory with totalitarianism or fascism. However, the contrary view was given a new lease on life by Karl Popper a few years later. Indeed, Popper even held Hegel responsible for the rise of Nazism.[14] Popper's unjustifiable claim, along with his poor "method" of proof, made his much-read chapter on Hegel an easy target for Hegel's friends. Thus, Walter A. Kaufmann (1951) was able to easily debunk Popper's arguments.[15]

However, the task of proving Hegel's political liberalism remained unfulfilled. In 1957, Joachim Ritter took an important step to remedy this problem as he popularized the longstanding legend that Hegel's entire political philosophy was deeply informed by the liberal ideals of the French Revolution of 1789, allegedly evidenced by his "unmistaken adherence and approval" of the Revolution "from the time of his youth up till his last years."[16] Zbigniew A. Pelczynski (1964) also argued that Hegel was

---

[12] Thomas. M. Knox, "Hegel and Prussianism," in *Philosophy* 15, no. 57 (1940). For Carritt's defiant response, see Edgar F. Carritt, "Hegel and Prussianism," in *Philosophy* 15, no. 58 (1940): 190-06. For their subsequent rejoinders, see E. F. Carritt and T. M. Knox, "Hegel and Prussianism," in *Philosophy* 15, no. 59 (1940): 313-17, 51.

[13] Herbert Marcuse, *Reason and Revolution: Hegel and the Rise of Social Theory* (Boston: Beacon Press, 1960—first published in 1941), 178.

[14] Karl R. Popper, *The Open Society and Its Enemies, vol. 2: The High Tide of Prophecy: Hegel, Marx, and the Aftermath*, (Princeton, NJ: Princeton University Press, 1971—first published in 1945). According to Russell, "Hegel's doctrine of the state ... justifies every internal tyranny and every external aggression that can be possibly imagined." Bertrand Russell, *A History of Western Philosophy* (New York: Simon & Schuster, 1945), 742.

[15] Walter A. Kaufmann, "The Hegel Myth and Its Method," in ed. Walter A. Kaufmann, *Hegel's Political Philosophy*, 137-71 (New York: Atherton Press, 1970). The first version of this article appeared in *The Philosophical Review*, October 1951. Subsequently, Kaufmann revised and published it in several different books.

[16] Joachim Ritter, "Hegel and the French Revolution," in Joachim Ritter, *Hegel and the French Revolution: Essays on the* Philosophy of Right, trans. Richard Dien Winfield, 35-89 (Cambridge: MIT Press, 1984), 45-7, also 59. The essays contained in this translation, which were written in different periods, were originally compiled in Ritter's *Metaphysik und Politik: Studien zu Aristoteles und Hegel* (Frankfurt: Suhrkamp, 1969).

essentially a liberal thinker throughout his life.[17] This claim was famously and unsurprisingly rejected by Hook, who aptly characterized Pelczynski's essay as an attempt to "rehabilitate" Hegel.[18] However, the academic tide was now beginning to favor Hook's opponents.

In 1968, Jacques D'Hondt contributed significantly to the distortion of Hegel's image. His main contribution in this regard consisted of the claim that Hegel was a "clandestine" activist, supporting the opponents of the reactionary Prussian regime (or the Restoration in general).[19] This false image of Hegel would soon be added to the itinerary of Hegel's rehabilitators.

Shlomo Avineri's *Hegel's Theory of the Modern State* (1972) was another influential contribution to the process of Hegel's rehabilitative distortion.[20] I think it is fair to say that Avineri's book has helped galvanize the image of Hegel as a liberal critic of the Prussian regime more than any of its predecessors. It is also fair to say that most of the contributions to Hegel's rehabilitation in the 1970s and 1980s involved *internal* readjustments and disputes, remaining within the new paradigm, forged into existence during the previous three or so decades.[21]

However, another paradigm emerged in 1979, when Charles Taylor basically pronounced Hegel's philosophy dead, but nevertheless brought it back to life as a useful reconstruction—useful *for us today*.[22] Although his reconstruction of Hegel as an expressivist-communitarian was generally rejected by Hegel's liberalizers, and not everyone was happy with his pronunciation, his attempt to reconstruct a useful Hegel succeeded in creating a new intellectual fashion. Two Hegel scholars, among others, namely, Steven B. Smith and Allen W. Wood, closed the next decade (the 1980s) with two influential contributions to this new fashion. The former

---

[17] Z. A. Pelczynski, "An Introductory Essay," in *Hegel's Political Writings*, trans. T. M. Knox, 3-137 (Oxford: Oxford University Press, 1964).
[18] Sidney Hook, "Hegel Rehabilitated?" in *Hegel's Political Philosophy*, ed. Walter Kaufmann, 55-70 (New York: Atherton Press, 1970—first published in 1966). Also see Sidney Hook, "Hegel and His Apologists," in *Hegel's Political Philosophy*, ed. Walter Kaufmann, 87-105 (New York: Atherton Press, 1970—first published in 1966).
[19] Jacques D'Hondt, *Hegel In His Time*, trans. John Burbidge (Peterborough, Ontario: Broadview Press, 1988).
[20] Shlomo Avineri, *Hegel's Theory of the Modern State* (Cambridge: Cambridge University Press, 1972).
[21] Some of the prominent contributions to this paradigm are the following: Raymond Plant, *Hegel* (New York: Routledge, 1973); Adriaan T. Peperzak, *Philosophy and Politics: A Commentary on the Preface to Hegel's Philosophy of Right* (Dordrecht: Martinus Nijhoff Publishers, 1987); Richard Bellamy, "Hegel and Liberalism," in *History of European Ideas* 8, no. 6 (1987): 693-708.
[22] Charles Taylor, *Hegel and Modern Society* (Cambridge: Cambridge University Press, 1979).

attempted to make Hegel a useful participant in the contemporary academic debates, as a liberal(ish) critique of the too-liberal (individualist) academics in the post-Rawlsian intellectual landscape.[23]

For his part, Wood, like Taylor, declared Hegel's metaphysics-logic "dead," by which he meant *absurd*, and so useless for us today. He even admitted that "to read Hegel" without his logic-metaphysics is "to read him in some measure against his own self-understanding."[24] By discarding the crux of Hegel's political *philosophy*, Wood imagined a transfigured "Hegel who still lives and speaks to us." This summoned specter of Hegel "is not a speculative logician and idealist metaphysician but a philosophical historian, a political and social theorist, a philosopher of our ethical concerns and cultural identity crises [i.e., alienation]."[25] But, claimed Wood in another context, "If we look closely at Hegel's discussion of modern ethical life, it is striking how little he concedes to ethical diversity, how little room he leaves for the impact of varying cultural traditions on the social and political structure of modern states."[26]

Apart from his confusing, often self-defeating, attempt to make Hegel useful for "our ethical concerns and cultural identity crises," Wood also failed to illustrate how Hegel was a (1) liberal (2) critic of the Prussian regime. In fact, he mostly assumed that both claims had been successfully defended previously by others. Based on this assumption, he made the following public announcement in 1991: "there is now a virtual consensus among knowledgeable scholars that the earlier [image] ... of Hegel as [a] philosopher of the reactionary Prussian restoration ... [is] simply wrong." The correct "consensus view" of the "knowledgeable scholars" is that Hegel was no servile apologist and that he kept "the liberal's state pretty much intact" in his mature political philosophy.[27]

Many scholars have subsequently pledged their allegiance to "the consensus view," while disagreeing with Wood and with each other on specific issues. Michael O. Hardimon (1994): "it is now generally recognized that Hegel was not the friend of the Prussian restoration he was once taken to be," and that he belonged "squarely in the camp of the moderate liberal progressives of his age."[28] Paul Franco (1999): "more

---

[23] Steven B. Smith, *Hegel's Critique of Liberalism: Rights in Context* (Chicago: University of Chicago Press, 1989).
[24] Allen W. Wood, *Hegel's Ethical Thought* (Cambridge: Cambridge University Press, 1990), 8.
[25] Ibid., 4-6.
[26] Ibid., 207.
[27] Allen W. Wood, "Editor's Introduction," in G. W. F. Hegel, *Elements of the Philosophy Right*, ed. Wood (Cambridge: Cambridge University Press, 1991), ix, xxvii.
[28] Michael O. Hardimon, *Hegel's Social Philosophy: The Project of Reconciliation* (Cambridge, UK: Cambridge University Press, 1994), 26-27.

Epilogue: "The Consensus View"

recent scholarship ... has uncovered historical and biographical evidence that Hegel's political views were ... moderately liberal or progressive," and that this has "long been the consensus view ... shared, as Allen Wood notes, by 'virtually every responsible scholar in the past generation.'" Moreover, "Hegel's political outlook has little in common with the reactionary Prussian state of 1819."[29] According to Terry Pinkard (2000), the following claims are flatly "false": "Hegel ... glorified the Prussian state, claiming that it was God's work ..., and was the culmination of all human history."[30] Also, Hegel supported the ideals of the French Revolution throughout his life.[31] Skipping many other attempts to rehabilitate Hegel, we note that Thom Brooks recently summed up the progress under our scrutiny as follows: the claim that Hegel's "views are consistent with liberalism" is now shared by the "overwhelming majority of commentators." Above all, "the debate about whether Hegel's political philosophy is either conservative or liberal is now over."[32]

I believe to have amply demonstrated that "the consensus view" of the "knowledgeable" and "responsible" scholars is flatly wrong. All proponents of this view also assume that Hegel was a great philosopher, who remains relevant and useful to us in some sense. I am not entitled to decide what each scholar might find relevant, useful, or else regard as great philosophical insight. In my view, Hegel was a largely incoherent charlatan. He was also an ambitious sycophant, who was only useful to himself, his acolytes, and his masters. This is the main reason why he was able to become the most famous philosopher in Germany.

---

[29] Paul Franco, *Hegel's Philosophy of Freedom* (New Haven: Yale University Press, 1999), 123, 364 n. 10.
[30] Terry Pinkard, *Hegel: A Biography* (Cambridge: Cambridge University Press, 2000), ix.
[31] Ibid., throughout.
[32] Thom Brooks, *Hegel's Political Philosophy: A Systematic Reading of the* Philosophy of Right, second edition (Edinburg: Edinburg University Press, 2013), 1. Brooks seems to agree with a tamed version of the consensus view. Other recent publications suggest a new focus: the debate over Hegel's political sympathies should be replaced with a more serious analysis of the much-neglected, even broadly rejected, *philosophical* (metaphysical or logical) aspects of his political philosophy. Three very recent publications suggest the (re)emergence of this trend: Eric Lee Goodfield, *Hegel and the Metaphysical Frontiers of Political Theory* (New York and London: Routledge, 2014); Thom Brooks and Sebastian Stein (eds.), *Hegel's Political Philosophy: On the Normative Significance of Method and System* (Oxford: Oxford University Press, 2017); Michael J. Thompson (ed.), *Hegel's Metaphysics and the Philosophy of Politics* (New York: Routledge, 2018). However, some scholars are still trying to clarify the sense in which Hegel was a liberal. See, for instance, Ludwig Siep, "Hegel's Liberal, Social, and 'Ethical' State," in ed. Dean Moyar, *The Oxford Handbook of Hegel*, 515-34 (Oxford: Oxford University Press, 2017).

BIBLIOGRAPHY

Works by Hegel

———. "Address on the Tercentenary of the Submission of the Augsburg Confession." In *Hegel: Political Writings*, edited by Laurence Dickey and H. B. Nisbet, 186-96. Cambridge, UK: Cambridge University Press, 1999.

———. "Hegel's Advertisement for the Publication of *The Phenomenology of Spirit*." In *Miscellaneous Writings of G. W. F. Hegel*, edited by Jon Stewart, 281-2. Evanston, IL: Northwestern University Press, 2002.

———. "Inaugural Address, Delivered at the University of Berlin (22 October 1818)." In *Hegel: Political Writings*, edited by Laurence Dickey and H. B. Nisbet, 181-85. Cambridge: Cambridge University Press, 1999.

———. "Inaugural Address: Delivered at Heidelberg on the 28th October 1816." In *Lectures on the History of Philosophy*, Vol. 1 translated by E. S. Haldane, xli-xliii. Lincoln: University of Nebraska Press, 1995.

———. "Maximen des Journals der deutschen Literatur." In *Gesammelte Werke: Jenaer kritische Schriften*, edited by Hartmut Buchner and Otto Pöggeler, 509-14. Hamburg: Felix Meiner, 1968.

———. "On the English Reform Bill." In *Political Writings*, edited by Laurence Dickey and H. B. Nisbet, 234-70. Cambridge: Cambridge University Press, 1999.

———. "Philosophical Dissertation on the Orbits of the Planets (1801), Preceded by the 12 Theses Defended on August 27, 1801." *Graduate Faculty Philosophy Journal* 12, nos. 1–2 (1987): 269–309.

———. "The Earliest System-Program of German Idealism." In *Miscellaneous Writings of Hegel*, ed. Jon Stewart, 110-12 (Evanston, IL: Northwestern University Press, 2002). (Note: Hegel's authorship of this work is highly dubitable.)

———. "The Tübingen Essay." *Miscellaneous Writings of Hegel*, edited by in Jon Stewart, 44-71. Evanston, IL: Northwestern University Press, 2002.

———. "Über die Englische Reformbill," *Allgemeine Preußische Staatszeitung*, nos. 115-118 (1831).

———. *Berliner Schriften, 1818-1831.* Edited by Johannes Hoffmeister. Hamburg: Felix Meiner, 1956.

———. *Die Verfassung Deutschlands.* In *Hegels Schriften zur Politik und Rechtsphilosophie*, edited by Georg Lasson, 3-136. Leipzig: Felix Meiner, 1913.

———. *Dokumente zu Hegels Entwicklung.* Edited by Johannes Hoffmeister. Stuttgart: Friedrich Frommanns Verlag, 1936.

Bibliography

———. *Early Theological Writings*. Translated by T. M. Knox. Philadelphia: University of Pennsylvania Press, 1971.

———. *Elements of the Philosophy of Right*. Edited by Allen W. Wood. Translated by H. B. Nisbet. Cambridge: Cambridge University Press, 1991.

———. *Faith and Knowledge*. Translated by H. S. Harris and Walter Cerf. Albany, NY: SUNY Press, 1977.

———. *Grundlinien der Philosophie des Rechts oder Naturrecht und Staatswissenschaft im Grundrisse*. Edited by Eduard Gans. Berlin: Duncker und Humblot, 1833.

———. *Hegel and the Human Spirit: A Translation of the Jena Lecture on the Philosophy of Spirit of 1805-6*. Translated by Leo Rauch. Detroit: Wayne State University Press, 1983.

———. *Kritik der verfassung Deutschlands*. Edited by Georg Mollat. Munich: Kassel, 1893.

———. *Lectures on Natural Rights and Political Science: The First Philosophy of Right*. Translated by J. Michael Stewart and Peter C. Hodgson. Oxford University Press, 2012.

———. *Lectures on the History of Philosophy*, Vol. 3. Translated by E. S. Haldane (Lincoln: University of Nebraska Press, 1995).

———. *On the Episode of the Mahabharata Known by the Name Bhagavad Gita by Wilhelm Von Humboldt*. Translated by Herbert Herring, 1-151. New Delhi: Indian Council of Philosophical Research, 1995.

———. *On the Scientific Ways of Treating Natural Law, on its Place in Practical Philosophy, and its Relation to the Positive Science of Right*, in *Political Writings*, edited by Laurence Dickey and H. B. Nisbet, 102-85. Cambridge: Cambridge University Press, 1999.

———. *Phenomenology of Spirit*. Translated by A. V. Miller. Oxford: Oxford University Press, 1977.

———. *Philosophy of Mind: Part Three of the Encyclopaedia of Philosophical Sciences*. Translated by William Wallace and A. V. Miller. Oxford: Oxford University Press, 1971.

———. *Philosophy of Nature, Part Two the Encyclopaedia of the Philosophical Sciences* Translated by A. V. Miller. Oxford: Oxford University Press, 1970.

———. *Philosophy of Right*. Translated by S. W. Dyde. London: George Bell and Sons, 1896.

———. *Philosophy of Right*. Translated by T. M. Knox. Oxford: Oxford University Press, 1952.

———. *Proceedings of the Estates Assembly of the Kingdom of Württemberg, 1815–1816*. In *Heidelberg Writings: Journal Publications*, translated by

Brady Bowman and Allen Speight, 32-136. Cambridge, UK: Cambridge University Press, 2009.

———. *Science of Logic* Translated by Miller. London: George Allen & Unwin, 1969.

———. *System of Ethical Life and First Philosophy of Spirit.* Translated by H. S. Harris and T. M. Knox, 97-177.Albany, NY: SUNY Press, 1977.

———. *The Difference Between Fichte's and Schelling's Philosophy.* Translated by H. S. Harris and Walter Cerf. Albany, NY: SUNY Press, 1977.

———. *The German Constitution.* In *Political Writings*, edited by Laurence Dickey and H. B. Nisbet, 6-101. Cambridge: Cambridge University Press, 1999.

———. *The German Constitution.* In *Political Writings.* Translated by T. M. Knox, 143-242. Oxford: Oxford University Press, 1964.

———. *The Jena System, 1804-5: Logic and Metaphysics.* Translated by John W. Burbidge and George di Giovanni. Kingston and Montreal: McGill-Queen's University Press, 1986.

———. *The Magistrates should be Elected by the People.* In *Political Writings*, edited by Laurence Dickey and H. B. Nisbet, 1-5. Cambridge, UK: Cambridge University Press, 1999.

———. *The Philosophy of History.* Translated by J. Sibree. New York, Dover, 1956.

———. *The Philosophy of Right.* Translated by Alan White. Newburyport: Focus Publishing, 2002.

———. *The Science of Logic.* Translated by George di Giovanni. Cambridge: Cambridge University Press, 2010.

———. *Vertrauliche Briefe tiber das vormalige staatsrechtliche Verhaltnis des Waadtlandes zur Stadt Bern: Aus dem Franzdsischen eines verstorbenen Schweizers.* Frankfurt: Jägersche Buchhandlung, 1798.

———. *Vorlesungen über die Philosophie der Geschichte.* Berlin: Duncker und Humblot, 1848.

Letters to and from Hegel

Butler, Clark and Christiane Seiler, ed., trans. *Hegel: The Letters* (Bloomington IN: Indiana University Press, 1984).

Hoffmeister, Johannes, ed. *Briefe von und an Hegel*, Vol. 1. Hamburg: Felix Meiner, 1952.

———. *Briefe von und an Hegel*, Vol. 2. Hamburg: Felix Meiner, 1953.

———. *Briefe von und an Hegel*, Vol. 3. Hamburg: Felix Meiner, 1954.

———. *Briefe von und an Hegel*, Vol. 4. Hamburg: Felix Meiner, 1960.

Bibliography

Hegel in the Reports of His Contemporaries

Nicolin, Günther, ed. *Hegel in Berichten seiner Zeitgenossen*. Hamburg: Felix Meiner, 1970.

Other Works

"Appendix to Chronicle." In *The Annual Register, Or a View of the History, Politics, and Literature, for the Year 1819*. London: Baldwin, Cradock, and Joy, 1820.

"*Gesetz über die Pressefreiheit vom 30. Januar 1817.*" In *Die Verfassungen des teutschen Staatenbundes seit dem Jahre* 1789, edited by Karl H. L. Pölitz, 373-77. Leipzig: Brockhaus 1847.

Adorno, Theodor W. *Hegel: Three Studies*. Translated by Shierry Weber Nicholsen. Cambridge: The MIT Press, 1993.

Althaus, Horst. *Hegel: An Intellectual Biography*. Translated by Michael Tarsh. Cambridge, UK: Polity Press, 2000.

Altmann, Wilhelm, ed. *Ausgewählte Urkunden zur Brandenburg-Preussischen Verfassungs und Verwaltungsgeschichte*. Berlin: R. Geartners, 1897.

Ameriks, Karl. *Kant and the Fate of Autonomy: Problems in the Appropriation of Critical Philosophy*. Cambridge, UK: Cambridge University Press, 2000.

Anderson, Frank Maloy. *The Constitutions and Other Select Documents Illustrative of the History of France, 1789-1901*. Minneapolis: The H. W. Wilson Company, 1904.

Aris, Reinhold. *History of Political Thought in Germany, 1789-1815*. London: George Allen & Unwin 1936.

Ashton, Bodie. *The Kingdom of Württemberg and the Making of Germany, 1815–1871*. London: Bloomsbury, 2017.

Avineri, Shlomo *Hegel' Theory of the Modern State*. Cambridge: Cambridge University Press, 1972.

Baack, Lawrence J. *Christian Bernstorff and Prussia: Diplomacy and Reform Conservatism, 1818-1832*. New Brunswick, NJ: Rutgers University Press, 1980.

Bachmann, Carl Friedrich. *Über die Philosophie meiner Zeit, zur Vermittlung*. Jena: Cröker, 1816.

———. *Von der Verwandtschaft der Physik und der Psychologie: Eine Preisschrift*. Utrecht, *Johannes* Altheer, 1821.

———. *System der Logik: Ein Handbuch zum Selbststudium*. Leipzig: F. A. Brockhaus, 1828.

———. *Über Hegel's System und die Nothwendigkeit einer nochmaligen Umgestaltung der Philosophie*. Leipzig: Vogel, 1833.

———. *Anti-Hegel*. Jena: Cröker, 1835.

Bibliography

Bartsch, Karl. *Ruperto-Carola: Illustrierte Fest-Chronik der V. Säcularfeier der Universität Heidelberg*. Heidelberg: O. Petters, 1886.

Beiser, Frederick C. *Enlightenment, Revolution, and Romanticism: The Genesis of Modern German Political Thought, 1790-1800*. Cambridge: Harvard University Press, 1992.

———. *Hegel*. New York: Routledge, 2005.

Bellamy, Richard. "Hegel and Liberalism." *History of European Ideas* 8, no. 6 (1987): 693-708.

Benecke, Heinrich. *Wilhelm Vatke in seinem Leben und seinen Schriften*. Bonn, Emil Strauß, 1883.

Bernasconi, Robert. "Hegel at the Court of the Ashanti." In *Hegel after Derrida*, edited by Stuart Barnett, 41-63 (London: Routledge, 1998).

Bigler, Robert M. *The Politics of German Protestantism: The Rise of the Protestant Church Elite in Prussia, 1815-1848*. Berkeley: University of California Press, 1972.

Black, Jeremy. *The Battle of Waterloo* (New York: Random House, 2010).

Bowie, Andrew. *Schelling and Modern European Philosophy: An Introduction*. London: Routledge, 1993.

Breuilly, John. *Austria, Prussia, and the Making of Germany, 1806-1871*. London: Routledge, 2011).

Bristow, William F. *Hegel and the Transformation of Philosophical Critique*. Oxford University Press, 2007.

Brooks, Thom and Sebastian Stein, eds. *Hegel's Political Philosophy: On the Normative Significance of Method and System*. Oxford: Oxford University Press, 2017.

Brooks, Thom. *Hegel's Political Philosophy: A Systematic Reading of the Philosophy of Right*. Edinburg: Edinburg University Press, 2013.

Brose, Eric Dorn. *German History 1789–1871: From the Holy Roman Empire to the Bismarckian Reich*. Providence: Berghahn, 1997.

Brown, Howard G. *Ending the French Revolution: Violence, Justice, and Repression from the Terror to Napoleon*. Charlottesville: The University of Virginia Press, 2006.

Burke, Edmund. *Reflections on the Revolution in France and on the Proceedings in Certain Societies in London, Relative to that Event*. London: J. Dodsley, 1790.

Carové, Friedrich W. *Ueber die Ermordung Kotzebue's*. Eisenach: Bärecke, 1819.

Carritt, Edgar F. "Hegel and Prussianism." *Philosophy* 15, no. 58 (1940): 190-06.

———. "Hegel and Prussianism: A Rejoinder." *Philosophy* 15, no. 59 (1940): 313-17.

———. *Morals and Politics: Theories of Their Relation from Hobbes and Spinoza to Marx and Bosanquet* (Oxford: Clarendon Press, 1935).
Cart, Jean-Jacques. *Lettres de Jean-Jacques Cart à Bernard Dumuralt, Trésorier du Pays de Vaud, sur le droit public de ce Pays, et sur les événements actuels.* Paris: Imprimerie du Cercle Social, 1793.
Cassirer, Ernst. *The Myth of the State.* New Haven: Yale University Press, 1946.
Chaloupek, Günther. "Friedrich List on Local Autonomy in His Contributions to the Debate About the Constitution of Württemberg in 1816/1817." In *Two Centuries of Local Autonomy*, edited by Jürgen Backhaus, 3-12. New York: Springer, 2011.
Chapman, Tim. *The Congress of Vienna 1814-1815: Origins, Processes, and Results.* London: Routledge, 1998.
Classen, Peter and Eike Wolgast. *Kleine Geschichte der Universität Heidelberg.* Berlin: Springer, 1983.
Coffin, Victor. "Censorship and Literature under Napoleon I." *The American Historical Review* 22, no. 2 (1917): 288-308.
Collier, Andrew. *Marx: A Beginner's Guide.* Oxford: Oneworld, 2004.
Constitution Des Königreichs Westfalen (15. 11. 1807). http://www.dircost.unito.it/cs/pdf/18071115_germaniaRegnoVestfalia_ted.pdf.
Cousin, Victor. "Souvenirs D'Allemagne." *Revue des Deux Mondes* (1866): 594-619.
———. *Oeuvres de Victor Cousin: Cours d'histoire de la philosophie morale. Fragments philosophiques*, Vol. 2. Bruxelles: Société Belge de Librairie, 1840.
Croce, Benedetto. *What Is Living and What Is Dead of the Philosophy of Hegel.* Translated by Douglas Ainslie. London: Macmillan, 1915.
Crouter, Richard. "Hegel and Schleiermacher at Berlin: A Many-Sided Debate." *Journal of the American Academy of Religion* 48, no. 1 (1980): 19- 43.
———. *Friedrich Schleiermacher: Between Enlightenment and Romanticism.* Cambridge: Cambridge University Press, 2010.
Cunningham, Clifford J. *Bode's Law and the Discovery of Juno: Historical Studies in Asteroid.* Cham, Switzerland: Springer, 2017.
D'Hondt, Jacques. *Hegel In His Time.* Translated by John Burbidge. Peterborough, Ontario: Broadview Press, 1988.
De Boer, Karin. "Hegel's Non-Revolutionary Account of the French Revolution in the Phenomenology of Spirit." *Epoché: A Journal for the History of Philosophy* 22, no. 2, (2018): 453-66.
DeGrood, David H. *Dialectics and Revolution*, Vol. 2. Amsterdam: B. R. Grüner Publishing Co., 1979.

Bibliography

Depré, Olivier. "The Ontological Foundations of Hegel's Dissertation of 1801." In *Hegel and the Philosophy of Nature*, edited by Stephen Houlgate, 257-81. Albany: SUNY Press, 1998.

Dettke, Barbara. *Die asiatische Hydra: Die Cholera von 1830/31 in Berlin und den preußischen Provinzen Posen, Preußen und Schleisen*. Berlin: Walter De Gruyter, 1995.

Dilthey, Wilhelm. *Die Jugendgeschichte Hegels und andere Abhandlungen zur Geschichte des Deutschen Idealismus*. Leipzig: B. G. Teubner, 1921.

Döll, Helmut. "Hegels Tod." *Zeitschrift für ärztliche Fortbildung* 79 (1985): 217-19.

Dorrien, Gary. *Kantian Reason and Hegelian Spirit: The Idealistic Logic of Modern Theology*. Chichester, UK: Wiley-Blackwell, 2012.

Dumas, Alexandre. *Celebrated Crimes*, Vol. 3. Translated by I. G. Burnham. Philadelphia: George Barrie & Son, 1895.

Dwyer, Philip G. and Peter McPhee, eds. *The French Revolution and Napoleon: A Sourcebook*. London: Routledge, 2002.

Ecker, Alexander. *Lorenz Oken: A Biographical Sketch*. Translated by Alfred Tulk. London: Kegan Paul, 1883.

Emerson, Donald Eugene. *Metternich and the Political Police: Security and Subversion in the Hapsburg Monarchy, 1815-1830*. The Hague: Martinus Nijhoff, 1968.

Epstein, Klaus. *Genesis of German Conservatism*. Princeton: Princeton University Press, 1966.

Fackenheim, Emil L. "On the Actuality of the Rational and the Rationality of the Actual." In *The Hegel Myths and Legends*, edited by Jon Stewart, 42-49. Evanston: Northwestern University Press, 1996.

Falkenheim, Hugo. "*Eine unbekannte politische Druckschrift Hegels.*" *Preussische Jahrbucher* 138 (1909): 193-210.

Fichte, Johann G. *Foundations of Natural Right*. Translated by Michael Baur. Edited by Frederick Neuhouser. Cambridge, UK: Cambridge University Press, 2000.

Findlay, J. N. "Foreword." In G. W. F. Hegel, *The Philosophy of Mind*, translated by William Wallace and A. V. Miller, v-xix. Oxford: Oxford University Press, 1971.

Follen, Eliza Cabot. *Life of Charles Follen*. Cambridge: Thomas H. Webb, 1844.

Ford, Guy Stanton. *Stein and the Era of Reform in Prussia, 1807-1815*. Princeton: Princeton University Press, 1822.

Forster, Michael N. *Hegel's Idea of a Phenomenology of Spirit*. Chicago, IL: Chicago University Press, 1998.

Bibliography

Förster, Eckart. "'To Lend Wings to Physics Once Again': Hölderlin and the 'Oldest System-Programme of German Idealism." *European Journal of Philosophy* 3, no. 2 (1995): 174-98.
Franco, Paul *Hegel's Philosophy of Freedom*. New Haven: Yale University Press, 1999.
Freitag, Sabine and Peter Wende. *British Envoys to Germany, 1816–1866*, Vol. 1, *1816–1829*. Cambridge: Cambridge University Press, 2000.
Fries, Jakob. "Wissenschaft der Logik von D. G. W. F. Hegel." *Heidelbergische Jahrbücher der Literatur*, no. 25 (1815): 385-93.
——. *Reinhold, Fichte und Schelling*. Leipzig: A. L. Reinicke, 1803.
——. *Von deutschem Bund und deutscher Staatsverfassung*. Heidelberg: Mohr und Winter, 1816.
Fulbrook, Mary. *Concise History of Germany*. Cambridge: Cambridge University Press, 2004.
Furet, François. *Revolutionary France, 1770-1880*. Translated by Antonia Nevill. Oxford: Wiley-Blackwell, 1992.
Gans, Eduard. "Preface to Hegel's *Philosophy of Law*." In *Eduard Gans and the Hegelian Philosophy of Law*, by Michael H. Hoffheimer, 87-92. Dordrecht: Kluwer Academic Publishers, 1995.
Gehring, Paul. "Um Hegels Landständeschrift: Friedrich List im Spiel?" *Zeitschrift für philosophische Forschung* 23, no. 1 (1969): 110- 21.
Geiger, Ido. *The Founding Act of Modern Ethical Life: Hegel's Critique of Kant's Moral and Political Philosophy*. Stanford: Stanford University Press, 2007.
Gentz, Friedrich. *Betrachtungen über die französische Revolution nach dem Englischen des Herrn Burke*. Berlin: Friedrich Vieweg dem Aelteren, 1793.
Gibbon, Edward. *Decline and the Fall of the Roman Empire*, Vol. 1. Edited by J. B. Bury. London: Methuen, 1925.
Girard, Philippe R. *The Slaves Who Defeated Napoleon: Toussaint Louverture and the Haitian War of Independence, 1801-1804*. Tuscaloosa: The University of Alabama Press, 2001.
Goldschmit, Robert. *Geschichte der Badischen Verfassungsurkunde: 1818-1918*. Karlsruhe i.B.: Braun, 1918.
Gooch, George P. *Germany and the French Revolution*. London: Longmans, Green, and Co., 1920.
Goodfield, Eric Lee. *Hegel and the Metaphysical Frontiers of Political Theory*. New York and London: Routledge, 2014.
Görres, Joseph. *Germany and the Revolution*. Translated by John Black. London: Longman, Hurst, Rees, Orme, and Brown, 1820.
Green, Jonathan Allen. "Friedrich Gentz's Translation of Burke's Reflections." *The Historical Journal* 57, no. 3 (2014): 639-59.

Gregory, Frederick. *Scientific Materialism in Nineteenth Century Germany*. Dordrecht: D. Reidel, 1977.

Grier, Philip T., ed. *Identity and Difference: Studies in Hegel's Logic, Philosophy of Spirit, and Politics*. Albany: SUNY Press, 2007.

Guyer, Paul "Thought and Being: Hegel's Critique of Kant." In *The Cambridge Companion to Hegel*, edited by Frederick C. Beiser, 171-210. Cambridge, UK: Cambridge University Press, 1993.

Gwee, Li Sui. "Night in Novalis, Schelling, and Hegel." *Studies in Romanticism* 50, no. 1 (2011): 105-124.

Habermas, Jürgen. *Theory and Practice*. Translated by John Viertel. Boston: Beacon Press, 1973.

Habib, M. A. R. *Hegel and Empire: From Postcolonialism to Globalism*. New York: Palgrave, 2017.

Hallesche Allgemeine Literatur-Zeitung 40 (1822): 313-17.

Hallische Jahrbücher für deutsche Wissenschaft und Kunst, Vol.4. Leipzig: Otto Wigand, 1841.

Hardenberg, Karl August. "Ideas for a Representative Constitution in Prussia." In *History of Germany in the Nineteenth Century*, Vol. 3, translated by Eden Paul and Cedar Paul and edited by Heinrich von Treitschke, 643-47. New York: McBride and Nast, 1917.

Hardimon, Michael O. *Hegel's Social Philosophy: The Project of Reconciliation*. Cambridge, UK: Cambridge University Press, 1994.

Harnack, Adolf. *Geschichte der Königlich preussischen akademie der wissenschaften zu Berlin*, Vol. 1. Berlin: Reichsdruckerei, 1900.

Harris, Errol E. "Hegel's Theory of Sovereignty, International Relations, and War," in ed. Donald P. Verene, *Hegel's Social and Political Thought: The Philosophy of Objective Spirit*. Atlantic Highlands, N.J.: Humanities Press, 1980.

———. "Hegel's Theory of Sovereignty, International Relations, and War." In *The Hegel Myths and Legends*, edited by Jon Stewart, 154-66. Evanston, IL: Northwestern University Press, 1996.

Harris, H. S. *Hegel's Development: Night Thoughts, Jena 1801-1806*. Oxford: Oxford University Press, 1983.

———. *Hegel's Development: Towards the Sunlight, 1770-1801*. Oxford: Clarendon Press, 1972.

———. "Introduction." In G. W. F. Hegel, *The Difference Between Fichte's and Schelling's Philosophy*. Translated by H. S. Harris and Walter Cerf, 1-75. Albany, NY: SUNY Press, 1977.

Harsin, Jill. *Barricades: The War of the Streets in Revolutionary Paris, 1830-1848*. New York: Palgrave, 2002.

Bibliography

Haym, Rudolf. *Hegel und seine Zeit: Vorlesungen über Entstehung und Entwicklung, Wesen und Wert der Hegelschen Philosophie*. Berlin: R. Gaertner, 1857.

Heine, Heinrich. *Der Salon*, Vol. 2. Hamburg: Hoffmann und Campe, 1834.

Henke, Ernst Ludwig Theodor. *Jakob Friedrich Fries: Aus Seinem Handschriftlichen Nachlasse dargestellt*. Leipzig: Brockhaus, 1867.

Henrich, Dieter. *Between Kant and Hegel: Lectures on German Idealism*. Cambridge, MA: Harvard University Press, 2003.

Heuvel, Jon Vanden. *A German Life in the Age of Revolution: Joseph Görres, 1776-1848*. Washington DC: The Catholic University of America Press, 2001.

Hicks, Peter. "The Napoleonic 'Police' or 'Security State' in Context." *Napoleonica: La Revue* 4, no. 1 (2009): 2-10.

Hobsbawm, Eric. *The Age of Revolution, 1789-1848*. London: Abacus, 1977.

Hoffheimer, Michael H. *Eduard Gans and the Hegelian Philosophy of Law*. Dordrecht: Kluwer Academic Publishers, 1995.

Hoffheimer, Michael H. "Hegel, Race, Genocide." *The Southern Journal of Philosophy* 39 (2001): 35-61.

Honneth, Axel. *The Struggle for Recognition: The Moral Grammar of Social Conflicts*. Translated by Joel Anderson. Cambridge, UK: Polity Press, 1995.

Hook, Sidney. *From Hegel to Marx*. New York: Columbia University Press, 1994.

——. "Hegel and His Apologists." In *Hegel's Political Philosophy*, edited by Walter Kaufmann, 87-105. New York: Atherton Press, 1970.

——. "Hegel Rehabilitated?" In *Hegel's Political Philosophy*, edited by Walter Kaufmann, 55-70. New York: Atherton Press, 1970.

Houlgate, Stephen. *An Introduction to Hegel: Freedom, Truth, and History*. London: Blackwell, 2005.

——. *The Opening of Hegel's Logic: From Being to Infinity*. Lafayette, IN: Purdue University Press, 2006.

Houlgate, Stephen, ed., *Hegel and the Philosophy of Nature*. Albany: SUNY Press, 1998.

Howard, Thomas Albert. *Religion and the Rise of Historicism: W. M. L. de Wette, Jacob Burckhardt, and the Theological Origins of Nineteenth-Century Historical Consciousness*. Cambridge: Cambridge University Press, 2000.

Humboldt, Wilhelm von. *Über die unter dem Namen Bhagavad-Gítá bekannte Episode des Mahá-Bhárata*. Berlin: Königliche Akademie der Wissenschaften, 1826.

Bibliography

Hyppolite, Jean. *Genesis and Structure of Hegel's Phenomenology of Spirit.* Evanston, IL: Northwestern University Press, 1974.

——. *Studies on Marx and Hegel.* Translated by John O'Neill. New York: Basic Books, 1969.

Ifergan, Pini. *Hegel's Discovery of the Philosophy of Spirit: Autonomy, Alienation, and the Ethical Life: The Jena Lectures 1802–1806.* Translated by Nessa Olshansky-Ashtar. London: Palgrave, 2014.

Ilting, K. -H. "The Structure of Hegel's 'Philosophy of Right'." In *Hegel's Political Philosophy: Problems and Perspectives*, edited by Z. A. Pelczynski, 90-110. Cambridge: Cambridge University Press, 1971.

Jackson, M. W. "Hegel, the Real, and the Rational." In *The Hegel Myths and Legends*, edited by Jon Stewart, 19-25. Evanston: Northwestern University Press, 1996.

Jaeschke, Walter. *Hegel-Handbuch: Leben, Werk, Schule.* Stuttgart: J. B. Metzler, 2010.

Jarrett, Mark. *The Congress of Vienna and its Legacy: War and Great Power Diplomacy After Napoleon.* London: I.B. Tauris, 2014.

Kain, Philip J. *Hegel and the Other: A Study of the Phenomenology of Spirit.* Albany, NY: SUNY Press, 2005.

Kant, Immanuel. *Critique of Practical Reason and Other Works.* Translated by Thomas Kingsmill Abbott. London: Longmans, Green & Co., 1879.

Kant, Immanuel. *Grounding for the Metaphysic of Morals.* Translated by James W. Ellington. Indianapolis: Hackett, 1993.

Karpeles, Gustav, ed. *Heinrich Heine's Life Told in His Own Words.* Translated by Arthur Dexter. New York: Henry Holt and Company, 1893.

Kaufmann, Walter A. "The Hegel Myth and Its Method." In *Hegel's Political Philosophy*, edited by ed Walter A. Kaufmann, 137-71. New York: Atherton Press, 1970.

Kelly, George. *Idealism, Politics, and History: Sources of Hegelian Thought.* Cambridge: Cambridge University Press, 1969.

Kennedy, Michael L. *The Jacobin Clubs in the French Revolution, 1793-1795.* New York: Berghahn Books, 2000.

Knecht, R. J. *Richelieu.* New York: Routledge, 2013.

Knowles, Dudley. *Hegel and the Philosophy of Right.* London: Routledge, 2002.

Knox, Thomas M. "Hegel and Prussianism." in *Philosophy* 15, no. 57 (1940): 51-63.

——. "Hegel and Prussianism: A Rejoinder." *Philosophy* 15, no. 59 (1940): 313-17.

Kojève, Alexandre. *Introduction to the Reading of Hegel: Lectures on the Phenomenology of Spirit*. Translated by James H. Nichols, Jr. Cornell: Cornell University Press, 1980.

Krell, David Farrell. *Son of Spirit: A Novel*. Albany, NY: SUNY Press, 1997.

Krieger, Leonard. *The German Idea of Freedom: History of a Political Tradition* (Chicago: University of Chicago Press, 1957).

Landständische Verfassung des Königreichs Württemberg vom 15. März 1815. http://www.verfassungen.de/de/bw/wuerttemberg/verfassung1815-i.htm

Leary, David E. "The Psychology of Jakob Friedrich Fries (1773-1843): Its Context, Nature, and Historical Significance." *Storia E Critica Della Psicologia* 3, no. 2 (1982): 217-48.

Leggiere, Michael V. *Napoleon and the Struggle for Germany: The Franco-Prussian War of 1813*, Vol. 1. Cambridge: Cambridge University Press, 2015.

Leo, Heinrich. "Der Hegelianismus in Preussen." *Zeitschrift für Religions- und Geistesgeschichte* 10, no. 1 (1958): 51-60.

Léon, Xavier. *Fichte et son temps*, Vol. 1. Paris: Armand Colin, 1922.

Levinger, Matthew. *Enlightened Nationalism: The Transformation of Prussian Political Culture, 1806-1848*. Oxford: Oxford University Press, 2000.

Lewis, Thomas A. *Religion, Modernity, and Politics in Hegel*. Oxford: Oxford University Press, 2011.

Longuenesse, Beatrice. *Hegel's Critique of Metaphysics*. Cambridge, UK: Cambridge University Press, 2007.

Lukàcs, Georg. *The Young Hegel: Studies in the Relations Between Dialectics and Economics*. Translated by Rodney Livingstone. Cambridge, MA: The MIT Press, 1975.

MacDonell, John and Edward Manson, eds. *The Great Jurists of the World*. Boston: Little, Brown, and Company, 1914.

MacGregor, David. *Hegel and Marx: After the Fall of Communism*. Cardiff: University of Wales Press, 2014.

Machiavelli, Niccolò, *The Prince*. Translated by James B. Atkinson. Indianapolis: Hackett, 2008.

Maliks, Reidar. *Kant's Politics in Context*. Oxford: Oxford University Press, 2014.

Mansel, Philip. *Paris Between Empires*. New York: St. Martin Press, 2001.

Marcuse, Herbert. *Reason and Revolution: Hegel and the Rise of Social Theory*. Boston: Beacon Press, 1960).

Bibliography

Mariña, Jacqueline, ed. *The Cambridge Companion to Friedrich Schleiermacher*. Cambridge: Cambridge University Press, 2005.

Markoff, John. *Abolition of Feudalism: Peasants, Lords, and Legislators in the French Revolution*. University Park: Pennsylvania State University Press, 1996.

Marx, Karl. *Contribution to the Critique of Hegel's Philosophy of Law*, in Karl Marx and Frederick Engels, *Collected Works*, Vol. 3, 3-129. New York: International Publishers, 1975.

Marx, Werner. *The Philosophy of F.W.J. Schelling: History, System, Freedom*. Bloomington: Indiana University Press, 1984.

Matthews, Bruce "Schelling: A Brief Biographical Sketch of the Odysseus of German Idealism." In *The Palgrave Handbook of German Idealism*, edited by Matthew C. Altman, 435-56. New York: Palgrave, 2014.

Maude, F. N. *The Jena Campaign, 1806*. London: Swan Sonnenschein, 1909.

McCarney, Joseph. *Routledge Philosophy Guidebook to Hegel on History*. London: Routledge, 2000.

McCumber, John. *Hegel's Mature Critique of Kant*. Stanford: Stanford University Press, 2014.

McDonald, Joan. *Rousseau and the French Revolution 1762-1791*. London: Bloomsbury, 2013.

McNeely, Ian. *The Emancipation of Writing: German Civil Society in the Making, 1790s–1820s*. Berkeley: University of California Press, 2003.

Montesquieu, Charles. *The Spirit of Laws*. Translated by Thomas Nugent. Kitchener, Ontario: Batoche Books, 2001.

Moran, Daniel. *Toward a Century of Words: Johann Cotta and the Politics of the Public Realm in Germany, 1795-1832*. Berkeley: University of California Press, 1990.

Napoleon's Conduct towards Prussia since the Peace of Tilsit: From the Original Documents Published Under the Authority of the Prussian Government. London: Henry Colburn, 1814.

Neuhouser, Frederick, *Foundations of Hegel's Social Theory: Actualizing Freedom*. Cambridge: Harvard University Press, 2000.

Niebuhr, Barthold G. *Preussens Recht wider den Sächsischen Hof*. Berlin: Realschulbuchhandlung, 1814.

Nietzsche, Friedrich. *On the Advantage and Disadvantage of History for Life*. Translated by Peter Preuss. Indianapolis, IN: Hackett, 1980.

Nipperdey, Thomas. *Germany from Napoleon to Bismarck: 1800-1866*. Translated by Daniel Nolan. Princeton: Princeton University Press, 1996.

Nohl, Herman, ed. *Hegels theologische Jugendschriften*. Tübingen: J. C. B. Mohr, 1907.

Bibliography

Nomer, Nedim. "Fichte and the Relationship between Self-Positing and Rights." *Journal of the History of Philosophy* 48, no. 4, (2010): 469-490.

Nusser, Karlheinz. "The French Revolution in Hegel's *Phenomenology of Spirit.*" In *The Phenomenology of Spirit Reader: Critical and Interpretive Essays*, edited by Jon Stewart, 282-306. Albany: SUNY Press, 1998.

Osiander, Andreas. "Sovereignty, International Relations, and the Westphalian Myth." *International Organization* 55, no. 2 (2001): 251-87.

Palmer, Alan. *Metternich: Councillor of Europe*. London: Faber & Faber.

Paulus, Heinrich. "Hegels Philosophie des Rechts." *Heidelberger Jahrbücher für Literatur*, no. 25 (1821): 392-400.

Pelczynski, Z. A. "An Introductory Essay." In *Political Writings*, edited and translated by T. M. Knox, 3-137. Oxford: Oxford University Press, 1964.

Peperzak, Adriaan T. *Philosophy and Politics: A Commentary on the Preface to Hegel's Philosophy of Right*. Dordrecht: Martinus Nijhoff Publishers, 1987.

Petry, Michael J. ed., *Hegel and Newtonianism*. Dordrecht: Kluwer Academic Publishers, 1993.

———. "Introduction." In G. W. F. Hegel, *The Berlin Phenomenology*, edited by M. J. Petry, xiii-xcvii. Dordrecht: D. Reidel, 1981.

———. "Propaganda and Analysis: The Background to Hegel's Article on the English Reform Bill," in *The State and Civil Society: Studies in Hegel's Political Philosophy*, ed. Z. A. Pelczynski, 137-58 (Cambridge: Cambridge University Press, 1984).

Pfleiderer, Otto. *The Development of Theology in Germany Since Kant, and Its Progress in Great Britain since 1825*. Translated by J. Frederick Smith. London: Swan Sonnenschein, 1890.

Pickus, Keith. *Constructing Modern Identities: Jewish University Students in Germany, 1815-1914*. Detroit: Wayne State University Press, 1999.

Pilbeam, Pamela. *The 1830 Revolution in France*. New York: St. Martin's Press, 1991.

Pinkard, Terry. *Hegel: A Biography*. Cambridge: Cambridge University Press, 2000.

———. *Hegel's Phenomenology: The Sociality of Reason*. Cambridge: Cambridge University Press, 1994.

Pinkney, David H. *The French Revolution of 1830*. Princeton: Princeton University Press, 1972.

Pippin, Robert B. *Hegel on Self-Consciousness: Desire and Death in the Phenomenology of Spirit*. Princeton: Princeton University Press, 2011.

———. *Hegel's Idealism: The Satisfactions of Self-Consciousness.* Cambridge: Cambridge University Press, 1989.
Plant, Raymond. *Hegel.* New York: Routledge, 1973.
Pradt, M. de, *The Congress of Vienna.* London: M. Carey, 1816.
Press, Steven Michael. "False Fire: The Wartburg Book-Burning of 1817." *Central European History* 42, no. 4 (2009): 621-46.
Prutsch, Markus J. *Making Sense of Constitutional Monarchism in Post-Napoleonic France and Germany.* Basingstoke, UK: Palgrave, 2013.
Puknat, Siegfried B. "De Wette in New England." *Proceedings of the American Philosophical Society* 102, no. 4 (1958): 376-95.
Pundt, Alfred G. *Arndt and the Nationalist Awakening in Germany.* New York: Columbia University, 1935.
Reichlin-Meldegg, Karl A. *Heinrich Eberhard Gottlob Paulus und seine Zeit*, Vol. 2. Stuttgart: Magazin, 1853.
Reiff, Paul Friedrich. *Friedrich Gentz, an Opponent of the French Revolution and Napoleon.* Urbana-Champaign: The University of Illinois Press, 1912.
Reill, Peter Hanns. "Barthold Georg Niebuhr and the Enlightenment Tradition." *German Studies Review* 3, no. 1 (1980): 9-26.
Riley, Patrick. *Will and Political Legitimacy: A Critical Exposition of Social Contract Theory in Hobbes, Locke, Rousseau, Kant, and Hegel.* Cambridge: Harvard University Press, 1982.
Ritter, Joachim. "Hegel and the French Revolution." In Joachim Ritter, *Hegel and the French Revolution: Essays on the* Philosophy of Right, translated by Richard Dien Winfield, 35-89 (Cambridge, MA: MIT Pres, 1984).
———. *Metaphysik und Politik: Studien zu Aristoteles und Hegel* (Frankfurt: Suhrkamp, 1969).
Rogerson, John W. *W. M. L. de Wette, Founder of Modern Biblical Criticism: An Intellectual Biography.* Sheffield, UK: Sheffield Academic Press, 1992.
Rose, J. Holland. "The Censorship under Napoleon I." *Journal of Comparative Legislation and International Law, New Series* 18, no. 1 (1918): 58-65.
Rosenkranz, Karl. *Georg Wilhelm Friedrich Hegel's Leben.* Berlin: Duncker und Humblot, 1844.
Rosenzweig, Franz. *Hegel und der Staat*, Vol. 2. Munich: R. Oldenbourg, 1920.
Rousseau, Jean-Jacques. The Social Contract *and Other Later Political Writings.* Edited and translated by Victor Gourevitch. Cambridge: Cambridge University Press, 1997.
Rupke, Nicolaas. A. *Alexander von Humboldt: A Metabiography.* Chicago: The University of Chicago Press, 2008.

Bibliography

Russell, Bertrand. *A History of Western Philosophy*. New York: Simon & Schuster, 1945.

———. *Philosophy and Politics*. London: Cambridge University Press, 1947.

Ryan, Edward. *Napoleon's Shield & Guardian: The Unconquerable General Daumesnil*. London: Greenhill Books, 2003.

Saine, Thomas P. "The World Goethe Lived In: Germany and Europe, 1750–1830." In *The Cambridge Companion to Goethe*, edited by Leslie Sharpe, 6-22. Cambridge: Cambridge University Press, 2002.

Sarlemijn, Andries. *Hegel's Dialectic*. Translated by Peter Kirschemann. Dordrecht: R. Reidel, 1975.

Schelling, Karl. F. "Schelling's Leben." In *Aus Schelling's Leben: In Briefen, 1775-1803*, edited by G. L. Plitt, 1-179. Leipzig: S. Hirzel, 1869.

Schmalz, Theodor. *Berichtigung einer Stelle in der Bredow-Venturinischen Chronik für das Jahr 1808: Ueber politische Vereine, und ein Wort über Scharnhorsts und meine Verhältnisse zu ihnen*. Berlin: Maurerschen Buchhandlung, 1815.

———. *Ueber des Herrn B. G. Niebuhrs Schrift wider die meinige, politische Vereine betreffend*. Berlin: Maurerschen Buchhandlung, 1815.

Schmidt, James. "Recent Hegel Literature: The Jena Period and the Phenomenology of Spirit." *Telos* 48 (1981): 114-41.

Schnädelbach, Herbert. *Philosophy in Germany 1831-1933*. Translated by Eric Matthews. Cambridge: Cambridge University Press, 1984.

Schopenhauer, Arthur. *The Two Fundamental Problems of Ethics*. Translated by Christopher Janaway. Cambridge: Cambridge University Press, 2009.

———. *The World as Will and Representation*, Vol. 1. Translated by E. F. J. Payne. New York: Dover, 1966.

Sedgwick, Sally. *Hegel's Critique of Kant: From Dichotomy to Identity*. Oxford: Oxford University Press, 2012.

Ségur, Philippe-Paul. *Defeat: Napoleon's Russian Campaign*. Translated by J. David Townsend. New York: New York Review Books, 2008.

Shklar, Judith N. "Hegel's *Phenomenology*: An Elegy for Hellas." In *Hegel's Political Philosophy: Problems and Perspectives*, edited by Z. A. Pelczynski, 73-89. Cambridge: Cambridge University Press, 1971.

Siep, Ludwig. *Hegel's Phenomenology of Spirit*. Translated by Daniel Smyth. Cambridge: Cambridge University Press, 2014.

———. "Hegel's Liberal, Social, and 'Ethical' State." In *The Oxford Handbook of Hegel*, edited by Dean Moyar, 515-34. Oxford: Oxford University Press, 2017.

———. "The Struggle for Recognition: Hegel's Dispute with Hobbes in the Jena Writings." In J. *Hegel's Dialectic of Desire and Recognition:*

Texts and Commentary, edited by O'Neill, 273-88. Albany, NY: SUNY Press, 1996.

Sietze, Karl Friedrich Ferdinand. *Grund-Begriff Preußischer Staats- und Rechts Geschichte als Einleitung in die Wissenschaft des Preußischen Rechts*. Berlin: Fr. Laue, 1829.

Simon, Walter M. *The Failure of the Prussian Reform Movement, 1807–1819*. Ithaca, NY: Cornell University Press, 1955.

Sinclair, Isaac. *Wahrheit und Gewißheit*. Frankfurt: J. C. Hermann, 1811.

Smith, Steven B. *Hegel's Critique of Liberalism: Rights in Context*. Chicago: The University of Chicago Press, 1989.

Snow, Dale E. Schelling and the End of Idealism. Albany: SUNY Press, 1996.

Soboul, Albert. *A Short History of the French Revolution, 1789-1799*. Translated by Geoffrey Symcox. Berkeley: University of California Press, 1977.

Stamm-Kuhlmann, Thomas. "Restoration Prussia." In *Modern Prussian History: 1830-1947*, edited by Philip G. Dwyer, 43-65. London: Routledge, 2013.

Stepelevich, Lawrence S. "Hegel and Roman Catholicism." *Journal of the American Academy of Religion* 60, no. 4 (1992): 673-691.

Stern, Robert. *The Routledge Guidebook to Hegel's Phenomenology of Spirit*. London: Routledge, 2013.

Stewart, Jon. *Hegel's Interpretation of the Religions of the World: The Logic of the Gods* (Oxford: Oxford University Press, 2018),

———. *The Unity of Hegel's Phenomenology of Spirit: A Systematic Interpretation*. Evanston: Northwestern University Press, 2000.

Stolleis, Michael. *Public Law in Germany, 1800-1914*. New York: Berghahn Books, 2001.

Suter, J. F. "Burke, Hegel, and the French Revolution." In *Hegel's Political Philosophy: Problems and Perspectives*, edited by Z. A. Pelczynski, 52-72. Cambridge: Cambridge University Press, 1971.

Sweet, Paul. *Friedrich von Gentz: A Defender of the Old Order*. Westport: Greenwood Press, 1970.

Tabak, Mehmet. *The Doctrine of Being in Hegel's Science of Logic*. New York: Palgrave, 2017.

Taylor, Charles. *Hegel*. Cambridge, UK: Cambridge University Press, 1975.

———. *Hegel and Modern Society*. Cambridge: Cambridge University Press, 1979.

Thompson, Michael J., ed. *Hegel's Metaphysics and the Philosophy of Politics*. New York: Routledge, 2018.

Tibebu, Teshale. *Hegel and the Third World: The Making of Eurocentrism in World History*. Syracuse: Syracuse University Press, 2011.

Toews, John E. *Hegelianism: The Path Toward Dialectical Humanism, 1805-1841*. Cambridge: Cambridge University Press, 1980.
Treitschke, Heinrich. *Historische und Politische Aufsätze*, Vol. 1. Leipzig: S. Hirzel, 1903.
———. *History of Germany in the Nineteenth Century*, Vol. 3. Translated by Eden Paul and Cedar Paul. New York: McBride and Nast, 1917.
Tunick, Mark. "Hegel's Justification of Hereditary Monarchy." *History of Political Thought* 12, no. 3 (1991): 481-96.
Vater, Michael G. and David W. Wood J. G., eds. *The Philosophical Rupture between Fichte and Schelling: Selected Texts and Correspondence, 1800–1802*. Albany, NY: SUNY Press, 2012.
Verene, Donald P. "Hegel's Account of War." In *Hegel's Political Philosophy: Problems and Perspectives*, edited by Z. A. Pelczynski, 168-80. Cambridge, UK: Cambridge University Press, 1971.
Vial, Theodore. *Schleiermacher: A Guide for the Perplexed*. London: Bloomsbury, 2013.
Vick, Brian E. *The Congress of Vienna: Power and Politics After Napoleon*. Cambridge, MA: Harvard University Press, 2014.
Villa, Dana. "Hegel, Tocqueville, and 'Individualism'." *The Review of Politics* 67, no. 4 (2005): 659-86.
Wahnich, Sophie. *In Defence of the Terror: Liberty or Death in the French Revolution*. Translated by David Fernbach. London: Verso, 2012.
Wallace, Robert M. *Hegel's Philosophy of Reality, Freedom, and God*. New York: Cambridge University Press, 2005.
Wangenheim, Karl August. *Die Idee der Staatsverfassung in ihrer Anwendung auf Wirtembergs alte Landesverfassung und den Entwurf zu deren Erneuerung*. Frankfurt: Kröner, 1815.
Wangenheim, Karl August. *Ueber die Trennung der Volksvertretung in zwei Abtheilungen und über landschaftliche Ausschüsse*. Stuttgart: (Publisher unavailable), 1816.
Ward, Adolphus William. *Germany, 1815-1890*, Vol. 1. Cambridge: Cambridge University Press, 1916.
Weech, Friedrich. "Welcker, Karl Theodor." In *Allgemeine Deutsche Biographie*, Vol. 41, 660–65. Leipzig: Duncker & Humblot, 1896.
Westphal, Kenneth R., ed., *The Blackwell Guide to Hegel's Phenomenology of Spirit*. Oxford: Wiley-Blackwell, 2009.
Whaley, Joachim. *Germany and the Holy Roman Empire: Volume I: Maximilian I to the Peace of Westphalia, 1493–1648*. Oxford: Oxford University Press, 2012.
Williams, David Lay. *Rousseau's Social Contract: An Introduction*. Cambridge: Cambridge University Press, 2014.

Bibliography

Williams, Robert R. *Hegel's Ethics of Recognition.* Berkeley, CA: University of California Press, 1997.

Winkworth. Susanna, ed. *The Life and Letters of Barthold George Niebuhr.* London: Chapman and Hall, 1852.

Wokler, Robert. "Contextualizing Hegel's Phenomenology of the French Revolution and the Terror." *Political Theory* 26, no. 1 (1998): 33-55.

Woloch, Isser. *Napoleon and His Collaborators: The Making of a Dictatorship.* New York: W. W. Norton & Company, 2001).

Wood, Allen W. "Editor's Introduction." In G. W. F. Hegel, *Elements of the Philosophy Right*, edited by Allen, W. Wood (Cambridge: Cambridge University Press, 1991).

———. "Fichte's Philosophy of Right and Ethics." In *The Cambridge Companion to Fichte*, edited by David James and Günter Zöller, 168-98. Cambridge: Cambridge University Press, 2016.

———. *Hegel's Ethical Thought.* Cambridge, UK: Cambridge University Press, 1990.

Yack, Bernard "Rationality of Hegel's Concept of Monarchy." *The American Political Science Review* 74, no. 3 (1980): 709-20.

Yovel, Yirmiahu. "Hegel's Dictum that the Rational is Actual and the Actual is Rational: Its Ontological Content and Its Function in Discourse." In *The Hegel Myths and Legends*, edited by Jon Stewart, 26-41. Evanston: Northwestern University Press, 1996.

Zeller, Eduard. *Theologische Jahrbücher in Verbindung mit Mehreren Gelehrten,* Vol. 4. Tübingen: Ludwig Friedrich Fues, 1845.

INDEX

(Since references to "Hegel" occur throughout, it is not indexed as such. For a detailed biographical and thematic indexing of "Hegel," see the detailed table of contents).

Abeken, Bernhard R., 21
Adorno, Theodor, 70
Alexander I, 114-15, 164
Altenstein, Karl von, 155-62, 169, 171, 174-77, 206, 210, 213-23, 243-51, 254, 256-62, 281, 291, 296-97
Althaus, Horst, 2, 3, 5, 11, 15, 21, 32, 33, 78, 102, 122, 157, 159, 218, 262, 292
Altmann, Wilhelm, 113, 156, 165
Ameriks, Karl, 66
Anaxagoras, 271
Ancillon, Jean Pierre Friedrich, 156, 226, 242
Anderson, Frank Maloy, 42, 80
Antigone, 68
anti-Semitism, 88, 154-55, 155, 180
Aris, Reinhold, 74
Arndt, Ernst Moritz, 83, 155, 169, 172, 317
Articles of the German Confederation, 113, 133, 139, 165
Ashton, Bodie, 134, 306
Asverus, Gustav 172-73, 177
Asverus, Ludwig C., 31, 173
Augsburg Confession, 260
Austria, 48, 49, 84, 92, 98, 113, 129, 133, 137, 171, 275
Avineri, Shlomo, 41, 45, 79, 82, 157, 172, 180, 182, 195, 197, 207, 288, 300

Baack, Lawrence J., 164
Bachmann, Karl F., 104
Bacon, Francis, 183
Baden, 96, 126, 129, 131, 133, 134, 136
Bähr, Karl, 235
Bamberg, 15, 19, 31-35, 78-80, 83, 91, 99, 102, 212
Bamberger Zeitung, 33, 35, 78, 99
Bastille Day, 5, 176, 252, 272
Battle of Aspern-Essling, 92
Battle of Fère-Champenoise, 94
Battle of Jena 30, 77, 91-92, 95
Battle of Regensburg, 91
Battle of Waterloo, 97, 111, 307
Beck, Karl, 171
Beckh, August F., 1
Beiser, Frederick C., 44, 55, 66, 74, 185
Bekker, Georg J., 226
Bellamy, Richard, 300
Benecke, Heinrich, 233
Berlin Yearbooks for Scientific Criticism, 246-48, 251-52
Bernasconi, Robert, 268
Bernese oligarchy, 11, 37
Beyme, Karl von, 288
Bigler, Robert M., 160
Black, Jeremy, 97
Boeckh, August, 248-49, 252
Boisserée, Melchior, 121
Boisserée, Sulpitz, 121, 123-25, 130, 135, 158
Börne, Ludwig, 251

Index

Böttiger, Karl, 24
Boumann, Ludwig, 238-39
Bouterwek, Friedrich, 25
Bowie, Andrew, 16, 101
Brinkmann, Karl G. von, 26
Bristow, William, 65, 66
Brooks, Thom, 152, 195, 196, 197, 207, 302
Brose, Eric D., 134, 155
Brown, Howard G., 79
Bund der Geister, 14
Burke, Edmund, 74, 307, 310, 319
Burkhardt, Auguste Theresia, 294
Burkhardt, Christiana, 33, 293
Burschenschaften 115, 137, 154, 163-64, 167, 169, 173-74, 177
Butler, Clark, 109, 172

Carové, Friedrich W. 172, 174
Carrier, Jean-Baptiste, 11
Carritt, Edgar F., 298-99
Cart, Jean-Jacques, 36-38, 40
Cassirer, Ernst, 46
Castlereagh, Robert S., 154
Catholic (Catholicism), 48-49, 115, 156, 228, 243-44, 260-61, 268, 271-74, 278, 283, 288
Chaloupek, Günther, 147
Chapman, Tim, 96
Charles X, 278
Cholera, 289-290, 292, 294
civil servants, 64, 144, 151, 199, 203
civil society 57, 68, 69, 147, 166, 189-90, 197-98, 203, 207
classes, *see* estates
coercion, 55, 65

Coffin, Victor, 80
Congress of Rastatt 41
Congress of Vienna 96, 169, 308, 313, 317, 320
Constant, Benjamin, 97
contractarian theory, 47, 58, 60-61, 148, 189, 190
corporations 68, 146-47, 149, 150, 166, 197-99, 201, 203-04, 207
Cotta, Johann F. von 134, 251, 281, 288-89, 315
Cousin, Victor, 136-37, 172, 224-28, 242-44, 247, 255, 279
Creuzer, Georg F., 34, 125, 133, 177, 245
Critical Journal of Philosophy, 25-26, 34, 53, 211
Croce, Benedetto, 298
Crouter, Richard, 120, 172, 219, 222
cunning of reason, 264

D'Hondt, Jacques, 4, 13, 157, 172, 180, 300, 308
Daub, Karl, 30, 34, 121, 123, 124, 125, 126, 127, 132-33, 136, 211, 258
De Boer, Karin, 71
De Wette, Wilhelm M. L., 116, 118, 120, 163, 171, 172, 177, 181, 186, 211, 213, 219, 222
DeGrood, David H., 173
demagogues (demagogic), 132, 155-56, 164-66, 168, 17-72, 175-77, 191, 206, 214, 216-17, 222-25, 227
democracy (democratic), 37, 39, 140, 143-44, 146, 149, 154-55, 158, 180, 189, 190, 197, 288

Index

Depré, Olivier, 20
Dettke, Barbara, 292
Devrient, Eduard, 245
Devrient, Therese, 245
Dilthey 4, 309
Directory of Five, 273
disciples (Hegel's), 23, 116, 179, 223, 231, 232, 238-39, 251, 253, 261, 263, 258, 265, 280, 291, 295-97, 302
Döll, Helmut, 292, 309
doppelsatz, 181-83
Dorrien, Gary, 66
Dumas, Alexandre, 164
duty, 12, 47, 53, 148, 152, 156, 157, 185, 187, 207, 208, 259, 285
Dwyer, Philip G., 80, 169

Ebert, S. H., 293
Ecker, Alexander, 154, 309
education, 56, 59, 63, 84, 85, 111, 151, 155, 157, 159, 169, 180, 188, 215, 254, 259, 284-85, 293
Emerson, Donald E., 114
England, 164, 169, 235, 250-51, 271, 273, 275, 279, 282-88
Erlangen, 28, 89, 90, 95, 110, 117, 118, 122, 125-27
Ernst II, 20, 234
Eylert, Rulemann F. 181

Fackenheim, Emil L. 182
Falkenheim, Hugo, 37
Fenner, C. W., 213
Fernow, Karl L., 22-23
Feudalism, 12, 43, 79, 143, 203, 286
Fichte, Immanuel H., 234
Fichte, Johann G., 3-4, 8, 16, 24, 28, 32, 41, 52-53, 55-56, 60, 63, 116, 159-60, 189, 220, 230, 235-36, 295, 296
Findlay, J. N., 238
Flatt, Johann F., 1, 2
Follen, Eliza Cabot, 224, 268
Follen, Karl, 171, 224, 267
Förster, Friedrich, 36, 172, 175-76, 248, 252, 294-96, 310
Forster, Michael N., 65
France 11, 38, 40, 42, 45-46, 48, 51, 71-74, 79-81, 84, 97, 114, 130, 163, 171, 173, 192, 224, 255, 260, 262, 272-74, 278-86
Franco, Paul, 61, 74, 180, 182, 195, 196, 301
Frederick Wilhelm III, 84, 92, 113, 115, 154-56, 162, 165, 168, 170, 173, 241, 260, 276
freedom of the press, 82, 83, 151, 154, 168, 205, 208, 215, 278, 288
freedom tree, 5-6
Freitag, Sabine, 154
French Republic, 41-42, 44, 95
French Revolution, 4, 5, 6, 7, 11, 39, 40, 46, 49, 50, 51, 56, 58, 62, 69, 70, 71, 74, 75, 78, 79, 115, 119, 156, 165, 183-85, 190, 192, 251-52, 271-75
Friedrich I, 30, 38, 133-34, 138, 140, 143, 147
Friedrich Wilhelm IV, 289
Fries, Jakob, 28, 30, 90, 95- 96, 102-03, 108-09, 111, 116-21, 124-25, 127, 129, 130, 132-33, 136-37, 145, 154, 163, 171, 177, 180, 184, 186, 188, 211-12, 215, 219, 234, 258
Frommann, Karl F. 120-21
Fulbrook. Mary, 114
Furet, François, 72

Index

Gabler, Georg A., 23, 232, 258, 297
Gans, Eduard, 69, 179, 182, 218, 223, 246, 248, 249, 254, 263, 279, 280, 281, 289, 290, 291, 292, 294, 295, 298
Gehring, Paul, 158
Geiger, Ido, 65
Gentz, Friedrich, 74, 114, 163, 165-66, 170, 184, 193, 253, 310, 317, 319
German Confederation, 113, 133, 164, 165, 177
German Empire, 41-45, 48, 51, 75, 77, 138, 139, 177, 275
Gibbon, Edward, 58
Girard, Philippe R., 79
Goethe, Johann W., 16, 21-23, 27-29, 32-33, 81, 106, 111, 129, 214, 230, 242, 245, 247, 255, 261, 262
Gogel, Johann N., 10
Gontard, Susette, 14
Gooch, George P., 74
Görres, Joseph, 83, 115, 118, 155, 170, 171
Göschel, Karl F., 280
Gregory, Frederick, 105
Grier, Philip T., 101
Gries, Johann, 27
Gwee, Li Sui, 101

Habermas, Jürgen, 70
Habib, M A. R., 268
Hardenberg, Karl von, 118-19, 155-56, 166, 169, 171, 175, 193, 210, 211, 213, 216-17, 219-20
Hardimon, Michael O., 193, 195, 301, 302, 311
Harnack, Adolf, 220, 311
Harris, Errol E., 207, 288

Harris, H. S., 2, 5, 6, 22, 24, 25, 36, 38, 40, 41, 44, 60
Haym, Rudolf, 39, 69, 135, 143, 157, 298
Hegel, Christiane, 1, 10, 13, 281, 292
Hegel, Georg W. F., *see* Contents, v-vii
Hegel, Immanuel, 292, 293
Hegel, Karl, 263, 280, 290, 292, 293
Hegel, Marie, 89, 137, 246, 247, 291, 292, 293
Heidelberg Yearbooks, 105, 111, 134, 138, 212
Heine, Heinrich, 229, 230, 297
Henke, Ernst L. T., 116, 118, 130, 137
Henning, Leopold von, 172, 175, 218, 250
Henrich, Dieter, 66
Herbart, Johann F., 258
Heuvel, Jon V., 83, 115, 119, 156, 165, 170
Hicks, Peter, 79
Hinrichs, Hermann F. W., 216, 220-21
Historical School 218, 249, 258
Hobbes, Thomas, 53-55, 61
Hobsbawm, Eric, 72
Hoffheimer, Michael H., 268, 290, 298
Hoffmeister, Johannes, 172, 173, 174, 175, 215, 227, 238
Hölderlin, Friedrich, 2, 5, 9, 10, 14, 15, 36
Holy Alliance 98, 113, 114, 115, 118, 163-65, 177
Holy Roman Empire, *see* German Empire
Homer, 29
Honneth, Axel, 61

Index

Hook, Sidney, 194, 195, 298, 299, 300
Hotho, Heinrich G., 179, 218, 223, 228, 231-32, 243-44, 246
Houlgate, Stephen, 20, 66, 243, 268
Howard, Thomas A, 120
Hufnagel, Caroline and Wilhelm, 25
Huguenots, 48
Humboldt, Alexander von 241, 259
Humboldt, Wilhelm von 116, 169, 218, 251, 253
Hyppolite, Jean, 65, 76

Ifergan, Pini, 60
Ilting, K. -H., 148

Jacobi, Friedrich, 2, 25, 26, 35, 102, 103, 107, 108, 111, 117, 118, 211
Jacobins, 79, 267, also *see* Terror
Jaeschke, Walter, 2, 14, 24, 136, 313
Jahn, Friedrich L., 155, 169
Jarrett, Mark, 96, 97, 114, 169
Jean Paul, 102
Jérôme I, 82
July Revolution, 262, 274, 278-81, 288, 290, 297

Kamptz, Karl von, 155, 173, 174, 175, 212, 224, 226, 247
Kant, Immanuel (and Kantian), 2, 5, 8, 11, 16, 23, 28, 30, 53, 56, 60, 64, 66, 67, 73-74, 103, 111, 152, 162, 180, 18-86, 192, 235-37, 296
Karl August, 114, 119, 129, 154, 163, 193

Karl Eugen, 1, 6
Karl Ludwig Friedrich, 126, 129
Karlsbad Decrees, 114, 163, 166, 168, 169, 171, 175, 179, 206, 215, 224, 257
Karpeles, Gustav, 230
Kastner, Karl, 29, 34
Kaufmann, Walter A. 182, 299
Kennedy, Michael L., 72
Kieser, Dietrich G. von, 154
Knebel, Karl L. von, 81, 107
Knowles, Dudley, 195
Knox, Thomas M., 172, 207, 299
Kojève, Alexandre, 65
Kolb, Jean J., 6
Köppen, Friedrich, 25, 26, 102, 103, 107
Kotzebue, August, 164, 165, 169, 170, 174, 186
Kracker, Johann, 117, 127
Krug, Wilhelm T., 252, 258

La Marseillaise, 5, 6
Lange, Christian, 30
Lasson, Georg, 40, 42
Le Moniteur, 81, 83, 212
Leary, David E., 28, 119
LeBret, Johann F., 1
Leggiere, Michael V., 92
Leo, Heinrich, 161, 172, 219, 290
Léon, Xavier, 4
Leutwein, Phillip F., 2, 5
Levinger, Matthew, 155, 156, 164, 165, 166, 169, 181, 184, 193
Lichtenstein, Martin H. K., 235
Loebell, Johann W., 255
Louis Philippe, 279
Louis XVI, 114, 156
Louis XVIII, 97

Luden, Heinrich, 154
Ludwig Fischer 33, 292, 293, 294
Lukàcs, Georg, 3, 4
Luther, Martin, 29, 183, 244

MacDonell, John, 218
MacGregor, David, 6, 175, 314
Machiavelli, Niccolò, 46, 48, 53, 62
Maliks, Reidar, 55, 74, 184, 185
Mansel, Philip, 279
Manson, Edward, 218
Marcuse, Herbert, 299
Marheineke, Philip K., 116, 218, 222, 256, 294, 295
Mariña, Jacqueline, 219
Markoff, John, 79
Martin, Christoph R. D., 121, 129-33, 177
Marx, Karl, 194, 199, 202, 203, 204
Marx, Werner, 16
Matthews, Bruce, 16
Maude, Frederic N., 31
McCarney, Joseph, 263
McCumber, John, 66
McDonald, Joan, 70
McNeely, Ian, 142
McPhee, Peter, 80
Mehmel, Gottlieb E. A., 118
Mendelssohn, Felix, 245
Metternich, Klemens von, 114, 154, 163, 165, 166, 184, 193, 226
Michelet, Karl L., 233, 238, 239, 280, 290, 292
Mollat, Georg, 40, 42
monarchical principle, 114, 129, 166, 192-93, 195, 271, 287
Montesquieu, Charles de, 48, 192

Moran, Daniel, 134

Nanette, Endel, 13-14
Napoleon, Bonaparte, 30, 31, 38, 45, 47, 62, 76-85, 91-97, 111, 113, 114, 115, 120, 122, 130, 133, 137, 138, 162-64, 166, 212, 265, 273
Napoleonic Code, 80, 82, 137, 275
Neuhouser, Frederick, 189
Newton, Isaac, 20, 21, 111, 237, 242
Nicolovius, Georg, 116, 117, 118
Niebuhr, Barthold G., 115, 124, 125, 126, 219, 226, 249
Niethammer, Immanuel, 19, 26, 28, 30, 31, 32, 33, 76, 78-82, 84-97, 107-10, 116, 117, 121, 122, 123, 125, 127, 135, 158, 212, 213, 214, 216, 292
Nietzsche, Friedrich, 271
Nipperdey, Thomas, 166
Nohl, Herman, 1
Nomer, Nedim, 55
Nusser, Karlheinz, 70, 316

Oken, Lorenz, 154, 171, 213
Order of the Red Eagle 115, 259, 281
Osiander, Andreas, 48
Ottilie, Goethe, 230

Palmer, Alan, 114
Parthey, Gustav, 231
Paulus, Caroline 89, 130
Paulus, Heinrich, 26, 30, 88, 94, 95, 111, 115, 116, 121, 123, 124, 125, 130, 134, 135, 136, 157, 158, 212

Index

Pelczynski, Zbigniew A., 41, 195, 299, 300
Peperzak, Adriaan T., 157, 300
Petry, Michael J., 103, 104, 242, 288
Pfleiderer, Otto, 30, 316
Piazzi, Giuseppe, 20
Pickus, Keith, 154
Pilbeam, Pamela, 279
Pinkard, Terry, 3, 5, 6, 11, 14, 38, 40, 65, 76, 99, 103, 104, 108, 157, 173, 226, 292, 302
Pinkney, David H., 278
Pippin, Robert B., 66
Plant, Raymond, 38, 300
Plato 2, 20, 63, 104, 225, 227
Popper, Karl, 296, 299
Pradt, M. de, 96
Press, Steven Michael, 137, 155
Prussia, 44, 45, 49, 113-15, 154-57, 168-72
Puknat, Siegfried B., 171
Pundt, Alfred G., 83

Raumer, Friedrich von, 123, 124, 256
Reformation, 271
Reichlin-Meldegg, Karl A. von, 135, 158
Reiff, Paul F., 114, 164
Reill, Peter H., 124
Reinhold, Karl L., 3, 8, 26, 28
Restoration, 95, 96, 98, 111, 114, 117, 118, 120, 122, 124, 127-132, 138-39, 141, 149, 153, 157, 163, 171, 179, 184, 192, 206, 276, 280, 281, 287, 298, 300
Rheinischer Merkur, 118
Richelieu, Cardinal, 46, 47, 48, 49, 52, 53
Riley, Patrick, 186

Ritter, Joachim, 299
Robespierre, Maximilien, 11 62, 72, 73, 273; also *see* Terror
Rödiger, Ludwig, 212, 234
Rogerson, John W., 116, 171, 181
Rose, J. Holland, 80
Rosenkranz, Karl, 2, 3, 7, 16, 38, 39, 215, 250, 281, 289, 296, 298
Rosenzweig, Franz, 73, 143
Rousseau, Jean-Jacques, 3, 7, 61, 62, 69, 70, 71, 72, 184, 189, 190, 267
Royal Academy of Sciences 160, 219
Royal Scientific Board of Examiners 216
Ruge, Arnold, 289, 290
Rupke, Nicolaas, A., 241
Russell, Bertrand. 229, 299
Russia 15, 98, 113, 164

Sack, Karl H., 222
Saine, Thomas P. 114, 129, 318
Sand, Karl L., 164, 168, 171, 173, 174, 181
Sarlemijn, Andries, 297
Savigny, Friedrich C. von, 218, 219, 223, 226, 245, 246, 249, 254, 258
Schelling, Caroline, 28
Schelling, Friedrich W. J., 2, 5, 6, 7, 8, 9, 11, 12, 13, 15, 16, 18, 19, 21, 23, 24, 25, 26, 28, 29, 30, 32, 34-35, 37, 41, 53, 78, 89, 100-06, 119, 120, 136, 137, 211, 226, 235, 236, 241, 242, 257, 305, 307, 310, 311, 315, 318-20
Schelver, Franz, 33, 34, 103
Schiller, Friedrich, 16, 22, 23

Schlegel, August 26, 28
Schlegel, Friedrich, 26, 186, 253, 255
Schleiermacher, Friedrich, 26, 83, 110, 111, 119, 163, 171, 172, 211, 216, 218-23, 226, 249, 254, 256, 258
Schmalz, Theodor von, 115, 116, 118, 258
Schmidt, James, 54, 66
Schnädelbach, Herbert, 297
Schnurrer, Christian F., 1, 2, 4, 5, 6
Schopenhauer, Arthur, 234-38, 240, 296
Schubert, Gotthilf H., 91, 102
Schuckmann, Friedrich von, 118-121, 123-26, 170, 224, 226
Schultz, Christoph L., 175, 214, 281
Schulze, Johannes, 176, 217, 243, 245, 248, 249, 254, 256, 257, 291, 292, 294, 296, 297
Schwarzott, Thomas, 19
Sedgwick, Sally, 66
Seebeck, Thomas, 106, 121
Ségur, Philippe-Paul, 92
Seven Years War 46
Shklar, Judith N., 74
Siep, Ludwig, 61, 65, 205, 302
Sietze, Karl F., 258
Simon, Walter M., 83, 113, 114, 115, 155, 156, 165, 169
Sinclair, Isaac von, 14, 77, 105, 110
Sixth Coalition 92
Smith, Steven B., 30, 197, 207, 301
Snow, Dale, 16
Soboul, Albert, 72

Society for Scientific Criticism 246, 248, 250, 252
Solger, Karl, 123, 229, 255, 295
Stamm-Kuhlmann, Thomas, 169
Steiger, Carl F. von, 4, 7, 11
Stein, Karl von, 84, 169
Stepelevich, Lawrence S., 244
Stern, Robert, 69
Stewart, Jon, 6, 36, 65, 212, 288
Stieglitz, H. W. A., 223
Stolleis, Michael, 193
Storr, Gottlob C., 1
Suter, J. F., 74
Sweet, Paul, 164

Tabak, Mehmet, 110
Taylor, Charles, 65, 300, 301
Terror, 4, 69, 72, 74, 183-84, 273, also see Jacobins and Robespierre
Thaden, Nicolaus von, 111-12, 213
The Committee of Public Safety 73, 273
The French Constitution of 1804, 80
Theodicaea, 276
Theseus, 47, 62
Thibaut, Anton F. J., 121, 123, 124, 130, 133, 135
Thirty Years War 44
Tibebu, Teshale, 268
Tieck, Ludwig, 255, 256
Tocqueville, Alexis de, 197
Toew, John E., 2, 83, 176, 233, 246, 248, 250, 254, 290, 295
Treaty of Lunéville, 42, 45
Treaty of Pressburg 30
Treaty of Westphalia 41, 44
Treitschke, Heinrich von, 134, 143, 166, 169, 193
Troxler, Ignaz P. V., 22, 106

Index

Tunick, Mark, 195
Twesten, August D. C., 110

Uhland, Johann L., 1

Varnhagen von Ense, 222, 223, 226, 243, 246, 247, 248, 250, 251, 252, 259, 281, 290
Vatke, Wilhelm, 233, 256
Vaud, 36-38
Vial, Theodore, 84
Vick, Brian, 96
Vienna Congress 98, 111, 113, 133
Villa, Dana, 197
Voigt, Siegmund F., 33
Voss, Johann H., 29, 30

Wahnich, Sophie, 72
Wallace, Robert M., 66
Wangenheim, Karl A., 134, 135, 143, 144, 145, 151, 161
War of Liberation, 93, 113, 114, 119, 131, 133, 163, 250
Ward, Adolphus W., 137
Wartburg Festival, 137-38, 154, 155, 156, 163, 180, 188, 267
Weech, Friedrich, 136, 320
Welcker, Karl, T., 136
Wende 154, 310
Westphal, Kenneth R., 66, 108
Whaley, Joachim, 41, 321
Wilhelm I, 134, 135, 151
Williams, David L., 62
Williams, Robert R. 61, 207
Windischmann, Karl J. H., 102, 104
Winkworth, Susanna, 124, 321
Wismayr, Josef, 87
Wittgenstein, Wilhelm L. G. von, 118, 119, 165, 171, 174, 175

Wokler, Robert, 69
Woloch, Isser, 79
Wood, Allen, W., 24, 55, 66, 180, 182, 185, 207, 301

Yack, Bernard 195
Yovel, Yirmiahu, 182

Zach, Franz Xaver von, 20, 234
Zeller, Eduard, 3
Zelter, Karl F., 245, 262
Zumpt, Karl G., 261
Zwilling, Jakob, 14